Petr Chalupský

A Horror and a Beauty: The World of Peter Ackroyd's London Novels

KAROLINUM PRESS
PRAGUE 2016

KAROLINUM PRESS, Ovocný trh 3–5, 116 36 Prague 1, Czech Republic
Karolinum Press is a publishing department of Charles University in Prague
www.karolinum.cz

Language supervision by Bernadette Higgins
Cover and layout by Jan Šerých
Typeset by DTP Karolinum Press
Printed in the Czech Republic by Karolinum Press
First English edition

The Cataloging-in-Publication Data is available
from the National Library of the Czech Republic

ISBN 978-80-246-3161-5
ISBN 978-80-246-3171-4 (pdf)

The original manuscript was reviewed by Christoph Houswitschka
(Department of English Literary Science, University of Bamberg)
Milada Franková (Department of English and American Studies,
Faculty of Arts, Masaryk University in Brno)
Šárka Bubíková (Department of English and American Studies,
Faculty of Arts and Philosophy, University of Pardubice)

All great art is born of the metropolis.
(Ezra Pound)

... fidelity to historical reality is a secondary matter as regards the value of the novel. The novelist is neither historian nor prophet: he is an explorer of existence.
(Milan Kundera)

Contents

Cue-Titles

Introduction:
Power, Majesty,
Darkness, Shadows

With cities, it is as with dreams: everything imaginable can be dreamed,
but even the most unexpected dream is a rebus that conceals a desire
or, its reverse, a fear. Cities, like dreams, are made of desires and fears,
even if the thread of their discourse is secret, their rules are absurd, their
perspectives deceitful, and everything conceals something else.
Italo Calvino, *Invisible Cities*

Peter Ackroyd is one of the most prolific contemporary British writers,
having written more than sixty books, including collections of poetry,
essays, novels, biographies, historical and literary non-fiction and books
for children. He is also the author of several television documentaries
and even of a libretto for an opera based on his favourite William Ho-
garth engravings. An exceptionally hard-working and diligent author
for whom writing has grown from profession and avocation to passion
and vital need, he maintains a rigid work discipline, the capacity for
which he believes he owes to his energetic and indomitable grandmother,
and boasts of never having missed a deadline: almost every day he takes
a taxi from his Knightsbridge apartment to his office in Bloomsbury near
the British Museum and Charles Dickens's house, an area he considers to
be London's holy territory, where he spends eight hours working, mostly
on three different books at once, usually a biography, a work of non-
fiction and a novel, which he insists is necessary for his sanity since if he
did only one thing at a time he would think he was wasting his time[1]. His
immense productivity, its intellectual, generic and imaginative variety,
his erudition and the breadth of his field of interest make Ackroyd one
of the most exceptional writers of his generation.

---

1   Cf. Emily Mann, "Tales of the city." *The Guardian*, 15 September 2007, "Retire? Only if my
     arms are chopped off first," an interview with Peter Ackroyd. *The Independent*, 12 July 2009,
     and Jody Rosen, "Peter Ackroyd's London Calling." *The New York Times*, 12 September 2013.

As is often the case with gifted individuals, Ackroyd's is a complicated personality and he has often been judged a controversial, eccentric or even grandiloquent figure. Facts about his life that he has stated in various interviews over time have contributed to the creation of this idiosyncratic persona: that he never met his father and was brought up as an only child by his single mother and maternal grandmother in a strict Roman Catholic household in a council house in working-class East Acton in west London; that he was a driven child whose intellectual tendencies were promoted by his mother and who wrote his first work, a play about Guy Fawkes, aged nine; that as a child he dreamed of being a Pope, a magician or a tap dancer; that he once saw a ghost; that he never wanted to be a novelist; that he never knows how his novels will end, relying on intuition and instinct rather than planning; that he does not read fiction, including that of his contemporaries, since he finds it too untidy; that he is gay, and his relationship with an American dancer, Brian Kuhn, lasted for more than twenty years until Kuhn contracted Aids in 1990 and died of it four years later; that nursing Kuhn was the only occasion which saw him leave London, for a cottage in the West Country; that he is happy and relieved to have led a single, celibate life for years as it allows him to concentrate on his work, which now matters more to him than love because it sustains him; that his workload nearly killed him in 2000, when, after he finished *London: The Biography*, he suffered a heart attack and spent a week in a coma; that he has always been a heavy drinker, dedicating the days to working and nights to drinking; that he leads a solitary life, hates to leave London and dislikes the countryside; that he is not a very outgoing person, he does not go to the theatre, concerts or the opera; that he does not read newspapers, is not interested in reviews, even though he once worked as a reviewer, does not like to discuss his finished books and hates literary festivals; that he is not interested in politics and has an aversion to commenting on the news, claiming that his opinions are of no consequence or value, and is therefore often criticised for his apolitical and aloof attitudes; that he is happiest in his study when reading, writing and doing research, aided by two assistants who fetch him the books and other materials he needs for his projects[2]. These shards of information about Ackroyd's background and life not only reflect his character and explain his reputation for eccentricity, they also help to

---

2   A complete list of interviews with and articles about Peter Ackroyd where all these facts are mentioned can be found in the Bibliography.

contextualise the intense focus in his work on London, the metropolis in which he was born and in which he has spent his whole life, the city whose culture, history, mythos and spirit are the objects of his intense passion and almost obsessive devotion.

Despite its numerous and openly criticised drawbacks, the metropolis has been one of the most common and popular objects of imaginative representation, celebratory as well as condemnatory, literature being no exception. "[T]o the literary imagination all the great cities are sacred [...], whatever suffering and inequity transpire in them,"[3] as in their multi-facetedness and contradictoriness they constitute a bottomless source of inspiration for artistic rendering. What urban literary works have in common is that "they reflect the discursive heteroglossia that resonates in the texture of each city, at the core of which lies an ultimate otherness on the personal, social, cultural and political levels that permeates and determines the modern city dwellers' everyday experience."[4] Their role is more complex than simply providing their readers with amusement and aesthetic enjoyment, for they can prove helpful in making the city more accessible by translating its baffling elusiveness into linguistic, stylistic and narrative devices that readers find familiar and comprehensible. Any city as big and diverse as London is too vast, chaotic, volatile and incoherent for its inhabitants to ever understand and know it in its totality. That is why these inhabitants "never experience the space of the city unmediated," but always through "symbolised and metaphorised" representational forms[5], which produce images and patterns that enable them, to some extent at least, to make sense of the city's innate convolutedness and heterogeneity. Novels and other literary texts may thus serve their readers as crucial psychic, spiritual and creative vehicles through which to approach and appropriate urban space, for they "in their way constitute the cities we live in as much as planners and builders and politicians and users do," and so they "become frames through which the disorderly, ungraspable material city can be mentally and imaginatively perceived."[6] Ackroyd's London novels do provide such a frame as they depict a distinctive and consistent chronotopic construct based on dramatisations of a set of their author's beliefs and convictions concerning the nature of the capital.

---

3   Harold Bloom, "Cities of the Mind," xi.
4   Petr Chalupský and Anna Grmelová, "Introduction: Urban Spaces in Literature," 2.
5   James Donald, *Imagining the Modern City*, 17.
6   John Clement Ball, *Imagining London: Postcolonial Fiction and the Transnational Metropolis*, 19.

He claims that each writer should have "a very strong sense of belonging to a possession of a particular territory,"[7] and his territory, which he transforms into an imaginative urban space in his novels, happens to be London. The fact that he is a Londoner who is well-acquainted with London's history is the main reason why Ackroyd chose the city to be the setting, theme and even character in most of his novels, being the ultimate landscape of his, and most of his central protagonists', imagination. He has always been a keen walker of the city streets even though, ironically perhaps, the outcome of these walks has been observation and gathering of experience and research material rather than epiphanic revelations or ideas for his work[8]. His relationship to London is not idealistic, idolising or purely aesthetic; he does not consider it a likeable, appealing or formally elegant city, but one built upon strictly pragmatic imperatives and as such often disrespecting or ignoring the wishes and needs of its citizens. For Ackroyd London is a heterogeneous city of contrasts and contradictions, a motley amalgam of joys and sorrows, a mighty apparatus generating, regulating and equalising positive and negative forces and energies, and he likes it precisely because of its variedness and as a unique historical phenomenon, always an independent, open, and infinite labyrinthine city (ML, 386–387). "Its power, its majesty, its darkness, its shadows," answers Ackroyd when asked what fascinates him about the city[9], stressing what he sees as its essential property: it defies an unequivocal, clearly delimited definition or appraisal, as its every dark side has its bright spot, every light its shadow. His London's charm and power rest in its ability to confront and subsequently reconcile these opposing tendencies and phenomena within the city's progressing continuum of human imagination, creativity and experience.

London's heterogeneity is inevitably reflected in the diversity of literary devices – genres, styles and modes of expression – inspired or instigated by the city, which attempt to capture as many of its aspects and metamorphoses as possible. In the same vein, Ackroyd's writing on and about London includes novels, biographies and non-fiction, mostly lectures, essays and historical books. Despite their formal differences, the relation between these works is complementary; their viewpoint and sub-

---

7 Anke Schütze, "I think after More I will do Turner and then I will probably do Shakespeare," an Interview with Peter Ackroyd.

8 "I always used to think I'd be filled with ideas as I walked, but it just doesn't happen" (Mann, "Tales of the city").

9 Five Minutes With: Peter Ackroyd, interviewed by Matthew Stadlen, BBC News website, 10 November 2013.

ject matter often correspond and overlap, and Ackroyd considers them equal in terms of their communicative value as well as their capacity for capturing the spirit of the city, seeing them as "single chapters in the book which will only be completed at the time of [his] death."[10] So he describes what he means by the term "Cockney Visionaries" in his lectures, inquires into the lives of the most significant of them in his biographies, while some others appear as characters in his novels; or, he frequently speaks about London's inherent inclination to violence and criminality in his non-fiction books, and various forms of crimes feature in all his novels set in the city, to mention just two examples. Although Ackroyd's biographies also fall into the category of his London works, their in-depth analysis would reach beyond the scope of this volume. However, references are made to the lectures, particularly to "The Englishness of English Literature," "London Luminaries and Cockney Visionaries," "William Blake, A Spiritual Radical" and "All the Time in the World," historical studies, especially *London: The Biography* and *Albion: The Origins of the English Imagination*, and to selected biographies and interviews. The central focus of this book is the portrayal of the city in his London novels, namely in *The Great Fire of London*, *Hawksmoor*, *Chatterton*, *The House of Doctor Dee*, *Dan Leno and the Limehouse Golem*, *The Clerkenwell Tales*, *The Lambs of London*, *The Casebook of Victor Frankenstein* and *Three Brothers*. His only novel set in the city but not discussed is *The Plato Papers*, a playful futuristic experiment which, unlike the above titles, does not elaborate much on Ackroyd's particular London chronotope.

Central to this chronotope is Ackroyd's concept of perpetual time, one in which the past and the present (and the future in consequence) are not only hard to distinguish, but in which the past can be found, in different forms, in or underneath the present reality. A related aspect of this space-time model is the intrinsic interconnectedness between certain territories of the city and the analogous events and actions that have tended to happen in them repeatedly in different historical periods. As most of these happenings are of obscure and/or violent nature, Ackroyd's London novels revolve primarily around the city's dark sides, its shadowy, subversive and vicious displays, its hidden, undercurrent lines of force, and the radical, desperate and defiant human acts that spring from them. This capital's, especially its East End's, marginality and liminality "makes it an ideal location for transgressions of all kinds of boundaries: legal (crime), natural (magic) and even temporal (the

---

10   An interview with Peter Ackroyd. *Bold Type*.

presence of the past)."[11] It is an internal as well as external subterranean world, mostly concealed from public view and scrutiny, yet which exists within the "official" world, in individuals' minds, in the privacy of their homes, pulsing beneath the silt of pretence, hypocrisy, play-acting and disguise. However, this cityscape is far from being a damned one, as good and evil exist there side by side, producing effects so diverse as terror, dismay, fascination and grace. It reflects Ackroyd's conviction that, both physically and metaphorically, "[i]f the underworld can be understood as a place of fear and danger, it can also be regarded as a place of safety [...], a place of fantasy" (*LU*, 3–4), and the idea of its "secret passages, of mysterious entrances and exits, of retreat and concealment, possesses an incurable charm" (*LU*, 7). Therefore, his stories render and dramatise those properties of the city and its life, present and past, as they are considered as one, which have been commonly overlooked and dismissed by its academic histories and other official discourses.

For this purpose, Ackroyd often plays with historiographic accounts by deliberately altering verified facts, inventing characters, events and texts and mixing them up with real historical ones, as well as by making paranormal happenings crucially affect the plots. The result is a peculiar universe in which, within a historically plausible framework, certain things, which lack support in either history or a rational worldview or both, are shown as not only possible, but natural and even inevitable. His is a poetics of the dark and the mysterious, yet one which manages to portray the city's obscurities as engaging or even enticing, not because it revels in violence or perversity, but through the use of a cleverly playful, inventive and subtly poetic language and imagery which impart to these Gothic elements a feel of ease and naturalness. Ackroyd began his career as a poet and assumes that when he turned from poetry to fiction "the same sensibility simply migrated into a different medium."[12] He professes what he identifies as the English tradition of not separating history from literary creation and since, after all, the very first historians were poets he strives to return to these roots and "restore the poetry of history."[13] His novels can be taken as more imaginative and less restrained exercises in the method which he also employs in his more ambitious projects – the histories of London and England.

---

11 Aleksejs Taube, "London's East End in Peter Ackroyd's *Dan Leno and the Limehouse Golem*," 93.
12 Lidia Vianu, "The mind is the soul," an interview with Peter Ackroyd, 5 October 2001.
13 Peter Ackroyd speaking about his six-volume series *The History of England* at the Royal Festival Hall, Part 1, 10 October 2011.

In order to understand the London of Ackroyd's novels it is necessary to be acquainted with the underlying postulates that shape his conception of the city as such. The first chapter introduces his fundamental ideas about London, its history and its position in and relationship with the English literary sensibility as he has presented them in his non-fiction. It also discusses his understanding of history, the historical novel and historical writing in general and compares them with some post-structuralist revisions of history and its textual representations, although he himself is rather sceptical of their legitimacy. Finally, it discusses the theoretical principles of his urban chronotope, which forms the basis of his London novels in terms of their setting, plot and character construction. Ackroyd's infinite, eternal, mystical and labyrinthine London defies any systematic categorisation or taxonomy, yet for the purposes of this study the most defining aspects of its novelistic projection have been identified – the uncanny, the felonious, the psychogeographic and antiquarian, the theatrical and the literary – which are individually examined in the five subsequent chapters. However, these aspects cannot be separated from one another as they are closely interconnected and as such they not only coexist but influence and determine one another. For instance, the uncanny often goes hand in hand with the psycho-geographic, the felonious with the theatrical, but all of them, though in varying degrees, can be traced in each of the discussed novels. A specific, prominent role is played by the city's literary character, namely its intertextual, metafictional, palimpsestic and apocryphal manifestations, which accompanies all the other aspects, and this is why it is treated last, in the sixth chapter, since it in fact summarises, generalises and completes what has already been elaborated in the preceding four. Ackroyd believes that for every writer dealing with the past, hard, factual evidence should be only one side of the coin, one which must always be complemented and balanced by "spiritual truth" if he or she aspires to understand the nature of history[14]. As this spiritual view often prevails over the factual in Ackryoyd's London novels they may not offer versions of the past that can boast historical precision or correctness, but they are ingenious, thought-provoking, evocative and, what he always stresses as paramount, enjoyable, and his fictional world is thus definitely worthy of close exploration.

---

14   Peter Ackroyd speaking at the Royal Festival Hall, Part 1.

Chapter 1
Ackroyd's London, Past and Present

The city, however, does not tell its past, but contains it like the lines of a hand, written in the corners of the streets, the gratings of the windows, the banisters of the steps, the antennae of the lightning rods, the poles of the flags, every segment marked in turn with scratches, indentations, scrolls.

Italo Calvino, *Invisible Cities*

London and the English Literary Sensibility

For Ackroyd London and English literature, or, more precisely, English literary sensibility, are two inseparable concepts which have affected and shaped each other from time immemorial. He explores and exemplifies them in detail in his two comprehensive studies, *London: The Biography* (2000) and *Albion: The Origins of the English Imagination* (2002), but his elemental ideas and theories can be found stated earlier, rather separately and therefore perhaps less coherently, yet all the more aptly and in a more articulate and outspoken manner, in his public lectures delivered during the 1990s, namely "The Englishness of English Literature" (1993), "London Luminaries and Cockney Visionaries" (1993), "William Blake, A Spiritual Radical" (1995) and "All the Time in the World" (1999). In these lectures Ackroyd clearly formulates what he believes defines and constitutes the intrinsic interconnectedness between the English and London's spirit and creative sensibility. More perceptibly than in his books, he is explicit when touching on more personal or polemical issues, such as the role of Catholicism in the development of English literary sensibility, the importance of spiritual radicalism for the formation of London's imaginative genius, his defining of himself by assuming a dismissive stance towards the notion of minority literature, or his criticism of the notion of postmodernism or postmodernist narrative tendencies in English literature. Therefore, these four short texts not only provide the reader with a lucid idea of Ackroyd's (primarily literary) London, but also make him/her familiar with their author's inward convictions and strong beliefs, which formatively determine the very conception of his distinct urban chronotope.

Two related terms prove especially crucial for understanding Ackroyd's vision of the above mentioned concurrent phenomena, i.e. London within the English literary sensibility and the English literary sensibility within London, and these are "patterns of continuity" and "heterogeneity." Following T. S. Eliot's remark that "the more truly native – even parochial – a literature is, the more universal it can become" (qt. in EEL, 329), Ackroyd sees almost no point in trying to establish any canonic, enclosed, invariable and generally valid national literary tradition or hierarchy, arguing that "a literature must be imbued with a powerful local presence before it can aspire to any kind of unique status" (EEL, 329). On the one hand, this need for a powerful local presence makes every literary work deeply rooted in the larger – temporal, spatial, social, spiritual and intellectual – conditions of its origin, in other words, inseparably bound to a certain historical period and its values, beliefs and ideas, both prevailing and undercurrent. Yet, on the other hand, he stresses that something like a characteristic genius can be traced in English literature throughout its development in the form of certain "lines of force which eddy through the language" (EEL, 330–31), and which are naturally imprinted in literary works written in this language. This English genius or spirit thus comprises certain, often diverse, forces, energies, tendencies and stimuli which, with varying intensity and chronological recurrence, (re)emerge in and determine the language and literature of a particular time and place. These patterns of continuity, or patterns of resonance and resemblance as Ackroyd also calls them (EEL, 331, 339), have been at work and persisted in English linguistic and literary traditions for centuries, gradually composing an inheritance that is impossible to avoid if one wishes to become part of this living continuum of human imagination, experience and wisdom. Although rather intangible, elusive or even speculative from a strictly scholarly perspective, for Ackroyd they represent an essential firm point in English, and in consequence London, history, which more often than not appears to him as "one of accident, confusion, chance and unintended consequences."[1]

---

1   Euan Ferguson, "I just want to tell a story," an interview with Peter Ackroyd. *The Observer*, 25 August, 2011.

Ackroyd thus, rather questionably and perhaps in part provocatively, strongly argues against two concepts popular in contemporary literary debates, which either defy or at least displace the idea of historical continuity – international writing and ahistorical categories of writing, such as African-American, gay or feminist writing (EEL, 329), precisely because these disregard any idiosyncrasies of national literary sensibility. At the same time, however, he warns against preserving the national literary tradition intact and inviolable by delineating and venerating a body of outstanding works from the past which, despite their exceptional qualities, have little if any relevance to what is written in the present. He claims that "[t]he Englishness of English literature is not some literary construct, some museum of the past, some enclosed hierarchical order" (EEL, 340), suggesting that such a sensibility is wholly devoid of elitism, exclusivity and impersonality, and that its continuous passage through time has created its own distinct recurrent patterns, flows and energies available for and close to anyone sensitive and sensible enough to let themselves be inspired or guided by this "line of force which is the very life and breath of the sentences we are writing now" (EEL, 340). It is a serious error to think we can learn about ourselves – our present-day culture, society, spirituality, creativity – only by reading modern literature which, in fact, can never be properly understood without examining the living inheritance of the historical tradition from which it stems. The great writers of the past, such as Chaucer, Shakespeare, Milton or Blake, Ackroyd insists, may therefore prove more substantial for this process of learning and understanding than their most celebrated and widely read contemporary successors.

Hand in hand with the patterns of continuity in the development of English sensibility goes heterogeneity, the tendency towards employing and combining a diversity of literary devices, such as genres, styles, perspectives and moods, of an often conflicting nature. This heterogeneity, which manifests itself across time as each historical period shows interest in using or adapting the styles and discourses of the past, and which Nikolaus Pevsner called the "'self-conscious choice of a mode of expression', the formal or playful use of a historical style" (qt. in EEL, 333), Ackroyd believes "is an intrinsic feature of the English literary inheritance" (EEL, 334). As such, it can be found at the core of the most complex and, simultaneously, inventively playful works, such as Sidney's *Arcadia*, Sterne's *Tristram Shandy* and Dickens's novels in the form of pastiche, parody, genre mixture or multiple narrative. While asserting heterogeneity as a recognisable feature of the English literary tradition,

Ackroyd is critical towards contemporary literary studies and histories as they have not only seemed to mostly disregard this tendency, but have often included it under recent cultural phenomena such as postmodernism or deconstruction. To attach these modern and fashionable labels "to such a familiar and ancient tradition," to "something which has always been close to the heart of the English genius" Ackroyd denotes an act of "cultural blindness or ignorance" (EEL, 333). And so he rejects the labelling of his books as postmodernist and prefers to see his approach as "belonging to a native London or English tradition that might, accidentally, have some things in common with postmodern culture."[2] For instance, mixing the high with the low, one of the features typically attributed to postmodernist sensibility, has for long been present in English culture through "the characteristic gift among English artists for the caricature of low or common life" (EEL, 332). Ackroyd therefore calls for a re-evaluation and revision of traditionalist approaches to the construction and interpretation of the history of English literature, which would be based, among others, also on the notions of patterns of chronological resonance and heterogeneity.

One of the crucial features of English literary sensibility that has been largely overlooked by modern literary criticism is an almost obsessive concern with theatrical display and spectacle. According to Ackroyd, the reason behind this is that twentieth century literary criticism has been dominated by a secular, or "dispossessed or displaced Protestantism," which means that "the themes and beliefs they explored in their reading of literature were largely taken from the values of a Protestant or Dissenting culture" (EEL, 334). The English liking for theatricality, variety and display, however, has its origins in the liturgy of the Catholic Church which makes use of and relishes collectively consumed linguistic ritual, spectacle and symbolism, as opposed to the more individualistic, solitary and unpretentious Protestantism. Ackroyd asserts that the tendency towards theatricality and all its heterogeneous manifestations, such as clownery, grotesque caricatures, pantomime humour and juxtaposition of varied moods and styles – serious and ludicrous, high and low – which is an intrinsic element of the English genius, can be traced back to medieval mystery and miracle plays, and, in consequence, to the Catholic Mass itself. It later infiltrated other literary genres and media of expression, most manifestly the novel, finding vent in the typically English combination of "pathos and comedy, tragedy and farce" (EEL, 335), the

---

2   Barry Lewis, *My Words Echo Thus: Possessing the Past in Peter Ackroyd*, 181.

"characteristic mixture of forms and styles, [...] in the unwillingness to maintain one mood for very long, in the manipulation of form for theatrical effect" (EEL, 338). English literary sensibility owes yet another of its defining aspects to Catholic tradition, which has been much neglected in the conventional histories of English literature, namely a respect for and drawing inspiration from the previous tradition. Unlike Protestantism, which stresses individual experience, conscience and relationship to God, Catholicism "tends to emphasize the significance of authority and historical tradition" (EEL, 336), which was also reflected in the idea of artistic originality as recreation, reinterpretation or readaptation of already existing works, stories and ideas that was followed until the end of the sixteenth century. And so the unique combination of heterogeneous incongruity with an awareness of being part of a continuous historical tradition has allowed the English sensibility to achieve "the symbolic re-enactment of certain visionary truths" (EEL, 337). Although Ackroyd admits that the Catholic inheritance cannot explain the English literary sensibility as a whole (as some of its aspects have emerged from the pre-Christian or Protestant traditions), he suggests that to ignore it may easily result in a reduced and simplistic, if not biased or tendentious, perspective.

The proposition of patterns of continuity running across and reemerging in different historical periods inevitably requires a reworking or redefinition of traditional chronology in favour of a less sequential and consecutively construed concept, and Ackroyd conceives it on the basis of a parallel between time and language, as the latter can be taken as a simulacrum of the first. Due to chronological resonance the past language and linguistic means of expression form a living inheritance, a line of force which still, at least latently, influences present-day writers: "all the previous structures of our language lie just beneath the one we are presently using, and if you reintroduce them you are able to open the readers' eyes to other realities and to other times which in similar fashion lie just beneath the one we are currently part of" (ATW, 369). If the patterns of continuity operate in other than a linear and chronological manner, the time within which they operate must be approached accordingly – as labyrinthine, at times circular, at times spiral, at times haphazard, but, most importantly, as a mass or continuum in which the traditional categories of the past and the present are not always easy to distinguish. It is only within this continuum of time that the historical tradition can truly attain its timeless momentousness. Therefore, the relationship between the past and the present is more intricate and one cannot be properly understood without the other. Ackroyd professes T. S. Eliot's idea that "[t]ime present and time past/ are both perhaps present in time future/ and time future contained in time past,"[3] inspired by Henri Bergson's notion of time as a unique "continuous flux" containing "a succession of states, each of which announces that which follows and contains that which precedes it"; this succession can "only be said to form multiple states" which are impossible to determine "where any of them finishe[s] or where another commence[s]. In reality no one of them begins or ends, but all extend into each other,"[4] resulting in "the perpetual present of the past."[5] The role of a writer is then to "introduce" time past to time present and vice versa, and possibly to introduce them both to time future, which is what the greatest writers have managed to do – "by the strength of their language, containing within itself all the potential and power of the past, they are able to intimate that time itself is an illusion" (ATW, 371). Their works, Ackroyd believes, "have conquered chronology" (ATW, 371), which is the sole achievement to which he also aspires.

A familiarity with Ackroyd's idea of the English literary tradition is essential for understanding his perception of London as all the aspects of English literary sensibility mentioned so far are also the very cornerstones of Ackroyd's conception of the capital as a literary city of unrelenting imaginary vision. It is primarily London time which strongly defies chronological and sequential linearity as most, if not all, happenings in and of the city are based on recurrence, influences and force patterns that either circulate through history, or run across the individual layers of time while evincing some regularity, or in a largely disordered, labyrinthine manner. As a result, the past and the present in the city cannot be viewed as separate, distinct temporal entities, but rather as overlapping or even interlocked parts of one perpetual continuum:

> We must not think of time as some continually flowing stream moving in one direction. Think of it more as a lava flow from some unknown source of fire. Some parts of it move forward, some parts of it branch off and form separate channels, some parts of it slow down and eventually harden. [...] It is as if the past and present were then locked in an embrace, like lovers. (LLCV, 343)

---

3 T. S. Eliot, *The Complete Poems and Plays*, 171.
4 Henri Bergson, *An Introduction to Metaphysics*, 11.
5 Anke Schütze, "I think after More I will do Turner and then I will probably do Shakespeare," an Interview with Peter Ackroyd.

What can be detected in the history of London, not only in its literary or cultural history, but also in its social, political and spiritual history, are certain supratemporal or perpetual tendencies, "patterns of habitation, and patterns of inheritance, which seem to emerge from the very streets and alleys of the capital," and which create the basis of its "sensibility which has persisted for many centuries" (LLCV, 343). In terms of place and space, the local presence of London's spirit manifests itself as the power of *genius loci*, the energy certain areas possess which makes particular events, acts or forms of human behaviour repeatedly occur on their territories.

The crucial defining aspect of London's creative genius is heterogeneity – the richness and diversity of forms, styles, moods and means of expression, both past and present – whose seemingly paradoxical or incongruent combination corresponds with the very nature of the city "where the extremes of the human condition meet, where one emotion or mood is quickly succeeded by another, where comedy and tragedy are to be seen side by side. This is the true London sensibility" (LLCV, 348). It is therefore inevitable that Ackroyd uses the novel as the medium most suitable for capturing and expressing the city's heterogeneity, contradictoriness and multiformity, as it is a genre which "quotes, parodies and transforms other genres, converting its literary ancestors into mere components of itself," thus becoming "a mighty melting pot"[6] whose potential to instigate something new or unexpected seems almost inexhaustible, and which best corresponds with the nature of London as he sees it – the pantomime-like tendency to combine "different strands of imaginative thought."[7] This heterogeneity, however, is not only a domain of the greatest works of the literary canon; on the contrary, its roots are to be found outside the official cultural and intellectual spheres, for instance in London's esoteric and occult traditions or in the sketches and melodies of the music hall.

Ackroyd calls the most outstanding personalities in the history of London, the artists, scholars and thinkers who thought of the city "as their spiritual home,"[8] "who saw elements of the sacred and the symbolic in their local circumstances,"[9] and whose work both reflects and projects a living example of these characteristic features because they "have

---

6   Terry Eagleton, *The English Novel*, 1.

7   Schütze, "I think after More I will do Turner and then I will probably do Shakespeare."

8   Schütze, "I think after More I will do Turner and then I will probably do Shakespeare."

9   Lidia Vianu, "The mind is the soul," an interview with Peter Ackroyd, 5 October 2001.

absorbed London culture and absorbed London's imagination,"[10] "London Luminaries" or, more frequently, "Cockney Visionaries." His list of visionaries includes traditional names, such as Chaucer, More, Newton, Blake, Turner and Dickens, together with those whose position within London's imaginative and spiritual traditions is perhaps more disputable and less widely acknowledged, such as John Dee, Nicholas Hawksmoor, Thomas Chatterton, Dan Leno and Charlie Chaplin, as what connects all these often dissimilar personalities is that

> [t]hey understood the energy of London, they understood its variety, and they also understood its darkness. But they are visionaries because they represented the symbolic dimension of existence in what Blake called 'Infinite London' – in this vast concourse of people they understood the pity and mystery of existence just as surely as they understood its noise and its bustle. (LLCV, 346–47)

The decisive criterion for obtaining this label is the person's boldness in compounding the city's contradictory aspects in forming their own creative vision; Ackroyd's visionaries successfully attempted to juxtapose and reconcile these aspects in their professional and personal lives. Their creative vision thus arises from their rejection of traditional categorisation and their capacity to transcend the clear-cut borderline between such opposites or extremes as the tragic and the farcical, the serious and the ludicrous, the serene and the spectacular, the dignified and the pathetic, the realistic and the grotesque, the sacred and the pagan, and make equal use of both polarities. Although for these individuals "visionary reality is much more real than the physical reality of life-in-time,"[11] such a vision by no means derives solely from unrestrained imagination, originality and defiance of conventions as it must be complemented with an awareness of historical tradition and one's position within it. Their greatness lies in their ability to embed their unique visions in this continuum of ideas and experience by drawing from, rather than ignoring or repudiating, the inheritance of the past. "There is an irrepressible energy and exuberance here which seems to me characteristic of great London artists, as if they always knew that they were part of something much larger than their own selves" (LLCV, 350), Ackroyd notes, believing this energy has been generated by the momentum of the patterns of resonance.

---

10 Daisy Banks, "Peter Ackroyd on London," *The Browser*.

11 Susana Onega, *Metafiction and myth in the novels of Peter Ackroyd*, 191.

A significant consequence follows from the fact that these visionaries have to face the task of depicting and rendering London's immense complexity – their work mostly lacks any deliberate and articulate moral stance or message. This is yet another reason why they have been largely overlooked by academic circles; it is also a tradition to which Ackroyd claims allegiance[12], as all he is trying to communicate to his readers is "a mood, an aspiration, a susceptibility to the past, but no message."[13] Because these Londoners need to incorporate and embrace in their vision as many of the city's opposites, contradictions and extremities as possible, there is not much space left to them for profound exploration and examination of the ethical side of their and their protagonists' values and beliefs, or the subtle and convoluted workings of the human psyche. Instead, they favour devices which tend to rather flatten their characters or impersonations, but which enable them to compose a panoramic yet dynamic image of London, such as caricature, spectacle and farce. "As city writers and artists they are more concerned with the external life, with the movement of crowds, with the great general drama of the human spirit. They have a sense of energy and splendour, of ritual and display, which may have very little to do with ethical judgement or the exercise of moral consciousness" (LLCV, 350). This does not mean that they would have absolutely no conscience or ethical sense, or that their work would be devoid of any moral anchorage; it is simply not their primary concern, and so if they are to comment on these issues they do so indirectly, using irony, satire, allegory, parable, allusion, or, for a more powerful effect, a combination of these. Ackroyd identifies himself with this tendency to evade psychological delving into characters' emotions, preferring rather to "explore them through the way in which they relate to their surroundings,"[14] especially to those within London.

All the stylistic, narrative, generic and linguistic heterogeneity of English literature that shows itself through such distinct yet intrinsically related phenomena as grotesque caricatures, clowneries, the mixing up and experimental use of past styles, theatricality, spectacle, heteroglos-

---

12 "... that morality idea comes from the desire of the literary critic to find moral lessons in literature. [...] A deep fear of pleasure, of course, lies at the heart of the academic study of literature. Whereas all I want to do is give people a bit of pleasure, a bit of slap and tickle. It's true! You don't learn anything from a novel, your ethical response aren't sharpened, your moral relations with the world aren't purified." Patrick McGrath, "Peter Ackroyd: Interview."

13 "Each book is a different reason to exist," Lidia Vianu's students' videoconference interview with Peter Ackroyd, 9 May 2006.

14 John Preston, "My work matters more to me than love," an interview with Peter Ackroyd. *The Telegraph*, 20 August 2006.

sia and Gothic excess, and in which the English sensibility truly resides, appears rather minor, if at all recognisable, to many, and as such is rarely mentioned in scholarly critical studies. The reason for this is that the heterogeneous combination of and oscillation between opposites, or even extremes, has its roots, to a considerable extent, in the lower and popular rather than the official cultural forms, those mostly ignored and dismissed by the intellectual elites. Nowhere is this tendency more obvious, he claims, than in London and its cultural tradition, no matter how strongly the city which, "within its very texture and structure [...] incorporates a diversity of human moods and actions, events and responses" (LLCV, 349) calls for diversity and variety of cultural forms and means of artistic expression in order to capture all its possible manifestations and metamorphoses. Yet, the very artistic forms and means of expression most corresponding with the city's multifaceted and polyphonic nature are precisely those which fall into the category of second-rate cultural and entertainment production, and so many manifestations of the true London creative sensibility have remained widely unacknowledged. Therefore, Ackroyd often concentrates on London's nineteenth-century popular culture, as the origins of many forms of popular fiction can be found in the printing technology, literacy and distribution centred on London in this period[15]. "Even the fears and obsessions and imaginative world of the Victorians continued to play on the minds and imaginations of Londoners throughout the twentieth century," and so "[a]ll the major genres of twentieth-century imaginative writing had at least some roots in Victorian London."[16] As a related example, Ackroyd uses the music hall tradition with its excessive theatricality based on folk humour, hyperbolic caricature, social satire, farcical scenes, impersonations and vocal imitations, spectacular cross-dressing and mock-dancing, improvisation, deliberate overacting, sudden switching between different moods and dramatic modes in or between acts and sketches, and frolicsome and skittish songs and ditties, which he believes so aptly catches the spirit of the city's ordinary life. He considers Dan Leno, the famous monopolylinguist and most popular music hall comedian of the late nineteenth century, one of the most outstanding Cockney Visionaries, and insists that to get to know the city's "real pathos and diversity, the scholar or critic should turn to the tunes of the London halls" as they are "charged with the real presence of place," and so "only a very blinkered culture can afford to ignore them"

---

15 Lawrence Phillips, "Introduction." In Lawrence Phillips (ed.), *The Swarming Streets: The Twentieth-Century Literary Representations of London*, 2.

16 Jerry White, *London in the Twentieth Century: A City and Its People*, 6.

(LLCV, 344, 345), and so every person sincerely in search of the essence of London's genius must avoid this mistaken narrow-mindedness.

There is one more feature that connects most of the Cockney Visionaries: because their visionary ideas were often misunderstood and unappreciated by their contemporaries, but largely also because they sought to understand their city through means other than those of the official cultural tradition, established reviewers and newspaper commentators criticised or even spurned them for their distance from reality, while, as Ackroyd notes, these critics simply disliked or found uncomfortable the essential heterogeneous qualities of London's vision, such as variety and energetic display (LLCV, 347). Therefore, there has been a unique, sometimes perhaps peculiar, yet always strong and significant, tradition in London reflecting those properties and tendencies of the city's life which resist taming, moralising and presentation by means prescribed by the official cultural establishment. This fundamentally London tradition

> is that of the energetic, individualistic, unfashionable artists who, more often than not, turn out to be native Londoners. They may be right-wing reactionaries or apolitical anarchists, but they always reject the values of the standard intellectual culture and, as a result, they are discounted, or attacked, or marginalised. It happened to Turner, it happened to Blake, it happened to Dickens in the second half of his literary career – which of course is enough to say that these establishment attacks are not only foolish but ultimately unsuccessful. (LLCV, 347)

Ackroyd's keynote is that the real artistic and literary tradition of London, with all its underlying patterns of resonance and continuity, has been persistently, if not indeed systematically, dismissed and overlooked, as it often developed alongside, and sometimes literally in opposition to, the standard, centralised and generally promoted one. This quality makes it democratic rather than elitist, inclusive rather than exclusive, open to new impulses, experience, themes and ideas as long as they resonate with the city's spirit and character, but also, very importantly, as long as they respect and revere the spiritual legacy of the past. The roots and sources of London's sensibility are thus a particular blend of the secret and the sacred, the underground and the manifest, and the pagan and the religious, which infuses it with its characteristic heterogeneity and variety. The crucial thing is, Ackroyd stresses, that this is an active, living inheritance that still operates below the surface of the present-day sensibility, affecting the language, imagination and behaviour not only of those who aspire to become truly London artists, but also all those who strive to understand what it means to be part of the city: "if we lose sight of our city – if we lose sight of our inheritance – then we lose sight of our own selves as well" (LLCV, 351).

As the continuous process of the shaping and employment of a London sensibility contains a strong element of radicalism, though spiritual and creative rather than political or social, Ackroyd considers William Blake the most emblematic representative of the visionary tradition. Blake's ideas, both in life and art, were in most cases radical, alternately subversive, reactionary and revolutionary, but he differed from the organised, typical London radicals of his time as he distrusted and despised rationalism, materialism and belief in future progress based on a denial of the past tradition, which means the principles that stood at the heart of their conception of a better England. Although Blake's visions looked into the future, it is difficult to label him as wholly modern and forward-looking because, apart from imagination and divine inspiration, he believed "in the paramount importance of historical and cultural inheritance" (WBSR, 357), as a result of which his radicalism "was an amalgam of various sources and ideas" (WBSR, 358), which, among the products of his resourceful genius, included such diverse sources of influence as literature, the Bible, folk and popular cultural forms, life experience, pagan and Christian cults and rituals, ancient wisdom, magic, occultism and sexual mysticism. Therefore, even in his radicalism, Blake was an individualistic solitary criticised, ignored or even mocked by most of his contemporaries, an artisan and artist whose work was ahead of its time as it surpassed its conventional thinking, but which was in large part derived from his historical and cultural inheritance and showed respect for the past and age-old values such as a belief in the spiritual and divine form, love and reverence. Rather than being a progressive, internationalist revolutionary agitator Blake is a split, seemingly internally inconsistent, personality, yet this ambivalence is at the same time the very constituent of the city's sensibility: he is a bardic figure, deeply rooted in the tradition of his nation, yet, at the same time, a prophetic visionary whose ideas and art appeal to people regardless of their time and cultural background. This kind of spiritual radicalism or dissent, Ackroyd argues, embodies a timeless, distinctly London tradition, it is "an emanation of the city we live in now" (WBSR, 363), one of the ways "of finding alternative sources of power" (WBSR, 364), which may not be successful, activated or visible immediately, but which crucially determines the city's genius in the long term.

Ackroyd, History and the Historical Novel

Although most of Ackroyd's works, at least in part, deal with the past it would be inaccurate to call him a purely historical writer. If nothing else, some of his novels, like *The Great Fire of London* (1982), *First Light* (1989), *English Music* (1992) and *Three Brothers* (2013), take place in the present or a very recent past and bear no features of a historical narrative whatsoever, nor is the rest of his fiction homogeneous in terms of its treatment of history. Leaving aside the conceit-novel *The Plato Papers* (1999), which mocks any period's preposterous attempts to restore the past as it really was, demonstrating that "[w]e are astounded by our ancestors and their misconception, but we may seem equally foolish to our successors" (*PP*, 126), Ackroyd's remaining novels can be loosely subdivided into two categories: those whose story is set wholly in the past, such as *Dan Leno and the Limehouse Golem* (1994), *Milton in America* (1996), *The Clerkenwell Tales* (2003), *The Lambs of London* (2004), *The Fall of Troy* (2006) and *The Casebook of Victor Frankenstein* (2008), and can be understood as examples of the genre of the historical novel, with a special subcategory created by *The Last Testament of Oscar Wilde* (1983), conceived as a quasi-document, a fictional diary allegedly written by Oscar Wilde and recounting the last months of his life; and those with multiple plotlines, one of which takes place in the present and the rest in the past, namely *Hawksmoor* (1985), *Chatterton* (1987) and *The House of Doctor Dee* (1993), which fall into the category only partially. What connects all these works, however, is the author's quest for the nature of the past, its representation in the form of mostly written history, the processes of obtaining our knowledge of what happened at times beyond our memory and life experience, and the intricate relationship between the past and the present. The past in his novels thus operates as a double agent – an object of inquiry and subsequent re-presentation as well as a crucial means of casting light on the present and on the human condition in general.

A London writer or chronicler is a more appropriate label for Ackroyd as novels that are both set in London and thematically deal with the metropolis represent a substantial part of his fiction and non-fiction. Therefore, it is prevailingly London's history, or, more precisely, the correlation between the past and the present within, but also beyond, the city that can be found at the heart of his London novels. This theme goes hand in hand with an exploration of how the history of and in the city is "made," how it works, how it gets recorded, preserved and passed on, but also how easily it gets distorted, obscured or completely lost. Ackroyd does not consider himself a scholar, not even a historian, but a writer for whom "history is not an academic discipline" but "a living presence which is on some occasions palpable," and whose task, in fiction and non-fiction alike, is to "dramatise and reinvent" this living presence for the audience[17]. It is precisely the often impalpable nature of the patterns behind the city's life in time, "the invisible agencies and the unseen powers that are not detectable by conventional history,"[18] that interest him far more than the concrete events and happenings which may be useful in terms of creating an attractive and gripping story, but which prove insufficient in terms of understanding the larger course of historical development. The result is a fictitious construct of alternative, or "heightened" as he prefers to call it, reality "in which the sacred forces of the world are as plain as any more familiar elements."[19]

The greatest strength of his London works results from the combination of their author's two crucial persuasions or premises. First, overtly or in a more subtle manner, they exceed the past by reaching into the present: they strive to demonstrate how the past is literally interwoven with, embedded in the present, that the past and the present are not separate, distinct periods but complexly interconnected moments of one continuum that transcends the prevalent historical concept of linear chronology. The present is thus shown as impossible to know or understand without a sensitive insight into the mechanisms and patterns of preceding events and developments. Second, they always strive to offer an unconventional, alternative or speculative re-presentation and interpretation of the past, to reveal the marginal, overlooked, unknown, disreputable histories that often problematise, contradict or disprove official records and versions. Such history is then subversive in both its form and content which, in effect, become inseparable and mutually determining. Although Ackroyd often speaks negatively and dismissively about his supposed involvement with recent theoretical and critical approaches, claiming that there is "no theoretical purpose behind [his] writing,"[20] his view of the past and history is not that far from their fundamental poststructuralist and postmodernist revisions.

---

17 Peter Ackroyd speaking at the Royal Festival Hall, Part 1, 10 October 2011.

18 Five Minutes With: Peter Ackroyd, interviewed by Matthew Stadlen, BBC News website, 10 November 2013.

19 Vianu, "The mind is the soul."

20 Half-ironically, Ackroyd admits that the notion of postmodernism may apply to his writing because it is so vague and broad that "it must apply to all writers after a certain date," but that it impinges neither upon his writing, nor upon his life. "Each book is a different reason to exist," Lidia Vianu's students' videoconference interview with Peter Ackroyd.

Being a writer whose principal theme is the past is not an easy role in, or perhaps already after, the period commonly referred to as postmodernity, during which the concept of history, its very nature and understanding, has been exposed to a strenuous critique and, consequently, has undergone an ultimate transformation. For many, however, a simplistic, one-sided variant of this critique has served as an instrument for denouncing and rejecting history as such, arguing that history is only fabulation, consisting of a multiplicity of subjective, biased truths and stories composed into a smooth, coherent narration using subjectively tainted narrative strategies, and therefore, as wholly objective truth about the past proves unobtainable, there is no point in vainly trying to seek it. However, despite all this, for many reasons, the main of which are discussed in the following paragraphs, it is vital for us, and all the more for a writer who is concerned with the past, to believe that some historical truth is, at least in part, obtainable, otherwise we find ourselves in danger of falling into what Julian Barnes calls "beguiling relativity,"[21] which may throw us into a void of values not only with respect to our historical knowledge, but also to the sense of who we are and why. In order to understand the fundamental premises of postmodernist deconstruction of history it is necessary to briefly touch upon the notion of historical discourse and its relation with the past.

People's urge to get to know, interpret, comprehend and possibly identify with their past is more than understandable as it is crucial and integral to their sense of both personal and collective identity. However, we are simultaneously aware that the actual past is always "beyond retrieval" for "all we have left are much-eroded traces and partial records filtered through diverse eyes and minds."[22] What we like to denote as the past is in fact in part a reflection of present needs and desires, a result of diverse, variously reliable but also variously motivated, processes such as recollecting past experiences, rewriting history, refashioning historical traces, and seeking some logic between and justifying particular past events. It follows that a distinction must be made between the past and history: while the first refers to what once really happened, the latter consists of a series of discourses about the bygone world which transform our knowledge of the past into narratives. The past as we "know" it in the form of history, or, more precisely, histories, is a discursive and narrative construct always crucially affected by the conditions and circumstances of its creation.

21   Julian Barnes, *A History of the World in 10 ½ Chapters*, 296.
22   David Lowenthal, *The Heritage Crusade*, 106.

It would of course be fatuous to deny the existence of the past. Similarly, it would be untrue and misleading to claim that all history is mere fiction or fabrication, that there is nothing credible enough in historical records and relics we can lean on in our attempts to bring the past back to life. The question rather is how we get to know and interpret this past, how we establish plausible and well-founded connections between historical data. The acts of reshaping, adapting and appropriating the past stem from our demand to make it convincing, logical, intelligible and, at least to some extent, interesting and gripping. The problem is that most historical facts are discontinuous, contingent or even timeless, and as such they do not make much sense of the past unless they are transformed and woven into stories, embedded in some interpretative framework and patterns of meaning. This process, however, happens "outside" these facts, in the realm of the historian's beliefs, assumptions and ideas about historical causality. "So, while individual statements may be true/false, narrative as a collection of them is more than their sum. The narrative becomes a complex interpretative exercise that is neither conclusively true nor false."[23] Therefore, history is a cultural product that always to some extent generates historical knowledge through the employment of the narrative. Moreover, due to its formal and organisational restraints, such as linearity, a sequential and limited number of perspectives, no narrative, though profound, detailed and compact, can ever capture the complexity and multiformity of real-life events. As a result, the historical truth may not only get distorted by being made intelligible and consequential, but also simplified when reduced to a narrative account of few dimensions.

It is inevitable that we see the past differently than people who actually lived in it as they did not experience their time in the way we present and interpret it now. As a result, the connections and conclusions present-day people construe and construct about the past are rooted in the world they live in – their way of thinking, background, self-image, assumed norms and value systems, reading experience, language capacity and imagination, all of which also affect how the narratives of history are composed and consumed. It naturally requires imagining and creative change to make the past's otherness believable, comprehensible and compelling to the contemporary audience. In order to bridge the temporal and mental gap between the past and the present, we have to introduce our cognitive processes, through which the past gets continuously

---

23 Alun Munslow, *Deconstructing History*, 12.

reshaped and revised, which means that no absolute, objective historical truth is attainable for us. This, however, does not mean that such historical knowledge is debased and useless as it operates with verified facts and data and thus always "casts some light on the past" and "elements of truth persist in it."[24] Every attempt at reconstructing and reinterpreting the past can thus be understood as another step in the unending process of approximating to its truthful image.

Moreover, no history is "innocent," in the sense of being independent of larger socio-political circumstances, as the purpose and motivation behind its creation also come into play, and so not only what history is but also for whom history is created determines its final form significantly. Every public discourse, history included, exists within the hierarchical systems of power which produce and sustain ideas through their "politics of truth," that means mechanisms of production, regulation, distribution, circulation and operation of statements, which enable an individual to distinguish between the true and the false[25]. The reasons for (ab)using or altering history are numerous and varied, from political and ideological to personal or aesthetic, but they have one thing in common – their motivation is to "distort or conceal" the historical truth rather than "reveal [it] to posterity."[26] Each historical period thus had a central, dominant evaluative perspective which caused some discourses and texts, and connected with these also some linguistic, literary and narrative devices and categories, to be deemed suitable and appropriate, while those expressing alternative or dissenting views were dismissed, ostracised and declared mendacious or even dangerous. However, in the course of time these central perspectives kept changing, lost their exclusiveness, and were replaced by "local patterns of dominance and marginality, which are all historiographically constructed and which must be historiographically read."[27]

What follows is the need to revise history as a centralised, totalising discourse by examining it with regard to the "evaluative hierarchies"[28] related to power within which it comes into being. To deconstruct the dominant histories means to point out all the possible influences and forces that helped construct them but are external to their ostensible subject matter – the past. By doing this, historical discourse, and the

---

24 David Lowenthal, *The Past is a Foreign Country*, 235.
25 Michel Foucault, *Power/Knowledge*, 131–133.
26 Michael Stanford, *An Introduction to the Philosophy of History*, 66.
27 Keith Jenkins, *Re-thinking History*, 44.
28 Jenkins, *Re-thinking History*, 31.

past along with it, is made open to reevaluation, reinterpretation and reappropriation by the marginalised, who have long been mere objects or instruments of other people's histories. All these deconstructive strategies "destabilize the past and fracture it, so that, in the cracks opened up, new histories can be made"[29] by stressing that history is a written discourse, a notional concept. As the same applies to fiction as well, historical novels, or novels concerned with the past, may play their part in this process through searching for and filling these cracks with imaginative potentials.

History's discursive and narrative character opens it to a plurality of perspectives, as a result of which many different stories can be made about the same past events. The meaning of such history thus derives not so much from the facts but from their textual representation. As Hayden White notes, "[h]historical situations are not inherently tragic, comic, or romantic," we only think of them as such "because these concepts are part of our generally cultural and specifically literary heritage. How a given historical situation is to be configured depends on the historian's subtlety in matching up a specific plot structure with the set of historical events that he wishes to endow with a meaning of a particular kind."[30] What comes out of this process is a subtle but unceasing rendering of past realities, as people in the past never really lived their lives in stories, they were not aware of any narrative logic which would draw connections between their disparate acts, and they obviously could hardly anticipate the ideological "centres" which would interpret their time in the future.

Historical narrative is therefore not only a biased but also a simplified version or representation of the past – what remains unsaid or obliterated are all those evasive, elusive, ungraspable or unproven occurrences, connections and causalities, what White calls the "historical sublime," by which he means "the celebration of the undiscoverable, possibly meaningless, and open-ended nature of the past."[31] Tracing, and subsequently presenting, the instances of the historical sublime, however, is not easy for traditional historiography, and rather calls for an experimental history whose central principle is to perpetually expose and confront everything that has been taken as given and indisputable. Such history is aware of its intertextuality, its authorialism and subjectivity, its always unfinished nature, its impressionistic and dialogic

---

29 Jenkins, *Re-thinking History*, 79.
30 Hayden White, *Tropics of Discourse: Essays in Cultural Criticism*, 85.
31 Munslow, *Deconstructing History*, 14.

character, and its being a mere link in a chain, a precursor to the next stage in the evolution of historical expression[32]. This does not mean that experimental history does not refer to the past and deploy facts and data, but rather the historical context is to some extent sidelined and not always verified or evidentially supported. The author-reader interaction thus becomes less restrained and controlled, more open and dynamic, a result of the combination of the author's creativity and the reader's interpretative liberty.

This shift in preference and focus requires changes and experiments in form, not only in the narrative but also in the linguistic, stylistic and generic perspectives. "History henceforth speaks in new ways – first person, the language of fiction and poetry, of tarot cards, pantomime, mystery, pastiche, entertainment and brevity."[33] The underlying premise of the absence of historical truth and lack of original meaning opens this "artwork history" to various alternative recreations and reinter-pretations, by which it also shifts the value of history and its larger consequences, social as well as intellectual. This "sceptical and ironic history"[34] by no means claims to be the only recognised one, but rather that which operates as parallel to, or perhaps complementary with, tra-ditional history, as it is exempt from the constraints of the imperative of producing reasonable and convincing versions of the past. Due to the considerably literary character of this experimental approach the borderline between such historical narrative and contemporary, post-modernist historical fiction, or fiction about the past, becomes blurred and practically indistinct.

Most of Ackroyd's London novels exemplify at least some of the above-mentioned deconstructive and revisionist tendencies and ap-proaches in their treatment of the past and history, both collective and individual, as being irrecoverable, ridiculing "the traditional attempt to authenticate historical and other such discourses by checking them for their fidelity to facts."[35] To begin with, the past as he perceives it is not a separated, sealed off entity but is "being constantly amalgamated into contemporary experience to suit the needs of such experience"[36] – there-fore, it resembles a centreless spectrum rather than a solid, compact, ordered structure with only one pivotal point. It consists of a countless

32   Alun Munslow, *The Future of History*, 182.
33   Munslow, *The Future of History*, 193.
34   Munslow, *Deconstructing History*, 2010, 223.
35   Brian Finney, "Peter Ackroyd, Postmodernist Play and Chatterton."
36   Finney, "Peter Ackroyd, Postmodernist Play and Chatterton."

variety of (hi)stories and fates which exist separately from one another, relate one to another, affect one another, overlap, get intertwined. Yet, at the same time, it is impossible to establish some hierarchy between them, none of them is more important, more correct or more truthful than the others (just as the colours of the spectrum cannot enter such relations) as there is no central discursive perspective that would impose such classifying hierarchies on them from the position of external authority and power. In this absence of hegemonic evaluative centres, what Jenkins calls "local patterns of dominance and marginality"[37] assume central significance within these (hi)stories. This shift of emphasis from centrality to locality naturally alters the whole concept of the past, whose real essence and value no longer reside in official records and versions, but are to be disclosed much deeper below their seamless surface and much further away from their prevalent truths. In such narratives, what is determining in one (hi)story has very little, if any, say in what should count as such in another, and a dominant value or viewpoint may easily turn into a marginal one in a different context. In *The Lambs of London*, for instance, transformations of such local patterns take turn rapidly as the story develops. Consequently, all the three main protagonists, Charles Lamb, Mary Lamb and William Ireland, keep incessantly switching positions of dominance and marginality under various circumstances: Charles at home, with his colleagues and as an aspiring writer; Mary in the relationship with her mother, with Charles and with William; and William in the relationship with his father, with Mary and as the "discoverer" of the Shakespeare papers. This principle liberates the more marginal historical characters, especially Mary and William, on two levels at once – not only are they freed from being mere objects of others' histories, as the story deliberately omits the perspective of those whose role in the exposure of Ireland's forgeries was more crucial according to traditional history, such as Edmond Malone, Richard Brinsley Sheridan and John Philip Kemble, but also, within their largely hapless fates, they are granted an opportunity to enjoy the feeling of being respected and listened to. The official historical version is thus destabilised as the focal point of the narrative is not only shifted but also fractured, as a result of which new connections and (hi)stories can emerge.

Ackroyd takes advantage of the discursive and narrative character of a history of past events, which calls for a plurality of perspectives with

---

37   Jenkins, *Re-thinking History*, 44.

the potential of generating a diversity of (hi)stories, in the sense of textual representations, by exploring new, unconventional, unsought for or speculative coincidences, connections and motivations. He believes that being a good writer is a necessary condition for being a good historian as it is impossible "to capture the drama and adventure of history" without bringing to it "gifts of narrative form and narrative style."[38] Only then can history "enthrall and inspire the reader in equal measure."[39] He insists that there is no substantial difference between a historian and a (historical) writer as both strive towards the same goal – to portray the grand general drama of the human spirit. Although he does distinguish between the poetic license of fictional narratives and the factual anchorage of historical texts, he thinks that the main problem of academic historians is that they address the readers' intellect without attempting to seize their imagination, himself claiming allegiance to the English tradition which considers historical writing to be a manifestation of literary skills as much as, or even more than, scholarship[40].

In his London novels the city's past comes to life through stories whose action is based on very few, if any, pieces of historical evidence and verified facts, such as Nicholas Hawksmoor's Satanist affiliation and sacrificial homicides in forming the pattern of the sites of his London churches, Edward Kelley's complicity in the decease of John Dee's wife, Dan Leno's, Karl Marx's and George Gissing's involvement as witnesses in an investigation of serial killings committed by a music hall performer in the early 1880s, the role of the mad nun of Clerkenwell in the deposition of King Richard II in 1399, the friendship between Mary Lamb and William Ireland and how this peculiar bond affected the tragic events in their lives, and Victor Frankenstein as a real-life member of the company around Percy Bysshe Shelley and Lord Byron while staying at Lake Geneva in the summer of 1816. He is, however, well aware of the limitations of narrative as a form in capturing the complexity and many-sidedness of the past, no matter how non-linear and multilayered the narrative may be. Even though he always emphasises the concept of London's past as

---

38 Peter Ackroyd speaking at the Royal Festival Hall.

39 Peter Ackroyd, "My epic search for our turbulent roots." *The Telegraph*, 25 August 2011.

40 In "My epic search for our turbulent roots," Ackroyd notes that there have been periods in the history and culture of England when historical accounts comprised fact and fiction, the latter involving imaginative narratives such as legends, myths, visions or folk tales, but also the authors' own ideas and beliefs. As examples he gives Venerable Bede, Layamon, John Milton, Tobias Smolett, Oliver Goldsmith, Edward Hyde, the 1st Earl of Clarendon, Thomas Macaulay and Edward Gibbon, who were able to address a larger audience precisely thanks to this approach, and whom he has taken as his model historians.

an ongoing continuum (or spectrum) whose sole focal point or power centre is the city itself, his novels' ambition is far from attempting to capture it as a whole. Instead, they concentrate on discrete events, incidents and fates from this continuum, "all the coloured beads which make the shape or a pattern,"[41] as if they were examined under a magnifying glass. Yet, the reader is never allowed to forget the humanity-transcending background entirely since, as the story progresses, the magnifying glass is lifted, and the lives of the individuals looked at in detail earlier "sink back" into the encompassing flow of the city's timelessness.

Therefore, rather than a seamless continuum, the history of the city as presented in Ackroyd's London novels is fragmentary, resembling a patchwork, an amalgam of mostly unrelated stories temporarily taken out of a continuum that is impossible to be textually rendered in its immensity. The best example of this history-as-patchwork narrative can be found in *The Clerkenwell Tales*, where the image of London during the turbulent year of 1399 is composed of diverse events, both known, documented and verified, as well as fabricated and imaginary, the latter largely prevailing, narrated from the perspective of twenty-two characters whose identities echo those of Chaucer's pilgrims. Not all of them happen to know one other and so their tales are only loosely related, one to another. Moreover, all these characters are marginal in terms of their historical significance, while the true personages from the point of view of traditional history, such as Richard II, Henry Bolingbroke and Robert Braybrooke, the Bishop of London, renamed as Robert Braybroke in the novel, are either only mentioned or appear as minor characters. The novel exemplifies its author's persuasion that the everyday, commonplace happenings and preoccupations of people in the past, such as their worries about health and money or what they found humorous, are much more interesting than the more sensational actions of and events involving those in power[42], claiming that researching such aspects of the past is more exciting as one "can come upon luminous and illuminating details which tend to be neglected by more academic historians or more professional historians."[43] Most of the tales are thus concerned with incidents and circumstances overlooked or dismissed by these academics as too implausible or unimportant to be of any consequence for the making of a coherent narrative account, while the historic moments and

---

41   Peter Ackroyd speaking at the Royal Festival Hall.
42   See for example Euan Ferguson's interview with Peter Ackroyd "I just want to tell a story."
43   Andy McSmith, "Rioting has been a London tradition for centuries," an interview with Peter Ackroyd. *The Independent*, 22 August 2011.

happenings are assigned the role of mere background framework. And so, instead of momentous acts the reader is offered some of the off-the-record and historically less visible events from the everyday reality of the time, from popular seasonal theatrical festivities, domestic murders and the tastes of brothel frequenters, to the conspiratorial activities of clandestine religious and political groupings.

Such an approach to textual representation of the past in fact bears all the earlier mentioned characteristic features of experimental history which are taken as fundamental in disclosing White's historical sublime: it is consciously intertextual, repeatedly pointing out and stressing its connection with and dependence on other texts and discourses, thus being a mere knot in the vast textual network of and about London, a link in the never-ending chain of historical representations of the city; consequently, the (hi)stories in these novels are only inconclusive fragments, as if bits of an almost impressionistic mosaic that can never be finished in a conventional manner as such a closure would fracture and distort the continual nature of the represented past; its presentation is overtly subjective, the action is always seen from the perspective of the protagonists, or, more precisely, from how Ackroyd makes them see it which, together with the numerous alterations of historical facts and data for the purposes of the narrative, makes the text an inherent extension of its author's ideas and notions; such a narrative is dialogic and pluralistic rather than monologic and authoritative, it operates through other, alternative, hypothetical, speculative and imaginary, possibilities offered to the reader for consideration, which call for further discussion and in fact are deliberately asking to be examined critically, questioned, contested or disproved. This unrestrained dialogic interaction between the writer and the past, the writer and the reader and, through them, the reader and the past inevitably sidelines the actual historical context in favour of foregrounding the sublime, that is the elusive, unknown, undiscoverable or meaningless, which is (re)constructed for the reader in the form of a coherent narrative.

In *Hawksmoor*, one of the two parallel plotlines is seen through the eyes of Nicholas Dyer, Ackroyd's mock-version of the real architect, Nicholas Hawksmoor, who is transformed, without any historical basis, into a devout Satanist and a believer in mystical reincarnation through a series of sacrificial acts performed in order to appeal to his dark deity to allow him to climb a transcendental ladder to higher spheres of transtemporal existence. This is to explicate the possibly unexplainable and meaningless – the enigmatic pattern formed by the sites of Hawksmoor's London churches. As the story proceeds and Dyer becomes more and more possessed with his wicked schemes, the narrative perspective grows even more biased and subjective, yet simultaneously more dialogically directed to the reader, and the same can be said about that of the present-day detective, whose name, ironically, is Nicholas Hawksmoor, who gets stuck in the case he investigates and retreats deeper and deeper into himself. It is not only the theme itself that provokes caution in the reader, but also several factual discrepancies, especially the addition of a made-up church to complete the supposedly occult pattern. By foregrounding the speculative, obscure and sensational elements Ackroyd gives up control over the process of the reader's consumption of the story and thus opens it to discussion and contestation, which is further underlined by the novel's open-ended, uncanny finale which takes place beyond physical space-time. In *Dan Leno and the Limehouse Golem* the mystical and occult is replaced by the intertextual, as almost all the protagonists of the story, real as well as fictitious, produce a text reflecting some of the novel's themes, in which they are inspired by having read a previously written text, most frequently De Quincey's "On Murder Considered as One of the Fine Arts" (1827). The novel extracts and examines a fragment from the fabric of London's (inter)textual network whose minute part it itself aspires to become, serving thus as a precursor to the subsequent thematically related textual representations. Moreover, in both novels the plot construction is determined and infused by the author's personal persuasion about certain inherent properties of the city, particularly the power of the *genius loci* and the theatrical nature of its life.

As imaginative and fictitious representations of past reality, Ackroyd's London novels feature other narrative, generic and linguistic forms than those of conventional, linear historical accounts. The theme of transhistorical recurrence is explored through the employment of parallel plotlines that take place in different historical periods yet which echo and resonate in one another, namely in *Hawksmoor*, *Chatterton* and *The House of Doctor Dee*. Moreover, through the motif of the power of the *genius loci*, a similar tendency can also be traced in *The Great Fire of London*, *Dan Leno and the Limehouse Golem* and *The Clerkenwell Tales*. Another less typical strategy of a historical narrative is the use of first person narration. Interestingly, all Ackroyd's major villains, Nicholas Dyer, Elizabeth Cree and Victor Frankenstein, are granted their voices in order to make their account more forceful and appealing. Yet, it is also used in both plotlines of *The House of Doctor Dee*, as it makes the novel's rendering of the protagonists' affiliation with the practice and discourse of mysticism and occultism more vivid and authentic. Therefore, his novels are often heteroglossic in the sense of displaying and confronting the "authentic linguistic speech variety"[44] inherent in actual language, by which they enrich and vivify the authorial speech. These discursive varieties are always determined socially, historically and professionally, for instance the imitation of historical English in John Dee's and Nicholas Dyer's narratives, Dan Leno's monopolylingustic music hall gags and impersonations, the interaction between the stage and the spectators during the performance of medieval mystery plays, or Audrey Skelton's vocal reincarnation of Dickens's Little Dorrit, to name just a few. The London of Ackroyd's novels materialises through a polyphony of voices and discourses, furthermore supported by the incorporation into the narrative of a mixture of literary styles, media and genres, such as poems, popular rhymes, theatrical performances, diary entries, trial records, and literary and historiographic commentaries. This is in full accord with his persuasion that "a writer must be free to explore every available form of writing," and the one he is interested in "includes those elements which have been generally classified as 'fact' and 'fiction'."[45] By means of this artistic license he freely achieves what experimental historians have to only very cautiously strive for – a pluralisation of the city's history that liberates it from appropriation by the dominant and powerful, as well as from the imperative of being plausible, reasonable and coherent if it is to be given any credit and recognition.

There is one more contemporary alternative approach to history that has been playing an interesting role in recent challenging of conventional historiography – counterfactual history, also known as "What if?" or virtual history. Its underlying principle is to imagine what would have happened if some events in the past had turned out differently. A counterfactual or "What if?" approach thus undermines the deterministic persuasion that past events were inevitable, and often the only possible, consequences of the given historical conditions and, by doing so, questions some of the most widely accepted causalities and long-held assumptions of traditional history. It can serve as "a tool to enhance the understanding of history, to make it come alive," and "reveal, in startling detail, the essential stakes of a confrontation, as well as its potentially abiding consequences."[46] Although they present virtual, hypothetical versions of

44   Mikhail Bakhtin, *The Dialogic Imagination*, 327.
45   Vianu, "The mind is the soul."
46   Robert Cowley, "Introduction," xi–xii.

the past they do not spring entirely from the realm of pure imagination as they work with facts and data in constructing stories whose plausibility can be deduced from historical evidence and records.

The basic premise of counterfactual history is simple: if we want to understand what happened, we need to understand what did not happen and why it did not happen. Theoretically speaking, the number of "What if?" versions of a past event is limitless, depending solely on the capacity of one's imagination. In practice, however, most of these versions are pointless as they are overly speculative or even completely fabricated, and as such depart too much from any possible outcomes. Therefore, Niall Ferguson stresses "the need of plausibility in the formulation of counterfactual questions."[47] In short, we only give consideration to those unrealised alternatives we believe could have happened under certain, plausible conditions and circumstances. He states the essential criterion for distinguishing probable alternatives from improbable ones as follows: "We should consider as plausible or probable only those alternatives which we can show on the basis of contemporary evidence that contemporaries actually considered."[48] Therefore, the possible alternative past constructed and explored, though only imagined, is ultimately anchored to actual historical reality.

The concept of counterfactual history is devoid of a belief in any all-defining deterministic principle, whether intellectual, cognitive, social or ideological, which would help us arrive at logical, in the sense of inevitable and unequivocal, conclusions in estimating and inferring the outcomes of larger historical processes. On the contrary, it presupposes that any historical progress, and especially that of human societies, evinces striking signs of irregularity, disorder and chaos, which must inevitably be reflected in its subsequent representations and reenactments. All we can do is acknowledge the potential, in the sense of probable and plausible, hypothetical scenarios, and thus not only explore alternative courses of history, but also learn to take into consideration a wider range of possible outcomes when anticipating future developments.

Counterfactual historiography focuses primarily on crucial and well-known events, partly also because of the condition of plausibility and the need for historical evidence, posing questions such as "What if Charles I had avoided the Civil War?," "What if there had been no American Revolution?," "What if Nazi Germany had defeated the Soviet Union?,"

---

47   Niall Ferguson, "Introduction," 83.
48   Ferguson, "Introduction," 86.

or "What if the Cold War had been avoided?"[49] The "What if?" subgenre of the historical novel is organically related to this method, and some works are based on altering the outcomes of the same or very similar affairs: Thomas Harris's *Fatherland* (1992) and *Archangel* (1998) explore "What if Nazi Germany had not lost the Second World War?" and "What if Stalin had had children?" respectively, and Harry Turtledove's *Ruled Britannia* (2003) toys with "What if the Spanish Armada had defeated the English navy in 1588?" However, the What if? historical novel, although it does exhibit some fidelity to actual historical reality, still belongs to the realm of fiction, and as such it does not have to trouble itself so much either with the imperative of plausibility or with the existence of evidence. Moreover, the rendered events and their protagonists need not always be of utmost historical significance. "What if? historical novels, then, are kind of historical novels squared, in so far as they fictionalise something which is already being fictionalized."[50] All this, of course, makes such fiction even more imaginative and therefore more subversive and iconoclastic than counterfactual history concerning the generally established assumptions of, mostly popular, historical consciousness.

All Ackroyd's novels dealing with the past, not only his London novels, are to some extent variations of a "What if?" narrative, working on the principle of elaborating on factual information and positing "an alternative reality in order to explore particular sets of historical phenomena."[51] His historical novels, that is those set entirely in the past, are all hypothetical and speculative stories, contemplating what the course of certain past events would have been like had some of their aspects or conditions been different. And so, *Dan Leno and the Limehouse Golem* explores what if Dan Leno, and also George Gissing and Karl Marx, had been interrogated by the police as potential witnesses who might have helped them identify the perpetrator of a series of ritual killings in late Victorian London, *The Clerkenwell Tales* elaborates on what if the clandestine alliance between the "mad nun" of Clerkenwell and the Bishop of London had played a role in the deposition of King Richard II, *The Lambs of London* toys with the idea of what if Mary Lamb had not only known William Henry Ireland personally, but had developed such a strong emotional bond with him that the disclosure of his forgeries brought about her mental collapse before she killed her mother, and *The Casebook of Victor Frankenstein* suggests what if the eponymous character

---

49   See Ferguson, "Introduction."
50   Jerome de Groot, *The Historical Novel*, 173.
51   de Groot, *The Historical Novel*, 173.

was not a product of Mary Shelley's imagination but a real person, more-over a member of the company around Lord Byron and Bysshe Shelley in which the famous sci-fi Gothic story originated. Ackroyd goes even further in his semi-historical novels, that is those with multiple parallel plots, which not only pose a what if question about the past, but also think of the present day consequences of such an alteration. *Hawksmoor* imagines what if the architect Nicholas Hawksmoor had been a homicidal occult Satanist, which could elucidate the mystical, topographic pattern formed by the sites of his London churches and why these churches still draw violent criminals to commit murders on their premises, *The House of Doctor Dee* asks what if Edward Kelly had had a hand in the sudden and untimely decease of Dee's wife, but mainly what if Dee had been successful in creating the homunculus, whose present-day reincarnation appears to be the person who inhabits the ancient house once belonging to the renowned scholar and magus. *Chatterton* represents yet another case, a meta-What if? of a sort, as it starts as a What if? mystery supposing Thomas Chatterton had only faked his death and continued writing poetry under other names, though this hypothetical version proves to be a blind alley as the evidence prompting it itself turns out to be fake.

However, Ackroyd does not aspire to write What if? history but fiction, the more imaginative and playful the better, and so he violates the plausibility maxim by deliberately ignoring the nonexistence of historical evidence which would support his hypotheses. On the contrary, as in cases of Hawksmoor, Dee and Frankenstein, he seems to revel in absolutely speculative, highly improbable, exaggerated and bizarre alternative histories, which in effect often go against the known facts and verified evidence. And so, when some factual data, particularly names, dates and the existence of certain persons, do not fit into or may even disprove his versions he either omits them completely or changes them freely for the purposes of his narrative (to which he explicitly admits only in the acknowledgement of *The Lambs of London*). Moreover, he never deals with significant, life-changing events, but concentrates either on rather minor or, for whatever reason, marginal historical characters, or on private, personal history which does not affect the larger, collective affairs of the community or nation, such as when he relocates John Milton from Restoration England to the savage lands of the New World in *Milton in America*. Ackroyd's What if? novels are thus "exercises in reconsideration that work as imagination renderings,"[52] whose primary purpose is, apart

---

52   de Groot, *The Historical Novel*, 173.

from amusing the reader and rather than exploring plausible courses of action, to expand the realm of the reader's imagination and bring to his/her attention those blind spots of the past which are in most cases excluded from official historical and literary historical surveys.

"Recent historians [...] have made deliberate and self-conscious attempts to restore narration to history,"[53] notes A. S. Byatt, and one of the reasons for this turn of the current has been the increasing popularity of historical fiction, as gradually the "idea that 'all history is fiction' led to a new interest in fiction as history."[54] Ackroyd's position in this debate is unique since he finds himself on both sides of the barricades: in his historical non-fiction he often relies on imaginative storytelling, while in his novels he fictionalises history by altering facts and incorporating speculative and made-up events into the narrative. Their aim, however, remains the same – not only to arouse interest in the past, but primarily to demonstrate that the past is not a distant, conserved, sealed-off entity, that it can be discovered in the present, and, most importantly, that it can prove very helpful in understanding the present. To achieve this in his novels, he employs most of the current, often labelled as postmodernist, tendencies in historical fiction, namely "parodic and pastiche forms, forms which fake documents or incorporate real ones, mixture of past and present, hauntings and ventriloquism, historical versions of genre fictions."[55] These allow him to use his poetic license in order to overcome the barrier of rational distrust and suspicion most readers feel towards uncanny and otherwise implausible elements in factual histories, and to show the spirit of the past, and even the past itself, to be closer to us than it may sometimes appear.

Ackroyd's London Chronotope

Any chronotopic universe a writer invents stems primarily from his or her need for creative freedom and control. The potential of imagining within the narrative a realm of limitless possibilities "bestows upon the author the opportunity to construct a verbal space endowed with psychological, ideational, and aesthetic dimensions that liberate him or her from the constructions of the ordinary time/space matrix of 'reality'."[56]

---

53 A. S. Byatt, *On Histories and Stories*, 38.
54 Byatt, *On Histories and Stories*, 38.
55 Byatt, *On Histories and Stories*, 38.
56 Carl Darryl Malmgren, *Fictional Space in the Modernist and Postmodernist American Novel*, 25.

The literarily appropriated space/place is outer as well as inner-world-ly, the latter allowing its "symbolic extension because there is so little that is inherently affective in [its] physical properties,"[57] and ensuring its being "soaked with signification, [...] identities, [...] and with living memory; thus turning those literary works which have taken up the task of charting this territory into living records of the lived time and space, of the lived chronotope."[58] This discursive space-time model is mostly not wholly made-up or fanciful, but somehow derived from really existing places and spaces. The result, then, is a particular amalgam of the actual and the fictitious, the familiar and the unknown, the plausible and the uncanny, as the narrative's "fictional configurations create a hybrid zone or interface generated by the conflation of the Real and the Imaginary."[59] The London of Ackroyd's novels is precisely such a lived hybrid zone, an interface between the city's physical reality and the writer's imaginative vision of it, between the inhabitants' commonplace experience and the paranormal phenomena he exposes his characters to, one which resembles the London of his non-fiction works, yet, at the same time, differs from it through the rendering of forces and events which surpass, if not even deny, its factual and empirical dimension.

His concept of London is based on his belief in the intrinsic inter-connectedness of particular temporal and spatial properties, namely an unorthodox understanding of time and the power of the *genii locorum* of the city. As Ackroyd's notion of time comprises a combination of cyclical, spiral and labyrinthine organisations, which resist a traditional chronological temporality that distinguishes strictly between the past, present and future, the events and actions of his London novels reduplicate, echo and reinforce one another in recurrent cyclical or spiral patterns, their occurrence to a large extent controlled by the energies of the places where they happen rather than merely by chronological successiveness. Sometimes, however, these events and actions take place in a haphazard manner, and even though they still do tend to repeat, they do so in patterns which are rather random, if not chaotic, than in relatively clearly perceptible circular or spiral ones. This labyrinthine aspect is caused by a unique human factor: although what most people do is largely driven by the momentum of the mythical space-time continuum, Ackroyd believes there are a few exceptionally strong personalities, his "Cockney Visionaries," who manage to assert their visions and ideas in spite of

---

57 Leonard Lutwack, *The Role of Place in Literature*, 35.
58 Wojciech Kalaga and Jacek Mydla, "Preface," 9.
59 Malmgren, *Fictional Space in the Modernist and Postmodernist American Novel*, 25.

these potent forces. Paradoxically, they are capable of doing so precisely because they understand the distinct temporal and spatial nature of their city, and it is precisely because their imaginative vision stems from this understanding that it can also transcend and break free from the cyclical recurrence. Through their ability to defy the city's tendency to shape its dwellers into its image, characters such as John Dee, Nicholas Hawksmoor, Thomas Chatterton, William Blake and Charles Dickens add yet one more dimension to the psychophysical structure of the city.

The space-time model of Ackroyd's fictitious London is a very specific and interesting variant of the Bakhtinian chronotope, one in which space and time form organically connected, complementary and mutually determining quantities (time being the fourth dimension of space), fused into a carefully thought-out, concrete whole that crucially affects the happenings in the city as well as its (re)presentation. As a result of this, time "becomes artistically visible; likewise, space becomes charged and responsive to the movements of time, plot and history."[60] Due to the above-mentioned properties of Ackroyd's literary London, time and space in his novels become ultimately inseparable determinants, functioning as two correlating axes whose coordinates form the interwoven lines of the matrix that underlines both the construction of the novel's setting and the production of its meaning. Such a chronotope is more than only "a formally constitutive category"[61] shaping the cityscape and narrative construction and, in consequence, determining the image of material reality and humanity in the literary work – it is also a crucial means of generating the work's themes and ideas. The ambivalence of this space-time literary model derives from the fact that in Ackroyd's novels London functions simultaneously as a setting, theme and character[62], as a result of which it also fulfils other purposes within the narrative than those proposed by Bakhtin.

Therefore, while performing its representational significance, Ackroyd's London also reaches beyond the limits of the traditional chronotope. The chronotope is an organising centre for all the substantial narrative events of the novel, one which concretises these events by embedding them into the novel's larger temporal and spatial framework. It is only within this chronotopic framework that the events of Ackroyd's novels relate to one another and thus assume their significance –

---

60 Mikhail Bakhtin, *The Dialogic Imagination*, 84.

61 Bakhtin, *The Dialogic Imagination*, 84.

62 Ackroyd has repeatedly admitted that the city of all his London novels becomes a character, a living being of a certain kind, e.g. in the *Bold Type* interview.

without his London and its particular temporal and spatial properties these events would appear isolated, fragmentary or contingent. This London also helps to hold the narrative together as the more abstract or figurative elements of the story, namely themes, ideas and symbols, are also tied to the chronotope which then helps them perform their role within this narrative. If taken away from this chronotope, most of these abstract elements would lose their "thought anchorage" as it not only allows them to have meaning but also elucidates and exemplifies them. Moreover, in Ackroyd's novels his concept of time becomes literally perceivable or palpable, often through how it affects place and space, as the main protagonists directly encounter its mostly uncanny manifestations, such as seeing ghosts, hearing voices from the past, experiencing transhistorical echoes and shifts in time. As such, his London chronotope functions "as the primary means for materializing time in space" and thus "emerges as a center for concretizing representation,"[63] one which makes the phenomenon of time and its effects tangible through artistic representation.

This space-time model in some respects transcends the scope of the chronotope as Bakhtin outlines it. The fact that Ackroyd's literary London assumes the roles of theme and character makes this chronotope not only define the literary work's artistic unity in relation to the actual rendered reality[64], but also represent both a peculiar, autonomous realm that to some extent produces meanings independently of this reality, as well as a certain form of distinctive identity, a metaphorical self that performs within the sphere of activity determined by its own spatial and temporal properties and their correlations. The first means that such a London functions as a kind of "meta-chronotope," a chronotope whose mechanisms and texture are laid bare, exposed to the reader while at the same time commented on by the implied author; it is a chronotope as a continuous process, always as if captured in the course of its making, which draws the reader directly into the focus of the power field of its potent energies; it is a chronotope which problematises itself by making its very construction and operation and their effect on the novel's characters and events, as well as itself, substantial subjects of inquiry; it is a chronotope that not only gives the events in the story and its characters' acts and utterances meaning in relation to the story's subject matter, the actual historical reality and the reality of the reader, but also in relation to itself,

63   Bakhtin, *The Dialogic Imagination*, 250.
64   Bakhtin, *The Dialogic Imagination*, 243.

making them mere devices for exploring a phenomenon that eludes the constraints of one particular historical time or place.

The latter complicates the whole concept even more as by making London in a certain sense a character in the story Ackroyd lets the chronotope work simultaneously within and without itself. The city as a character is, of course, of a different kind than the human protagonists or their supernatural incarnations because it operates above them, on a higher level of symbolic abstraction and supra-temporal pattern. This is most apparent in *Hawksmoor* and *The House of Doctor Dee*, where in the end London transforms into the decisive factor of the plot development, the true mover in resolving the story's mystery, specifically the "culprit" in the murders investigated by Detective Hawksmoor, and the agent of John Dee's house's transhistorical echolalia. If as a chronotope it allows the human characters to act and have a meaningful existence, as a character it challenges, surpasses and eventually engulfs them, becoming thus a "supra-character" into which they all naturally merge, and which then articulates, in its encompassing abstraction and immateriality, a universalised form of their individual experience. And so, if a traditional chronotope materialises time in the space of the narrative, Ackroyd's London questions and undermines the rational and the material by rendering them as governed by heterogeneous and uncanny forces. By the parallel processes of the materialisation of the intangible and the immaterialisation of the physical, such a chronotope both establishes and subverts its relationship with the extratextual reality.

As Bakhtin notes, a number of different chronotopes may be found within one literary work, entering a complex network of interactions with one another, and frequently one of them is made more dominant and as such embraces or includes the others. What proves to be crucial is that their relationships are based on mutual inclusiveness and coexistence, as a result of which these chronotopes can be, on the one hand, interconnected and interwoven, but, on the other hand, they may also replace or contradict one another, thus operating in an ongoing dialogue. Yet, no matter how complex these relationships are, they never interfere in the relationships inside the individual chronotopes. "[T]his dialogue cannot enter into the world represented in the work, nor into any of the chronotopes represented in it; it is outside the world represented, although not outside the work as a whole. It enters the world of the author, of the performer, and the world of the listeners and readers."[65] This dialogic

---

[65] Bakhtin, *The Dialogic Imagination*, 252.

chronotopic mechanism is essential for Ackroyd's writing as it establishes both the physical foundations and the thematic framework of his fictitious representation of the city. His London chronotope can be seen as an encompassing one within the realm of his London novels, one which includes in itself many other chronotopes that are minor in terms of their impact upon the story and narrative as a whole. However, there is one significant departure from Bakhtin's description which is caused by the meta-chronotopic character of Ackroyd's model: the minor chronotopes and their interrelationships not only help to constitute the major chronotope and allow it to mean, but also serve as devices for a more thorough and graphic rendering of the represented reality. Although they do not affect the outside of the work in any other form than that of another dialogue, this time between the author, the text and the reader, these relationships do enter the world represented, as they actually co-determine it and thus are to be found in its very fabric.

Most of Ackroyd's minor chronotopes are heterotopic in nature, in the sense of Michel Foucault's definition of heterotopias – as places of otherness, which are both real and imaginary, mythic, physical and mental, existing in and outside time. They can be seen as "counter-sites" in which "all the other real sites that can be found within the culture are simultaneously represented, contested, and inverted. Places of this kind are outside of all places, even though it may be possible to indicate their location in reality."[66] As such, the heterotopia is a place that not only stands for itself, but also reflects and juxtaposes other places, thus displaying a multiplicity of meanings, some of which may be contradictory, incompatible or mutually exclusive. It follows that heterotopias are also heterochronic in their relation to time as they do not relate to its chronological organisation, but are rather "linked to slices of time" and begin "to function at full capacity when men arrive at a sort of absolute break with their traditional time."[67] This heterogeneity inevitably manifests itself in two prevailing tendencies which themselves are contradictory in nature: the first is represented by heterotopias of a temporal mass which is being infinitely accumulated and built up, for instance cemeteries, museums and libraries; the latter are temporal, or temporary, heterotopias of fleeting and transitory character, which do not incline to the continuous and the eternal, but to the seasonal and the transient, and as such get activated only at certain, though usually regularly repeating, times of the year, for instance

66   Michel Foucault, "Of Other Spaces," 24.
67   Foucault, "Of Other Spaces," 26.

festivals, fairs and seaside resorts. Heterotopias differ from public places in their being simultaneously inclusive and exclusive, as they "always presuppose a system of opening and closing that both isolates them and makes them penetrable,"[68] which means that they contain in themselves a moment of exclusion, either obvious or latently hidden. Some of them require permission, the undergoing of a certain ritual or purification, or the making of a special gesture to get into them, for instance a prison, a sanctuary and a sauna, while others are seemingly easily accessible, though mere entry does not guarantee one the identity of an insider, but rather that of a passing visitor, for instance publicly open churches and the guest bedrooms on farms. Heterotopias necessarily function and signify in relation to their outer spaces, which always unfold between two opposite poles: either they create "a space of illusion,"[69] a sealed and enclosed space which is deliberately all the more illusory and fanciful than, and thus detached from, outside reality, such as a cabaret or a brothel; or they create "a space of compensation,"[70] one that is other than ours in that it is more perfectly organised, thus rendering the outside space as disorderly and ill-conceived, such as dissenting religious communities.

Heterotopias of almost all the above types that function as minor chronotopes within the major chronotope of the city can be found throughout Ackroyd's London novels. In *The Great Fire of London* the most notable ones are the prison and the film location near the Thames where the latest version of *Little Dorrit* is being shot, which both, apart from their primary functions, reflect the city and the condition of its more neglected and marginalised inhabitants. Although both these places have a system of closing which prevents outsiders from entering them freely, these limits are eventually broken through, either from inside, when Little Arthur short circuits the security system, opens the prison gates and lets his inmates flow into the streets, or from outside, when Audrey and the homeless tramps set the film sets on fire. The crucial heterotopia in *Hawksmoor* is Little St Hugh, the church beside Moorfields in which Detective Hawksmoor finally meets the murderer who calls himself the Architect and who proves to be the reincarnated spirit of the architect Nicholas Dyer. The fact that this church does not exist in reality enables Ackroyd to make it a place simultaneously realistic and imaginary, in and outside time. In the novel's closing scene it transforms into a mythical, supratemporal or transhistorical gate through which the

---

68 Foucault, "Of Other Spaces," 26.
69 Foucault, "Of Other Spaces," 27.
70 Foucault, "Of Other Spaces," 27.

two main protagonists, historically separated by almost three centuries, merge and become part of the city's eternal continuum.

The most complex of Ackroyd's heterotopic minor chronotypes is the mysterious house Matthew Palmer inherits in *The House of Doctor Dee*, as it is not only linked to and contains various slices of time, but it also allows them to echo and pervade each another. The chronotope of the house thus serves as a miniaturised and condensed symbolic version of the London chronotope, in which the weight of the accumulated time and history of the city, physically and metaphorically, compresses space and affects the lives of its inhabitants. Several interesting heterotopias feature in *Dan Leno and the Limehouse Golem*, such as the prison and Solomon Weil's study, but those which best reflect, while also contesting and inverting, places that are geographically located in reality and yet somehow stand beyond these places are the Reading Room of the British Museum and Dan Leno's music hall. The former is, like Dee's house, a perfect example of a heterotopia of accumulated time, one deliberately built to store and preserve the past's wisdom and experience, as well as to remain insusceptible and insubordinate to momentary time upheavals; the latter represents a site of hilarity, distraction and escape, existing in real time and space yet separated from the outside world by a protective "wall of illusion": although they derive from, reflect and dramatise city life, the London in them is both familiar and other, close and distant, ostensibly tangible and enticingly ephemeral, pathetically serious yet brimming with laughter. Arguably, his most heterotopic novel in terms of its chronotopic construction is *The Clerkenwell Tales*. The actual composition of the individual Tales/chapters is based on a series of heterotopias within the late fourteenth-century London setting, such as the churches, the convent, the prison, the bishopric, the pub and the brothel, inhabited or frequented by at least some of the members of its miscellaneous cast of characters. However, the most profoundly elaborated heterotopia is the Clerkenwell fairground, the carefully delimited site of annual markets, festivals, celebrations and popular festive theatrical performances, whose heterogeneity and tendency to excess challenge the conventional law, order and stable social hierarchies and temporarily liberate the participants from their restraint.

Undoubtedly, there is a dividing line between the actual world and its representation in a literary work, and so no matter how faithful to reality this work strives or appears to be it "can never be chronotopically identical with the real world it represents."[71] The London of Ackroyd's novels

---

71   Bakhtin, *The Dialogic Imagination*, 256.

is modelled on the real London in which he lives, or, rather, on how he sees, interprets and imagines it and its past, and so in many respects it resembles the city which he describes or refers to in his most celebrated non-fiction books, namely *London: The Biography* and *Albion: The Origins of the English Imagination*. Yet certain deviations from this London are striking and set the stories free from the constraints of historical truthful ness and from the need for a rational or logical explanation of its events and developments. To name his most frequently employed devices: he changes some historical facts, such as names, dates, chronologies and biographical data; he brings together people who in reality never met; he puts real historical personalities into made-up events with fictitious or literary characters and also inserts these characters into real historical processes; he alters and adapts the topography of London for the purpose of the narratives; and in the resolutions of his plots he often relies on various paranormal and occult phenomena and manifestations.

However, despite this clear boundary the two realms keep entering into a relationship of mutual influence. The real world, and the writer's experience along with it, interferes in the world of the work as a model for its setting, landscape, characters, relationships and actions, as a crucial source of inspiration for the process of its creation, and the represented world of the work, and naturally the work itself, enters the real world through its dialogical interaction with the author, readers and critics. Complex and elaborated chronotopes such as Ackroyd's London can enrich the real world through the creative and critical reception of its readers by offering alternative, fresh and original perspectives and interpretations of this world and its more intangible and perplexing aspects in particular. Bakhtin calls this "a special *creative* chronotope inside which this exchange between work and life occurs, and which constitutes the distinctive life of the work,"[72] and problematising and questioning the habitual and conventional perceptions of how and where we live lies at the core of such exchange in the case of Ackroyd's London novels and assures their viability.

There is yet another dimension of this exchange, or dialogic interaction, between the work and the outside world – the relation between the author and the chronotopes of the world he/she represents. Regardless of the degree of his/her involvement in the story, the author always finds him/herself outside the represented world, which is outside the time and space in which the narrated event happens, though somehow tan-

---

72 Bakhtin, *The Dialogic Imagination*, 254, emphasis in original.

gentially since it is, after all, he/she who represents this world through the chosen narrative perspective and authority. As soon as the author, in whatever form, as a character, an alter-ego, a doppelgänger or a narrative voice, decides to enter the realm of the work, his/her self is automatically transformed and redefined according to the needs and the internal logic of the narrative, which are inevitably other than those of the outside world. As a result, the identity of this projected author can no longer be the same as that of the real author, and becomes something like an image of the author, an outcome of the creative process rather than its originator. Ackroyd's self-projection into his stories, either in the form of characters who bear some of his personal traits or, more frequently, in the form of an authorial narrative voice, can be traced in most of his London novels, yet nowhere else is it as strong as in the final chapter of *The House of Doctor Dee*. At first, the narrative voice is that of John Dee, a few pages later it starts taking turns with that of Matthew Palmer, after which the assumed narrator-author takes over, alternately discussing with Dee and Palmer, while also offering metafictional commentaries on the difficulties and peculiarities involved in producing a sensible representation of the city's past and its distinct temporality. Although this narrative voice truly reminds one of Ackroyd, it is still a created image, a narrative device that can function only in the novel's ambiguous and eerie chronotope of mystical supratemporality and supraspatiality, and as such it represents a lure used by the writer to make readers fall prey to his playful conceit of presenting the fictional world as if it were identical with reality.

In terms of both ideas and composition, Ackroyd's London chronotope is a highly complex, elaborate and cohesive narrative construct, a distinct space-time literary model, yet one which by no means attempts to provide a finite or comprehensive image of London in (and out of) time. In this sense such a fictional realm as a social space shows adherence or relates to both a modern as well as a postmodern creative sensibility, though Ackroyd would dislike such categorical labelling. On the one hand, it falls into the literary tradition of late modernity whose heterogeneous city "allows for multiple interpretations, multiple representations of space in the same site," rather than to that of postmodern social space where only a few or even "no new concepts are applied, no vision of the city as a whole is produced."[73] Ackroyd's concept of London attempts to compose and explicate a vision of the city in a certain whole-

---

73   Paul Smethurst, *The Postmodern Chronotype: Reading Space and Time in Contemporary Fiction*, 53.

ness, a milieu which is elusive, multiple and diverse from within, but relatively compact and seamless from without. In his vision, this mystical, eternal city, despite the countless blasts of history, always stands tall and majestic in the end, as if above the currents of the mundane, everyday existence of its inhabitants. On the other hand, a distinction must be made between London and the London in this literary representation: however universal and homogeneous Ackroyd's city appears to be, his chronotopic model is derived precisely from its inherent heterogeneity and variability, tendencies which are to be found at the very heart of the city's force fields. Paradoxically, these forces, which on the level of time-confined human societies defy ordering and pacification, drive the city's evolvement in the transhistorical dimension of a supratemporal space-time continuum. In addition to this, Ackroyd's London novels entertain various non-linear temporal arrangements that further disrupt and confuse the relationship between the outside world and its artistic representation. Therefore, in a rather postmodern fashion, these novels offer a self-contained yet ultimately inconclusive rendition of reality, as they concentrate on the heterogeneous particularities of individual and disparate fates and events, and only through them do they testify or predicate about the functioning mechanisms of the city as a whole.

According to Paul Smethurst, organising narrative time in various non-linear ways and juxtaposing disparate time-spaces is quite common in postmodern novels, yet this approach is far from new as it can already be found, most noticeably, in modernist fiction, utopian fiction, sci-fi and fantasy stories[74]. What connects all these cases – the disorderly temporality of the conscious and unconscious mind in modernist writing, the secluded and ahistorical utopian world, the technologically advanced future where time is perceived differently thanks to such inconceivable abilities as time travelling in sci-fi, and the made-up fantasy world in which time assumes other than chronological forms and properties as a result of supernatural forces and phenomena – is the fact that they are examples of imaginative projections, extensions or (re)constructions of reality in invented or mental realms in which non-linear time and temporal displacements serve rather as distancing literary devices whose primary purpose is to detach from the real world the narrative and the world represented in it, which has therefore little if anything to do with these representations. In the postmodern novel, however, the employment of unorthodox temporal concepts transcends the formal level of

---

74   Smethurst, *The Postmodern Chronotype*, 173–174.

the narrative as it is mostly not motivated by a desire to distance the represented world. They are rather incorporated into its very texture, explicitly contesting the western social, scientific and cultural notion of reality and time rather than removing it from the reader's temporal and spatial experience. In chronotopes composed thus, the alternative time organisations do not allow the narrative to evade or escape reality but are made part of it, thus rendering the habitual, conventionally taken for granted and rationally explicable principles and mechanisms of its functioning insufficient, fallacious or even unworkable.

This is not to say that in the postmodern novel these non-linear forms of time do not appear as, for example, metaphors, as means of making the setting more imaginative and original, or as stylistic devices creating a less conventional structuring of the plotline. Yet all these have a rather supportive role as the underlying chronotopic principle of these narratives is to implement such forms of time into the otherwise realistically modelled social space, thus making the nature of time, its relation to space, and, along with that, the whole understanding and perception of reality their crucial themes. An important consequence follows from this implementation: once non-linear time is made and explored as reality, the story is very difficult, if not impossible, to read and interpret in a linear manner, and so it requires the reader to free him/herself of preconceptions about the flow of time as directional. Nowhere else is this problematisation of temporal linearity more frequent and resourceful than in contemporary fiction dealing with the past and challenging the notion of historical time, whose re-presentation undermines the very premises of traditional, academic historiography. Several more or less related alternatives for linear historical time have been proposed by authors of postmodern historiographic metafiction, including Ackroyd. However, the exposition of the workings of such forms of time is by no means the sole purpose of these texts, as they mostly serve as a stepping stone or pretext for the exploration of wider thematic concerns: to open up the past to multiple interpretations and, by doing so, to undermine the assumption of its (de)finiteness and conclusiveness; and, through looking back to the past, to cast light on the present, to make us reassess who we are, where we came from, and what we take for the true, fixed and real.

All Ackroyd's London novels attempt to problematise the linear concept of time, but three of them do so more overtly than the others: *Hawksmoor*, *Chatterton* and *The House of Doctor Dee*. They are all based on a multiple time-frame consisting of two or three more or less discrete yet interconnected narratives taking place in the same settings; they all contain a historical chronotope as well as a contemporary one, while the properties of and happenings in the first help to understand those of and in the latter; and they all produce meaning through transhistorical parallelism, echoing and resonance resulting in recurrent and intersecting motifs, patterns, events and utterances, and/or seemingly uncanny coincidences. As some of the most crucial passages of these novels take place outside the temporal and spatial reality of the material world, they introduce and bring into confrontation various alternative concepts of social time. They assume the form of a ghost story – their characters see the ghosts of the dead, hear voices from the past, communicate with them, or even traverse from their historical period into a perpetually enduring space-time continuum, where they meet with other similarly disposed time-crossing individuals – yet one whose purpose is not to scare but to transcend historical time by creating something of an "achronotope," a spatial construct outside the perceivable flows of time whose *modus operandi* delivers the final blow to the idea of the exclusive dominance of chronological temporal causality in the processes of historical development. Naturally, such texts presuppose a certain kind of reader, one who is willing and able to imagine and admit not only that such time patterns may exist and exercise power over the fates of the stories' protagonists, but also that our life may be governed by forces which defy a rational or logical explanation.

In order to achieve this effect, by putting his heroes into the chronotopes of non-linear temporality Ackroyd lets them come to the conclusion that pure rationality would always bring them to a dead-end street of misconception or even ultimate incomprehension of their life situation, and in consequence, of the nature of London and the world in general. Nicholas Hawksmoor, Charles Wychwood and Matthew Palmer in their respective cases realise that due to the mythical functioning of time any "rational methodology is undermined [...] because there appears to be no beginning from which to start plotting the events and so solve the mystery."[75] Under these circumstances, they have to rely on other "methodologies" or approaches to reality, those which are conventionally deemed at best as irrational and alternatively focused, such as intuition, imagination, sensibility, occultism and visionariness. What also connects these otherwise dissimilar personalities is that they find themselves part of a larger, metaphysical, supratemporal pattern of the city, which stretches over and runs across different time layers, which

---

75   Smethurst, *The Postmodern Chronotype*, 191.

perpetually intertwines the past with the present (and with the future), and which manipulates them with forces that are way beyond their conscious control. Ackroyd is far from rejecting rationality altogether, he rather suggests that alone it may prove insufficient for understanding certain aspects and regularities of human existence, particularly the nature of time and its relation to space. As his fictional world is characterised by heterogeneity, by juxtaposition and the combining of diverse or even contradictory elements and tendencies, its temporal framework must inevitably conform to this principle. The complexity of his London chronotope rests in that "it brings together conflicting forms of time"[76] – linear, cyclical, spiral, labyrinthine, trans-historical, mythical, occult – and, at least fictionally, he confirms the validity of the non-linear forms, by which he transforms his narrative into an idiosyncratic vision of a timeless, everlasting city.

What is symptomatic of Ackroyd's London chronotope is an awareness that its temporary properties are inseparable from the location and environment in which they occur and operate, that the untraditional organisation and forms of time go hand in hand with a distinct concept of space and its complex and heterogeneous composition and fabric. The world of his London novels is built around the three essential dimensions of human life: historicality, sociality and spatiality. This fictional world always exists and is firmly embedded in time, no matter how alternatively conceived, and this historical framework defines it and crucially impacts all its inhabitants and events; it is also a social world occupied by individuals and communities who form more or less complicated and intricate networks of relationships, and therefore its functioning and character are determined by various societal interactions, practices and patterns. However, the complexity of this milieu lies in the fact that these two existential qualities are complemented by a third – spatiality – and they are understood as simultaneous, interdependent and organically interwoven. All the action in these novels not only unfolds in time and involves a cast of human characters and their diverse relationships, but it is also inherently bound with the space in which it occurs, and which becomes an essential component of the characters' lived experience: on the one hand, this space is historically and socially produced and shaped, it evolves and transforms in and as a result of time as well as according to the wishes and needs of its inhabitants; on the other hand, this space affects the social and historical reality that takes place within its territory through forces

---

76   Smethurst, *The Postmodern Chronotype*, 194.

which have a potential to alter the flows of time in it and attract a certain kind of people to inhabit it, and certain kinds of events to happen there.

Such a chronotope, created in the three-dimensional co-ordinate system of historicality, sociality and spatiality, is therefore impossible to explore, interpret, not to say comprehend from three separate perspectives revolving around their individual axes – the fact that one dimension determines and is determined by the other two always needs to be taken into consideration and the system therefore must be approached in its wholeness. Ackroyd's construction of his fictional London is in accord with recent theoretical spatial revisions which are trying to reassess, and possibly even to redefine, who we are, where we live and how we study our history and society, i.e. that we "are first and always historical-social-spatial beings, actively participating individually and collectively in the construction/production – the 'becoming' – of histories, geographies, societies."[77] This is precisely what Ackroyd's London exemplifies: it is a world in which the historical, societal and spatial factors are constitutive in an incessant interconnection and co-action, one which is produced simultaneously by its being in time, by its inhabitants' acts and practices, and by the distinct properties of its space, both physical and social.

Drawing on Henri Lefebvre's classification of three different moments of social space: the perceived space (or Spatial Practice), the conceived space (or Representations of Space) and the lived space (or Spaces of Representation), Edward W. Soja distinguishes what he terms Firstspace, Secondspace and Thirdspace. The first two are in fact identical with Lefebvre's perceived space and conceived space: the former is the concrete, material space that can be empirically perceived, measured and described, one that is produced by people's everyday routines and routes; the latter consists of the mental projections or re-presentations of the former, conceived in ideas about and other cognitive forms of space by urbanists, architects, geographers, cartographers, planners and other scientists. It is a rational, knowledge-based conceptualised space, a discursively produced system of (mostly) verbal signs, and as such it reflects the distribution of power in society and serves the needs of its dominant ideology. Although Secondspace is wholly ideational and discursive and primarily created, its imagined geographies tend to be presented as real, as a result of projections and impositions of power, mostly through the assertion of the primacy and supremacy of reason and rational logic over

---

77   Edward W. Soja, *Thirdspace: Journeys to Los Angeles and Other Real-and-Imagined Places*, 72–73.

other modes of thought. Ackroyd's novels undermine this assertion, and so his protagonists often challenge the proposed hegemony of some forms of London's imagined geographies, most explicitly in *Hawksmoor* where the architect Nicholas Dyer repeatedly questions the validity and viability of his rationalist Enlightenment colleagues' designs, or in *The House of Doctor Dee* where John Dee is trying to discover the mystical, original, lost London buried underneath the current city and unknown to its official cartographers.

Soja, however, focuses chiefly on Lefebvre's lived space, which he further elaborates upon and extends in his concept of Thirdspace. On the one hand, lived spaces comprise and encompass the materially perceived spaces and the mentally conceived spaces; on the other hand, they surpass them in scope and meaning, as a result of which they are "[s]imultaneously real and imagined and more," "objective and subjective, material and metaphorical, a medium and outcome of social life."[78] Lived space is therefore that of inhabitants, that of scientists, planners and ideological designers, but also, and most importantly, that of artists, philosophers, scholars and individualistic spatial practitioners, that of those who hold an alternative or dissident view of social reality. It is a space of those "who seek only to describe rather than decipher and actively transform the worlds we live in,"[79] and through their ideas and imagination to reassess and possibly appropriate them. For Lefebvre, lived spaces are produced through social and spatial practices that are internally and personally motivated, and which simultaneously help constitute and shape their users' identities.

Lived space is distinct from and much more intricate and complex than the other two spaces because it not only contains them as two separate moments of social space, but also combines and transforms and, as a result, revises and re-presents them, contesting the traditional spatial binary dialectic as such. It is therefore difficult if not impossible to "be dealt with separately in convenient forms of technical and academic compartmentalisation."[80] It transcends the physical space by "making symbolic use of its objects,"[81] and thus teems with symbols and symbolic communication arranged in more or less coherent and comprehensible systems that overlay the perceived material reality. Also, although it contains the spatial representations of ideology and power, thanks to its

78 Soja, *Thirdspace*, 11, 45.
79 Soja, *Thirdspace*, 67.
80 Stephen Hardy, *Relations of Place*, 24.
81 Soja, *Thirdspace*, 68.

profound and sometimes hard to decode symbolism, the lived space provides a vital ground for the "clandestine or underground side of social life," attempting "to retain, if not emphasize, the partial unknowability, the mystery and secretiveness, the non-verbal subliminality, of spaces of representation,"[82] which are products of operations of mind other than those behind the conceived spaces. The simultaneity of other spaces, real and imagined, within the lived space, together with the absence of hierarchies among them, allows for the generation and opening up of "counterspaces" to the prevailing conceptions of socio-spatial reality. Within the lived space, these formerly dominated and marginalised spaces become loci of resistance and counter-power, platforms for struggle, liberation and emancipation, as well as sanctuaries of individuality and unchallenged otherness, which no longer solely occupy the peripheries. Lived spaces thus blur the often taken-for-granted borderlines between the binary oppositions whose (de)valuation constitutes our habitual and prevalent ontological and epistemological assumptions: the private and the public, the individual and the collective, the subjective and the objective, the mental and the physical, the rational and the spiritual, the intellectual and the imaginary, making them work in a paradoxical yet all the more efficient complicity in the production of social space.

Soja's Thirdspace adapts Lefebvre's concept of the lived space to the more contemporary reality of modern, predominantly urban, space. It can be understood as a kind of meta-space that contains and recombines all other spaces in a simultaneous coexistence, one which is fundamentally heterogeneous and permanently shifting, and which in its multiplicity unites, juxtaposes, confronts, and reconciles aspects and perspectives previously considered incompatible and inconsistent. Such space is therefore intrinsically contradictory as it is composed of opposites that all come together within it, yet whose *modus operandi* rests in an incessant creative process of drawing "selectively and strategically from the two opposing categories to open new alternatives."[83] These new, often marginal, emancipatory or subversive alternatives are precisely what defines Thirdspace and imparts to it its radicalism of thought and focus, in terms of both political and personal scope. However, as bell hooks points out, there is a "definite distinction between the marginality which is imposed by oppressive structure and the marginality one chooses as a site of resistance, as location of radical openness and possibility."[84] Thirdspace

82 Soja, *Thirdspace*, 67.
83 Soja, *Thirdspace*, 5.
84 bell hooks quoted in Soja, *Thirdspace*, 98.

thus allows for deliberate activity and socio-spatial production of meanings at the margins of the habitual terrains of Firstspace mundane everydayness, and also of the Secondspace power centres and the reach of their imposed representational systems.

It follows that Thirdspace is both familiar and ultimately other, publicly visible but containing hidden secrets, "a space that is common to all of us yet never able to be completely seen and understood, an 'unimaginable universe'."[85] Although Thirdspace offers countless worlds to explore, getting to know them separately as exclusive domains provides too fragmented and totalising a perspective and makes its openness and heterogeneity inaccessible. Therefore, it is an ever-changing, disharmonious space of incongruities that resists being known and expressed by standard, sequential cognitive and recording methods and systems of representation, which only amplifies the "incapacity of language, texts, discourses, geographies and historiographies to capture fully the meanings of human spatiality." In the complexity and internal variability of Thirdspace, Soja concludes, spatial knowledge "is achievable only through approximations, a constant search to move beyond what is known."[86] This all-inclusive, simultaneous and volatile meta-space inevitably presupposes as well as implies non-traditional temporal patterns which would make the incoherent and discontinuous spatiality possible and also better suit the diverse modes of social production of this space. As Lefebvre notes, such space "embraces the loci of passion, of action, of lived situations, and this immediately implies time. Consequently it may be qualified in various ways: it may be directional, situational or relational, because it is essentially qualitative, fluid and dynamic."[87] What Thirdspace opens up to alternative or even radical reinterpretation and reinvigoration are not only approaches to spatial knowledge and its social implications, but also to historical knowledge by strengthening our awareness that the workings and organisation of time may be, like our social space, more complicated and differently layered than we have assumed.

Although various forms of Firstspace and Secondspace can naturally be found within Ackroyd's novels, it is above all the concept of Thirdspace to which his London chronotope as a whole addresses itself. It is a meta-space (meta-chronotope) that contains countless other spaces (chronotopes, heterotopias) in a historical-social-spatial arrangement of

---

85 Soja, *Thirdspace*, 56.
86 Soja, *Thirdspace*, 57.
87 Henri Lefebvre, *The Production of Space*, 42.

heterogeneous simultaneity, diversity, incoherence and contradiction, which is inherently generated and perpetuated by the incessant encounters, clashes, collaborations or even reconciliations of what are generally perceived as opposing, incongruous and mutually exclusive principles and forces, as a result of which some of its manifestations may appear paradoxical – real and imagined at the same time. It is a milieu where the realistic and the fabricated, the rational and the uncanny, the knowable and the unfathomable, the public and the personal, the powerful and the powerless, the hegemonic and the peripheral, the official and the subversive, not only exist one next to the other, but, though sometimes only temporarily, also turn their binary relation upside down and invert their customary hierarchy of significance and priority, thus altering the mechanisms of the narrative's production of meaning and its potential interpretative perspective. This London as a historical-social-spatial rendering of the undersides of the city's social life is chiefly occupied, and produced, by characters whose worldview and perception of reality are dissimilar to or dissenting from the mainstream, and particularly in discord with those holding positions of power and authority within the society's governing institutions, such as artists, writers, directors, architects, comedians, bibliophiles, scholars, philosophers, aspiring essayists and journalists, errant scientists, heretics, anarchists, clandestine conspirators and sectarians, criminals, solitary detectives, occultists, mystics, visionaries, eccentrics and lunatics. What connects all these diverse individuals is that by their acts they create domains of resistance and liberation, be they physical, imaginary or both. Ackroyd's chronotopes are thus sites of (not necessarily political) counter-power which enable their inhabitants to challenge the widespread false assumptions and preconceptions about, prejudices against and dismissive attitudes towards their, often willing, marginality and otherness.

Although most of these chronotopes, and their inhabitants, are not concealed from public scrutiny, due to their marginality and otherness, and also their contradictoriness, irrationality, radicality and obscurity they are prevented from ever being known and understood completely by the majority society and its prevailing, officially approved methods of enforced rationalism and systems of representation. Ackroyd's novels capture this unknowability and the impossibility of presenting unbiased and authentic history, personal as well as collective, both in their content and form. The protagonists of the stories come to the realisation that the world around them is to be grasped only if the myth of omnipotent rationality and all-recording language is abandoned in favour of alternative, "non-rational," approaches and philosophies valuing intuition, unrestrained imagination and sensuousness. And so they retort to practices such as alchemy, mysticism, visionariness, magic, imaginative self-fashioning, experimentation on the verge of the law and ethics, but also to forgeries, frauds, conspiracies and homicides in order to cope with and make sense of the city and their existence and role within its distinct historical-social-spatial continuum. This does not mean that Ackroyd rejects rationality altogether, rather that reason, logic and alternative methods and devices of cognition are viewed as two sides of one coin, as different yet not wholly exclusive, even complementary, ways of obtaining knowledge that is impossible to achieve in its totality and finality. His protagonists' excursions beyond the reach of empirical rationalism, and, in a more extreme form, also beyond the limits of legally and socially acceptable behaviour, can be understood as their attempts at what Soja (following Lefebvre) calls the approximations of spatial knowledge, which inherently involves social and temporal dimensions – the more paths to this knowledge one is able to walk along, Ackroyd suggests, the more accurate or faithful these approximations may become. On the formal level, his novels demonstrate that such (hi)story-telling is not viable entirely through traditional narrative and language forms and structures. Therefore, they make use of multiple plots, multiple-perspective narrations, time inversions, supra-temporal parallelisms and inconclusive, equivocal endings, which are prone to ambiguous interpretation as they witness a gradual disappearance of realistic elements and their replacement by a transposition to the realm of paranormal phenomena or hallucinatory mental states. This "thirdspatial" London chronotope as an ontological and epistemological concept is then fundamentally evasive, ephemeral, unfinished, always in process and open to further complementation and elaboration, but also to problematisation and re-revision.

Chapter 2
Uncanny London

If I tell you that the city toward which my journey tends is discontinuous in space and time, now scattered, now more condensed, you must
not believe the search for it can stop.
Italo Calvino, *Invisible Cities*

"What is now proved was once only imagined," claims William Blake in
"The Marriage of Heaven and Hell,"[1] stressing the need for excessively
productive imagination in all spheres of human creativity, while also
pointing out that the logic of imagery and the logic of rational reason
operate differently and at different paces. These two logics have always
been at work, cooperating in a distinct sort of unspoken agreement, the
former prompting and stimulating the latter, moving humankind forward in terms of both technological progress and self-awareness. By (re)
presenting the paranormal, "characters and their authors are in different
ways projecting a new model of subjectivity," notes Marina Warner, and
adds that "[i]n some unprecedented way, the various operating dynamics
of magic stories – time shifts, ubiquity, hypnosis, possession, metamorphosis itself – now charge the currents of popular culture more densely
than at any time since the first high wave of the Gothic in the late eighteenth century."[2] Ours is indeed an age that is highly suspicious of the
myth of the ultimate rational explicability of the world, and the uncanny
has gained larger recognition by becoming a frequent subject of modern
philosophy and art. In literature, the increasing popularity during the
past four decades of genres and narrative styles such as fantasy, horror,
Neo-Gothic, magic realism and the carnivalesque is solid enough evidence that numerous writers have responded to this tendency by placing

---

1   William Blake, "The Marriage of Heaven and Hell," 77.
2   Marina Warner, *Phantasmagoria*, 378, 379.

the spiritual alongside, or even above, the material, thus continuing the long tradition of intersecting the esoteric and the literary.

The tradition of Western esotericism is long, diverse but historically discontinuous, its developmental paradigm being rather of a dormant nature[3]. Yet, what almost all these currents have in common is their reliance on the written word to pass on knowledge from one generation to another. As their etymology suggests[4], the esoteric and the occult are supposed to bear and reveal certain inner, metaphysical knowledge intended for a limited and select audience. Since the practitioners often found it impossible or undesirable to transmit their tradition in a direct, official manner, such teaching and initiation mostly took place through encoded or symbolic literature and art. An apt example is that of alchemical texts which, more than others, employ most of the elemental literary figures in order to better express the peculiar, exotic, ambiguous and enigmatic images, phrasings and symbolism through which they fuse science, literature, mythology and religion[5].

The early literary works featuring such forces were ancient mythologies which attempted to impose structure and order onto a disorderly or incomprehensible reality by defining enemies and aliens, issuing warnings and offering advice[6]. Therefore, the reason and motivation for their employment of supernatural creatures and phenomena transcend mere entertainment and stirring up of the imagination. Yet, this tendency can by no means be restricted only to classical and popular myths and mythologies. A concern with the suprasensual and ethereal can be found in the writings or private activities of authors who lived in times favourable to the matters of the immaterial world, as well as those whose era proclaimed itself as overtly rational[7]. Therefore, literature has always served as a reflection and mediator of people's experience as well as a source of an alternative reality which defies the rules and principles of the material world.

---

3 This means that it can reemerge, with different intensity, in different historical periods, and allows individuals, groups or communities "to rediscover or reawaken a particular archetypal paradigm latent within a tradition without any direct contact with such lineage" (Arthur Versluis, *Restoring Paradise: Western Esotericism, Literature, Art, and Consciousness*, 143).

4 The Greek *esotero* means "more within" or "further inside," the word occultism derives from the Latin *occulo* meaning "to conceal."

5 Versluis, *Restoring Paradise: Western Esotericism, Literature, Art, and Consciousness*, 86.

6 Marina Warner, *Managing Monsters: Six myths of our time*, 19.

7 The mathematician and logician Lewis Carroll and Arthur Conan Doyle, the creator of a literary epitome of rational reason and emotionless logical deduction, for instance, were both keen on the possibilities of the new media, especially photography, to capture and make visible spirits and apparitions.

Still, the occurrence of mystical and occult themes and motifs in modern literature is rather scarce, and there have been only a few recognised writers concerned with some of the Western esoteric traditions. From those writing in English we can mention William Butler Yeats, Hilda Doolittle, Charles Williams, C. S. Lewis, J. R. R. Tolkien or Dion Fortune[8]. These rather sporadic voices, however, demonstrate that the Western literary and esoteric traditions are more closely related than it may at first sight seem, and, in cooperation perhaps even more powerfully than individually, they creatively and often unconventionally explore the infinite possibilities of the imagination and the limitless forms human (un/sub) consciousness can take when searching for experience mere material existence proves impotent to provide. The end of the twentieth century is marked by an increased interest in the psychic and occult, and the British literary scene from the late 1960s to the present has been no exception to this rule, as various forms of dealing with the supernatural or paranormal feature in the works of writers such as John Fowles, Angela Carter, Salman Rushdie, Jeanette Winterson, Marina Warner, John Banville, Graham Swift, Charles Higson, Iain Sinclair and Peter Ackroyd.

Ackroyd's conviction that the history of London is largely incomplete without involving its enigmatic and mystical manifestations and happenings represents one of the pillars of his conception of the city, both in the past and in the present and the future[9]. In his view, it is precisely the intrinsic interconnectedness of and incessant encounters and tensions between the city's rational and public and irrational and hidden sides that have always generated its formidable material, intellectual and spiritual forces and thus considerably shaped its development. "The city itself remains magical; it is a mysterious, chaotic and irrational place which can be organised and controlled only by means of private ritual or public superstition" (*LB*, 207). His novels exemplify a recent tendency of historical fiction that "has delved deeper into the cultural genealogies and 'psychogeographies' that intimately connect our presents/presence with the past."[10] One

---

8 The most extreme of them is Fortune, herself a practicing magus, whose novels are composed as a particular blend of fiction and a manual or handbook of magical practices and paranormal phenomena.

9 "This fascination with the spiritual side of things goes back, he thinks, to his Roman Catholic upbringing." John Preston, "My work matters more to me than love," an interview with Peter Ackroyd. *The Telegraph*, 20 August 2006.

10 Therefore, Ackroyd prefers to write what he calls "religious or spiritual fiction," as opposed to "secular fiction," and his way of doing this is by illuminating and celebrating "the sacredness of time and passage of time." "Each book is a different reason to exist," Lidia Vianu's students' videoconference interview with Peter Ackroyd, 9 May 2006.

of these linking elements across time levels is people's unflagging need for an alternative approach to themselves and the world around them, other than that held and promoted by the prevalent ideology of the current political and social establishment. The idea that the history of the capital cannot be separated from its occult, esoteric and mystical traditions also forms the basis of all his London novels, in which the great historical events always take place off-stage, forming a mere background for the author's "private mythology of London."[11] Ackroyd's idiosyncrasy is his foregrounding of the city's "unofficial" history, its enigmatic, obscure or otherwise irrational aspects and phenomena. His novels always revolve around some mystery through which the city's underside manifests its lines of force and, therefore, the theme and discourse of the irrational plays a significant role in them: a combination of occultism and serial murders; mysticism, communication with spirits and alchemical experiments; mysterious identities related to the motif of forgery; or the myth of the homunculus combined with the theme of the doppelgänger.

This feature, however, is logically not an isolated characteristic of Ackroyd's vision of London, but is firmly embedded in the complex structure of his distinct urban chronotope, inevitably overlapping and interfering with its other defining constituents, in particular with the notion of the literary dimension of London's history, which is in part created through the texts produced by its inhabitants. All his London works, fiction as well as non-fiction, reflect their author's insistence that the irrational has always been an integral part of the city's texture and thus has deeply affected its life, its inhabitants' acts and their desire to transform them into autonomous narratives. As this is a recurrent process, during which new stories appear while past events are reinterpreted from different points of view or in the light of newly discovered facts, these affairs have become immortalised in London's palimpsestic mythology. Although he can hardly be labelled an occult writer, Ackroyd assumes a significant position among writers concerned with the city's mystical aspects as he has demonstrated an intense sensibility to the esoteric and paranormal and to their close relation to the written word. His works, therefore, represent a unique contribution to the process of (re)writing London from the fresh perspective of long marginalised arcane phenomena and practices, which only the city could have ever produced and which, in return, have in large measure transformed the city in their image.

---

11 Barry Lewis, *My Words Echo Thus: Possessing the Past in Peter Ackroyd*, 75.

London the Obscure

For Ackroyd, London's history has always been a story of its two faces: the official, public, rational city and the unofficial, hidden, shadowy city existing somewhat behind or below the commonly presented and experienced version. Therefore, he insists, in order to approach the city in its wholeness it is necessary to get acquainted with its histories other than the official one, those of its more undercurrent tendencies, manifestations and phenomena, which are sometimes enigmatic and irrational and always heterogeneous in nature. As for centuries London's identity has been inseparable from manifold forms of occultism, esotericism and mysticism, their accounts represent a significant insight into the city's concealed happenings, which have often affected or determined the more manifest ones. Following this tradition, Ackroyd's London novels explore and reveal the city's continuous preoccupation with the occult and esoteric, and thus allow light to be cast on "those neglected quarters of the city and their forgotten histories, whose very peculiarity often acts as a welcome corrective to the more anodyne aspects of London's carefully managed past"[12] and, by doing so, to assume a more complex perspective on its past and present development.

The roots of London's modern esoteric and occult traditions can be traced to the Renaissance, when the English Reformation allowed a gradual secularisation of everyday life by focusing on the practical, pragmatic aspects of Christianity, which inevitably deprived it of some of its former metaphysical charms. As this transformative process was most immediate in the capital, average Londoners were the first to experience the personal consequences of the growing insistence on self-reliance and the absence of a helping hand from the Church. Many of them thus looked for solace elsewhere, often in what may have appeared to be relics of pre-Christian mythology and medieval superstition. Sixteenth-century London thus witnessed a concurrence of a progressive development of modern natural sciences and philosophy, as well as a spontaneous recourse to age-old superstitious folk beliefs. That is why the city attracted not only many prominent scholars and philosophers, but also "an emerging class of occult professionals,"[13] ranging from wise women and seers to sorcerers and witches. However, no unequivocal line between these two groups existed as many thinkers and proto-scientists of this time

---

12 Merlin Coverley, *Occult London*, 14–15.
13 Coverley, *Occult London*, 18.

often resorted to various mystical and occult teachings and traditions in order to complement or support the scientific claims of their "official" branches. Arguably the most gifted of these was Dr John Dee, a scholar at Elizabeth's court, promoted to the role of "intelligencer,"[14] a distinguished mathematician, astronomer and navigator, but also a practicing alchemist, deeply concerned in astrology, the study of the Cabbala and other ancient forms of mysticism and symbolism[15].

After the Elizabethan era, London's tradition of bridging the rational and the irrational was less persistent, chiefly due to the revolutionary changes English society underwent in the following century, with the notable exceptions of Isaac Newton, who devoted much of his vigour and writing to alchemy, and Sir Christopher Wren. As Surveyor General, Wren developed for London a precise geometrical plan of a radial system of wide, modern thoroughfares running from one centre. Yet, what might appear to be a product of rational logic and purely scientific calculation was in fact also rooted in "the unacknowledged traditions of Freemasonry, the Cabbala, and the 'sacred measurements' of the Bible."[16] The key unit of measure of this New Jerusalem was a "cubit,"[17] and the major apexes of the design were set in locations of spiritual and occult significance. Interestingly, these facts have been largely overlooked as the role of occult architect was instead allotted to Wren's younger colleague and former pupil, Nicholas Hawksmoor, who in planning his churches used similar measurements. His "dark" reputation, however, is a relatively recent phenomenon that was acquired retrospectively, particularly thanks to Iain Sinclair's *Lud Heat* (1975), which suggests that the locations and certain architectonic details of these churches have a mystical meaning derived from the architect's secret preoccupation with ancient religious and occult teachings.

During the Age of Reason much of the occult tradition remained largely latent in effect, emerging only sporadically, through a few re-

---

14 A term denoting "a seeker of hidden knowledge, philosophical and scientific." (Benjamin Wooley, *The Queen's Conjuror: The Life and Magic of Dr Dee*, 62).

15 Dee was the owner of one of the most voluminous libraries in Europe, which included numerous copies on occultism and mysticism. He himself summarised his occult theories in two influential books, *Monas Hieroglyphica* (1564) and *De Heptarchia Mystica* (1582–83), and established an unofficial esoteric centre in his mother's cottage in Mortlake to which he moved from London in 1565.

16 Especially in accordance with principles laid down in the Old Testament Book of Numbers, Ed Glinert, qt in Coverley, *Occult London*, 42.

17 This unit was based on the length of the forearm (measured from the elbow to the tip of the middle finger), the Biblical cubit is usually estimated as approximately 18 inches (45 centimetres).

markable individuals as well as through the reemergence of local superstition and legends[18]. London occult circles of the second half of the
century were dominated by two mystics of foreign origin – Emmanuel
Swedenborg, who frequently returned to the city, eventually dying in
Clerkenwell in 1772, and Chayim Samuel Jacob Falk, known as "Rabbi
Falk, the Ba'al Shem of London," who lived in London for forty years
after fleeing Germany where he was to have been burned alive for sor-
cery in 1742. These two neighbours in Welclose Square often met to discuss their occult, Cabbalist and alchemical preoccupations, and their
ideas also inspired works by visionary romantic writers, most notably
William Blake's radical spiritualist poetry and Mary Shelley's novel
Frankenstein[19].

In spite of its façade as a time of rational pragmatism and firm social
cohesion, the Victorian era witnessed an increasing interest in esoteric
practices alongside another wave of rapidly progressing technologies
and natural sciences[20]. And so, in 1875 Reverend Charles Maurice Davies
claimed that in the mist of London there was "an element of the mysterious and occult utterly undreamed by the practical people."[21] Gradually,
the quest for spirits and the invisible moved from the seclusion of laboratories, studies and drawing rooms, where various enthusiasts carried
out their spiritualist, mesmerist or clairvoyant experiments and private
séances, to the spheres of social debate, media and entertainment. Yet, it
was not until the very end of the century that a truly consistent revival of
London's esoteric and occult traditions took place, and the period "between 1890 and the beginning of World War I saw a remarkable eruption
of creative energy and speculation, a fantastic mélange of alternative and
progressive ideas wedding ancient beliefs and modern science,"[22] offering
thus a remedy for the deepening spiritual crisis of Western civilisation[23].

---

18 Thanks to the development of popular mass media and cultural forms, early and mid-Victo-
    rian London experienced the appearance of several legends and superstitious beliefs whose
    popularity spread and was sustained via their coverage in the press and their rendering in
    music-hall performances and variety shows, such as the legend of Spring-Heeled Jack, whose
    nocturnal rages occupied London's popular imagination for most of the century.

19 Coverley, *Occult London*, 49–59.

20 "In many ways, the most brilliant inventors of the Victorian age were at a loss to account for
    the marvels they made and were seeking ways to explain them, and many of them applied
    metaphors according to the logic of the imagery, psychic and paranormal, evolved during the
    course of a long history of speculation about spirits through concepts of ether, pneuma, light,
    immateriality, and so forth" (Warner, *Phantasmagoria*, 254).

21 Charles Maurice Davies, *Mystic London: or, Phases of Occult Life in the Metropolis*, 284.

22 Gary Lachman quoted in Coverley, *Occult London*, 69.

23 Chief of these movements and organisations was the Theosophical Society and the Hermetic

The World Wars, however, brought an abrupt end to this heyday, interrupting the tradition for more than half a century.

In the pragmatic, post-WWII climate the uncanny was again moved to the margin of interest as a dubious enterprise, a distraction rather than a legitimate source of knowledge. Yet, with the postmodernist diversion from a purely rational grasp of the world, the situation began to change, London "witnessed an occult revival,"[24] and so, once again, within the teeming metropolis "the not-so-secret or hidden world of the occult" could be found[25]. A concern with the deliberate geometrical patterns of buildings and monuments, hypothetically with a larger religious or mystical significance, as well as with the hidden and disappearing aspects of the city assumed a prominent position in its literary manifestations, such as Chris Street's project entitled *Earthstars: The Geometric Groundplan Underlying London's Ancient Sacred Sites and its Significance for the New Age* (1990)[26]. However, as the esoteric and occult are inevitably unorthodox, radical and underclass, by entering mainstream media and texts they run the risk of being appropriated by the popular culture industry and the public discourse through selective simplification and commodification[27]. Though temporarily banished from public view, occult currents in London are tenaciously resilient and continue to exist behind its official face, ready to erupt in new forms, with new intensity, and to offer an original, alternative perspective of what appears mundane, familiar and indisputable, one which Ackroyd identifies as key to comprehending the spirit of this eternal, illimitable city.

His London is thus founded on the perpetual encountering of the rational and irrational principles, neither of which is attributed any truth value. All his books exemplify his belief that in order to approach and

---

Order of the Golden Dawn, the first inspired by the Eastern philosophies and spiritual principles, the latter rooted in the Western esoteric tradition, prevailingly that of the Cabbala. The growing popularity of these two movements' teachings attracted London's most prominent luminaries, including writers such as W. B. Yeats.

24 Coverley, *Occult London*, 96.

25 Francoise Strachan, *The Aquarian Guide to Occult, Mystical, Religious, Magical London and Around*, ix.

26 Inspired by Alfred Watkins's 1920s texts developing the idea of "ley lines," a network of straight tracks on which the city was built, Street proposes a secret and sacred, triangular geometrical system with its main axis located in "overlooked suburban spaces, rather than within the city's official centre," on which he "shows London to be at the centre of a national, even global, web of interconnected sites whose alignments reveal the true pattern underlying our familiar landscape" (Coverley, *Occult London*, 100, 101)

27 Iain Sinclair gives Will Self's "Psychogeography" column in the *Independent* as an example of this danger. In his interview with Stuart Jeffries (*The Guardian*, April 24, 2004), Sinclair notes that despite its title Self's column "has got absolutely nothing to do with psychogeography."

comprehend the city, it is necessary to reconcile them in a seemingly paradoxical symbiosis, and thus adopt a "parodic or irreverently playful attitude to history over an ostensibly normative mimesis."[28] Although it would be absurd to make a clearly arranged taxonomy of Ackroyd's connections between London and its occult tradition, it is at least possible to trace certain interconnected fundamental principles or properties around which his treatment of this uncanny city is organised: the main of these are a mythical, cyclical, spiral or labyrinthine conception of time that denies chronological linearity and "rather works forwards and backwards at the same time,"[29] resulting in a myotical timelessness in which the past and the present are no longer clearly distinguishable; an emphasis on the influence of the genius loci, the inexorable energy of certain areas that have retained a power that determines a recurrent pattern of events happening in them; the significance of various individuals who are ahead or out of their time, or "Cockney Visionaries" as he prefers to term them, who, in different historical periods, inhabit the city and affect its life through a genius and foresight that enables them to embrace the mystical and occult forces embedded in the city's texture; the practices of occultism, esotericism and radical sectarianism within the city and their impact on its public life; and the capacity of the imagination to perform acts comparable to transcendental magic. Apart from demonstrating the ways in which he explores London's esotericism and mysticism in his works, this chapter attempts to illustrate how the author incorporates the theme and discourse of the irrational into his narrative technique in order to make it not only more elaborate, but also to challenge the readers' most taken-for-granted assumptions about the world by offering alternative modes of its interpretation. Moreover, it also argues that Ackroyd's employment of the esoteric makes his novels more attractive to read and, through his hybridising and pluralising of them, revivifies the genre of the (post)modern historical novel and instigates his readers' interest in the city and its history. It is thus also through his writing that London's "magical energy survives still" (*LB*, 507).

---

28   Suzanne Keen, "The Historical Turn in British Fiction," 171.

29   Susana Onega, *Peter Ackroyd*, 45.

Wandering and Wondering in Eternity – Mythical Time

Ackroyd's concept of mythical time, based on circular or spiral recurrence and a labyrinthine intersecting of different time levels, is by no means restricted to his fiction, but proves essential for his understanding of the process of London's historical development. In the preface to his *London: The Biography*, Ackroyd plainly expresses what he thinks best captures the city's existence and evolvement in time, though, as he himself admits, the whole sense of time in London is complicated as it primarily reflects the workings of the imagination[30]. For him, the city "defies chronology," which is the reason why "this book moves quixotically through time, itself forming a labyrinth" (*LB*, 2). From this perspective, London history is not a seamless, sequential account but a "search of those heights and depths of urban experience that know no history and are rarely susceptible to rational analysis" (*LB*, 2). Instead of following it year by year, Ackroyd probes various iterative, periodically, regularly or not, reemerging patterns of events, acts, habitation and sensibilities across time that are related to one another thematically rather than causally, and that have been repeatedly incited by operations evading rational grasp. Thus, the traditional linear understanding of time, though not rejected altogether, is shown to be ultimately incapable of capturing the complexity of the city's past.

Seen from this perspective, in the course of time London has always been a distinct yet strangely familiar city – the outward, visible developments of its modernisation and rebuilding may have made it look different, but underneath the surface a more sensible observer would recognise familiar patterns of urban existence which have remained unchanged for ages, such as the atmosphere of certain places or its inhabitants' moods, habits and gestures. Therefore, the city has and has not changed at the same time. The disordered intersecting of time sequences inevitably reflects in the process of gaining urban experience, which is accumulative rather than gradual and sequential, each Londoner being imposed upon by a mass of shared living inheritance generated by the momentum of the recurrent forces. "Ackroyd portrays London as an eternal city, one beyond the confines of time, which maintains itself by interaction with its population and exists as an inspiration for those receptive to its mythic qualities."[31] He has proposed several metaphors

---

30 See "Interview between Peter Ackroyd and Julian Wolfreys" (21 December 1997) in Gibson, Jeremy, Wolfreys, *Peter Ackroyd: The Ludic and Labyrinthine Text*, pp. 249–63.

31 David Charnick, "Peter Ackroyd: *The Plato Papers*."

for the working mechanisms of such temporality, for instance, that of a lava flow moving in many streams of varied velocity and in different directions, which suggests that not all occurrences in time are predestined to be reduplicated or perpetuated (LLCV, 343). Another is that of "a house with many rooms" in some of which the past is introduced to the present, while in others the present is introduced to the past, only for both to eventually be introduced to the future. All these metaphors, and all Ackroyd's works, attempt to capture "that spectral and labyrinthine world where the past and the present cannot necessarily be distinguished" (ATW, 368). Moreover, as the present and the past imbue each other and human experience layers and accumulates, "every period has a different sense of time" (ATW, 369), depending not only on the memory and weight of the previous happenings, but also on the current modes of evoking time and approaches to its measuring. Therefore, the patterns of mythical time resulting in what may be termed "perpetual time"[32] stem from the invariability of the very essence of the human condition, and so it is legitimate to use the past to illuminate the present just as the present can help to get hold of the past, as neither can be understood without the other. Accordingly, his London novels attempt to render and dramatise selected minutiae embedded within the city's immense past/present experience.

In *The Great Fire of London* this complex model is only suggested and rather fragmentarily outlined, yet both the defining aspects of Ackroyd's time, the circular/spiral and the labyrinthine, are presented in the novel. When Spenser is contemplating the sinister atmosphere of the old prison, he comes to the conclusion that the very existence of sites of confinement is a product of the city's temporal cyclicality: "Such places will always exist – once the Marshalsea, now here. Only a small time – an historical moment – separated the two; and they represented the same appalling waste of human life. Nothing had really changed in society which had such places as its monuments" (*GFL*, 57). The two physically and temporally different places are therefore connected through their metaphysical affinity, as they are merely two recurrent materialisations of the same mental conception, and as such they are not separated by any substantial historical time distance. However, Spenser also feels himself part of a much less graspable pattern of the city, one defined by its human dimension. When walking around the crowded streets, he has the sensation that other people "also, became part of him – as though he

---

32 David Charnick, "Out of time: Peter Ackroyd's perpetual London."

contained them all within himself at the same time as they directed him forward. The pattern was one, within and without" (*GFL*, 37). This dimension makes the time structure of the city even more amorphous and directionless, rooted not only in its territorial properties, but also in its inhabitants' imaginations and creativity, which are presented as the only means through which human beings can possibly make their imprint on the larger space-time framework of their existence.

Hawksmoor thoroughly probes the mythical conception of time, as a result of which its temporal composition is far from linear and the distinction between the present and the past becomes blurred. Much of the story is constructed through the juxtaposition of two mirroring, parallel plotlines, separated by about two hundred and fifty years in time. The two narratives grow to echo each other in all their basic components, having the same manner of killing, the same places, the same type of people falling victim to a serial killer, related characters with the same names, and a similar personality and character traits for the main protagonists – although both like to think of themselves as sensible, pragmatic and self-controlled men, in reality they cannot help trusting and relying on their intuition and instinct, some sixth sense which often prompts them to act against the principles of reason and logic. As a result, they are solitaries who prefer to work alone, their behaviour and opinions are sometimes interpreted as eccentric and old-fashioned, and they are treated by their colleagues and superiors with a peculiar mixture of respect, distrust and mild ridicule. Apart from these, the book abounds with other repetitions which link the two plotlines and emphasise their doppelgänger effect, such as motifs, moods, phrases and rhymes. The structural parallelism is also enhanced by the echoing of the last words of one chapter at the beginning of the subsequent one. All these devices "may be said to function as temporal bridges, rendering ineffectual the time gaps that logically exist between the two stories."[33]

However, what appears to be a manifestation of a simple cyclicality of time gradually transforms into a more intricate shape as the two protagonists become more and more time-conscious, aware of their own position within the larger scheme of London, and cosmic, perpetuity. While at the beginning of their stories these men are preoccupied with accomplishing their goals within a traditional time chronology, Hawksmoor with solving his cases as soon as possible and Dyer with having his churches live on after his death, towards the end, as they renounce and abandon

---

33 Susana Onega, *Metafiction and myth in the novels of Peter Ackroyd*, 47.

the imperatives of pure rationality, they experience an epiphanic revelation concerning the necessity of using immaterial means to achieve
material aims, through which they find themselves capable of assuming
a detached view and seeing their selves transcend earthbound space-time
reality and become part of the mass of a radiating time flow extending
across and interconnecting different historical periods. And so Dyer is
seen turning on his bed, feeling "cut down out of Time," eventually running "to the end of [his] Time" and kneeling down as his "Shaddowe
stretched over the World" (*H*, 206, 209), while the desperate Hawksmoor
comes to understand that the pattern "was growing larger; and, as it ex-
panded, it seemed about to include him and his unsuccessful investigations" (*H*, 189), and reaches a timeless state in which his mind and body
are set free from the constraints of mechanical physical laws: "At such
times the future became so clear that it was as if he were remembering it,
remembering it in place of the past which he could no longer describe.
But there was in any case no future and no past, only the unspeakable
misery of his own self" (*H*, 199). This at first only intensifies his troubles,
but then it allows him to see them in a clear light and thus approach
them in a manner more appropriate to their existence within the labyrinthine time-patterns.

At the end of the story the time structure of the narration collapses
completely, giving way to a cryptic fusion of not only different time levels
but also of their dwellers' psyches. As Nicholas Hawksmoor follows the
traces and, most importantly, studies Dyer's diary, he begins to reveal the
significance of the occult scheme of the *loci delicti* and focuses his attention on finding the mysterious vagrant who calls himself the Architect.
As the novel progresses to its resolution, the space-time gap that separates the Architect and Hawksmoor diminishes and the two men rush
through the streets of the city towards the place of their spiritual union,
eventually encountering each other within the walls of the nonexistent
Little St Hugh in what appears to be an eerie time loop devoid of all laws
that govern the rationality and coherence of the physical world, peopled
by countless individuals from diverse periods:

> And his own Image was sitting beside him, pondering deeply and sighing,
> and when he put out his hand and touched him he shuddered. But do not
> say that he touched him, say that they touched him. [...] The church trem-
> bled as the sun rose and fell, and the half-light was strewn across the floor
> like rushes. They were face to face, and yet they looked past one another
> at the pattern which they cast upon the stone; for when there was a shape

there was a reflection, and when there was a light there was a shadow, and when there was an echo, and who could say where one had ended and the other had begun? (*H*, 216–217)

It is what the detective is feeling as he is experiencing his merging into the body of the city's perpetual continuum of shared human experience, at first through becoming one with the Architect, and then with all the figures inhabiting this "transcendental meeting place,"[34] joining them in their silent motion, both backwards and forwards, closer and further apart. This culminates when he is reborn as a new being, a child "begging on the threshold of eternity" (*H*, 217). The voices of the Architect and Hawksmoor merge into a single mystical voice belonging to neither of them but to some supra-temporal reincarnation, perhaps that of Dyer, floating within the city's mythical timelessness. As a result, the orthodox conception of history disintegrates, "the past and the present begin to become unnervingly similar and our notion of the present as a secure and, by implication, superior perspective is undermined."[35] Therefore, as the novel (in)concludes, more questions than answers remain, yet one thing is indisputable: Hawksmoor manages to find his "culprit" by patiently and correctly reading and interpreting Dyer's book. His understanding of the true nature of London time is thus achieved, in the best tradition of Western esotericism, through an initiation into secret occult wisdom by the means of encoded written words.

A similar parallelism can be found in *The House of Doctor Dee*, Ackroyd's most overtly spiritualist novel. When Matthew Palmer inherits an old house in Clerkenwell that once belonged to the eponymous Elizabethan mathematician, astrologer and occultist, he immediately gets drawn into its eerie history. He gradually learns that the house stands as if outside time as it repeatedly echoes certain behaviour patterns, ideas or utterances from the past. The house is a time-concentrating place where different historical periods coexist and time itself is running in diverse directions, which is reflected in the novel's "structural alternation of narrative voices and periods," and so "the further Matthew seems to be traveling backward in the course of investigating Doctor Dee's life, the further Doctor Dee seems to be traveling forward into the future."[36] Haunted by the spirits and voices of the house, Matthew is compelled to experience life situations analogous to those of John Dee four centuries before. Ackroyd draws sev-

---

34 Onega, *Metafiction and myth in the novels of Peter Ackroyd*, 56.
35 Richard Bradford, *The Novel Now*, 83.
36 Onega, *Metafiction and myth in the novels of Peter Ackroyd*, 115.

eral resemblances between the two main protagonists, of which the most notable is their understanding of time as an eternal process comprising cyclically recurrent events, which in effect become coincident, simultaneous or mutually permeated in some mystical, fifth dimension in which the notion of time transforms into a maze where the human spirit and experience of different periods encounter one another in a rather haphazard manner. When carrying out his research concerning the house and its distinguished one-time owner, Matthew feels he has "become part of the continuing historical process, as mysterious and unapproachable as any other period," viewing "the past as [his] present, so in turn the present moment became part of the past" (*HDD*, 13). John Dee, likewise, sees himself involved in greater patterns of history – assuming that "the past is restored around us all the time, in the bodies we inhabit or the words we speak," he believes that "there are certain scenes or situations which, once glimpsed, seem to continue for eternity" and that a really strong personality endowed with profound mental energy can incarnate into "the true spiritual body" (*HDD*, 26, 39, 68) that stretches over all times.

As in *Hawksmoor*, a significant part of the narration in *The House of Doctor Dee* is that of detection, though not of murders or some other crime, but of the relationship between the past and the present and, in consequence, of sacred knowledge which would allow the grasping of this uncanny connection. Matthew's learning about Doctor Dee's life, beliefs and teachings can be understood as a spiritual quest through which he becomes initiated into esoteric wisdom which, as in Hawksmoor's case, is achieved by his reading of occult texts, and which is later confirmed by his own transcendental experience. He learns about the theory and history of the homunculus, a fully artificial human form created in a glass tube, the dream of most Renaissance alchemists, including Dee, its recurrent existence in different historical periods, and the fact that it is not aware of its past or future existence until it returns home, always "at the end of its thirty years" (*HDD*, 125). He himself experiences a mysterious event which can be interpreted analogously – nearing his thirtieth birthday, he arrives home and finds in his garden a small boy looking like himself as a child, an image he suddenly recalls from photographs with his father. Ackroyd even seems to make a parallel between the intricate workings of time and the process of attaining wisdom through the written word:

> Once upon a time I was afraid of libraries. Those shelves of books formed
> a world which had, almost literally, turned its back upon me; the smell of

dust and wood, and faded pages, induced in me a sense of melancholy loss. Yet I began to repair my life when I became a researcher and entered the past: then one book led to another book, one document to another document, one theme to another theme, and I was led down a sweet labyrinth of learning in which I could lose myself. It has been said that books talk to one another when no one is present to hear them speak, but I know better than that: they are forever engaged in an act of communion which, if we are fortunate, we can overhear. (*HDD*, 129)

It is only through actively roaming this Babelian labyrinth of seemingly disparate pieces of knowledge that one can at least glance at the larger temporal patterns, as well as one's own position within the labyrinthine body of London's perpetual continuum, in which the most outstanding visionary ideas are preserved in eternity. And so Matthew eventually acknowledges the possibility that Dee's spirit and personality could exert some mystical influence on the present house and its new resident, admitting that "perhaps there is a kind of intelligence or vision which never really dies" (*HDD*, 262), which allows its possessor to be set free from the narrow limitation of his or her time's conventions and dogmas by revering and expounding the past, activating the present as well as anticipating the future.

Ackroyd's persuasion that John Dee was such an exceptional individual who, "in one way or another, belonged to every time" (*HDD*, 132), resonates on almost every page of the novel and his spirit affects the lives of all the characters that find themselves under the spell of the house. In the final chapter, symptomatically entitled The Vision, the two voices of Dee and Matthew coalesce in the universal mythical voice of the city, only to be subsequently accompanied by the narrative voice of Ackroyd himself. What has long seemed to be an imaginative ghost story turns out to be yet another confirmation of the author's mythical conception of London as, "a holy city where time never was" (*HDD*, 272), in which the past, the present and the future coexist, intertwined through the eternal power of the human imagination. To achieve this intertwining in a manner that would reflect and celebrate this essential property of the city is what Ackroyd strives to accomplish in his fiction. And so the novel ends with its author's assumption of the prophetic voice of the city, a London writer's mock-prayer for the eternal spirit of the city to descend upon him and help him accomplish his task, an appeal which also invites readers to wander/wonder with him: "Come closer, come towards me so that we may become one. Then will London be redeemed, now and for ever, and all those with whom we dwell – living or dead – will become the mystical city universal" (*HDD*, 277). It is the city's imaginative energy and vision which make it truly surpass the restraints of chronological linearity and immediate causality.

Various practical manifestations of this concept of time are scattered in all Ackroyd's London novels, most evidently in *Chatterton*. Through the use of the supra-sensual, the novel dramatises this invisible yet all-encompassing world of shadows and voices existing crosswise the individual time layers, especially through the ghost-figure of Thomas Chatterton which appears, with different effect, to other potentially visionary writers in the story – George Meredith, Harriet Scrope and Charles Wychwood. Such a world is also necessarily a supra-temporal one in which the past, the present and the future coexist and intermingle to such a degree that they are no longer distinguishable, suggesting thus that "history is unknowable, and in being unknowable it can never be given teleological or epistemic closure."[37] Charles's soul leaves this world in order to join those of Chatterton and Meredith in a transcendental and, from a literary point of view, intertextual one; Chatterton lives on through his masterful forgeries and mysterious death, inspiring new people to study his life and write biographies of him, though each biography seems to describe a "quite different poet" (*C*, 127), as they simultaneously always reflect the personalities of their authors; and Wallis's painting immortalises not only its author, the person portrayed and the model, but all those whose lives were somehow affected by it, including Charles, whom his son Edward still sees in the painting, thanks to which he believes that his father "would never wholly die" (*C*, 230). It is a psycho-physical world in which not time but visions, ideas, beliefs and dreams are the true measuring criteria of value and durability, and thus constitute and propel this distinct space-time labyrinthine continuum's defining dimension of eternity.

Where Suffering Seems to Linger – *Genius Loci*

A mythical concept of time is not the sole factor which causes the notable recurrence of certain happenings, phenomena or tendencies within the history of London. It is supported by what may be called the spirit of the place, the persistent effect of latent yet powerful energies through which certain places in the city have retained their particular atmosphere and

---

37 Alex Murray, *Recalling London: Literature and History in the work of Peter Ackroyd and Iain Sinclair*, 37.

character, and that have for centuries attracted the same kinds of people to settle in them. Ackroyd is convinced that there are areas within the city that are subject to peculiar temporal and special conditions as a result of which their *genius loci* has crucial influence on both the events happening in them and their inhabitants' lives, making the city "a place of echoes and shadows" (*LB*, 655). It is as if these areas were spellbound by some half-forgotten, atavistic forces, the power of which, according to Ackroyd, should never be underestimated. In his writings he describes numerous such areas dominated by this "topographical imperative,"[38] many of them associated either with the suffering of the poor and the outcast, such as the vicinity of St. Giles-in-the-Fields and Hawksmoor churches, which "can in their turn seem woeful or haunted" (*LB*, 496). Others are associated with the esoteric and mystical, such as Bloomsbury, which for centuries has been a place of congregation for controversial occult orders, secret sects and radical spiritual groups, because of what Ackroyd denotes as "a congregation of aligned forces, by coincidence or design" (*LB*, 463) still remaining at work up to the present day, as the Swedenborg Society and famous occult and astrological bookshops are still to be found in the neighbourhood of the British Museum. What Ackroyd strives to do is to "disclose a definite pattern of continuity" (LLCV, 346) which would help him understand the history and essence of the city, which often seems too uncontrolled and chaotic to contain or act according to any underlying structure of its functioning and development. And so he believes that these patterns of continuity and inheritance represent the axis around which a record of the city's past may be recreated. This theory forms the basis of all his London novels and is also what best demonstrates the complementariness of his fiction and non-fiction works[39].

As Ackroyd always concentrates on the obscure side of the city, the settings of his novels are frequently places that "emanate misery" and where "suffering seems to linger" (*LB* 498, 496). In the plot of *Hawksmoor* the disastrous consequences of the operation of these sinister forces are followed over two and a half centuries. Ackroyd mentions two of Nicholas Hawksmoor's churches, St George's-in-the-East and Christ Church, in *London: The Biography*, because they have always attracted the city's va-

---

38 "Each book is a different reason to exist," Lidia Vianu's students' videoconference interview with Peter Ackroyd, 9 May 2006.

39 The various parts of London that repeatedly appear in Ackroyd's (and, of course, other London writers') works are explored in detail in Ian Cunningham's *A Reader's Guide to Writers' London*.

grants and other outcasts, and therefore have witnessed an uncommonly high number of crimes and other dismal events. The fictitious architect, Nicholas Dyer, is well aware of this when he offers his verbose commentary on one of the miserable parishes in which his new church is being erected:

> Here in Angell Rents next the Ratcliffe High-way was Mr Barwick barbarously killed, his Throat being cut, the right side of his Head open'd and his Scull broke [...] The Murtherer was afterwards hang'd in Chains near the place of his Crime – thus it is called Red Cliff, or Ratcliffe, the hanging Dock opposite my Church [...] there was one Boy who killed his whole Family in Betts-Street and was taken in Chains to the Dock to be hang'd [...] Destruction is like a snow-ball rolled down a Hill, for its Bulk increases by its own swiftness and thus Disorder spreads: when the woman nam'd Maggot was hanged in Chains by here, one hundred were crushed to Death in the Tumult that came to stare upon her. (*H*, 93)

Dyer's words contain a peculiar mixture of disgust and fascination, a superior contempt for the miserable place as well as for those who inhabit it, though he also feels a kind of pleasure and satisfaction that the pattern of the ominous forces which have governed the area would expand its scope to his church. In the spirit of the novel's parallelism Dyer's soliloquy also anticipates forthcoming actions when he expresses his belief that the ghost-figure who reportedly haunts the place is not an apparition of the victims, but of "an ancient Murtherer returning to the Spot of his old Glory" (*H*, 93).

The fact that it is not the first time that murders have been committed on the sites of certain churches does not surprise Hawksmoor since he has already grown "to understand that most criminals tend to remain in the same districts, continuing with their activities until they were arrested, and he sometimes speculated that these same areas had been used with similar intent for centuries past" (*H*, 115). Like Dyer, the detective muses on the criminal history of Ratcliffe Highway and the area around St George's-in-the-East, pointing out a pattern of continuity stemming from the fact "that certain streets or patches of ground provoked a malevolence which generally seemed to be quite without motive" (*H*, 116). He gradually comes to realise that in order to understand the murders he is investigating he must get acquainted with the history of the sites where they were committed, which brings him to the study of Dyer's architectural designs. The dark magnetism of Dyer's/Hawksmoor's churches, which attracts violence and suffering, together with the mystical symbolism of the murders and their sites, make Hawksmoor abandon the purely rational deduction he has been so proud of and assume a more intuitive approach that allows him to disclose the larger schemes and hidden forces behind the homicidal acts and to identify the true "culprit" – the city.

A similar pattern is seen in *Dan Leno and the Limehouse Golem* with the replication of the Ratcliffe Highway murders. Once again, Ackroyd's insistence on the power of the *genius loci* and his rejection of a chronologically linear understanding of time operate concordantly. It is the spirit of "the same power-concentrating places"[40] that magnetises certain people and events rather than some rationally explicable causes. The Limehouse of the novel is a poverty-stricken, shadowy area and its negative energy recurrently materialises in various violent acts, culminating in a series of ritual murders in and around the Ratcliffe Highway. This area, as Dyer notes in *Hawksmoor*, was already notorious for barbarous killings in the early eighteenth century, but it became infamous because of the slaughter of the Marr family in 1811. This part of London thus "becomes a brooding presence behind, or perhaps even within, the murders themselves" (*DLLG*, 38). In *Dan Leno and the Limehouse Golem*, the dark spirit of the area comes to life in 1880 when several representatives of the margins of Victorian London society become victims of a homicidal force, the seeming invisibility of which causes the newspapers to label it the Limehouse Golem. However, in the case of Elizabeth Cree the power of the *genius loci* does not operate in an eerie, rationally unfathomable manner as she is overtly inspired by De Quincey's romanticising account of the Marr murders and consciously plans to commit her killings in the same place and using a similar method, wishing to become, like John Williams in De Quincey's essay, "an avenging angel of the city" (*DLLG*, 38). And so, although Elizabeth willingly follows the vicious tradition of the area, her homicidal acts are still, according to Ackroyd, a result of the impact of the dark territorial forces which breed such a monstrosity. She herself is well aware of this power, noting that "[i]nfinite London would always minister [to her] in [her] affliction" (*DLLG*, 192).

The novel also shows that the forces of the spirit of a place are not simply one-sided, attracting only evil or only good. The mysterious pyramid in the grounds of St Anne's church has drawn the city's "lost souls," like homeless tramps, insane individuals or violent criminals, and Elizabeth Cree leaves the mutilated body of one of her victims on this pyramid, yet

---

40   Onega, *Peter Ackroyd*, 68.

it has also inspired those in pursuit of profound knowledge, like occult scholars or scientists – Charles Babbage, for instance, is said to have chosen this location partly because of his fascination with the pyramid and its potential interpretation in terms of mathematical calculus. In either case, those who get trapped in these lines of force are always people who somehow stand outside of the category of conventional citizens. There is one more place in the novel that has a crucial, and mainly beneficial, impact upon most of the characters' lives – the Reading Room of the British Museum – where the fates of its frequenters, real and fictional, encounter and intersect one another, be it physically or not. The Reading Room thus becomes a miniaturised version of London, a focal point of the city's spiritual energies, the murmuring hums of which "set up a whispering echo like that of the voices in the fog of London" (*DLLG*, 46). Ackroyd presents it as a milieu disposing of some almost occult power, which, for example, manages to befriend such different persons as the materialist atheist Karl Marx and the cabbalistic spiritualist Solomon Weil. It is therefore not surprising that the mystery of the Limehouse Golem brings there many people who believe it is "the spiritual centre of London where many secrets might finally be revealed" (*DLLG*, 269), an emblem of the mutual inseparability of intellect and spirituality, a true source of the city's *geist*.

In *The House of Doctor Dee*, Matthew Palmer comes to understand the significance of the power of place when he moves into the ancient house in Clerkenwell. From the very beginning of the story the area breathes an atmosphere of mysteriousness and emanates energies which immediately affect all who find themselves in their force field. Approaching Clerkenwell, one of "the old centres of the city" (*HDD*, 1), on the tube Matthew begins to experience this "deeper sense of oblivion" as "[e]ven the passengers seem to be transformed, and the general atmosphere of the carriage becomes more subdued and, on occasion, more fearful" (*HDD* 1), and when in Clerkenwell Green he feels as if the "somehow bereft" area was "as if [...] separated from the rest of the city" (*HDD*, 10–11). As he starts to investigate its history he discovers certain persistent "subterranean layers" of London that still assert themselves through various eerie or hidden manifestations upon the city's "official" face, mostly in the form of a transhistorical recurrence of identical or related phenomena, for instance, Matthew watches in fascination as the police lead three prostitutes from one of the "nondescript office entrances" of a building on the site of which a medieval brothel used to stand (*HDD*, 17). He acknowledges that certain areas have tended to attract similarly-minded or focused people, a realisation which is only confirmed when he learns the history of his recently inherited house, which for centuries was the site of miscellaneous religious, occult and spiritualist sects and practices, whose inhabitants' steps, as one of them remarks in his account, were directed, often without them being able to foresee "the dreadful consequences," by "some power, benign or menacing, which resided there" (*HDD*, 222).

Like the British Museum Reading Room, Doctor Dee's house represents a condensed version of the city's spirit and shaping forces, "both the microcosmic replica of 'London eternal' and its centre."[41] Through revealing the secrets of the house Matthew begins to understand the operating mechanisms of the mythical city, to discover their occurrence within himself, and to get to know the feeling of being exposed to the uncanny power fields that force him to return to certain parts of London that are laden with the weightiness of past events and ancestral lives. So he visits the old Hoxton mental asylum by Wharf Lane where Charles Lamb used to visit his sister while she was temporarily detained after she had killed her mother, or the site of the former Marshalsea Prison in Southwark[42], and frequents them despite the oppressive presence of accumulated human experience. Those patient and tenacious enough are rewarded through being involved in this cumulative process, and Matthew gradually becomes aware of his merging with the house/city's spiritual and mystical body:

> The sense of peace, even in the middle of the city, was so strong that I presume it came from some powerful event in the past. Or perhaps it was simply that people like myself had always chosen this place, and over the years it had accepted the stillness of its visitors. [...] There was a sense of continuing power, of living force here. It was beyond death; it was the condition of the world. [...] It occurred to me then that this was really a city under the ground. It was the eternal city for those who are trapped in time. I was still kneeling beside the memorial in Red Lion Square, but now I seemed to be entering the stone wall of the basement in Cloak Lane. I was becoming part of the old house. (*HDD*, 43–44)

To submit to these living forces allows a transcendence into the city's timelessness and an experiencing of its dimension of eternity. Ackroyd thus exploits the motif of the fictitious haunted house once inhabited by the famous Renaissance scholar and mystic as a metaphor

---

41 Onega, *Peter Ackroyd*, 60.
42 Both these places appear in other Ackroyd's novels, namely in *The Lambs of London* and *The Great Fire of London* respectively.

for the supratemporal workings of London's *genius loci*, perpetuated and deeply embedded in the city's texture and crucially reflected in its dwellers' lives.

The district of Ackroyd's specific interest is Clerkenwell, a place strikingly prone to replicating the patterns of its past preoccupations. Over centuries, Clerkenwell has witnessed diverse, often concurring, forms of subversive, occult and radical activities, and attracted an incredible range of eccentric and visionary individuals, from the outcast and insane to scholars, writers, philosophers and "religious and political dissidents of every stripe."[43] Its irresistible spirit explains why in *The House of Doctor Dee* the house once supposedly belonging to John Dee is located there, though it is generally known that he in fact lived in Mortlake, which "reinforces Dee's status as a Cockney visionary."[44] The house still contains the concentrated power of its past events and inhabitants, which Ackroyd believes has been a distinctive property of the whole area, and which he likes to illustrate on a number of examples of activities and practices continuing in the same spirit over centuries. Apart from its theatricality and dramatic representations, from medieval times Clerkenwell was, for instance, "known, and identified, through its sacred or spiritual affiliation" (*LB*, 457), the site of various religious institutions, foundations and orders. As it was originally situated outside the city walls, it became a natural home for those who "wish to be separate and separated" (*LB*, 458), for dissenting and radical groups and individuals, and so it has witnessed many instances of unrest and riots, as well as attempts at their suppression or pacification. A related continuity is that of the tradition of radical, or at least unorthodox and oppositional, publishing, as already in the seventeenth century the local printers "were denounced for issuing 'blasphemous and seditious' literature" (*LB*, 462), and, later, it was in Clerkenwell that Lenin edited and published his revolutionary journal *Iskra*, where the Communist newspaper, the *Morning Star*, had its offices, and where, since the 1990s, the *Big Issue*, the magazine published to raise support for the homeless and unemployed, has resided (*LB*, 462–63). Therefore, as Ackroyd believes that the *genius loci* never ceases to operate in such an area, in the concluding paragraphs of the chapter "London's Radicals" in *London: The Biography* he poses the prophetic, rhetorical question of whether it was wise of property developers and speculators to choose this "shadowland" for their modernising designs (*LB*, 469).

---

43 Lewis, *My Words Echo Thus: Possessing the Past in Peter Ackroyd*, 130.
44 Lewis, *My Words Echo Thus*, 75.

The House of Doctor Dee is not Ackroyd's only novel set in this area. With his exceptional eye for detail, in *The Clerkenwell Tales* he brings to life medieval Clerkenwell in the unsettled year of 1399, with all its idiosyncrasies: tremendous energy, religious extremism, political radicalism, theatrical performances, and enigmatic events. Through a network of interrelated metafictional historiographic sketches rather than a continuous narrative, the reader is exposed to the operations of multiple undercurrent forces of the city – occult sectarians, heretics, secret plotters and spies alongside aberrant clerics and lunatics. Against the historical background of the time, the reader follows a clandestine fellowship of respected city officials who seem to be conspiring with an apocalyptic heretical sect, the predestined men, as both the groups, though for different reasons, are eager to get rid of the king. All this is foreseen by Sister Clarice, a nun endowed with prophetic powers, and the story gradually unfolds another mystery – that of the relationship between the "madly divine" cloistress and the political plotters. The novel thus dramatises both the earthly and paranormal activities of the city's "underworld spirits" (*CT*, 2), whose secret, offstage operations are often made "public" by the folk imagination in countless popular songs and refrains that reverberate in the streets, and which, in Ackroyd's view, are "the true melodies of London" as they "posses that spirit of place" (LLCV, 345).

Variety, Energy and Darkness – Cockney Visionaries

London as a "city of vision and prophecy" (*LB*, 752) has been home to several remarkable personalities who seem to have disposed of a special gift to see the city in its wholeness, who found themselves "living outside London time" (*LB*, 465), and who thus stood apart from, because far ahead of, the mainstream thinking and conventional beliefs of their time. As a result, they were seen, at best, as harmless eccentrics, and as dangerous radicals in the worst case, and as such were strenuously criticised, dismissed or mocked by their contemporaries because they always rejected, explicitly or not, being a part of the official cultural establishment. These "London Luminaries" and/or "Cockney Visionaries," in Ackroyd's view, occupy the greater cyclical processes of history as they are endowed with a remarkable capacity of imagination that enables them to glance, or at least anticipate, eternity. Their understanding of the role of imagination as "a staging ground for action, and not only for escape"[45] was exceptional and forward-looking, no matter how natural or taken-for-granted it may appear today. All these visionary Londoners, either by birth or by circumstances, were able to become part of the city's immense body of human experience and creative energy and, thanks to their exceptional sensibility, approached the city in its diversity and captured, simultaneously, its light and dark sides. It is precisely this ability to understand both London's oppressive misery and its bright liveliness that made them visionary as it helped them grasp the city's mystical patterns of existence in the infinite dimension of its perpetual transformation and renewal. This dimension allows them to create timeless, prophetic visions while acknowledging and drawing on the legacy of past traditions. That is why their works abound with "stylistic variety, display, heterogeneity" (LLCV, 348), properties so characteristic of London's nature and spirit, and represent the city's living imaginative inheritance, which Ackroyd also professes.

Ackroyd's visionaries can be classified into three categories: the first group is represented by outstanding London artists, mostly, yet not exclusively, writers, "who in their art have expressed the true nature and spirit of this place" as they "have recreated all the variety, the energy and the spectacle which this city expects and demands of its inhabitants," and "have expressed the horror, too" (LLCV, 342). Ackroyd has written separate biographies of most of them, namely *T. S. Eliot: A Life* (1984), *Dickens* (1990), *Blake* (1996), *Shakespeare* (2004), *Chaucer* (2005), *Turner* (2006), *Wilkie Collins* (2012) and *Charlie Chaplin* (2014). The second group are visionary scientists, scholars and philosophers, the subjects of Ackroyd's *The Life of Thomas More* (1998) and *Newton* (2007); and the third are diverse, often peculiar and eccentric, individuals, "the dreamers and the antiquarians" (*LB*, 757), whom the official historical records rendered nameless, but whose acts and thoughts resonate with the city because they elude purely rational explanation, and therefore they appear in all his novels. What connects them all is that in their personalities, and, consequently, in their spirit, imagination and work, we can find the most essential characteristic of the city – the juxtaposition, fusion and sometimes perhaps reconciliation of opposites or even extremes of human life: "To hear the music of the stones, to glimpse the spiritual in the local and the actual, to render tangible things the material of intangible allegory, all these are at the centre of the London vision" (*A*, 307). It is precisely this vision that Ackroyd's London novels strive to chronicle.

---

45   Arjun Appadurai, *Modernity at Large: Cultural Dimensions of Globalization*, 7.

Representatives of all these three groups of visionaries are scattered throughout Ackroyd's fiction, from dubious sorcerers, conjurors and prophets to renowned writers and thinkers. What connects these sometimes very distinct personalities is their potential to devote themselves to challenging visions that somehow transcend the historical time in which they emerge. Arguably the two most notable London writers for Ackroyd are two very different individuals – William Blake and Charles Dickens, though, interestingly enough, neither of them appears as a character in his novels. While the former was a truly mystical and prophetic poet, a solitary spiritual radical who opposed and rejected almost all the conventions and values of his society, and in whose "visionary imagination [...] there is no birth and no death, no beginning and no end, only the perpetual pilgrimage within time towards eternity" (*B*, 3), the latter was a celebrity for much of his productive life and made a significant, and largely esteemed, contribution to all spheres of public debate. Yet, like his predecessor, though by slightly different – more rational and pragmatic – means, Dickens also aspired to a realisation of his revolutionary vision, and not only on the aesthetic and personal levels, of a mental and structural transformation of English society into a more humane establishment, a vision that by far transcended the limits of most of his contemporaries' imagination and foresight. In his Postscript to *Dickens*, Ackroyd notes that the writer's exceptionality consists in his life-long "struggle to maintain a vision of the coherence of the world" resulting in "his energetic pursuit of some complete vision of the world" motivated by "so great a concern for the central human progress of the world, yet such a longing for transcendence also" (*D*, 576, 577). This applies to all Ackroyd's visionaries: they possess the capacity to see their occupation as part of a supra-temporal continuum across individual time layers. Their conation partly caters for and is fuelled by the rationalist idea of limitless progress and development, but it also always contains some transcendental, spiritual momentum essential to elevate it to perpetuity. Two related yet dissimilar examples of such individuals can be found in the protagonists of *The House of Doctor Dee* and *The Casebook of Victor Frankenstein*.

Ackroyd's Dee and Frankenstein share an insatiable hunger for knowledge. They both represent Faustian characters eager to learn ceaselessly in order to disclose all the secrets and mysteries of the world, even at the cost of their own happiness, as such a pursuit can easily be turned into an all-absorbing obsession[46]. Doctor Dee's ability to combine rational

---

46 While studying at Cambridge, for instance, Dee devoted eighteen hours a day to work and learning, allowing only four hours for sleep and two for meals (Wooley, *The Queen's Conjuror*, 12).

principles with a belief in the power of the esoteric, which he perceives to be essential if complex knowledge and understanding are to be achieved, makes him see beyond the horizon of material existence. Only a scholar who perceives scientific research and experimentation within a larger scope composed of various alternative, non-rational perspectives can enter the vast, timeless tradition that claims "no necessary disparity between the various forms of occult and experimental understanding" (*LB*, 502–3). Ackroyd repeatedly points out that the "pursuit of knowledge has always been one of the city's defining characteristics, even though it may take unfamiliar forms" and that "in London it is impossible to distinguish magic from other versions of intellectual and mechanical aptitude" (*LB*, 501). Therefore, Ackroyd's Renaissance thinker is not only a respectable mathematician, astronomer, engineer and geographer, but also a person who believes that he can speak with spirits and angels through a magic crystal, that he can discover the original, ancient city of London preserved intact deep below the existing one, or that he can create the homunculus, the everlasting creature that would serve as both divine illumination and guardian spirit to those whose efforts deserve it. "He believed the world to be imbued with spiritual properties [...] Each material thing is the visible home of a universal power, or congregation of powers, and it was the task of the enlightened philosopher and alchemist to see these true constituents" (*HDD*, 133). As a true visionary, Dee strives to compose a work based on the wisdom gained from invoking and learning about and from these spiritual forces. This, however, is an immensely complicated quest that might lead a zealous devotee like Dee astray, making him infatuated with a blinding, self-consuming obsession with the promise of black magic

What almost ruins Dee eventually restores him to life – a belief in otherworldly powers makes him rediscover the humanistic belief in the paramount importance of getting to know oneself and the power of human affection. Deceived and betrayed by his would-be friend Edward Kelley, Dee eventually admits his blindness and indifference to those who really like him, yet this awakening is mightily aided by the appearance of the supernatural forms of the two persons who suffered most from his neglect and whom he lost in part due to his obsession: first, the ghost of his father torments him with a fearful vision of a loveless world which devours all he has ever had or cared for, and in which he sees himself being executed and descending to hell; fortunately, after some time, he is visited by the ghost of his late wife who on her deathbed promised to return to her husband in order to reveal to him another possibility of attaining harmony with the cosmos, "a different road to wisdom, not the 'total' knowledge of the cabbalist that creates *homunculi* and a world without love, but rather the *docta ignorantia* of the hermetic magus and of the radical craftsman."[47] Only after having been exposed to this vision of an unselfish world does Dee understand that visionary transcendence is impossible without acknowledging basic humane and humanistic values. Symptomatically, it is his willingness to engage in activities reaching beyond physical existence that allows Dee, and his modern double Palmer, to realise that in order to disclose the mystery of the universe it is first necessary to come to terms with private feelings, fears and deeply-hidden secrets, that "God is within man [...] and he who understands himself understands the universe" (*HDD*, 133). However, Ackroyd goes further than that in his toying with the reader – having explained the mystical lore of the creation of the homunculus he implies that Matthew might be the latest avatar of this perpetually recurrent, supertemporal being, thus suggesting that Dee's involvement with dark powers may have produced wished-for results after all. The novel's central conceit, that the modern characters, including the narrator/writer himself, are reincarnations of Renaissance occult practitioners or even of their occult makings, adds to the specific dynamism of both its mystical subject matter and the corresponding symbolism and parallel narrative structure.

At the beginning of *The Casebook of Victor Frankenstein*, the central character, with his urgent yearning for ultimate knowledge, appears to be Dee's mythical disciple. An experienced Ackroyd reader is not in the least surprised that the semi-derelict, deserted pottery factory, which Victor Frankenstein transforms into a secret laboratory for his ill-fated project, is located in Limehouse, one of those "woeful" districts of London, notorious in the past for its violence and social deprivation. Moreover, in London he finds himself in the intellectually and spiritually inspiring atmosphere of Romantic turmoil as his company consists of notable champions of radical political ideas and outstanding thinkers and poets such as Percy Bysshe and Mary Shelley, Lord Byron, Samuel Taylor Coleridge and William Godwin. However, what distinguishes Frankenstein from Dee is his reluctance to admit that other than scientifically rational processes might be at work in his experiments, as he dismisses Shelley's claim that "the great poets of the past were philosophers or alchemists. Or magicians. They cast off the vesture of the body, and in their pursuits, became pure spirit" (*CVF*, 9). Having rejected the spir-

---

47   Onega, *Peter Ackroyd*, 61.

itual principle, Frankenstein falls prey not to the monster created in his laboratory but to the monsters in his unconscious: on his nighttime ramblings between Smithfield and Limehouse he becomes haunted by nightmarish shadows and fearsome murders and the reader gradually understands that "the dark agent of desolation" (*CVF*, 253) he pursues is not in fact a dead man restored to life but "[his] double, [his] shadow, without which [he] would not exist" (*CVF*, 259). Unlike Dee, Frankenstein has no ghosts or other paranormal manifestations to prevent his self-absorbing obsession from developing into a psychotic state during which his mind loses touch with reality and replaces it with phantasmagoric embodiments of unconscious fears and desires, but this is chiefly because he repeatedly refuses to acknowledge the existence of an immaterial dimension of the world. Only after his disputes with Byron's personal doctor, John Polidori, whom Ackroyd, for the sake of the plot, transforms into a Jewish cabbalist who believes in the ancient legend of the Golem, does Frankenstein realise the significance of the spiritual aspects of human existence. Although the novel starts as a variation on Mary Shelley's celebrated novel, it turns out to be an absorbing psychological thriller exploring the Jekyll-and-Hyde theme of doubles, doppelgängers and split personality. Frankenstein's progressive madness can be understood as an effect of the strenuous suppression of his irrational self, which dooms him to end up as a tragically deluded idealist rather than a mystical visionary.

What Ackroyd describes as Cockney visionariness lies at the core of *Chatterton*, for its story, even more than in his other London novels, is based on a dramatisation of an idea rather than on its characters' lives and development. The two protagonists crucial for this rendering, Thomas Chatterton and Charles Wychwood, both possess the capacity to sustain and materialise such a vision, and only untimely death prevents them from leaving an indelible mark in the tradition of the London/English visionary imagination. The exceptional youth's forged Rowley poems astonished and inspired a whole body of succeeding poetry, and so the ghost or spirit of his creative genius won its place in eternity, making its appearance to gifted writers of generations to come. However, only those who are sufficiently sensitive and altruistic benefit from such visitations, which the novel demonstrates on two different personalities – Harriet Scrope and Charles. Scrope is arrogant, self-centred and unprincipled, making use of other people and stealing other people's ideas for her own interest and profit, so seeing Chatterton's ghost torments her as she is afraid she is either becoming insane or getting punished for her deceptions. Charles, on the other hand, values imagination, creativity and independent humanity over material gain and trifling rivalry. For him Chatterton represents an underrated poetic prodigy, an inspiration for all other unrecognised poets to persist in trying to realise their vision, as he explains to Andrew Flint, who sold his talent for commercial success, in his final, passionate speech:

> And why is it, Andrew, that some people try all their lives to become writ-ers or poets, even though they are too ashamed to show their work to any-one? Why do they keep on trying? Why do they write and write, putting their poems and stories away as soon as they're finished? Where does *their* dream come from? [...] I'll tell you what it is. It is a dream of wholeness, and of beauty. All the yearning and all the unhappiness and all the sick-ness can be taken away by that vision. And the vision is real. (*C*, 152–3, emphasis in original)

It is the beauty contained in the vision's wholeness, in the complexity of a harmonising union of opposites and extremes clashing incessant-ly within the pulsing urban milieu that makes Chatterton and Charles Wychwood prototypes of Cockney Visionaries, as, despite failures re-sulting from their being misunderstood and dismissed by others, they retained the capacity to capture the spirit of London and reconcile it with the universal human condition.

In other Ackroyd's London novels these visionaries appear either as a source of influence and inspiration for their protagonists or author, like Charles Dickens in *The Great Fire of London* and Geoffrey Chaucer in *The Clerkenwell Tales*, or as background or merely mentioned characters, such as Christopher Wren in *Hawksmoor* and Charles Lamb and Thomas De Quincey in *The Lambs of London*. In this respect, *Dan Leno and the Limehouse Golem* has a specific position as it features several instances of both these types of appearance. The first is represented especially by Thomas De Quincey and Charles Babbage: De Quincey's famous essay, "On Murder Considered as one of the Fine Arts," has an impact on some of the novel's characters, both real and fictional, like George Gissing, Dan Leno, Elizabeth Cree and Inspector Kildare; Babbage's visionary project of the Analytical Engine, the mechanical predecessor of modern computers, makes a crucial contribution to the city's timeless mass of imagination and thus suffuses the spirit of Limehouse, where his manu-facture and workshops were located, but it also affects young Gissing who is carrying out research on the invention for the essay on Babbage he is supposed to write for the *Pall Mall Review*, and which brings him to the area where "the Golem" seeks its victims.

The second type is represented by Karl Marx, George Gissing and Dan Leno, but due to their age at the time of the story only the last mentioned clearly demonstrates his visionary potential. The novel catches Marx some two years before his death and, being on the police blacklist of suspected revolutionaries, the elderly philosopher, economist and socialist is no longer publicly active, devoting his time to reading, studying and attending the theatre with his daughter. Gissing, on the other hand, is an aspiring writer of twenty three, who has only recently published, at his own expense as he did not find a publisher, his first novel, *Workers in the Dawn* (1880). Although Ackroyd attributes to him the potential of a visionary since the Yorkshire-born youth moved to London to experience "a time of extraordinary mental growth, of great spiritual activity" (*DLLG*, 143), at this point in his life he is used in the story rather for his almost scandalous personal life, thanks to which he can be made a suspect in the investigation of the serial murders of prostitutes. And so, aged thirty in the novel[48], Dan Leno is the only one of these three at the peak of his powers, being the most popular comedian and impersonator of his time, a perfect representative of the tradition of London "monopolylinguists – in other words comedians or actors who play a number of quick-change parts in the course of one performance" (LLCV, 344). His ability to cheer up, move or calm the crowds of spectators and make them forget their daily worries, his imagination and ability to improvise, his sense of detail and gimmick which he used to adapt a wide range of scenes and spectacles from urban life for the stage, or his exceptional quick-wittedness and intuition make him a prototypical London artist. Once again, combining within himself and his art all the contradictory attributes of London life and, at the same time, always comprising and emanating the very essence of humanity, "so plain and yet so haughty, with such a grand air and such a pitiful sniffle, ebullient in defeat and absurd in victory" (*DLLG*, 169), Ackroyd's Cockney visionary Leno smoothly makes his way in the city's eternity.

Yet another approach to this theme can be found in *Three Brothers* where uncanny elements play a determining role, and the narrative foreshadows their significance at its very beginning by pointing out that Harry, Daniel and Sam Hanway were born "with a year's difference of

---

48 In reality, George Wild Galvin, which was his real name, was ten years younger, born in 1860, not in 1850 as Ackroyd claims in the novel, and in 1880 when the story takes place he was not yet known under his stage name Dan Leno, which he adopted in 1884.

age [...] at the same time on the same day of the same month" (*TB*, 1), as a result of which they have developed a certain "invisible commun-ion" (*TB*, 1). It is an instinctual, innate, unconscious bond, some kind of a sixth sense due to which they sense the physical presence of the other brothers without seeing or hearing them, they can hear them without their being physically present, or have an indistinct foreboding of what might happen to them in the near future. It is a capacity beyond any rational control, one they do not actually wish for, yet one they cannot but submit to. The dreamy, impractical and unsociable Sam is especially prone to irrational behaviour and to seeking out various ways to escape the mundane reality of an uncomfortable domestic life and a routine job in a local supermarket. Endowed with exceptional sensitiveness and im-agination, he frequently comes to inhabit a timeless, "floating world" (*TB*, 46), where physical laws do not apply and material and immate-rial things lose their essence and melt, and where imaginary people and places exist as if they were part of the real one. Therefore, he feels he has been chosen to experience miracles, such as seeing a stone post hovering several feet above the ground or tears running down from the blue eyes of the statue of a lady in the church of Our Lady of Sorrows.

This culminates when Sam becomes a handyman in the convent ad-jacent to the church as the abbess, Mother Placentia, gets fond of the extraordinary "young man who sees visions in the heart of London" (*TB*, 50). The reader does not know how long his eerie "stay" at the convent took in reality, but the tranquil days of gardening and feeding tramps and beggars end abruptly: one day after having an ominous vision of fire and destruction he finds out that the convent and all the nuns and home-less people have vanished. Sam's mind is occupied with such visitations and daydreams almost constantly, but his far more rational and prag-matic brothers are not immune to them either. Harry experiences two such occasions, the first when he observes a luminous structure rising from his sleeping would-be wife, Guinevere, and taking on her shape, the second when he spots a fierce-looking apparition of his late father in the back garden of his luxurious house, as if the ghosts of the two people whom he has betrayed most came to prevent him from taking any further treacherous steps. Daniel encounters a nun in Limehouse who seems to be coming to look after Sparkler, and who tells him to be grate-ful for his good spirit, yet whether this nun was real or a mere product of Daniel's imagination remains unclear. Similarly unclear is the identity of the good spirit, although an interpretation of an appeal to Daniel to ap-preciate Sparkler as a close friend suggests itself. The circle of enigmatic coincidences resulting from the brothers' communion closes when on the same day they leave this world, two physically and one mentally. Symptomatically, Harry and Daniel, who did not obey the otherworldly warnings and advice, die, while the visionary Sam receives a letter from Our Lady of Sorrows suggesting that he come back to live in the convent.

Poets of Power and Darkness – Ackroyd's Occultists

Ackroyd's mystical London as an intricate and multifarious apparatus is a paradoxical phenomenon in itself: it has been officially built and developed on strictly reasonable and practical principles, but, despite and maybe also because of this, it has always resisted any absolute control over itself, thus creating "the conditions of its own growth" and playing "an active part in its own development like some complex organism slowly discovering its form" (LLCV, 342). Such conditions and form, however, have often diverted from officially promoted doctrines rooted in causal logic and pragmatic calculation and sought their foundations in less rational areas of the natural world and human enterprise. Therefore, the city has also been governed and perpetuated by mutually related uncanny tendencies and paradigms, as a result of which it has produced, or at least attracted, a countless number of individuals, or groups, whose minds are preoccupied with the urge to disclose, clarify, make use of, and sometimes even abuse, the paranormal mechanisms at work in the capital's texture, and whose activities and practices fall into the category of occultism and esotericism. A few exceptionally gifted individuals who were able to transcend the limits of this field and make it part of a larger and more complex vision were discussed in the previous chapter. Yet, Ackroyd's London novels are peopled with many other less endowed and prophetic but similarly inclined, or possessed enthusiasts and practitioners.

While some of Ackroyd's later London novels literally revolve around the themes and motifs of occultism, occult rituals and practices, in *The Great Fire of London* the author's approach to this subject matter appears more restrained, treating it rather within the notion of the city's intertextual character. This is already suggested at the beginning of the novel, when the slightly drunk Spenser is trying to explain to his uninterested wife why he believes Dickens best understood London and its inhabitants: "He was a great man, you know, he knew what it was all about. He knew that in a city people behave in different ways like, oh, I don't know, like they were obsessed" (*GFL*, 16). It is as if Spenser was talking about himself and some of the other characters from his story as they all give way, or even become addicted, to some irrational obsessive mania, be it filming a book, seeking sexual adventures, fighting an abstract conspiracy or tracing the identity of their new internal voice. The connection between the literary and the occult is made clear during the séance Audrey attends and where, with the feeble help of Miss Norman, an irritable, businesslike parody of a spiritualist who is ironically described as a "clairvoyant and spiritual counselor [...] well-known in the mediumistic circles for her pragmatic approach to the spirit world, which she tended to address as if she were a customer in Harrods" (*GFL*, 38), she passes out and starts uttering the words of Amy Dorrit, in spite of the fact that she has never read Dickens's novel. Later she even has fits during which she "becomes" Little Dorrit, and "she would kneel on the floor, and pray for her father and for herself, pray to God that they would reap their just reward and that it would not be taken from them" (*GFL*, 113). It is only after his own experience of being rejected, misunderstood and abandoned that Tim begins to appreciate, if not envy, Audrey's quest, feeling he also "needed guidance, and he would take it from wherever it came" (*GFL*, 143). The recourse to "institutional" esotericism is depicted as the desperate escapist act of those at odds with the pressures of stressful and alienating city life, rather than a serious means of its comprehension. The occult and the mystical therefore play a twofold role in the novel: while Spenser's epiphanies when he comes to see himself as part of London's supra-temporal spiritual continuum enable him to better understand the city and his own position in it, Amy's psychotic possession has a devastating effect upon her as she grows more and more insecure and paranoid about her own identity.

In *Dan Leno and the Limehouse Golem* the motif of the occult is introduced through the character of a Jewish-German scholar, Solomon Weil, an expert in the Cabbala and owner of a large library of esoteric texts. Ironically enough, Ackroyd makes this fictional character befriend another German thinker living in London whose materialistic worldview is much more remote from Weil's spiritualism, Karl Marx. The two elderly men get on surprisingly well and they meet at Weil's place in order to exchange ideas on various matters of Judaic traditions and cabbalistic teachings. Although Weil correctly assumes that Marx's sudden interest rather disguises his attempt "to atone for his vindictive assaults upon his own old faith" (*DLLG*, 64), he finds this atheist revolutionary a pleasant and erudite companion for conversation. In his late search for his once rejected native spiritual tradition, the novel's Marx lets the Limehouse "magician" enlighten him about the intricate relationship between the visible and invisible worlds. As this explication sounds too foreign to Marx, Weil soon turns the conversation to their common interest, the music hall and its songs, to illustrate his abstract ideas on a concrete, and more accessible, example, pointing to the similar metaphorical imagery in music hall and cabbala terminology, as well as the fact that these music halls often occupy the sites of former chapels and churches. He then proceeds to clarify how the visible materialises the invisible through reference to one of the most famous legends of ancient Jewish lore – the golem – in order to exemplify that the material realm can be seen as a mere projection of the spiritual one, a visible manifestation of human hopes, wishes, expectations and beliefs, and that it is therefore essential to look underneath the visible surface in order to fully understand the world around: "Of course we do not have to believe in golems literally. Surely not. [...] But then what do we do? We give it life in our own image. We breathe our own spirit into its shape. And that, don't you see, is what the visible world must be – a golem of giant size" (*DLLG*, 68), he explains in the scene climaxing Ackroyd's conceit of making Marx a confused pupil of a fictional mystic. The Golem, Weil implies, does not exist physically but only in the narratives which provide it with a tangible shape, thus being "only a textual trace, a shared, communal memory, given life only through the articulation of its possibility."[49] And so, when after Weil's murder the public imagination, though on a false textual premise, nicknames the homicidal force "the Limehouse Golem," identifying it as an incarnated emblem of the city's miserable condition, the search for the killer assumes the larger, mythical dimension of "a search for the secret of London itself" (*DLLG*, 88), thus echoing the message of the lesson Weil delivers to the famous philosopher.

A related approach can be found in *The Casebook of Victor Frankenstein*, in which Ackroyd ascribes esoteric tendencies to the Romantic poets Shelley and Byron during their and their friends' visit to the dungeon of the fictitious Chateau de Marmion at Lake Geneva: while the former experiences vivid, tormenting visions and almost swoons, the latter, inspired by the raging storm outside, organises a séance, believing that "[a]ll lakes are haunted [...] Large bodies of water attract lost souls" (*CVF*, 367). Most importantly, without any historical evidence Ackroyd makes John Polidori, Lord Byron's personal physician and a would-be

---

49   Jeremy Gibson and Julian Wolfreys, *Peter Ackroyd: The Ludic and Labyrinthine Text*, 205.

writer, a devout occultist who not only uses exorcism in treating his master's ailments, but who is also well acquainted with the ancient wisdom of renowned cabbalistic texts, such as that of the creation of the golem. He reveals his interest in the mystery of this mythical artificial "creature of the Kabbalah, made of dust and red clay" (*CVF*, 306), by telling the company the legend of Rabbi Loew and claiming he maintains a correspondence with certain Jewish scholars in Prague in an effort to learn the secret ritual words which, when pronounced directly to the golem, are supposed to bring it in or out of life. His most captivated listener is Victor Frankenstein, who foolishly believes that he could make use of these words in order to deactivate his monster, and so he pleads with Polidori to find them out for him as soon as possible. However, the reader cannot be sure if this account is reliable as it is all described by the, at that time, semi-insane Frankenstein, and thus Polidori's discovery of the exact wording of the magic spell may be a product of the narrator's sick imagination, as is the existence of his killing creature itself. As in *The Great Fire of London* and *Dan Leno and the Limehouse Golem*, the occult matters appear to be treated ironically in the novel, as the séance turns out to be an almost comical failure and the teaching of the Jewish lore proves useless in stopping the monster, but Ackroyd rather demonstrates what happens if they are appropriated by those who are not sufficiently suited to handle them properly, such as unbelievers, lunatics, opportunist converts and keen amateurs.

Hawksmoor presents a more complex and thorough, though by far no less ambiguous, treatment of the theme of occultism, as it derives from the recent popular "rediscovery" of Nicholas Hawksmoor as one of the most unacknowledged and misinterpreted figures in the history of English architecture. Ackroyd's version of the architect is wholly fictitious since, as he admits, Dyer's language and thoughts are "a patchwork of other people's voices as well as my own [...], an echo from about three hundred different books as well as my own."[50] His rendering of this myth is very much indebted to Iain Sinclair's 1975 book *Lud Heat*. In this quasi-treatise Sinclair proposes a well-elaborated, symbolic arrangement of Hawksmoor's London churches, forming cryptic geometrical patterns of lines of force, consisting mostly of triangular and pentacle figures, possessing and emanating energies which can negatively affect the lives of those who happen to inhabit the areas where they intersect. Although he admits that these churches are only one of many systems of energies

50   Patrick McGrath, "Peter Ackroyd: Interview."

within the city, he sees each of them as an enclosure of malignant force, trapping their victims, "a sight-block, a raised place with an unacknowledged influence on events enacted within their nome-lines."[51] This he supports with the fact that a series of ritual murders have been committed in their vicinities, such as the 1811 Ratcliffe Highway Murders, the 1888 Jack the Ripper Murders, and the slaying of Abraham Cohen in 1974, concluding that this evidence points to their sinister topographical significance. Sinclair also takes note of other aspects of the churches, such as the location of the mysterious-looking pyramidal structures in their grounds, seeing them as "removed brains" which "must be activated by the chanted word of need to animate the shell of the building, to bring life to the beast," or that they "live in accordance with so many sacred conditions,"[52] such as their being located on the former sites of worship and inhumation, but also by rivers, springs and underground streams, water being the element of sex, change, maternal suicide, dominance and dark purifications[53]. Whether all these are mere coincidences and fabricated speculations or not, thanks to Sinclair, Hawksmoor's churches have come to assume a crucial position within modern London's occult lore.

From what is known about Nicholas Hawksmoor's life and work he can be seen as a prototypical Ackroyd Cockney visionary: he was an individualist, mostly solitary in designing his architectural projects, relying on his intuition and private reading rather than institutional schooling, believing in synthesis and integration rather than categorisation and purity of form. His architectural method rested in combining what was then thought to be largely incompatible or contradictory, which is why his works often met with critical disapproval and public dismissal[54]. The result was an eclectic style concerned with synthetising tradition with innovation, antiquity with modernity, paganism with Christianity, rationalism with elements more esoteric in nature[55]. Adhering to inventiveness and variety rather than canonical rules, Hawksmoor never produced any consistent style as he frequently adopted a range of models and styles, which, however, no matter how radically subversive they may have appeared, always reflected "what he saw as the contemporary virtues of

---

51 Iain Sinclair, *Lud Heat*, 19.
52 Sinclair, *Lud Heat*, 34, 36.
53 Sinclair, *Lud Heat*, 36.
54 Vaughan Hart, *Nicholas Hawksmoor: Rebuilding Ancient Wonders*, xi.
55 The influences shaping his work were not only architectonic and cultural, ranging from Egyptian, Greek, Roman, early Christian and Gothic to Baroque and Palladian, but also intellectual and spiritual, including such diverse areas as ancient philosophy, Church of England theology, freemasonry, advances in scientific theory and contemporary Whig politics.

Reason, Monarchy and Faith."[56] Like Milton, Blake or Dickens, he was thus capable of creating a prophetic vision while remaining firmly rooted in the spirit of his native cultural tradition.

He was familiar with the scientific discoveries of his age as can be seen in the volumes he owned, namely on mathematics, geometry, geography and civil engineering, which encouraged him to contribute to the "contemporary advancement of what he went on to term 'the Science of Architecture'."[57] Even his frequent use of elements of antique funeral and ornamental iconography, such as pyramids, obelisks, altars, mausoleums and urns, was largely for memorial purposes, though his fascination with the architecture of death certainly did play its part. Moreover, the stylistic variety of his churches was also determined by his desire to respect and reflect the context of the surroundings in which they were located[58]. However, there are several reasons why his life and work still remain enigmatic: unlike his more respectable colleagues, he produced no comprehensive theoretical study which would explain his style; he had no pupils or disciples who would carry on putting his ideas into practice or make them known to the public, and therefore he is known as Wren's and Vanbrugh's assistant rather than an independent architect; he neither received university education nor travelled abroad in order to extend his knowledge, so most of his ideas and inspiration must be deduced from his wide-ranging collection of books; and his sacral architecture uses several pagan, antique or primitive Christian elements. And so, in the absence of certain pieces of information, in a time once again inclined to the spiritual and irrational, the myth of an obscure architect plotting secretly in the shadow of Sir Christopher Wren could come into existence. Although Hawksmoor was neither an "Ancient" nor a "Modern," but rather "followed the classical ancients but in a modern way,"[59] there is in fact no evidence to support his modern diabolical image. He strongly relied on his imagination ("Good Fancy"), but always regulated by and in tune with the contemporary imperatives of rationality ("Strong Reason"), and validated by empirical testing ("experience and tryalls"), his aim being to build a "timeless architecture" based on the combina-

---

56 Hart, *Nicholas Hawksmoor*, 7.

57 Hart, *Nicholas Hawksmoor*, 16.

58 The churches in the poorer areas, such as Spitalfields, Wapping and Limehouse, are plain in ornament and sombre in mood, "intended to stand as beacons of Christian morality," while those in the richer ones, like St George in Bloomsbury, show stylistic magnificence, heavy ornamentation and the iconography of their royal patrons. (Hart, *Nicholas Hawksmoor*, 170, 185).

59 Hart, *Nicholas Hawksmoor*, 244.

tion of his own vision and the enduring legacy of historical models[60]. Be it as it may, he managed to accomplish his aim as the architecture of his London churches fascinates people almost three centuries after their construction.

The plot of *Hawksmoor* stems from Sinclair's interpretation of Nicholas Hawksmoor's London churches and pushes it to more extreme conclusions. The reader soon understands that occultism and black magic play a crucial role in the story as Nicholas Dyer, the novel's version of the real architect, confesses that he is a secret Satanist and adherent of an occult science. For this conceit Ackroyd uses a similar strategy as with, for instance, Dan Leno, Thomas De Quincey or the Lambs – he changes some of his character's personal data. And so, like the real Hawksmoor, Ackroyd's Dyer is a pupil, assistant and later a colleague of Wren, he assists his teacher and master in designing and building St Paul's, cooperates with Vanbrugh, and, most importantly, he is commissioned as the principal architect upon the passing of the 1711 act of parliament to build new churches in London. However, while Hawksmoor was born around 1661 in Nottinghamshire and died in 1736, Dyer is supposed to have been born in 1654 in London and died in 1715, which is three years before Hawksmoor's first church, St Alfege in Greenwich, was completed. Also, Dyer is appointed to erect seven new parish churches, while in reality the plan was fifty; and while Hawksmoor managed to complete only six of his designs, Dyer manages one more, "finest of all, the church of Little St Hugh beside Moorfields" (*H*, 214). These alterations allow Ackroyd to employ his poetic license in making up his (semi-)fictitious protagonist's character and psychological profile.

Dyer's view of the world is deeply sceptical, bordering on the nihilistic concerning human nature, which he sees as intrinsically evil and therefore ultimately irreformable, claiming that "Humane life is quite out of the Light and that we are all Creatures of Darknesse" and that "we sin necessarily and co-actively" (*H*, 11, 21). Such a persuasion inevitably shapes his architectural vision, which is based on a few underlying maxims that stress that cities are embodiments of condensed evil ("it was Cain who built the first City"), that architecture which aspires to eternity should possess occult significance ("not only our Altars and Sacrifices, but the Forms of our Temples, must be mysticall"), and that the miseries of human life must be reflected in quality architecture, which is subject to "Harmony or to Rationall Beauty" rather than to "a full Conception

---

60 Hart, *Nicholas Hawksmoor*, 247.

of Degenerated Nature" (*H*, 9). A convinced Satanist, he cherishes all ancient buildings supposedly dedicated to the deity of darkness and consecrated by human sacrifice according to the satanic teaching that "Humane life, either in desperate sicknesse or in danger of Warre, could not be secured unless a vyrgyn Boy suffered instead" (*H*, 21). He hopes that his churches would join this tradition if he implements mystical power-invoking elements such as pyramids, sepultures and subterranean labyrinths, next to his sacral and sovereign forms, and if he supplies the sites of his churches with the corpses of innocent people killed for the sake of pleasing their infernal patron.

In defiance of the demands of the "Rationall and mechanicall Age" in which he lives Dyer addresses himself to "Mysteries infinitely more Sacred" and "the Guardian Spirits of the Earth" (*H*, 22–23), secretly designing his churches on principles of Satanist mysticism and black magic[61], believing they would "provide an immutable form of spiritualism, a dark bond between the occult and certain areas of London that remain unbroken,"[62] while for appearance's sake he disguises them as seemingly adhering to mainstream philosophical and scientific principles. These are, most of all, represented by Sir Christopher Wren, the most outspoken proponent of rationality, appropriateness and austere and pious moderation in the novel. For Dyer, Wren is the embodiment of the prevalent values he does not acknowledge, and he prefers the esoteric and paranormal instead, often identifying himself against people like his former master:

> ... there are those like Sir Chris. Who speak only of what is Rational and what is Demonstrated, of Propriety and Plainness. [...] Men that are fixed upon *matter*, *experiment*, *secondary causes* and the like have forgot there is such a thing in the World which they cannot see nor touch nor measure: [...] the Existence of Spirits cannot be found by Mathematick demonstrations, but we must rely upon Humane reports unless we make void and annihilate the Histories of all passed things. (*H*, 101–102, emphasis in original)

Dyer dislikes the "Moderns" and extols the "Ancients," yet his profession of the Ancients' wisdom rests in a selective and biased interpretation of their philosophy and art, foregrounding only those aspects that suit his

---

61 This pattern, Ackroyd admits, is wholly made up and the churches do not form it in reality. (Anke Schütze, "I think after More I will do Turner and then I will probably do Shakespeare," an Interview with Peter Ackroyd)

62 Murray, *Recalling London: Literature and History in the work of Peter Ackroyd and Iain Sinclair*, 46.

worldview and morbid urges. As he reveals to Vanbrugh, "the Ancients knew how Nature is a dark Room, and that is why their Plays will stand when even our Playhouses are crumbled into Dust" (*H*, 179), which is why he can but imitate their ideas in order to achieve true authenticity in his architecture. Yet this must not be executed in an explicit, obvious manner, but encoded through the use of mystical and occult symbols and schemes, which he further explains to his less gloomy colleague: "I build in Hieroglyph and Shadow, like my Ancients. [...] I wish my Buildings to be filled with Secresy, and such Hieroglyphs as conceal from the Vulgar the Mysteries of Religion" (*H*, 180). What these "Mysteries of Religion" involve and who all "the Vulgar" are, however, remains concealed from those who are influential enough to thwart his intentions. Dyer thus manages to fulfill his ingenious and daring plan of inscribing his subversive doctrine onto the very epitomes of official power and faith.

There is also a personal dimension to Dyer's architectonic designs. Believing that "all Humane events depend upon the Starres" (*H*, 21), he is obsessed with the idea that his soul is condemned to reincarnate from one body to another until in one of them it manages to accomplish a work, the greatness of which would be comparable to the act of God's creation of the universe, and that acquiring power over earthly matters automatically ensures an ability to affect the acts of God. Therefore, he arranges his churches in triangular and pentagram-star patterns[63] corresponding to the position of key stars in the sky, "thereby magically aligning the churches with the seven planets and the seven circles of the heavens,"[64] the result of which should be a power-concentrating, magical structure through which he hopes "to submit to his will the seven planetary daemons who control them and prevent his transcendental ascesis," with the aim of "establishing a current of sympathetic magic between heaven and earth that would function as a magical ladder to heaven"[65] which his soul could safely climb to an eternal harmony of the Self:

> ... in this Pattern, every Straight line is enrich'd with a point at Infinity and every Plane with a line at Infinity. [...] the seven Churches are built in conjunction with the seven Planets in the lower Orbs of Heaven, the

---

63 A more detailed exploration of these spatial patterns can be found in chapters "The Carto-graphic Fictional Space of *Hawksmoor*" and "Sacred Heterotopias: An Alternative Reading of the Urban Sphere of *Hawksmoor*" of Zénó Vernyik's *Cities of Saviors: Urban Space in E. E. Cumming's* Complete Poems, 1904–1962 *and Peter Ackroyd's* Hawksmoor, 90–115.

64 Lewis, *My Words Echo Thus*, 39.

65 Onega, *Peter Ackroyd*, 46.

seven Circles of the Heavens, the seven Starres in Ursa Minor and the seven Starres in the Pleiades. Little St Hugh was flung in the Pitte with the seven Marks upon his Hands, Feet, Sides and Breast which thus exhibit the seven Demons – Beydelus, Metucgayn, Adulec, Demeymes, Gadyx, Uquizuz and Sol. I have built an everlasting Order, which I may run through laughing: no one can catch me now. (*H*, 186)

In devising his churches as well as in choosing their locations, Dyer thus combines the principles of white and black magic in order to concentrate as many kinds of energies as possible to ensure the talismanic effect will be potent enough to transcend the gap between the physical and the spiritual realms[66]. As Onega notes, "the fact that his act of recreation of the cosmogonic act has been achieved by evil means is immaterial, for according to occultism [...] the true God is the totality of everything, containing all good and evil and reconciling all opposites."[67] The novel puts forth the idea that the eclectic and enigmatic architecture of Dyer's/Hawksmoor's churches may have been the result of the architect's attempt to establish what esotericism sees as a harmonious balance between the two opposite poles of life – the material, rational and empirical and the immaterial, irrational and intuitive. The resulting approach pursues aims that resonate with Ackroyd's concept of an infinite, supratemporal London. The only remaining variable is the ethical stance of the protagonist, his or her opting for good or evil, for moral or morally dubious acts, which, however, as the ending of *Hawksmoor* suggests, has only a negligible impact on the prospective success of such an enterprise. However, what seems immaterial from the esoteric point of view proves determining for the image of the city the novel presents: unlike in the other discussed Ackroyd novels, the darkly obscure London in *Hawksmoor* is remarkably dehumanised, devoid of the energetic experience of its dwellers, as the major focus is put on its topography and material objects. "In the process, all the human inhabitants of this London are marginal and borne down upon by the extreme uncanniness of the inanimate city, which becomes both monolithic and acutely disturbing."[68]

The House of Doctor Dee is probably Ackroyd's most occult novel in

---

66 Onega offers an in-depth elaboration of the esoteric and occult significance of the theological and philosophical belief behind Dyer's churches in *Metafiction and Myth in the Novels of Peter Ackroyd*, pp. 50–58.

67 Onega, *Metafiction and myth in the novels of Peter Ackroyd*, 54.

68 Lawrence Philips, *London Narratives: Post-War Fiction and the City*, 148.

essence, yet, as in the other cases, his exploration of this theme is not an end in itself. Once again, Ackroyd creates a protagonist on the basis of an existing historical personality, but, unlike in *Hawksmoor*, he does not have to make up a speculative background to link this protagonist with esoteric and mystical practices. Therefore, his John Dee is much more faithful to his model, their dates of birth and death are identical, as is their interest in numerology, astronomy, alchemy and spiritualism, and the works his Dee writes and the people he is acquainted with have bases and counterparts in his real life. What he changes, however, are some crucial facts and circumstances concerning Dee's alliance with Edward Kelley, the notorious charlatan and conman who made his career at the court of Emperor Rudolf in Prague. It is true that Kelley paid a visit to Dee's house and eventually managed to impose himself on the respectable Elizabethan scholar by convincing him of his exceptional skills as a medium scryer (though in reality he was brought to Dee's attention by another person, a certain Mr Clerkson, and at first introduced himself, for unknown reasons, as Edward Talbot[69]). It is also true that despite his initial mistrust and suspicion, Dee eventually fell for this exceptionally resourceful and educated youth who could see visions in magic crystals, because he believed that "crystal gazing, properly and devoutly conducted, [...] was a way of beholding the universe in all its glory, and understanding its manifold and mysterious workings,"[70] that by the prophecies and appeals of the mostly celestial beings from these visions Kelley manipulated Dee to his ends, and that from the beginning there was a tension between Kelley and Dee's wife, who did not believe him in the least.

In most other aspects Ackroyd deviates from historical records, in addition to the already mentioned relocation of Dee's house from Mortlake to Clerkenwell it is not known that Dee and Kelley tried to discover the lost ancient city of London; in his designs Kelley was not so much tempted by Dee's fortune and knowledge of "how to transform base metals into gold by using the philosopher's stone"[71] as driven by his lust for Dee's attractive young wife, whose name was Jane and not Katherine (which was actually the name of one of the Dees' daughters). Ackroyd does not mention Kelley's wife, Joanna, and, interestingly, he also omits from his story the most sensational period of the two men's cooperation – the nomadic continental journey through Poland, Germany and

---

69 For a more detailed description of Dee and Kelley's first encounters see Woolley, *The Queen's Conjuror*, 141–172.

70 Woolley, *The Queen's Conjuror*, 168.

71 Lewis, *My Words Echo Thus*, 76.

Bohemia which they undertook with their whole families, and which cul-
minated in Kelley's spiritistic masterpiece trick when he persuaded Dee
that the angel Uriel wished the two men should share their wives. The
most crucial deviation, however, is the drawing of a connection between
Dee's wife's death and Kelley's plotting. In Ackroyd's version, Katherine
dies in London while Dee is still regularly meeting Kelley for their scry-
ing séances or suburban explorations. Moreover, she dies from unspeci-
fied causes, yet much suggests she was poisoned by Kelly who saw her
as an obstacle to winning more of her husband's trust. In reality, the
two men parted in February 1589 and never saw each other again, Kelly
settling in Prague, entering the service of Emperor Rudolf, while Dee
returned to England to find his cottage in Mortlake in ruins. Although
the Queen's favour was not restored to its previous extent, in 1595 she
appointed him Warden of Christ's College in Manchester, where in
March 1605, his wife and two daughters became victims of the plague[72].
Dee's wife thus died more than a hundred and sixty miles away from
London, and more than sixteen years after Kelley vanished for good
from her husband's life.

Although the theme of occultism is virtually omnipresent in the novel as its plot revolves around John Dee and his present-day disciple of
thought and spirit, it is less of an aim than a means through which Ackroyd articulates his message concerning the true nature of wisdom and
understanding. Ackroyd attributes to his protagonist two maxims expressing the essence of what Dee calls "the true gold of wisdom" (*HDD*,
133): first, everything in the world, including material things, possesses
spiritual properties, hidden powers which must be disclosed and explored by every person who aspires to attain complex knowledge about
this world; second, every person is an abode of both humanity and divin-
ity, and so in order to understand the universe one must first understand
oneself. Dee's problem is that the more he becomes preoccupied, and
later possessed, with the secrets and mysteries of the former, the more
he neglects the latter. As a result, he grows too "infatuated with the poetry of power and darkness, which in turn made him susceptible to the
demands of envy and ambition" and "he lost sight of that sacred truth
he wished to investigate" (*HDD*, 133), as only a simultaneous fulfillment
of both these requirements ensures one's harmony with oneself and the
world. Yet these maxims are analogous to those Ackroyd identifies as
crucial for anyone who wants to feel at ease in London: an acceptance of

---

72 Woolley, *The Queen's Conjuror*, 296–297, 319.

the interconnectedness of its material/rational and immaterial/irrational sides, and the finding of one's own position within its mass through understanding how these two principles compose one's personality and thus affect the formation of one's identity.

The final chapter, entitled "The Vision," opens with Dee walking the streets of London endowed with the humanistic vision presented to him by the spirits of his father and his wife. Having thus met both the above requirements, he finds himself a part of the city and the city a part of himself, a city which has never been so beautiful, a city which seems "to glow with the heat of that flame which dwells in eternity" (*HDD*, 273). At the end of the chapter, however, Dee's first person narration switches to the authorial voice, and it is Ackroyd who is then walking through this eternal city, as "the light of the imagination" is filling its "every corner and every quarter, every street and every house" (*HDD*, 276), along with all its present and past inhabitants, including his novel's characters. It is the city as a process, a continuum that resonates in the novel's main protagonists, and the writer himself, and they "do not connect to one another but are connected by the flow of London through them both."[73] And so, once again, "[a]lchemy and other arcana are nothing but metaphors for a writer who wishes to explore the transformations wrought by times and texts,"[74] and a novel dealing with various forms of magic and mysticism concludes with a celebration of London and Ackroyd's own contribution to the ongoing project of grasping its complexity – his "literary spiritism" that seeks to cast light on the present by invoking the spirits of the city's past.

A concern with the esoteric also determines the formal structuring of Ackroyd's narratives by making it more elaborate and thus open to interpretation. This is especially apparent in *Hawksmoor* and *The House of Doctor Dee*, which are built around an archetypal mythical conception: both Dyer and Dee believe in a cosmological vision that could remove them from the world of matter to a transcendental level and thus ensure their transmutation from a mortal physical body into an eternal, spiritual one. The mythical pattern manifests itself in an all-pervading duality and complementarity of characters, names, events, and utterances that perpetually reduplicate in the co-temporality of time. In addition, the duality is reflected by the structural organisation of the novels in which chapters depicting the contemporary world alternate with those taking place

---

73 Gibson and Wolfreys, *Peter Ackroyd: The Ludic and Labyrinthine Text*, 194–95.
74 Lewis, *My Words Echo Thus*, 80.

in the early eighteenth and late sixteenth centuries respectively, while in the final chapter the protagonists and their narrative voices, along with that of the author, leak into one another in an unearthly reincarnation inhabiting the realm of the city's mythology. As both the novels feature mystical patterns, for attentive readers their structure also invites occult symbolic interpretation. Onega, for instance, shows how the chapter division of *The House of Doctor Dee* corresponds to the arrangement of the four elements in the hieroglyphic monad[75], a symbol invented by John Dee to signify the unity of the universe. Yet, in *The House of Doctor Dee* the occult significance goes beyond the level of its formal structure as the eponymous house itself represents an esoteric symbol: separated from the rest of the neighbourhood, the house is an eerie microcosm somehow disconnected from the outside world, a place haunted by mysterious echoes, voices and apparitions, where even the shadows either fall at a strange angle or do not exist at all. It is also repeatedly compared to the human body, with huge, mystical arms outstretched over London, which can be seen as "a striking example of the *monas hieroglyphica*, the materialization of Doctor Dee as Cosmic Man or *anthropos*."[76] The house serves as a gateway to another dimension of human experience in the city, to the realm of the occult and uncanny, and as such it possesses several properties which may function as cryptic signs inviting esoteric interpretations, such as the four colours of its doors or the fact that the larger part of the house, three stories specifically, is buried under the ground[77]. However, no matter how alluring these interpretations are, Ackroyd is far from forcing them on the reader – they are simply inherent in his novels for those who wish to discover them.

---

75 For Onega's more complex scrutiny of the two novels' occult formal structure and symbolism see the chapter "A Dream of Wholeness and of Beauty" of *Peter Ackroyd*, pp.43–65, and the chapter "*English Music* and *The House of Doctor Dee*" of *Metafiction and Myth in the Novels of Peter Ackroyd*, pp.116–130.

76 Onega, *Peter Ackroyd*, 59.

77 Onega suggests some of these interpretations in chapter "A Dream of Wholeness and of Beauty" of *Peter Ackroyd*, pp. 59–60.

The Divine Spark that never Dies, or Making the Dead Speak – the Magic of the Imagination

The playfulness of Ackroyd's novels consists not only in his altering of received historical facts and data in favour of his "could-have-been" renderings, but also in his purposeful employment of mysterious and irrational elements within the novels' narrative frameworks. Due to this juxtaposition or confrontation of diverse points of view, his imaginative narratives avoid the trap of becoming self-consciously about themselves as they always explore certain aspects of the world they mediate. The central of these aspects is the proposing of an alternative conception of reality based on a mystical interpretation of events. Such an approach to writing might be considered disruptive and subversive, "but it is difficult to be subversive in a society that refuses to listen"[78] – and the popularity of his books proves that the perspective he offers is hardly one to be dismissed as irrelevant. However, in the context of the Western esoteric tradition and its literary reflection, Ackroyd cannot be denoted as an occult or esoteric writer, as the theme and perspective of the irrational represents only one axis of a much more complexly construed London chronotope. Ackroyd always emphasises the paramount role of the spiritual dimension in human life and acknowledges the significance of various obscure, unofficial, and subversive undercurrents and practices in the history of the city, but his eccentrics, visionaries and mystics, though they may pursue some secret knowledge, in reality rely on the magic of their imagination, rather than on images of magic. Therefore, Ackroyd's exploration and depiction of London's uncanny manifestations is in fact one of his means of mapping the workings of the English imagination within the city.

The uncanny element of Ackroyd's narratives centres on his "imaginary projections," a device he has developed into a "key aspect of his approach to the presentation of textual realities,"[79] one which exists solely in the realm of imagination, but one which through an explicit collaboration between the narrator and the reader invites or even lures the latter "to share the damaged viewpoints of John Dee, Matthew Palmer, Elizabeth Cree, and Victor Frankenstein."[80] The theme of human imagination

---

78 Marguerite Alexander, *Flights from Realism: Themes and Strategies in Postmodernist British and American Fiction*, 202.

79 David Charnick, "Peter Ackroyd's Imaginary Projections: A Context for the Creature of *The Casebook of Victor Frankenstein*," 54.

80 Charnick, "Peter Ackroyd's Imaginary Projections: A Context for the Creature of *The Casebook*

permeates all of Ackroyd's London works, but two of his novels, *Chatterton* and *The Casebook of Victor Frankenstein*, celebrate it in an especially explicit and straightforward manner. Although in terms of thematic concerns and structural parallelism *Chatterton* is similar to *Hawksmoor* and *The House of Doctor Dee*, its metafictional and intertextual focus allows it to elaborate on what the former only mentions and the latter merely touches on in its ending: the power and timelessness of the imagination. *Chatterton* explores this theme on several related levels and through characters from three different historical periods. When Charles Wychwood gets hold of the curious portrait his mind becomes possessed with a desire to disclose the mystery of the young forger's death. As a person prone to daydreaming and fantasising, and who unconditionally believes in the permanence of poetry and imaginative genius, he relies on his imagination and wishful thinking rather than on a systematic detection, which leads him astray even before the investigation begins: "already, in his imagination, he had solved the secret of Thomas Chatterton and was enjoying the admiration of the world" (*C*, 60). Yet, despite its failure, Ackroyd suggests that his way proves more beneficial for other people than if it were based merely on rational deduction and the patient collecting of clues because it inspires them to discover their better selves. Chatterton is fascinated by the power and potential of the imagination when he is planning to compose his mock-medieval poems, through which he would "perform a Miracle," "bring the Past to light again," "become one of those Dead and could speak with them also" (*C*, 83, 85). And some ninety years later, George Meredith admires Chatterton as a poet who actually created a new world and helped others to better understand the past because he "invented an entire period and made its imagination his own" (*C*, 157), and so he believes that being the model for Henry Wallis's painting would win him immortality as he has been made part of the Chatterton legend.

Charles's conclusions about Chatterton's faked suicide and subsequent secret poetic career are all wrong; Chatterton's poems fail to make an impression on London publishers and editors, and Meredith, rather than gaining immortality, loses his beloved wife to Wallis, though none of this matters greatly, as it is the imaginative vision which outlives their earthly setbacks. "Reality is the invention of unimaginative people" (*C*, 39), Harriet Scrope remarks, and, accordingly, every page of the novel demonstrates Ackroyd's conviction that in the realm of artistic

---

of *Victor Frankenstein*," 67.

creation, imagination has a higher value and status than anything else, and one's belief in its potentiality takes precedence over the moral and conventional norms of the outside world as it aims to reach higher goals. The novel features several manifestations of the supernatural and paranormal, but they all seem to be primarily generated by the all-powerful magic of the human imagination and, as Murray notes, rather than as a theme, they serve as "an element of narrative logic" and "a form of representation,"[81] tied to other concepts that underpin the book's narrative structure, such as temporality and spatial energies.

The Casebook of Victor Frankenstein also professes the sovereignty of visionary excess by exploring the ambivalent common edge of creative imagination and social and scientific progress. For this purpose the story brings together a scientist, Victor Frankenstein, engaged in exploring the power of electricity, and radical Romantic writers, such as Shelley, Byron and the Godwins, who long for revolutionary social change but who are also captivated by the idea of galvanism and its use for occult rather than scientific purposes. As Frankenstein admires Shelley's spirit and creativity and Shelly is fascinated by the results of Frankenstein's experiments, the nature and effects of the imagination and electricity are described in similar terms. And so Frankenstein compares Shelley's imagination to "the voltaic battery from which lightning issued forth" (*CVF*, 8), the poet himself claims the imagination to be "the creator," "the seed of new life" and "divine spark, leaping across chaos" (*CVF* 46), his wife, Mary, strongly believes that "without the imagination [...] the human frame is dust and ashes" (*CVF*, 263), while the novel's Humphry Davy calls the electric current "the spark of life, the Promethean flame, and the light of the world" (*CVF*, 29), or as "[s]ome vast principle of power [that] animates infinity" (*CVF*, 243). However, like *The House of Doctor Dee*, the novel demonstrates two versions of the power of the imagination: the divining – creatively unbound and prophetic – power which inspires great literary works, such as those by the Shelleys and Byron, or outstanding scientific discoveries, such as Davy's and Galvani's; and the destructive – obsessive and possessive – power which brings about Frankenstein's fatal metamorphosis from eager scholar to unscrupulous "dark agent of desolation" (*CVF*, 253), imprisoned in his sick dreams and "longings for sublimity and power" (*CVF*, 407), and which lacks the essential touch of humanity which would allow it to produce visionary ideas of lasting significance.

---

81 Murray, *Recalling London*, 39, 40.

Ackroyd's use of the esoteric and occult is not motivated by his desire to reject rationality altogether or to shock readers, but primarily to variegate his stories and the traditional perspective of the historical narrative in general. The theme and the discourses such approach produces challenge most readers' assumptions about the world and, in effect, help to both pluralise and hybridise the genre. The spiritual and the rational are always depicted as inseparable and complementary; their simultaneous interference is necessary in order to approach the defining points of human identity. Ackroyd's obsession with occult matters is rather a plot device subsidiary to the author's true concern – a resurrection of the past through "the necromancy of words and language."[82] What all his protagonists have in common, whether his beloved London or its visionaries and eccentrics, is the immense power of their imagination, as if they all believed in Shelley's words that "[w]hat can be imagined, can be formed into the image of truth. The vision could be created" (*CVF*, 102). It is the imagination in its endless poetic, scientific and philosophical varieties, the unceasing creative spirit that truly transcends materiality and allows an individual to perceive life through an alternative and possibly enriching prism[83]. Although Ackroyd's novels feature diverse forms of the uncanny, their supreme magic rests in the multiplicity of histories and destinies brought to life thanks to the power of his imagination. "So who in this world can make the dead speak? Who can see them in vision? That would be a form of magic – to bring the dead to life again, if only in the pages of a book" (*HDD*, 258), muses Matthew Palmer, and bringing back to life London and its inhabitants in the tradition of what his creator calls the English imagination seems to be the spiritual or esoteric force Ackroyd espouses above all.

82 Lewis, *My Words Echo Thus*, 80.
83 In the chapter "The Eye of the Imagination" of *Phantasmagoria*, Marina Warner draws a similar parallel between the deep strata of the spiritual and the logic of the imaginary.

Chapter 3
Felonious London

It is true that the city is accompanied by two projections of itself, one celestial and one infernal; but the citizens are mistaken about their consistency.

Italo Calvino, *Invisible Cities*

Ackroyd's interest in London's underside is most manifest in his persistent attempts to depict and analyse the interconnectedness between the city and the miscellaneous crimes it has witnessed daily since its foundation. The vast and populous city, with its anonymity, crowded streets, poor and derelict districts, abandoned areas and constructions full of dark nooks and makeshift shelters for tramps and other homeless people naturally represents a locus where violence and criminality thrive beyond any conceivable institutional control. As Ackroyd sees violence, criminality and everything related to it as an inseparable, if not characteristic, component of urban life, all his London works, though in various ways and to various extents, deal with crimes and the roles the city plays in allowing or even inciting them. This, as he claims, does not spring from his conscious liking of these violent acts, but from a long tradition of various London Gothic narratives[1]. His London would therefore be incomplete without crime and so he not only makes it one of his central themes, but also inevitably employs certain aspects of traditional crime and detective narratives which he incorporates into his distinct narrative style.

---

1 "I'm not exactly obsessed with it myself. Most of these things are ways of engaging the readers' attention." Anke Schütze, "I think after More I will do Turner and then I will probably do Shakespeare." An Interview with Peter Ackroyd.
"I'm not a very melancholy sort of person. So again, it's rather a surprise to me when these things keep emerging in book after book after book. I suppose they come from some hitherto unexplored recesses of my personality, but where, it would be hard to say." Patrick McGrath, "Peter Ackroyd: Interview."

Although his concept of the fictional treatment of crime is unique, Ackroyd is by no means the only contemporary British writer to focus on crime and make use of crime narratives in his works. Ever since the early 1960s, when John Fowles published *The Collector* (1963), in which the plot hinges on a kidnap, crime as a theme and the subsequent employment of various crime narratives have appeared frequently in British mainstream fiction. Many of the most acclaimed British writers, such as Graham Swift, Martin Amis, Julian Barnes, Ian McEwan and Irvine Welsh, have managed to establish crime and crime narratives in their novels and short stories either as a significant constituent of the plot, or as the very core or trigger of the action. However, Richard Bradford argues that these established novelists sometimes employ the conventions of crime writing in order to exploit them for other artistic purposes, as they "frequently experiment with crime writing [...] not so much to revivify the subgenre as to make use of its hidebound conventions as a background to their superior talents; in short, they are slumming."[2] Although none of these novels are purely detective or crime stories, and some of them do not even treat the conventions of the genre seriously, they still show how useful the discourse of crime narratives has been for the development of modern fiction, exploiting their never-ending potential to reinvent themselves with the times[3].

Ackroyd's perspective on the development of London locates aspects of its "unofficial" history as being as, or even more, important than its "official" ones. Therefore, in *London: The Biography*, he always tries to look into hidden, obscure, or otherwise irrational forces, elements and mechanisms and, consequently, discover their impact on the city's more obvious manifestations. He regards London from the perspective of themes and phenomena such as murders and other violent crimes, the city's smells, its voraciousness, its poor, the outcast, or the visionaries who inhabit it, and therefore references numerous "true crime" narratives[4]. However, since Ackroyd attempts to provide a biography of the city, he simultaneously makes countless references to relevant texts produced at different historical moments in its "lifetime." The most frequently cited are Arthur Morrison's *A Child of the Jago* (1896), Thomas De Quincey's "On Murder Considered as one of the Fine Arts" (1827), William Godwin's *Caleb*

---

2   Richard Bradford, *The Novel Now*, 107.
3   Christiana Gregoriou, *Deviance in Contemporary Crime Fiction*, 44.
4   These crime records and texts include titles such as *The Murder Guide to London*, *The London Hanged*, *The Rookeries of London*, *London's Underworld*, *The Four Stages of Cruelty* and *The Newgate Calendar*.

Williams (1794), Dickens's *Oliver Twist* (1837–39) and *Barnaby Rudge* (1841) and Shakespeare's *Much Ado About Nothing* (1598–99). Using all these sources, Ackroyd explores the most crucial themes concerning the city's crimes and punishments: the history of London prisons and places of execution; the history and variety of London murders; the ways in which London criminality was made a subject of contemporary drama; the history of forces of crime-control, public executions and other punishments. It is, above all, through this complementariness of the factual and the fictitious that Ackroyd's biographical London comes into being. The knowledge gained through the author's research is mixed with quotations from contemporary records, stories that really happened, as well as literary and other artistic representations of crime. The result is a London crime narrative of its own kind, one which is perpetually renewed for as long as the city, in which "money and blood run together" (*LB*, 295), stands.

By focusing on the subterranean aspect of city life Ackroyd consciously follows the tradition set by his admired literary predecessor, Charles Dickens. In *Dickens*, Ackroyd mentions how the young writer was absorbed by the issues of a twopenny weekly in which he read stories and sketches of London lowlife, which from early on shaped his narrative genius. Ackroyd also continually reminds the reader how the narratives of crime, violence and other manifestations of the city's wretchedness repeatedly appear in Dickens's novels: the depiction of the London underworld, which he calls "the poetry of darkness and isolation" (*D*, 133), in *Oliver Twist* (1837–39), resurfaces in various forms in *Nicholas Nickleby* (1838–39), *Barnaby Rudge* (1841), *Little Dorrit* (1855–57), and *Bleak House* (1852–53)[5]. Dennis Porter claims that *Oliver Twist* is above all a crime novel as it deals extensively with the environment and inner structure of the London criminal underworld[6]. It is this ability to naturally acquire, become familiar with, and employ such a variety of discourses that makes a London writer an exceptional chronicler of the city, one whose narration in fact aspires to be absorbed into the city's "official" discursive network.

Ackroyd is therefore a specific example of a writer who often makes use of crime narratives in his novels. They combine his interest in literature and history with his fascination with the recurrent pattern of

---

5   Ackroyd considers *Bleak House* Dickens's novel which most powerfully suggests London's darkness while, at the same time, it promotes the positive values of duty, love and charity. "In all respects it conveys a haunted city, half pantomime, half graveyard, and full of ghosts and unseen presences." Daisy Banks, 'Peter Ackroyd on London', an interview, *The Browser*, 2013.

6   Dennis Porter, *The Pursuit of Crime: Art and Ideology in Detective Fiction*, 18–19.

crimes and other forms of violence in London, especially the possible ways in which these discourses can intertwine. What connects his non-fiction books, in particular *London: The Biography*, and his novels is his concern for the enigmatic, off-the-record history, "a concentration on alternative, marginalised and unofficial experiences that offered alternative and often competing perspectives on official histories," and fascination with "underworld and carnivalesque narratives."[7] Various types of murders feature in *The Great Fire of London*, *Hawksmoor*, *Dan Leno and the Limehouse Golem*, *The Clerkenwell Tales*, *The Lambs of London*, *The Casebook of Victor Frankenstein* and *Three Brothers*, two different forms of organised crime determine the plotlines of *The Clerkenwell Tales* and *Three Brothers*, while literary forgery crucially influences the plots of *Chatterton* and *The Lambs of London*. Ackroyd's novels are therefore peopled by numerous individuals who personify the dark side of the city, such as visionaries, occultists, members of secret sects, music-hall performers, murderers and other criminals, and their pursuers – police inspectors and detectives. Moreover, as Ackroyd always strives to offer a wide range of viewpoints on his subject matter, the reader is confronted with a variety of discourses dealing with crime in the form of quotations from newspaper articles, entries from a murderer's diary, extracts from a late Victorian trial report, cabaret performances depicting these crimes, psychological insights into the criminals' psyches, or a modern criminologist's reflections on the nature of various crimes. As a result his works adopt an "irreverently playful attitude to history over an ostensibly normative mimesis."[8]

Ackroyd thus makes use of crimes and crime narratives in both his non-fiction and fiction, namely in those works concerned, directly or indirectly, with London. These texts, and the fact that they repeatedly echo one another, best demonstrate the ways in which he employs the theme and discourse of crime and detection within his most characteristic narrative strategies. Ackroyd believes that crime and violence are deeply imbedded in the city's texture and therefore inspire some people to repeat them, and numerous others to write about them, either in the form of factual recordings or fictional stories. Such narratives in fact perpetuate the crimes and, consequently, form new sources of inspiration for their readers as well as other writers, who, having read them, might produce crime narratives of their own. Ackroyd is fascinated not only by those crimes that have repeatedly been recorded but also by people's incessant

---

7   Nick Bentley, *British Fiction of the 1990s*, 12.
8   Suzanne Keen, "The Historical Turn in British Fiction," 171.

urge to transform them into miscellaneous narratives and, in his novels, develops his own versions as a part of this never-ending process.

Serial Killings and the London Gothic Psychothriller

Although all his London novels revolve around crimes, *Hawksmoor* and *Dan Leno and the Limehouse Golem* are specific even within this context as their framework plots are borrowed from the genre of crime fiction: an investigation of a series of murders in the former, and the first-person narration of a mass murderer, recording her perceptions and interpretations of her acts, in the latter. Ackroyd therefore observes some practices characteristic of crime fiction, while, at the same time, he perpetually undermines its key aspects by employing various postmodernist narrative strategies, such as mixing crime narratives with the genre of the historical novel, inserting parallel and side stories featuring both fictional and real historical characters, inserting intertextual and historiographic references alongside mysterious and occult phenomena, and applying the conception of identity as being fluid and superficial. As a result, readers are given neither a crime story nor an historical novel in the traditional sense, but specific postmodernist permutations of both combined in one. The specific choice of crime fiction within this narrative strategy is crucial since crime fiction has an indisputable readership potential and is the popular genre most able to blur the still distinctive polarity between popular and "valuable" culture. As Christiana Gregoriou claims, by appealing to a cross-section of the population, "contemporary crime fiction changes one's perspectives and challenges one's perceptions, necessitates questioning of one's attitude towards murder, capital punishment and the state of our culture."[9] The effect of Ackroyd's novels is to a large extent conditioned by his ability to naturally employ popular discourses and narratives in order to give support to his ideas without disturbing the novels' elaborate structures. This chapter will also attempt to demonstrate that in Ackroyd's fictions crime narratives effectively help to hybridise the genre of the historical novel and, by doing so, contribute to the genre's invigoration and vivification.

A narrative strategy typical of all Ackroyd's fictions is a mixing of the historiographic and the fictional, namely concerning the novels' settings and their protagonists. Although his novels take place in realistic parts of

---

9   Gregoriou, *Deviance in Contemporary Crime Fiction*, 158.

London in given historical periods, there are always made-up, non-existent places in which crucial turns of the plot occur. This strategy is most effective in bringing together historically recognised as well as invented characters who inhabit a certain area of the city, and who encounter one another often without knowing their true identities. The fates of characters such as Sir Christopher Wren, Karl Marx, George Gissing and Dan Leno are thus influenced by fictional ones like Nicholas Dyer, Solomon Weil, and Elizabeth and John Cree, which makes the novels both more playful and authentic. The fact that the real characters feature in criminal stories only underlines this strategy's effect for it makes the narratives more interesting, and perhaps even more plausible, for the readers.

Ackroyd makes use of a similarly dual perspective of London in his novels through the simultaneous exploration of the historical and the mystical, the rational and the irrational. This perspective enables him to explore the lives of people inhabiting the underside of the city. Such a choice of characters is by no means exceptional in postmodernist variants of historical narratives since these protagonists "are anything but proper types: they are ex-centrics, the marginalized, the peripheral figures of fictional history [...] Even the historical personages take on different, particularized, and ultimately ex-centric status."[10] Though crime narratives are not always invariably urban, the city's milieu offers them a world of limitless possibilities, which can be conveniently transformed and rewritten into "a solidly realized but metaphorically heightened city-space, with violence itself often taking on symbolic force in scenes of grotesque, sometimes surreal destruction and viciousness" which becomes "an ultimately unknowable terrain, to be grasped only in a fragmentary way."[11] Yet through the theme of crime Ackroyd explores one more characteristic feature of the city – the determining effect of the always simultaneously operating rational and irrational forces upon their inhabitants' perception and understanding of the world in which they live. It is the coexistence of these forces that crucially affects the *genii locorum* of particular areas, especially through the recurrent generating of happenings of a felonious character.

The interconnection of the city's rational/irrational duality and criminality is most apparent in his novel *Hawksmoor*. Its plot consists of two seemingly different story lines set some two hundred and fifty years apart: a first-person narration supposedly written between 1711 and 1715 by the

10   Linda Hutcheon, *A Poetics of Postmodernism*, 114.
11   Lee Horsley, *Twentieth Century Crime Fiction*, 70–71.

architect Nicholas Dyer, a fictional device taking on Nicholas Hawksmoor's historical role; and a third-person narration describing the detective Nicholas Hawksmoor's investigation into a series of murders committed in London of the 1980s in the vicinities of the churches built by
the actual Hawksmoor. Ackroyd transforms the early eighteenth-century
architect into a merciless serial killer and devout Satanist, by which the
historical story line assumes its particular dynamism and suspense. The
motive behind Dyer's homicides is not primarily his delight in violence
as he displays no special pleasure in committing the murders, but rather
sees them pragmatically as inevitable steps in the process of reaching his
"higher" aim – pleasing his diabolical deity which, as he believes, would
then allow him, through the mystical power-concentrating pattern of
the sites of his churches, to achieve the transtemporal immortality of his
soul. And so, in order to endow these sites with dark energy he kills innocent, and often almost helpless, people whose corpses he then buries
as sacrifices in the foundations of his churches. His mind is undoubtedly
that of a psychopath as he is incapable of feeling compassion or remorse
not only for his victims, but also generally for anyone who suffers but
somehow stands in his way and must therefore be disposed of, his parents included.

For most of its course the second plotline resembles a traditional
narrative of detection as it describes the daily routine of the detective
Hawksmoor's work while providing occasional insights into his solitary mind. Only when he is dismissed from the case and starts realising
the larger, transcendental dimension of the investigated murders does
the seemingly conventional detective story give way to the account of
Hawksmoor's search for intangible and uncanny clues that would help
him identify and bring him closer to the mysterious perpetrator who
appears to be a modern reincarnation of Dyer's evil self. However, the
function of these circumstances is to form a necessary background for
the novel's final twist, for as the two historically separated narratives alternate throughout the book, new parallels are revealed and similarities
echoed, in the process of which the historical time gap between them
is rendered irrelevant and the otherness of the two main protagonists'
lives decreases, so that eventually they merge into a single voice belonging to neither Dyer nor Hawksmoor. In order to solve the case Hawksmoor must at first understand the nature of the city where these crimes
were committed, especially its material as well as spiritual existence
within and without time. The narrative thus transforms from one predominantly about crime and investigation to one which seeks to explore

London's mystical and occult patterns – the narrative of crime detection plays a crucial role in making the narrative of the historical city more original, attractive and challenging.

What connects *Hawksmoor* with another Ackroyd novel that also captures London's shadowy aspects, *Dan Leno and the Limehouse Golem*, is the motif of a serial killer, this time accompanied by even deeper insights into the killer's wounded psyche, as the novel "highlights juridical issues [...] and intertwines them with the emergence of the unconscious of the law itself as well as of the individual."[12] These "dark artists" and their homicidal acts have a highly subversive effect upon the genre of the historical novel as they have "a destabilizing effect" even within the genre of crime fiction[13] since "[f]amiliar motivations for murder – greed, ambition and jealousy – no longer prove adequate to account for the incalculable repetitive form."[14] The East End milieu appears in several distinct microcosms that are interconnected through the motif of a series of ritual murders. Several representatives of the margins of Victorian London society – prostitutes, a Jewish scholar, and a second-hand clothes shop owner's family – become victims of a homicidal force labelled the Limehouse Golem by the newspapers. Moreover, the murder plotline is made more complex by having two levels – the public and the private – with the same perpetrator. The former is represented by the deliberately spectacular and ritually showy serial killings, performed in order to appear on the front pages of newspapers and draw the attention of as large an audience as possible. The murderer sees her acts as an exciting game both with public opinion and, especially, with the police, showing off her limitless dominance and "creativity," and providing misleading clues whose investigation makes the detectives appear even more incompetent in the eyes of ordinary Londoners. The latter is a domestic homicide; the murderer poisons her husband because he dared to defy her obstinate refusal to fulfill her marital obligations by having an affair with their housemaid. This murder is offstage, undercover and discreet, carefully plotted to give the impression of a sudden, accidental decease. Ironically, it is a minor flaw in covering the tracks after this almost non-violent crime that eventually brings Elizabeth Cree before the court.

However, the novel exceeds the limits of a mere murder story as a substantial part of the narrative deals with the murderess's social and

---

12 Sidia Fiorato, "Theatrical Role-Playing, Crime and Punishment in Peter Ackroyd's *Dan Leno and the Limehouse Golem* (1994)," 65–66.

13 Horsley, *Twentieth Century Crime Fiction*, 118, 141.

14 Martin Swales, "Introduction," xiii.

emotional background, with her unfortunate childhood and adolescence due to her dysfunctional relationship with her domineering, abusive and bigoted mother. The narration thus follows Elizabeth Cree's progress from bullied child of the poverty-stricken Lambeth slums, via her career as a music-hall comedian, to her life as a respectable middle-class wife, and her character often evokes pity, sympathy and understanding rather than condemnation or contempt. Yet, gradually the reader realises that she is a merciless homicidal monster willing to destroy anyone who might threaten her dreamt-of self-projection. By making Elizabeth Cree's hapless fate central to his novel, Ackroyd also explores the significant potential of the genre of crime fiction as an instrument of social critique and protest against established power structures. As the story progresses, rather than the actual murders, London, or, more precisely, the social condition of London's most impoverished areas and some of its possible devastating consequences, becomes its central theme. It is furthermore elaborated upon through real-life characters, such as Karl Marx, George Gissing and Dan Leno, who are not only involved in the investigation as either witnesses or suspects, but who also offer their personal insights into the city's poverty and material deprivation. While Marx, Gissing and John Cree try to cope with the question of social injustice in their writing, and Leno in his comic performances, Elizabeth seeks a way with a much more immediate and noticeable effect. Therefore, one possible explanation for her monstrous acts can be that by killing some of its members she symbolically erases the world of her social humiliation from her life. On a more general level the Golem may be described as the materialised evil spirit of the dismal consequences of the Industrial Revolution on the city's weak and vulnerable, similarly as the representation of vagrancy in *Hawksmoor* may be interpreted as a metaphor "for the impermanence of the human condition and the voracious metabolism of the city" resulting in a "sense of estrangement from an increasingly unrecognizable and alienating urban landscape"[15] one century later.

The motif of serial killing also appears in *The Clerkenwell Tales* and *The Casebook of Victor Frankenstein*, but these two novels do not read as detective stories but rather as specific versions of the London Gothic psychothriller. *The Clerkenwell Tales*, set in London in 1399, might be taken as a jigsaw mystery constructed like a mosaic through the individual tales,

---

15   Laura Colombino, *Spatial Politics in Contemporary London Literature: Writing Architecture and the Body*, 6.

which echo those narrated in Chaucer's *The Canterbury Tales*. The novel is another example of Ackroyd's love of the arcane city as the plot develops around the mad visions of Sister Clarice, an illegitimately born nun of the Clerkenwell convent, which prophesy the downfall of the king as well as doom for the sinning and superstitious public, and stir up hatred and fear. However, while Henry Bolingbroke leads his revolutionary army against Richard II, the reader follows a fellowship of respected city officials who seem to be conspiring with a secret, apocalyptic heretical sect, the predestined men, as both the groups, though for different reasons, are eager to get rid of the king. This sect of "foreknown" ones, considered the most dangerous of their ilk at that time, see themselves as the only true followers of Christ, absolved of all sin, whose actions are "prompted wholly by the spirit of God. They could lie, commit adultery or kill, without remorse" (*CT*, 37). The powerful men thus use the simple-minded young fanatics as pawns to kill inconvenient people and to set fires in a circle of five London churches, symbolising the five wounds of Christ, to invoke the last judgement and the day of the apocalypse. All this is foreseen by Sister Clarice and so the author gradually puts forth another mystery – that of the relationship between the mad nun and the city authorities.

The late fourteenth-century London of *The Clerkenwell Tales* is a world dominated, to a large extent, by various dubious forces such as religious visionariness and fanaticism, clandestine conspiratorial societies, court intrigues and omnipresent rampant superstition, a world which is impossible to know unless one removes the veil from its "official" face. Against this background Ackroyd constructs two murder stories which are not only essentially different in terms of the nature and motivation of the offences, but also ostensibly unrelated in terms of the novel's subject matter. The first is a classic domestic murder: a young wife, Anne Strago, poisons her elderly husband in order to inherit his business and marry his young and handsome apprentice, Janekin. Yet the homicide is disclosed and when Anne is questioned she claims that it was Janekin who committed the murder and he is then tried without being granted the opportunity to prove his innocence as he is of too low an estate. The second is the story of William Exmewe, one of the foremost representatives of the city and a generally respected citizen, who in reality is an unscrupulous plotter, the brains of a fanatical religious terrorist sect, an opportunist double agent, and a callous psychopathic serial killer who cold-bloodedly murders anyone who stands in his way or who could reveal his true identity. Exmewe's justification of his acts, "[t]o kill is to be free.

We are far above the law. We are the realm of love. When love is strong, love knows no law" (*CT*, 181), is clear evidence that his is a deranged and dangerously self-deluded mind. What connects the two murder plotlines is the role of the city in them: "There was an ancient belief, however, that murder could never be concealed in London and that it would always find its season to appear" (*CT*, 34), Ackroyd notes, suggesting that although the city seems to prompt these crimes by offering its perpetrators the veil of anonymity, in the end it always somehow helps to expose and convict them. And so, as Exmewe is arrested, accused of treason, imprisoned and ritually punished in public disgrace, the reader is left with the feeling that justice will eventually reach Anne Strago as well.

Combining the first-person narration of a self-deluded, and half-insane, serial killer with a discourse of mysticism, spiritualism, mystery and a hunt for the inexplicable, *The Casebook of Victor Frankenstein* primarily consists of elements of two historically distinct genres: the urban Gothic and the psycho-thriller. Ackroyd had already used a similar strategy in *Hawksmoor*, *Dan Leno and the Limehouse Golem* and *The Clerkenwell Tales*, and in all these works his protagonists find themselves at an impasse with their reasoning and logic and are thus forced to accept that the world around them, namely the city of London, is also governed by forces lying beyond the limits of rational comprehension, which, to varying degrees, has an immediate impact on their psyches. Naturally, the Gothic represents an ideal vent for this clash between the rational and irrational and, as writers such as Patrick McGrath, Charles Higson and Diane Setterfield demonstrate[16], can effectively capture the postmodern sensibility. Therefore, the collapse of the *grand récits* "seems to be particularly suited to the Gothic because it questions the notion that one inhabits a coherent or otherwise abstractly rational world,"[17] and the fundamental horror of postmodern Gothic rests in the fact that "the loss of belief in metanarratives marks out a final limit and then substitutes a plunge into limitlessness, an ultimate meaning as meaninglessness."[18]

The Gothic is a largely complex and versatile mode of narration which exists in numerous distinct modifications, but, as with each genre, it is also distinguished by certain recurrent features and characteristic narrative strategies. One of these is that the setting, its topography

---

16 All McGrath's novels follow the Gothic mode of narration, elements of Gothic or neo-Gothic fiction can also be found in Higson's *Getting Rid of Mister Kitchen* (1996) and Setterfield's *The Thirteenth Tale* (2006).

17 Andrew Smith, *Gothic Literature*, 11.

18 Fred Bortiny, "Aftergothic: Consumption, Machines, and Black Holes," 296.

and atmosphere, corresponds not only with the mood of the story, but also reflects the individual characters' states of mind and ways of thinking. In order to vividly capture this reflection, in *The Casebook of Victor Frankenstein* Ackroyd employs, apart from the necessary fear- and horror-evoking scenes and motifs, two other such strategies. The first is the novel's narrative voice, a first person narration oscillating between a sincere, rationally detached teller of his humble *confession cum apologia* and what has been termed the "mad monologist," an ultimately unreliable, self-centred Poean narrator who is unable to distinguish between reality and vision or dream, and who rejoices in a carefree transgression of the "ethical and social norms of a given culture," having a "pathologically limited capacity to communicate with others," and a paranoid character "with a propensity to justify unjustifiable actions."[19] The mad monologist is a skilled and manipulative speaker who can integrate elements of the grotesque and reflections on his own madness into a highly self-conscious testimony, but who also strives to present and defend his "case" persuasively in an emotionless, objective-sounding, almost legal argumentation. The fact that a reader of the Gothic is always kept in uncertainty as to whether what he/she is reading really happened or merely occurred in the narrator's hallucinatory psyche gives the narrative a specific tension and playfulness by perpetually obscuring the narrator's perception[20]. The second strategy Ackroyd employs is locating the story in a prevailingly urban setting, in the very heart of early nineteenth-century London. The reader follows the obsessed/possessed Victor Frankenstein through the nocturnal metropolis's back-streets, dark nooks, derelict districts and abandoned workshops, a milieu inhabited by the city's underground types and outcasts, such as muggers, drunkards, vagrants and gravediggers.

The multiple-personality, homicidal first-person narrator of *The Casebook of Victor Frankenstein* represents the central conceit of the novel. At first glance, Ackroyd's Frankenstein is a character closely related to its original model, a Faustian scholar with an immense hunger for knowledge, eager to solve all the mysteries of the universe and by restoring human life "determined to prove that nature can be a moral force, an agent for good and for benevolent change" (*CVF*, 127). He appears to be one of the admirable visionaries that inhabit Ackroyd's London. This, however,

19 Rudolf Weiss, " 'Hell is a city much like London': Postmodern Urban Gothic in Charles Higson's *Getting Rid of Mister Kitchen*," 57.

20 For a further exploration of the hallucinatory narrative perspective in Gothic fiction see David Punter and Glennis Byron, *The Gothic*, 293.

is the author's narrative trick, a strategy aimed at evoking the delusion in readers that the way in which the narrator presents himself corresponds with what his personality is really like. The construction of the narrative voice is a key constituent in the game Ackroyd plays with his readers – he deliberately presents a character only seemingly identical with the original in order to blunt their alertness and make them believe what the narrator says, and thus make them an easier target for the "shocking" effect of the final disclosure. At the same time, he leaves hints in the text that shatter the narrator's carefully created self-image and help reveal his true character. Unlike Mary Shelley's temperate, in places even humble and later sincerely miserable, protagonist who devotes the rest of his life to the destruction of the monster he created, Ackroyd's variant shows signs of almost pathological ambition and self-complacent arrogance. When conceiving the project of bringing the dead back to life he considers himself "to be a liberator of mankind, freeing the world from the mechanical philosophy of Newton and of Locke" (*CVF*, 66), suggesting that his selfish desires and aspirations lie at the core of his enterprise, rather than any benefit to humankind. When he learns about the murders his creation committed in London, he comes back to the city not out of despair but out of scholarly interest, "curious about the nature of [the monster's] exploits, since he may thus have displayed something of his debased temperament" (*CVF*, 200), as if the casualties were an inevitable component of his ominous experiment; and when he is eventually about to disclose the story of his life to Doctor Polidori, instead of feeling guilt and regret, he can "hardly wait to tell the story of [his] success" (*CVF*, 400).

These are not the only clues pointing to the narrator's unreliability and revealing that his seemingly credible eloquence serves in fact as a manipulative device to impress the audience, disguising his true intentions and mental condition. From the very beginning of the novel the reader can feel a suspicion that Frankenstein has difficulties in distinguishing between what is happening while he is awake and when he is dreaming. At the end of the third chapter, the narrator describes his dream in which he was being buried in a coffin only to realise that someone was lying in there beside him; a few chapters later he retells a similar story in which he was kneeling by his bed to discover that he was not there alone but with a "gigantic shadowy form" (*CVF*, 104) stretched out upon the bed and coming uneasily to life. At the same time, however, he keeps insisting that on his walks through the streets of London he is often accompanied by someone he hears and feels but cannot see, "some image, some phantasm [...] keeping up with [his] rapid strides" (*CVF*, 32). Ackroyd also hints at his narrator's long-term problems with alcohol by letting his servant Fred suggest that his master actually drinks more than he chooses to admit. The fact that Frankenstein has not mentioned his tendency to drink only further discredits his self-proclaimed "exhaustive" account of what happened in reality. In the most powerful of his fits, the one provoked by the horror of restoring the late Jack Keat to life and intensified by a subsequent excessive consummation of spirits, Frankenstein ends up ranting lines from *The Rime of the Ancient Mariner* (1798) in a feverish, delirious state from which he never fully recovers.

When eventually he starts taking laudanum to soothe his restless spirit and spends much of his time in opium-induced dreams, Frankenstein transforms into an exemplary "mad monologist" narrator confined to the realms of his hallucinatory mind. His mental state is, however, a mere culmination of the preceding traumatic events, caused largely by the progression of his mental illness – multiple-personality disorder. In addition to the mentioned paranoid idea of his being accompanied by a shadow form, Frankenstein's double personality is shown when he is testing the power of the electric fluid on himself, which animates in him a mysterious "secret voice" (*CVF*, 175) which he does not recognise as his own. The voice expresses the conviction that external things can only manifest their existence as an inherent part of the observer's psyche, and demonstrates that the other self is endowed with such vast might that it can never be controlled or overpowered by its conscious counterpart. This disclosure of the possibility that some events have taken place entirely in the narrator's deranged imagination automatically casts doubt on the credibility of the story's central motif – the creation of the revived corpse. Did it really happen or was it a mere phantasm engendered, for instance, by the man-made monster from *Melmoth the Wanderer* that so fascinated Frankenstein when he watched the theatrical adaptation of Maturin's novel. From this perspective, some utterances in the novel become susceptible to alternative interpretation: Bysshe's "you are a stranger everywhere, Victor. That is your charm" (*CVF*, 329) might thus refer not so much to his absorption by natural science as to his mental otherness; or Frankenstein's statement claiming that "the English, despite their air of business and practicality, were a wholly credulous and superstitious nation" (*CVF*, 368) can be understood as the speaker's triumphant mockery at how easily he deceived the Shelleys and Byron by acting as an amicable and endearingly absent-minded companion.

The fact that the monster represents a materialisation of the dark side of its "creator's" schizophrenic personality rather than an outcome of some dubious scientific experiment becomes more and more apparent throughout the novel, especially in his "conversations" with the creature. "There is no substance without a shadow" (*CVF*, 225), he replies to Frankenstein's objection to his being sought out and contacted by the monster against his will, suggesting that he has always been there with him due to the "adamantine bond" (*CVF*, 253) that ties them ominously to each other. Frankenstein at first naively argues that his follower is automatically subordinate to his intentions and wishes, but when the monster informs him that nothing would ever stop him from causing unceasing misery in his life since "the wilderness in [him] is greater" (*CVF*, 257) than any on earth, Frankenstein finally understands who the actual master of the situation is and that he will never escape this fearful shadow double. Once he reconciles with his condition, he becomes a more attentive listener to what his other self tells him and discovers that their thinking is strikingly similar, "as if there were a connection between [them] that surpassed the ordinary power of sympathy" (*CVF*, 373). As his mental disorder progresses, Frankenstein begins to feel fascinated rather than repulsed by the hideous agent of desolateness in himself, in this way manifesting the ultimate loss of the last bits of control he is able to exercise over his conscious acts.

Because of this, it is logical that Frankenstein turns his hatred towards Doctor Polidori, the only person around him who can detect the true nature of his split personality. Once again he attempts to deceive the reader by presenting Polidori as a very annoying person who keeps spying on Frankenstein and even intruding himself into his household in order to learn his secret. In reality, Polidori correctly diagnoses Frankenstein's psychological disturbance and deliberately tells him the story of Monro, a clerk in holy orders who lost his faith but hypocritically continues taking part in services and preaching and therefore "decides to commit a crime of malignant evil, without motive" (*CVF*, 385) which would redeem him from a life of living a lie. The murder he commits, however, does not bring the desired effect as he feels no guilt, shame or remorse but rather a pride so great that he wishes to boast to the world about it. He does this directly from the pulpit and ends up in a mental institution. The affinity between Frankenstein and Monro turns out to be closer than it at first seems – Frankenstein is also eventually overwhelmed by the desire to narrate his story to someone. When Polidori tells him that there is no monster and that he has merely been living in his imagination, it infuriates Frankenstein and he not only confesses to being a homicidal maniac but also murders the doctor brutally on the spot. The true motives behind his acts remain obscure but the most likely suggests a parallel to Monro in that Frankenstein failed in his project, lost his belief in it yet continued experimenting anyway, and the murders were committed to set him free from his disgraceful existence. Whatever the motives, Ackroyd's Frankenstein is a patient in a mental asylum and his "mad monologue," recorded in the inmate's diary, is made public by the hospital superintendent.

Crime Re-written

London's most attractive aspects for Ackroyd are its volatility and multi-facetedness, which are best manifested through the diverse fates of the people who have happened to live in it. His London is always inseparable from its inhabitants, their experiences, and, most importantly, their imaginative production that somehow reflects this experience, from amateur and folk creation to the works of professional artists, thinkers and scholars. Being a writer and literary scholar himself, Ackroyd's attention is naturally drawn primarily to literary and textual representations, both official and well-regarded as well as ignored, underground and dubious, all of which offer a distinct insight into the city's history and development. His approach thus reveals that one of the many possible Londons can be discovered through reading and juxtaposing a great variety of the texts its inhabitants have produced. He further emphasises that the city itself can be understood and therefore read as a text, one in which both factual and fictitious narratives are interwoven, the polarity between them blurred. It is apparently no ordinary text but one that is constantly being written and re-written. London as a text thus represents a complex, multi-layered palimpsest, which is highly unstable and variable and is being perpetually inscribed on and overwritten, as new textual layers multiply and are laid upon previous ones.

One of the best examples of the city-as-a-text can be seen in the literary exploration of London's fascination with murder. Murder is always shrouded in mystery and so it stirs people's curiosity and imagination, and all the more so in a populous city. It provokes ambiguous feelings in them – an eagerness to learn the truth and uncover the identity of the perpetrator, but also an enjoyment of the case being unsolved as they can follow how it is reported in various, mostly popular, media,

and also think up and share their own solutions, which further discredit and mock the official investigation, while simultaneously they
tend to glorify and idealise the criminal. "The essential point remains
that crime, and in particular murder, enlivens the urban populace. That
is why, in London mythology, the greatest heroes are often the greatest criminals" (*LB*, 269). What makes the theme especially attractive
is that more often than not there appears to be some intrinsic connection between homicidal forces and the city's topography, more or less
directly indicating the areas' complicity in the crime by allowing it to
occur within their confines. The fact that certain areas in London, such
as Spitalfields, Whitechapel and Islington, have repeatedly witnessed
murders, moreover often of a similar kind in terms of motive and execution, leads Ackroyd to note that it is as if the spirit or atmosphere of the
city itself played a fortuitous if malign part in them (*LB*, 265). Be it as
it may, violent urban crimes have always been a fruitful inspiration for
artists, writers in particular. Ackroyd mentions that Charles Dickens, for
instance, liked to hear criminals' stories (*D*, 188), which he could later
rewrite within the framework of his novels. Therefore he several times
visited prisons, especially Newgate Prison which features in some of his
novels, confessing to a "horrible fascination" for it[21]. In the chapters
"A Rogues Gallery" and "Horrible Murder" of *London: The Biography,* he
refers to several texts which sought to both record and bring to life the
city's greatest crimes, including Thomas De Quincey's celebrated essay,
"On Murder Considered as one of the Fine Arts." He claims that all
these texts, although they often differed significantly in their accounts
and interpretation, contributed to the immortality of the crimes in question as they perpetuated them in the narratives. All these written records
of London criminality represent unique crime narratives showing how
deeply rooted violent crimes are in the very texture of the city. Therefore, as people have always been attracted by accounts of brutality in
the city, for many writers these murders challenged them to re-write the
city that fascinated them from its darkest side.

Ackroyd also takes advantage of this fact in his novels as most of them
revolve around a violent crime, usually a murder, and explore its possible connection with the place where it was committed. Some of them,
however, are concerned directly with the relationship between these
crimes and their textual representations, and the actual process of their
being re-written and reenacted in the form of affirmative or contending

---

21   Donna Dailey and John Tomedi, *Bloom's Literary Places: London*, 85–86.

narratives, themselves inspired by previously written texts dealing with the same or related felonies. The most telling example is *Dan Leno and the Limehouse Golem*, in which Thomas De Quincey's "On Murder Considered as one of the Fine Arts" becomes a central text that inspires or otherwise influences most of its protagonists' fates. First, there is young George Gissing in the Reading Room of the British Museum, aspiring to win recognition as a writer and reading De Quincey's work as an inspiration for his own essay, "Romanticism and Crime," in which he admires De Quincey's ability to transform the killing monster into some kind of Romantic hero. Sitting next to him, we can find John Cree studying De Quincey while musing on his own still unfinished work, a social drama about the soul-destroying misery of the London poor. Then there are the newspaper interpretations of the murderer and her acts, picking up on the false clues she arranged and creating a new myth that a creature similar to that found in Yiddish lore has been killing innocent people in the night-time London streets, which form an independent, fictitious narrative of the mystery. In order to achieve greater historical accuracy and authenticity for the story, Ackroyd also reproduces extracts from the records of the trial of Elizabeth Cree during which she is sentenced to death for poisoning her husband.

Ackroyd contributes to this palimpsest by creating his own crime narrative in the form of a diary supposedly kept by the serial killer. Elizabeth Cree is not only inspired by the account of the Ratcliffe Highway murders in the plotting of her own homicidal schemes, she further develops the idea of the killer as artist and forges her husband's diary in order to pin the blame on him, in which she often quotes De Quincey's words. She especially chooses those words which help her to project herself as the city's great performer, "a solitary artist, who rested in the centre of London, self-supported by his conscious grandeur" (*DLLG*, 30). This faked diary represents an artistic enterprise of its own kind, since it combines psychological explorations of the murderer's mind with elements of a detective thriller, a narrative strategy which is becoming increasingly popular in contemporary crime fiction and which can be labelled "criminal mind style."[22] The reader can thus trace the motives behind the murderer's acts, her elaborate preparations for them, the perverse logic which determined and explained the selection of her victims, as well as the social and economic circumstances which enabled the birth of such an unscrupulous human monster. However, by making Eliza-

---

22 Gregoriou, *Deviance in Contemporary Crime Fiction*, 70–78.

beth Cree's narrative perspective dominant – hers is the only first-person narration in the novel, Ackroyd manages to both engage and subvert the principles of the detective thriller. He engages the genre's typical morality which "has no respect for equality, privacy, [...], a morality of unequivocal self-assertion tempered only by an entirely personal sense of decency,"[23] yet he deliberately offers the villain's perspective, which invites the reader's identification with her and in effect contributes to the novel's playfulness. Gregoriou argues that in order to portray the criminal mind crime writers employ "deviant linguistic structures" through which they are "in fact demystifying their criminal behaviour; they are justifying it, or putting readers in the position of sympathising with the criminal."[24] The crime narrative in *Dan Leno and the Limehouse Golem* therefore adds further dimensions for possible readings to the historical novel, such as a psychological study of a pathological mind, social critique, and an exploration of the theatrical nature of the city's life.

Another example of Ackroyd's fictitious, or at least semi-fictitious, re-enactment of a famous London murder is the unfortunate life-story of Mary Lamb in *The Lambs of London*. In 1796, Mary Lamb, who had previously suffered a mental breakdown, probably in a fit caused by the long-term strain of caring for her family, killed her mother with a kitchen knife, as a result of which she had to be kept under permanent supervision for the rest of her life. Her younger brother, Charles Lamb, became her guardian, the siblings lived together and later they even adopted an orphan. They collaborated on several books for children, including the most famous *Tales from Shakespeare* (1807). Ackroyd's novel depicts the days and months that preceded this tragic event and, as in his other historical novels, he brings together a variety of really existing and fictional characters – apart from the Lambs and their parents, there are other historical personages such as William Ireland, Richard Brinsley Sheridan and Thomas De Quincey, though the inclusion of the last mentioned is historically inaccurate as De Quincey was in reality only eleven years old at the time of the murder[25]. This rather short novel skillfully portrays a late eighteenth-century London of eager entrepreneurs, doubting scholars and bohemian artists, a promising yet merciless urban world of ambition and hope, but also of failure and disappointment, an environ-

---

23 Jerry Palmer, *Thrillers. Genesis and Structure of a Popular Genre*, 5.

24 Gregoriou, *Deviance in Contemporary Crime Fiction*, 90.

25 As we have seen with the year of birth of Dan Leno in *Dan Leno and the Limehouse Golem*, or with that of Nicolas Dyer/Hawksmoor in *Hawksmoor*, such deliberate manipulation with precise historical data is Ackroyd's favourite game with the reader.

ment that would exert enough pressure on an aspiring young writer to resort to a crime in order to fulfill his or her dreams.

In *The Lambs of London* Ackroyd is rewriting two officially unrelated crimes, Mary Lamb's matricide and William Henry Ireland's Shakespeare forgeries, by linking them through the intersection of the novel's two plotlines. Making use of the two events' time coincidence and the fact that the true motive behind neither of these acts is known for sure, he suggests that the consequences of the latter could have played a substantial part in instigating the former. Ackroyd makes his Mary befriend William, consider the young man exceptionally thoughtful and spiritually mature for his age, and gradually find in him a confidant in whose company she can at least temporarily shake off the burden of her domestic and household duties and worries. She puts so much trust in his accounts of how he got hold of the Shakespeare papers that when she learns about her friend being a counterfeiter she suffers a nervous breakdown, one consequence of which is her rash and extreme reaction to her mother's habitual chiding, resulting in the astounding murderous act. Yet, altering or speculating about the past is not the novel's only refreshing aspect – equally important is that most of the action is seen through the characters of Mary and William. And so, although they are not given a first-person narrative voice the reader still gets an insight into their minds, obtaining thus a rather marginal perspective of the events in terms of traditional historical accounts, one which may allow a reassessment of the gravity of their crimes in the light of the "newly revealed" circumstances.

In his works Ackroyd strives to provide exemplifications of how the individual narratives that crimes inspire resist any hierarchy in terms of chronological sequence or factual importance. He shows that they can be scattered and read again in whatever preferred order, always offering an alluring perspective on what actually happened or rather, what might have happened. The fact that these homicides fascinated their contemporaries as much as they fascinate readers more than a century later has resulted in their being mythologised in their modern literary representations. Moreover, as is typical of all mythologies, what really matter are no longer the actual acts but the different ways in which they are narrated[26]. We will never be able to discover what precisely happened on the Ratcliffe Highway or in the Lambs' and the Crees' households, and it is

---

26 Richard Guard notes that the effect of these murders and their subsequent mythologising was so strong that [n]ot only did Ratcliffe Highway receive a new name (it was first renamed as St George's Street and became The Highway in 1937) but public outrage was such that it led to significant pressure for a full-time police service" (*Lost London*, 152–153).

in fact no longer relevant, for the murders live on in their ability to stir people's creative potential. In accordance with the postmodernist conviction that we can never fully know any historical event, the mythology of London crimes represents an ongoing process of history's narrative recreation. This process has always been affected by the prevailing values and perspective of the period in question, such as De Quincey's romanticising glorification, or Gissing's admiration for his predecessor's literary gift. The murders in Limehouse, Ackroyd notes for instance, later indirectly inspired the dark atmosphere of the London underworld in Oscar Wilde's *The Picture of Dorian Gray* (1890). Then there is Ackroyd's own contribution to the process of re-writing famous London murders in the form of his novel, in which he takes up De Quincey's project of making horrible factual events into fine art, and readers can only wait anxiously to see who will be the next to come up with his or her new version.

Assuming a Story – the Narrative of Detection

So far we have been dealing with Ackroyd's use of crime narratives that give an account of the act or explore the psychology of the criminal. A crucial component of crime stories is, of course, the narration of investigation and detection, which incorporates into the story another discourse, with its own characteristic tone, vocabulary, pathos and inner logic. While in the depiction of crime the writer can often give free range to his or her imagination in order to make the plot more exciting for the reader, the character of the detective is expected to possess certain qualities required in his or her real-life counterparts in order to make the fictional process of investigation realistic and plausible. This is the reason why, for instance, Dickens arranged to meet various members of the Detective Department at Scotland Yard, and of these, "Inspector Field was later assumed to be the original Inspector Bucket in *Bleak House*, and there is no doubt that Dickens was sufficiently impressed by him to turn him into yet another token of his always-admiring interest in the efficiency and doggedness of the London police" (D, 326). In the two Ackroyd novels that feature a description of an actual murder investigation, *Hawksmoor* and *Dan Leno and the Limehouse Golem*, the narrative roles of the investigators, the present-day Detective Nicholas Hawksmoor and his late Victorian precursor Chief Inspector Kildare, are substantially different, though neither of them accomplishes, for various reasons, what crime fiction detectives are expected to – the solving of their cases.

Detective Hawksmoor, one of the two main protagonists of the novel, at first resembles a typical, or even stereotypical in terms of some late twentieth century detective fiction, representative of such a character – an experienced, slightly eccentric and antisocial loner without a family, dressed in ill-fitting clothes, inhabiting a small shabby rented flat, obsessed with solving his cases by using methods often misunderstood or disapproved of by his senior colleagues and considered old-fashioned by the younger ones. The reader does not meet him until the second part of the book, yet his appearance changes the narrative instantly as we follow him through all the formal stages of a murder investigation, such as examining the corpse, searching the crime scene and consulting the pathologist. However, the reader soon realises that this is not a conventional detective story with a conventional detective as the traditional discourse of investigation and detection is more and more frequently interrupted by Hawksmoor's thoughts and ideas, which in effect reveal the detective's/the author's theory concerning the relationship between the particular areas of the city and the events happening within them. It is this gradually increasing emphasis on the operations of the detective's mind which allows the narrative to shift from the material reality of the investigation to the actual theme of the novel – the transtemporal connection between the crimes and the sites where they occurred.

As was shown in the previous chapter, an important aspect of Ackroyd's London is his conviction that there are areas within the city that are subject to peculiar temporal and special conditions as a result of which they retain a particular *genius loci*. This repetitive parallelism of events supports Ackroyd's insistence that the present is merely the past revisited and "the question of chronology is immaterial, for time is cyclical and human actions are endlessly accumulated and repeated around the same power-concentrating places."[27] Such a persuasion inevitably affects the story by diverting its focus from the realistic and rational to the paranormal, as a result of which even a seemingly traditional narrative, such as that of crime detection, assumes an unconventional, hybridised form. In *Hawksmoor*, this reflects the detective's gradual dismissal of and departure from traditional procedures and methods of murder investigation in favour of mere intuition, as thanks to this sensitivity to the magnetising properties of certain London territories he comes to realise that the churches have not witnessed such crimes for the first time, and that

---

27 Susana Onega, *Peter Ackroyd*, 68.

in order to understand the motives behind them he will have to consult the obscure history of their locations.

The detective also articulates Ackroyd's belief in the narrative potential of crimes as he insists there must be a story behind the murders that will help him to find the culprit. When his assistant impatiently asks what they will do next, Hawksmoor gives him an answer he does not really comprehend: "We do nothing. Think of it like a story: even if the beginning has not been understood, we have to go on reading it. Just to see what happens next" (*H*, 126). Simultaneously, Hawksmoor is aware that such a story can be highly unpredictable as the murderer can play a game with the detective, just as a writer can deliberately puzzle the reader: "Of course I want to stop him. But I may not have to *find* him – he may find me" (*H*, 127, emphasis in original). This is why he often relies on his intuition, to his assistant's unconcealed uneasiness. Hawksmoor's prediction proves to be correct and the murderer "finds" him by sending him a prompt in the form of a plan outlining the area of the churches in which the murders were committed. As he follows the clues and reads Dyer's secret diary, Hawksmoor begins to understand the occult significance of the scheme of the loci delicti and focuses his attention on finding the mysterious vagrant who calls himself the Architect. The narrative once again changes, this time into that of a thriller as Hawksmoor gradually uncovers the killer's psyche and understands his intentions. Ackroyd thus employs the conventional crime fiction device of a detective trying to understand the criminal by thinking in a similar mode, as a result of which the detective becomes a double of the criminal[28]. As the novel progresses, the story loses its rational grounding and the reader learns that Hawksmoor is in fact pursuing Dyer's supertemporal reincarnation and the other, deviant side of himself. The detective is no longer the criminal's double as the two merge into a single, mystical self. Ackroyd plays a game with the reader in the end by leaving his narrative of crime detection inconclusive, suggesting that neither the detective nor the murderer, but the city itself is the central subject of the story.

In *Dan Leno and the Limehouse Golem*, save for his being a bachelor and leading a rather lonely life, Chief Inspector Eric Kildare differs from his twentieth-century counterpart in almost every respect. Being Hawksmoor's predecessor by some hundred years and a member of the newly established Criminal Investigation Department, Kildare lacks the experience and knowledge Hawksmoor obtains from studying the his-

---

28 Gregoriou, *Deviance in Contemporary Crime Fiction*, 59.

tory of London crime's detection as he himself is one of its pioneers. Therefore he relies entirely on the well-tried procedures for this kind of investigation – gathering evidence, looking for witnesses, interrogating suspects, and establishing hypotheses. As a result, in contrast to Hawksmoor's case, the reader is offered a crime narrative of mechanical and almost punctilious precision. What is more, Kildare seems to lack Hawksmoor's intuition, a detective's sixth sense, which he demonstrates by not picking up on the clues the suspects and witnesses give him. Interestingly, all Kildare's key witnesses are real historical personages, which exemplifies the freshness of Ackroyd's entwining of the historiographic and the fictional. Karl Marx, the first of these, directs attention towards the victim, the motive, and the possible perpetrator: "The Jew and the whore are the scapegoats in the desert of London, and they must be ritually butchered to appease some terrible *god* [...] Murder is part of history, you see. It is not outside history. It is the symptom, not the cause, of a great disease" (*DLLG*, 92–3, emphasis in original). What Marx is suggesting is that it must have been the dreadful living conditions of the area that gave birth to the homicidal evil, but Kildare listens to the elderly philosopher merely out of politeness and remains persuaded that the killer is an educated man since he has studied De Quincey's essay as inspiration for his murders for "there are too many resemblances for it to be entirely natural" (*DLLG*, 204). Later on, when he is talking to Dan Leno, he recalls seeing a scene in which Leno was almost strangled on stage by another performer, but completely ignores Leno's remark that the performer was a woman. Even when he appears to show some insight into the case, especially when he notices the curious theatricality of the murders, he immediately rejects the idea despite Leno's expert confirmation that the atmosphere the murders provoked resembles "some kind of penny gaff or theatre of variety" (*DLLG*, 205).

Kildare's main flaw is that he does not, unlike Hawksmoor, Marx and Leno, understand that crimes are inseparably connected with the areas in which they are committed, that the nature of the evil echoes that of the city, and that in Lambeth and Limehouse it is the combination of poverty and cheap theatricality that crucially determined the slaughters. His investigation therefore turns into speculation and fruitless theories. This is also the reason why the narrator treats him ironically at the end of the novel, as "a diminished Sherlock Holmes who thinks smoking a pipe will help him "cogitate" but does not."[29] His lack of trust in the

---

29 Onega, *Peter Ackroyd*, 69.

power of the *genius loci*, his ultimate misunderstanding of the city's character, leaves him without a story behind the murders and consequently without a solution. In the end, although he prides himself on being keen on progressive ways of thinking, he not only deems the case insoluble, but even starts to be inclined to believe in some intangible Golem-like force behind the murders. Symptomatic of his incompetence as a detective is that he is literally deaf to what other people suggest to him about the possible causes of the killings. And so he ignores his friend George Flood's insightful idea that he "must look for a material cause" (*DLLG*, 259) behind the seemingly irrational acts, as if he could not believe that a London Underground civil engineer could ever surpass a professional detective in ingenuity, just as, perhaps partly out of his conceitedness and disdain for the elderly radical philosopher and mere music hall comedian, he dismisses Marx's and Leno's theories. As a result, he misses the crucial connection between the murders and the condition of the city, foolishly persisting in the belief that they were committed by a machine-like killing monster who eventually "fled the country on a steamship and was probably somewhere in America" (*DLLG*, 268).

Like *Hawksmoor*, *Dan Leno and the Limehouse Golem* subverts traditional detective fiction, this time by mocking the investigator's inability to find the perpetrator by making lay characters more resourceful and foresighted concerning the character of the crimes and, consequently, by giving the final say in the novel to Dan Leno, a person of well-developed intuition and empathy. If, as Gregoriou argues, the reading of crime fiction can be viewed as a manifestation of Bakhtin's notion of carnival, during which readers become both voyeurs of and participants in the violence of the novel they read[30], then *Dan Leno and the Limehouse Golem* doubles this effect. It offers carnivalesque pleasure in the observation of both the elaborately performed violence and the farcically awkward endeavours of the incompetent police officer, and thus allows readers to side with the felonious and subversive forces rather those of law and order. It also deals with the very carnivalesque and theatrical side of the city, which in fact acts as an agent that helps to restore the order that was violated by the imminent threat of murder in a more effective and smooth manner than the institutions of the state apparatus. The heterogeneous and ungovernable phenomena and manifestations of the city, Ackroyd seems to suggest, can only be truly pacified or done away with by means of a related nature.

---

30 Gregoriou, *Deviance in Contemporary Crime Fiction*, 101–2.

Ackroyd's employment of a mock-criminal aspect in the form of a parody of the traditional narrative of detection also composes a significant part of the narrative structure of *Chatterton*. The parallel between finding out the identity of a person from a painting and the process of solving a criminal case is suggested by Charles, who is determined to "investigate that picture" and to "solve the mystery" (*C*, 17), teasingly calling Philip "Holmes." Yet, it is Charles who sees himself as a modern personification of the detective genius, even though this label would be more fitting, or at least slightly less far-fetched, for his friend. Among other things, Philip is rational, organised, and patient enough to collect and scrutinise different pieces of evidence so as to be able to see the problem from different points of view. Moreover, Philip is the one who actually "solves" the case, though not because he sees himself as a detective but out of sheer curiosity and thanks to basic common sense rationality. Not only does he recognise who the portrayed man is supposed to be, he also keeps looking for more information about and references to Chatterton even after Charles believes he has unravelled the mystery. In his own imagination Philip is already "enjoying the admiration of the world" (*C*, 60), but he is also willing to listen to the real owner of the manuscripts. Charles, on the other hand, has only one characteristic in which he might resemble the most famous detective personages – his eccentricity and peculiar habits like eating pages of books rather than reading them – otherwise he is a perfect example of an anti-detective: he is a dreamer, easily excitable, impulsive, overenthusiastic, impatient, credulous, deluded and prone to be driven by wishful thinking rather than rational analysis. As a result,Charles always misses crucial clues and jumps to conclusions without any sufficient evidence which, as it accumulates, leads his "investigation" completely astray. No matter how likeable Charles appears as a person, his absolute incompetence as a detective allows these parts of the novel to be read as a parody of classical narratives of detection and in consequence makes the reader suspicious of his interpretations of the findings. Therefore, it is rather the reader whom Ackroyd puts into the role of his literary investigator, though one whom he simultaneously repeatedly confuses by providing deliberatively misleading or speculative clues[31].

---

31 For a more detailed analysis of the novel as a parody of famous detective narratives see Berkem Gürenci Sağlam's *"The Mystical City Universal": Representations of London in Peter Ackroyd's Fiction*.

London Confined

Criminality and violence go hand in hand with various forms of punishments imposed on the perpetrators and suspects by the city authorities, and so the prison soon became one of the most popular symbols of the city's dark sides. There have been more prisons in London than in any other European city[32]. "From the penitential cell in the church of the Knights Templar to the debtors' prison in Whitecross Street, from the Clink situated in Deadman's Place, Bankside, to the compter in Giltspur Street, London has been celebrated for its places of confinement" (*LB*, 251). Even though it is not as old as the metaphor of the world as a prison, the roots of the image of the city as prison run back to the second half of the seventeenth century. As Ackroyd notes, when in 1670 the most famous and horrifying Newgate Prison was reconstructed and enlarged in order to accommodate different criminals in separate premises of the building, the prison became a condensed miniaturised version of the sinful city and "no more lucid demonstration could be given of its intimate connection with London" (*LB*, 241). Surrounded by the mystery of the unknown, associated with unutterable suffering and death, praised for performing justice but also condemned for excessive cruelty and numerous acts of injustice, the prison "has inspired more poems, dramas and novels than any other building in London" (*LB*, 238). Writers and playwrights such as Daniel Defoe, John Gay, William Godwin, Charles Dickens and William Morris either made use of their own first-hand experience with the institution in their work, or were influenced by its practices and the narratives these had incited in order to make direct or indirect comments on the very condition of the city.

"Prisons are closed and secretive societies because it is only under these conditions, of complete submergence in the system, that the arduous processes of self-assessment and rehabilitation are supposed to do their work" (FEP, 74), comments Ackroyd on how the punitive institution acquires its identity. Here, the parallel between the city and the prison suggests itself: in both cases it is an enclosed, thoroughly organised and ordered space which perpetually, directly as well as indirectly, shapes its inmates and their lives. In his *Discipline and Punish* (1975), Foucault characterises the prison as a transforming "apparatus intended to render individuals docile and useful, by means of precise work upon their

---

32   By the end of the 17th century there were eighteen prisons in London (Dailey and Tomedi, *Bloom's Literary Places: London*, 55).

bodies," which "merely reproduces, with a little more emphasis, all the mechanisms that are to be found in the social body."[33] To a certain extent, the prison can thus be viewed as a miniaturised, condensed version of the social body of the city, which only adopts, adapts and officially institutionalises its most effective controlling mechanisms and procedures.

Foucault identifies three essential principles that must be in operation if the prison is to be successful in transforming individuals: "the politico-moral schema of individual isolation and hierarchy; the economic model of force applied to compulsory work; the technico-medical model of cure and normalization."[34] All these principles simultaneously lie behind the operations of the city's social, political and economic structures. Even within crowds the city dwellers find themselves isolated from one another due to the anonymity of city life but also because the stressfulness and complicatedness of such a life forces them to enclose themselves in a shell of their own worries and anxieties. The necessity of institutionalised work is another defining aspect of urban existence since it is impossible to live there on what the land offers. Work is therefore a means of disciplining the citizens, forcing them to deserve the luxury of their lives. Yet it also serves as a crucial source of pleasure and satisfaction as it provides an opportunity to rise in the city's social hierarchy. Finally, an individual's life is far from autonomous as it is constantly supervised and directed so as not to diverge from the administrative norms and rules that establish and perpetuate the order of the city. Foucault's idea of the prison as the Panopticon, a place and space of "at once surveillance and observation, security and knowledge, individualization and totalization, isolation and transparency,"[35] is thus perfectly applicable to the experience of modern urban life.

The prison represents the central emblem of official authority and power, a symbol of the order of the city which is, however, not always perceived as desired but rather as forced upon its inhabitants against their will. Therefore, the great heroes of London have often been those who freed themselves from the confinement of the prison, which was not celebrated as the liberation of an individual criminal, but rather as a manifestation of universal defiance of the forcible pacification of all the spontaneous, heterogeneous undercurrents of urban life which must be kept under control if the city authorities are to perpetuate their idea of order. And so, for instance, when Jack Sheppard, a thief and robber, who repeatedly managed to escape from Newgate Prison, was sentenced

---

33 Michel Foucault, *Discipline and Punish*, 231, 233.
34 Foucault, *Discipline and Punish*, 248.
35 Foucault, *Discipline and Punish*, 249.

to death his execution was eagerly watched by one of the largest crowds London had ever seen. It was not so much a concern for this violent and unscrupulous man that drew the crowds and "transformed the atmosphere of the city" into a prevailing mood "of genuine collaborative excitement" (*LB*, 245), but an escapist, plebeian fascination with the story of his successful resistance to the most noticeable symbol of institutional authority and social domination. "We might then equate the experience of the prison with the experience of the city itself" (*LB*, 245), Ackroyd concludes, as the former allows a visible materialisation of the latent, indomitable carnivalesque tendencies concealed under, and always ready to disrupt, the seemingly civilised surface of the latter.

No other sites or buildings in the city have evoked such ambivalent if not downright contradictory feelings and emotions, rapidly oscillating between fascination and hatred, as the places of confinement. Taken by many as the most striking manifestation of official authority and its impact on ordinary citizens, the target for those who felt the need to release their rage against their heartless mistreatment by the powerful of the city and the world and to even the score with the abstract and inviolable power hidden behind it, the prison often became, "the first object of London rioters who were determined to destroy the order of the city" (*LB*, 240). Thus, the prison not only generates incessant clashes between the city dwellers' rational and irrational, conscious and unconscious impulses and acts, but also intensely stirs their imagination. "Allusions to the world as a prison run deep through London writing" (*A*, 312), Ackroyd observes, and some of his novels may be taken as a continuation of this tradition.

In *The Great Fire of London* the connection between the city, its inhabitants' lives and a prison, and also between a prison and the texts and artifacts the city produces and inspires, plays a most crucial role, as almost all its main protagonists are somehow related to prison, or to a no longer existing prison, or to both. The as yet little recognised film director Spenser Spender is a great lover of London who wishes to dramatise the very spirit of the city in a feature film. He decides to make a film of Charles Dickens's *Little Dorrit* (1855–57), as he believes that the Victorian writer knew what the city and its inhabitants are truly like, which he vainly tries to explain to his wife: "You see, Lettuce, Dickens understood London. He was a great man, you know, he knew what it was all about. He knew that in a city people behave in different ways like, oh I don't know, like they were obsessed" (*GFL*, 16). As the novel centres around London and the harsh life in the Marshalsea debtors' prison, Spenser plans to use the streets of the city and the interiors of a contemporary

London prison as the film's setting. "These two aspects of the film – the prison and the city – were the ones which would lend it atmosphere and authority" (*GFL*, 106). He feels that the plot's almost caricatured and often melodramatic theatricality will be most authentically captured by the cinematic combination of London streets and the institution of confinement, namely the contrast between the vitality and spaciousness of the first and the dingy gloominess of the latter, the two intersecting aspects that constitute the core of each city's life.

Even though Spenser's choice of the prison as the place to capture one of these two defining aspects of the city is an appropriate one, his inability to understand the correlation between them proves fatal both for his film and himself. In his film he plans to render the prison in contrast to the city. "The street scenes in London had been going well, and he wanted to contrast the rough and open life of the city with the bright but enclosed life of that city's debtors – its victims" (*GFL*, 120). However, while the opposition between London's openness and the prison's enclosedness is a logical and justifiable one, that between the roughness of the first and the brightness of the latter is very doubtful, as it presents the prison almost as a sanctuary, a place of seclusion and safety in the turbulent and merciless city, rather than one of utter despair and suffering. As Spenser does not comprehend the spirit of the prison, the prison somehow strikes back by resisting being idealised during the filming:

> As [Spenser and the actors] walked across the central area of the prison, or banged their cell doors, or ran up and down the metal staircases, to prearranged signals, a tremendous shout rang out. The landings shook under their feet, and the cries and noises echoed around the old building, sending the small birds screaming out through the roof. It was as if all the ghosts of the prison had risen up together, creating that bright, unearthly light which shone from the wing and corrupted the daylight outside. (*GFL*, 121)

It is as if Spenser's misconception awoke some atavistic forces of the old site, which rise up to show him the true nature of the place. Ackroyd ironically uses the word "bright" once again, but this time negatively connoted in connection with the corrupting "unearthly light" which contrasts with the actual brightness of the outside world. And so a minor incident in the prison when an arc-light falls down and hurts one of the technicians, prompting the whole crew to go on strike, in effect triggers a series of unpleasant consequences which eventually bring disaster to the film and its director. The prison as a metaphor of the city's darkest forces claims its victims also among those who, for whatever reason, fail to acknowledge and respect their potency.

Other characters in the novel are also connected with prisons in some way. Rowan Phillips, a tutor in English literature at Cambridge University, who is writing a critical study of Charles Dickens, decides to find the site where the old Marshalsea prison used to stand, which he believes might help him approach the background and inspiration of Dickens's *Little Dorrit*. A homosexual, Rowan moves to Gray's Inn Road not only "to be close to his 'material'" (*GFL*, 10), which is his official reason, but mainly because in his fantasy the big city life offers freedom and frequent opportunities for anonymous sex. Obsessed with his persistent search for sex, he realises that searching for topographical traces of Dickens's life and work in London might both distract his thoughts as well as help him find an appropriate object of his longing. A prisoner of his sexuality, Rowan sets out to find the prison where the writer of his academic interest spent the most sorrowful moments of his childhood. Timothy Coleman, a young Londoner whom Rowan accidentally meets during his quest, assists Rowan to find the site of the Marshalsea prison, at first out of kindliness and curiosity but later, as his relationship with Audrey deteriorates, as a surrogate he becomes interested in the old prison and in all the traces of the no longer existing city centre. A prisoner of a dysfunctional intimate relationship, discovering the site of the old prison and other lost places of London allows him to reconstruct his broken identity and the integrity of his self. Audrey Skelton, who gets possessed by the fixed idea of being an incarnation of the eponymous heroine of Dickens's novel, wanders at night around the site of the old prison, "looking for clues, some kind of old marks" (*GFL*, 97) which might help her understand and empathise with the person she believes resides in her body. In *The Great Fire of London*, the city and the prison coincide to capture the various traits of its characters' distorted psyches and states of mind.

Finally, there is Arthur Feather, or Little Arthur as he is nicknamed due to his dwarfish physiognomy, a grotesque, Dickensian almost half-witted creation, whose highly fragile and unstable psyche is definitively harmed when the "Fun City" amusement arcade where he works is closed as part of the cost-saving arrangements of the owning company. Having killed a little girl from the neighbourhood in one of his fits of compulsive obsessive psychosis which urged him to "save" her from the snares of the hostile world, he ends up in the same prison where, in one of its no longer used wings, Spenser and his crew are making the film. When the prisoners hear about the actors' strike they are exhilarated since they take it as an act of rebellion against the system that deprived them of their freedom, an "attempt to disrupt or dislodge the established world" (*GFL*, 66). Moreover, believing that the actress performing Little Dorrit is another reincarnation of "his" girl, Little Arthur decides to rescue her no matter what it takes. Getting out of the prison thus becomes for him an act of defiance against the outside world, namely the city which had taken away his only pleasure – the lights of his Fun City, and which "had brought her here to mock him, to show him that he was powerless to help her" (*GFL*, 147). Arthur therefore escapes from his cell in order to short-circuit the electricity system of the prison and set the little girl of fantasy free, which switches off the emergency signals, security cameras and the electronic locks of the cells and allows the prisoners to stream out into the London streets. This fictitious event, Lewis notes, echoes not only the Great Fire of 1666, but also two other events in the city's history: the fire that destroyed the original Marshalsea Prison in 1885, and the torching of Newgate Prison which released about three hundred prisoners during the anti-Catholic Gordon riots of June 1780[36]. In the climax of the story law and order are undermined as the border between the prison and the city is violated, yet the person who caused it is sitting and laughing contentedly amongst the cables, ironically remaining ignorant of the fact that the consequences of his deed made his dream that "the lowly shall be exalted" (*GFL*, 147) come true, at least temporarily.

The inseparable connection between London and its prisons also appears in *Dan Leno and the Limehouse Golem*. The novel opens with the hanging of the serial murderer, Elizabeth Cree, in Camberwell Prison, and the narrator provides the reader with several customs associated with this ceremony, such as the exact time it used to be performed, the other prisoners' ritual howling in honour of the executed, the placement of the coffin so that the condemned had to pass it on his/her way to the gallows, and the reverence with which the clothing of the dead was treated, which, in the days of public execution, was sold in pieces to the superstitious crowd who believed it to possess magical power. As after 1868 executions in England were no longer performed in public, Elizabeth Cree's hanging in 1881 takes place within the walls of the prison and her white gown is handed to the governor of the prison who takes it home, puts it on his naked body and lies down on the carpet with an almost

---

36   Barry Lewis, *My Words Echo Thus: Possessing the Past in Peter Ackroyd*, 24.

ecstatic sigh. And so, even though the punishment was withdrawn from public scrutiny to bring it, among other reasons, "under the veil of administrative decency,"[37] in its more private and subdued forms, a morbid fascination with the prison and the happenings it hosts remains deeply rooted in the psyche of the city's inhabitants.

The parallel between the city and a prison is not only dramatised through deplorable criminals and perverted governors. Interrogated by Chief Inspector Kildare, Karl Marx places the murder of Solomon Weil into a wider socio-historical context of London, pointing out the role its social and economic conditions play in driving its most deprived dwellers to violent crimes and stressing the external aspects behind the very homicidal act. "[T]he streets of this city are a prison for those who walk in them" (*DLLG*, 93), notes Marx, as the impoverished are literally imprisoned in the slums and the poorest areas of the East End. The German philosopher elaborates on this comparison even further by claiming that "in the prisons of England, more convicts die at the hands of their fellows than by the judicial process" (*DLLG*, 93), which can also be interpreted metaphorically as the number of those the city, as a prison, in effect kills is far greater than those whom it convicts and punishes, if not reforms. The large capital in which the accumulation of immense wealth exists right next to manifestations of great poverty makes social differences more apparent and their consequences more disastrous. The poverty-stricken city underworld with its unbearable living conditions is thus identified not only as an accomplice of these crimes, but also as a prison and executioner of those who find themselves entrapped in the vicious circle of destitution, misery and despair.

George Gissing, another innocent person whom Kildare suspects of a murder committed by Elizabeth Cree, even ends up in a police prison cell for a night. The unfortunate young writer at first bitterly realises how mistaken he was when he naively believed that he could become the sole author of his fate and fashion his life like the plots of his fiction, as he finds himself a "prey of 'circumstances' trapped in a narrative over which he had no control" (*DLLG*, 146). However, his gloomy thoughts are eventually diverted by a copy of the *Weekly Digest* and its story of the ancient city of London that was recently uncovered during some construction works, and he immediately fantasises that the remnants of this buried city might have been used for the building of the very walls of his cell, stretching thus the *genius loci* of the ancient metropolis as far as Lime-

---

37   Foucault, *Discipline and Punish*, 263.

house where it mingles with that area's *genius loci*, represented by Charles Babbage's Analytical Engine and the mystery of the slaughtering Golem. Gissing imagines himself as a victim of these atavistic forces, a "sacrifice, waiting in an antechamber for the doom prepared" (*DLLG*, 147). As an ingenious and sensitive observer of the city, one of those whom Ackroyd labels as "London Visionaries," Gissing understands not only the supra-temporal and transcendental connection between the ancient, lost London and the new one, but also the specific position of places of confinement within the spiritual and mythical framework of the city.

Yet another image of the city as a prison is presented in *The Clerkenwell Tales*. Sister Clarice is, in a way, doomed to remain a prisoner within the city; as one of the infants born of the forbidden union between a nun and a monk, she spent her childhood in the Clerkenwell convent's secret, subterranean rooms, hidden from the eyes of the religious and political authorities until she was old enough to become a nun herself and enter the convent without arousing suspicion or provoking a scandal. Endowed with a prophetic insight into the city's and the kingdom's future, Sister Clarice, or the "mad nun of Clerkenwell" as she is labelled by Londoners, is kept in her convent cell for most of the time, though as her prophecies spread around the London streets she soon becomes an object of fear and hostility for many, as well as a source of solace and hope for others. Having visited the female prisoners of the Mint beside the Tower of London, Clarice, facing the main building in the yard in front of the prison, makes a short speech claiming her body to be her prison house and foreseeing "a day when all doors would be opened and all locks would be broken" (*CT*, 46). Prompted by her previous visit to the prison and her life-long experience as a prisoner of fate, Clarice envisions the utmost act of liberation of herself and all the oppressed from the confinement and restraints of everyday life, from the wearisome burdens imposed on ordinary people by social and political institutions represented, more than anything else, by the city. The prophetic unlocking of the prison gate thus symbolically stands for the freeing of not only an individual but of the whole capital and its denizens in general. Only a city like London, Ackroyd seems to suggest, could ever have produced such a peculiar phenomenon as Sister Clarice, and only there could she have found such a keen and convinced audience.

Sister Clarice's diabolical prophecies eventually attract the attention of the authorities when they turn more political, and it is predictable that she soon becomes the target of the magistrates' preventive countermeasures. "The city will take her, be sure of it. They wish to keep her silent until they know what will befall" (*CT*, 151), notes Thomas Grunter, the physician, alluding to the connection between the city, political power and the maintenance of order at all costs. After one of her speeches about the degeneracy of the city, addressed to ordinary citizens, she is arrested and sent to the prison at the London bishopric for speaking against the king and "inciting the citizens of London against the spiritual lords of the city" (*CT*, 156), where she is questioned harshly by the Bishop of London and accused of blasphemy and witchcraft. Once again, Clarice draws a parallel between her life, the city and the prison. She indicates that there is not much difference between her previous life and her stay in the prison as both helped her to be disciplined and chastised and thus liked more by her God, only to illustrate a more general likeness between the city and the prison. When the Bishop objects to such a comparison by claiming that that one can move freely around the city, she tells him that the "old, foul and thick sins of London surround you" (*CT*, 160), suggesting that she has been referring to psychological rather than physical confinement, identifying the city as a site imprisoning its powerful in a mental cell of moral corruption and unscrupulous hunger for power, and in consequence also its powerless. The fact that the whole dispute is a mere sham staged deliberately in order to deceive the squire Gybon Maghfeld, a witness of the act who would then spread the account of the interrogation in the London streets, only ironically underscores the metaphor's poignancy.

In Ackroyd's novels the prison is used, sometimes in literal but more often in metaphorical senses, to depict several defining aspects of the condition of London. On the basic level, it represents the harshness, cruelty and misery of the city's mundane everyday life, namely the often merciless fates of those who are forced to linger at the bottom of its social and economic ladder. In short, the prison is the site of the darkest, underworld manifestations, the evil atavistic forces residing latently in the very texture of the city's social body. Moreover, it reflects the distribution of political power from both ends of the hierarchy: the governing elites imposing their power over the freedom of the condemned, but also the condemned resisting official authority by attempting to escape or otherwise violate the procedure of confinement achieved through institutional mechanisms. The prison thus becomes an object of fear as well as glorification for the disempowered, one inciting respectful reverence as well as temporary, carnivalesque reversals of the city life's order. Yet, as Ackroyd shows, such a celebratory attitude must have its limits and should never stretch to idealisation, which the prison always defies and which consequently proves fatal for those who are prone to be blind to its true nature.

On a more private, personal level, the metaphor of London as a prison captures the quintessential loneliness, and the despair resulting from it, of its less happy and fortunate inhabitants who feel isolated, misunderstood, ignored and thus lost in the larger framework of the city's life. Rowan Phillips and Little Arthur in *The Great Fire of London*, George Gissing in *Dan Leno and the Limehouse Golem*, Hamo Fulberd in *The Clerkenwell Tales* and William Ireland in *The Lambs of London* are only a few of the many Ackroyd characters who find themselves imprisoned in their lonely existence within the indifference of the anonymous and uncaring city, helplessly carried away by its invincible currents. These people often in consequence trespass the law or at least their own moral principles in order liberate themselves from the suffocating constraints of such confinement. This feeling is probably most forcefully articulated by Mary Lamb in *The Lambs of London*, for whom the prison of the city has miniaturised and transformed into the house arrest of living with her captious and heartless mother who rebukes her daughter whenever she does not comply with her rigidly conventional ideas of proper behaviour. "This is not a house of correction, Mother. We are not your prisoners" (*LL*, 123), Mary cries out in despair when her mother is callously scolding their servant, yet due to the conventionally prescribed respect towards parents her defiance for long remains only verbal before it assumes an extreme, homicidal form. Mary's example thus demonstrates how the city-prison effectively consumes its weaker "inmates/lambs," arousing in them sinister impulses which their otherwise docile and calm disposition would have never allowed to surface.

Vivifying Crimes, Vivifying the City

Ackroyd returns to a considerable focus on London's criminal element in *Three Brothers*, as much of the novel's story is set against a backdrop of organised crime. The capital's underworld is depicted as being dominated by a network of various local gangs whose bosses have absolute command of most of their area's dishonest and dark dealings, ranging from prostitution and blackmail to arson and homicide, yet which also includes a few solitary petty criminals, pimps, swindlers, small-time thieves and pickpockets, who are trying to grab their bit of the action without interfering with the gangsters' plans. The novel also depicts the seemingly more refined, yet no less unscrupulous, environment of the economic and political criminality of the rich and powerful, which mostly takes the form of white-collar crime, such as divulging secret information for gain, profiteering from government properties and real estate, fraud and bribery. Moreover, as it is often the case in reality, the novel shows these two criminal worlds as notably interconnected as the interests of those who pull the strings in them often converge and overlap.

Despite this intricate background of lawlessness, the story of the three Hanway brothers is framed by crimes of a personal nature, independent of any kind of organised criminal structures. In the beginning, their family breaks down when the mother is sentenced to three months' imprisonment for soliciting and offending public morals after she resumes occasional prostitution in order to help the family's funds, an activity with which she had supported herself even before she met her husband. In the end, Harry, the most ambitious and successful of the brothers, but also the most cold-blooded and calculating, murders his superior's wife, who is also his mother-in-law and mistress, when she threatens to reveal their affair to his wife/her daughter. Paradoxically, his own journalistic career gets started when he prevents a crime by stopping a deranged man from setting a church on fire. He makes a story of the incident for the local newspaper where he has served as an ordinary messenger boy up to that point and consequently becomes a news reporter, rushing "after stories of burglaries and assaults" (*TB*, 18), for which he obtains information at the magistrates' court, where he also discovers the real reason his mother left the family. Daniel, the most gifted and reflective of the brothers, gets unknowingly involved with the city's criminal underworld when he meets, and later starts an intimate relationship with, Sparkler, a pickpocket, con man and gay prostitute. Due to his emotional indifference, Daniel shows little if any interest in his lover's personal life, his criminal activities included, seeing him rather as a source of relaxing pleasures and as someone who provides him with the opportunity to be introduced to the milieu of London's gay community.

What truly connects all the story's protagonists' struggles in the city is the fact that they are affected by the far-reaching consequences of the almost omnipresent network of organised crime. The fact that most of its criminal and obscure activities happen in and around Limehouse links the novel with *Dan Leno and the Limehouse Golem* and *The Casebook of Victor Frankenstein*, in which the area also functions "as a powerful spatial idea" and "a microcosmic manifestation of a wider idea of the East End."[38] The person who connects London's underworld and the sphere of political

---

38   Paul Newland, *The Cultural Construction of London's East End: Urban Iconography, Modernity and the Spatialisation of Englishness*, 106, 107.

and economic criminality is Asher Ruppta, a notorious gang leader and one of the city's powerful criminal masterminds, the smart yet ominous figure responsible for most of the twists in the fates of the three brothers. Ruppta most noticeably interferes in Harry's life, first when Harry, with the help of his girlfriend Hilda, tries to investigate the secret illegal cash flows between Ruppta and Cormac Webb, a junior minister in the Department of Housing, and later when Harry's investigative report is turned down by Sir Martin Flaxman, the proprietor of the *Chronicle*, as he himself has a score to settle with Ruppta and does not want to needlessly irritate his former business ally. Eventually, Ruppta destroys Harry's reputation, though posthumously. When in collaboration with another gang leader, Pincher Solomon, Ruppta blackmails Flaxman, the infuriated newspaper owner murders him in his own house. Yet the whole incident leaves his nerves shattered and in effect causes his massive heart attack, making him unable to manage his company, thus driving Harry into the insidious arms of the unpredictable and vindictive Lady Flaxman. Sam, the most withdrawn and peculiar of the brothers, is employed in Ruppta's office, unaware that his mother once lived with his employer and even had his child. As he never asks questions and always does what he is told, he gets "promoted" to courier, which means the "odd-job boy" (*TB*, 125) collecting rent from the tenants of Ruppta's properties, through which he befriends Sparkler who is one of these tenants in Britannia Street. Although Daniel never has contact with the criminal boss, even his life gets changed by Ruppta's enterprise: after Pincher Solomon's "jackdaw" steals Sparkler's diary with a list of his clients, which includes Sir Martin Flaxman, the devastated Sparkler leans on Daniel, who soon loses interest in his once slick but now emotionally volatile boyfriend and abandons him in his distress.

However, no matter how prominent a role the motif of crime plays in the novel's plot, it gradually turns out to be rather supportive in terms of its overall thematic composition, which is dominated by the portrayal of the invariable, perpetual character of the city and what it takes for an individual to live, persist and thrive under the weight of its demands. As in Ackroyd's other London novels, the protagonists who resort to crime are those who are not in accord with the city and its inheritance, either because they are too weak and insecure to bear these demands, or because they are too callous, complacent and disdainful to ever realise their existence, as in Harry's case, or to acknowledge their legitimacy, as in Daniel's. And so, ironically, the innocently ignorant and unconcerned Sam is the only one who survives physically and mentally intact, as if his visionary capacity, though he is largely unconscious of possessing it, made him resistant to yielding to the city's felonious tendencies, be it as a prey or a perpetrator.

The theme of violence and crime is one of the most suitable to demonstrate the interconnectedness of the city's rational and irrational sides. Moreover, the employment of crime narratives makes Ackroyd's fiction not only more complex, but also more intriguing and, consequently, more vivid, as they inevitably add a "whodunit" and/or "whydunit" and/or "howdunit" aspect to the novels' plots, making the reader turn away from historiographic facts and get engulfed by the process of the disclosure of the crime. Such a modified narrative, however, requires a special, more intimate, conspiratorial relationship between the narrator and his reader, one in which "the writer and the reader are essentially participants in a ritual, with the writer as celebrant and the reader as communicant."[39] The writer thus gains the opportunity to both guide and misguide the reader, a strategy Ackroyd repeatedly makes use of in his novels to destabilise the normative reader-writer relationship by giving him or her deliberately false clues and by mixing the rational with the irrational in the course of the investigations.

To some extent, Ackroyd's novels can therefore be read as particular alternative variants of crime narratives, which characteristically undermine one of the key conventional aspects of these genres – the conclusive and revealing ending. This strategy links him with other contemporary writers working against the background of this generic form, such as Paul Auster, whose *The New York Trilogy* (1988) both appropriates and dismembers the conventions, and simultaneously defamiliarises the genre itself[40]. Although the reader is presented with intriguing cases and encouraged to chase up clues with the detectives and to expect a satisfactory resolution, the process of investigation somehow goes astray as rationality gives way to "arbitrariness and mysticism."[41] As a result, Ackroyd's investigators' quests "mushroom into a metaphysical search for truth itself", ending up "not with a solution, but in dissolution."[42] This is what happens in the case of the Dyer/Hawksmoor incarnation in the non-existent church of Little St. Hugh in *Hawksmoor*; and it can also be found in the celebration of London's theatricality as the emana-

---

39   Robin W. Winks (ed.), *Detective Fiction, A Collection of Critical Essays*, 207.

40   Siobhan Chapman and Christopher Routledge, "The Pragmatics of Detection: Paul Auster's City of Glass," 244.

41   Lewis, *My Words Echo Thus*, 177.

42   Lewis, *My Words Echo Thus*, 178.

tion of the carnivalesque aspect of life, which is vital for the characters' ability to recharge their strength to struggle on with their fates in *Dan Leno and the Limehouse Golem*. In neither of the novels does the detective successfully solve the case as he is in part outwitted by the murderer and in part overcome by the crime's mysteriousness and the lack of rational explication for it. Similarly, the final revelations of the true perpetrators in *The Clerkenwell Tales* and *The Casebook of Victor Frankenstein*, or of the circumstances of the main criminal guru's death in *Three Brothers* do not disentangle the novels' central mysteries and neither do they answer the reader's central questions. Ackroyd is not a detective or psychothriller writer and, although all the considered novels revolve around murders, the reader sooner or later recognises that their true theme is London and not the actual crimes. However, his pluralising approach that treats all narratives and discourses as equal and autonomous and does not make any of them subordinated to the others demonstrates that crime narratives have a considerable potential to vivify the city which represents the paramount object of interest in his fiction.

The revisionist, or postmodernist, pluralisation of discourses and narratives has not resulted in mainstream fiction authors automatically turning to writing detective novels and thrillers, but some have considered that these genres offer an unusual and therefore enriching perspective on numerous themes and subject matters, for instance by "setting up a contrast between our fascination with death, violence and gross illegality and our regulatory attendance to an ideal, a world involving a spectrum from day-to-day normality [...] to our reliance upon those agencies, usually the police, who protect us from it."[43] Ackroyd is a writer who acknowledges the significance of the hybridisation of the genre of the London novel as one of the crucial means of retaining its diversity of styles and perspectives, and by doing so he confirms Martin Priestman's belief that various forms of crime narratives represent a natural environment for the still necessary bridging of the gap between high and low-brow literature[44]. As a result, crime, detection and their fictional representations make some of the most significant constituents of the polyphony of voices and narratives that forms the very essence of Ackroyd's discursive and intertextual London.

---

43   Bradford, *The Novel Now*, 109.
44   Martin Priestman, "P. D. James and the Distinguished Thing," 257.

Chapter 4
Psychogeographic
and Antiquarian London

... each man bears in his mind a city made only of differences, a city without figures and without form, and the individual cities fill it up.
Italo Calvino, *Invisible Cities*

As the preceding chapters demonstrated, Ackroyd's London is not only a physical but also a mental concept, one in which the material and the psychic always coexist and operate in an inherent correlation. Following the tradition of Charles Dickens, who transformed the topography of the London he knew and moved in a city of his mind in his works[1], though avoiding the "principle of binary opposition (or contrasted parallelism) in which the thematic polarity closely correlates with the spatial arrangement of the world"[2] of most of his novels, Ackroyd transforms the city he has lived in all his life into a distinct psycho-spatial-temporal fictional construct. Not only do his characters inhabit this London, but the more sensitive and open-minded ones read the city as a text, by moving through and thinking about it; they absorb and internalise its distinct properties and mechanisms, and by doing so become conscious of its transtemporal character as well as of their own position within the body of its past and present development and collective experience. Most of them are keen walkers, more or less eccentric and frenetic, and always peculiar loners who explore and map the city's topography, discovering its hidden, obscure, uncanny, forgotten or vanished aspects, phenomena, texts and discourses, and store up, interpret, confront or even reshape its miscellaneous narratives.

---

1   For a more detailed survey of London places and areas which feature in Dickens's novels see Donna Dailey and John Tomedi, *Bloom's Literary Places: London*, 72–87.
2   Zdeněk Beran, "Allied to the Bottom of the River": Stratification of the Urban Space in Charles Dickens's *Our Mutual Friend*, 27.

However, there are also those who are not naturally predetermined to establish such an affinity with the urban milieu, and who find themselves helpless and hopeless when faced with its daily pressures and imperatives, remaining blind to its more attractive or mysterious sides. The city inevitably gets reflected in all these individuals' minds and psyches, as each of them creates his or her own "London of the mind" whose functions vary greatly, ranging from a means of mere mental escapism, to a mode of self-understanding and personal transcendence. For Ackroyd, "the past, the imagination, and the topography of the city form 'lines of force' and a literary 'psychogeography'."[3] His treatment of the relationship between the city and its dwellers' states of mind and mental processes thus employs a particular combination of psychogeography and antiquarianism embedded in and crucially determining the stories' narrative framework.

Psychogeography

What is the relationship between the territory an individual inhabits or temporarily occupies and this individual's mind? How does a sense of place and space affect one's mood, feelings and behaviour? What is the actual correlation between the physical topography of a place and the "mental map" one conceives while experiencing this place? These are only a few of the many questions to which psychogeography attempts to respond. From the essence of these queries it is apparent that such a search prefers the more intangible, ambiguous and ephemeral explorations of effects which often defy any rational or logical explication. Guy Debord describes psychogeography as the "study of the specific effects of the geographical environment, consciously organised or not, on the emotions and behaviour of individuals,"[4] yet this deliberately broad definition poses further questions, particularly those concerning the very nature of this enterprise – is it an artistic movement, a narrative strategy, a set of loosely related ideas, a spatial practice, an avant-garde movement, or a subversive political act? As the answer may be all these, psychogeography, above all, represents a challenging tool for a new, and potentially more radical, reflection and redefinition of modern urban experience, be it for aesthetic, psychological or political purposes, on the

---

3 Lawrence Phillips, "Introduction," 4.
4 Guy Debord, "Introduction to a Critique of Urban Geography," 8.

public level, as well as providing, on the personal level, a "virtual map to the topography of one's consciousness."[5]

Its characteristic features are urban walking, a spirit of political subversion of the authorities and their politics and ideology, a focus on the mysterious and the occult, and a preoccupation with rediscovering the past as a means of casting light on the present. Providing a direct experience with the urban terrain, the act of unrestricted walking, wandering or strolling proves vital for all the psychogeographic practices, because it gives one a certain freedom of motion and spirit to explore the "[l]andscapes of the id"[6] – the more forgotten, disreputable, marginal areas overlooked by both the city's visitors and its inhabitants. Such walking then becomes an act of radical opposition to the officially promoted ways of exploitation and consumption of the city's terrain. It is a moving in which the physical dimension is intrinsically interwoven with the mental, in which planning of a journey gives way to randomness, intuitiveness and immediateness. It also fuses the present and the past, seeing the city as a "place of dark imaginings [...] allied to an antiquarianism that views the present through the prism of the past and which lends itself to psychogeographical research that increasingly contrasts a horizontal movement across the topography of the city with a vertical descent through its past."[7] Psychogeographic walking can be thus understood as an act of defiance against the (post-)modern condition that allows, or even causes, the traces of the old city to be obliterated and sunk into oblivion. From the pragmatic perspective, such an act is an ineffective and nostalgic one, as it cannot and does not attempt to save the vanishing aspects and properties of these areas, going against the current of time, and against the grain of the conventional notion of urban progress and development, as "[t]he solitary walker is, himself, an insurgent against the contemporary world, an ambulatory time traveller."[8] And so the avid practitioners of psychogeography are a set of reclusive and, in the eyes of many, eccentric, individuals rather than a social group of common interest and agenda.

In literature psychogeography has been in large part focused on London and Paris. Walking the Parisian streets and boulevards has been associated primarily with the character of the *flâneur*, examined especially in the works of Charles Baudelaire and Walter Benjamin. The rich, fash-

5   M. Hunter Gates, *Understanding Will Self*, 8.

6   Iain Sinclair, *Lights Out for the Territory*, 306.

7   Merlin Coverley, *Psychogeography*, 14.

8   Will Self, *Psychogeography*, 15.

ionable and decadent *flâneur* strives to aesthetise and elevate his aimless strolling to an art form, watching the spectacle of the elegant arcades, and logically shows no interest in the peripheral parts of the city. His experience of the city is thus elitist, eclectic and nostalgic. What *flânerie* and psychogeography have in common is that they are primarily motivated by a "search for experience, not knowledge," one which "remains somehow pure, useless, raw."[9] On the contrary, the psychogeographic approach to London has been much less self-complacent and showy, more egalitarian, and politically subversive, seeing walking as a reactionary act undermining the city's power-holding authorities by deliberately straying from the officially approved and promoted routes and territories in favour of its shabby backstreets, courtyards, waste-grounds, enclosures and other urban "no man's lands."

Psychogeography's prominent contemporary representatives are Iain Sinclair, J. G. Ballard, Stewart Home and Will Self, the first mentioned being particularly responsible for its current revival and popularity[10]. Sinclair has reestablished and adapted the figure of the *flâneur* for the rigours and challenges of his London expeditions, claiming that the concept of aimless urban strolling has been superseded by "the age of the stalker," by "walking with a thesis. With a prey," the stalker being "a stroller who knows where he is going, but not why or how."[11] His writings reconstitute London's topography "through a superimposition of local and literary history, autobiographical elements and poetic preoccupations."[12] For him, walking the streets becomes a continuous research into the hidden layers of modern urban experience carried out through an ultimate immersion in the gravity field of its lines of force, resulting in a peculiar combination of spiritual visionariness, political discontent and artistic creation[13]. The output of such undertakings is inevitably fragmentary, inconsistent, and inconclusive, based on layering

---

9 Edmund White, *The Flâneur: A Stroll through the Paradoxes of Paris*, 47.

10 The accounts of Sinclair's eclectic, vigorous and surreally manic wanderings are recorded in detail in non-fiction books he authored, co-authored or edited. The most notable of these are *Lights Out for the Territory* (1997), its pictorial version composed in collaboration with the photographer Marc Atkins, *Liquid City* (1999), an attempt to encompass the wider city along the M25, *London Orbital* (2002), and the collection of psychogeographic essays on the vanished London he edited, *London: City of Disappearances* (2006).

11 Sinclair, *Lights Out for the Territory*, 75.

12 Coverley, *Psychogeography*, 12.

13 "Walks for their own sake, furiously enacted but lacking agenda [...] Walks as portraits. Walks as prophecy. Walks as rage. [...] Walks that release delirious chemicals in the brain as they link random sites (discrete images in an improvised poem). Savagely mute walks that provoke language" (Mark Atkins and Iain Sinclair, *Liquid City*, 15).

and revising rather than complementation, on the practitioner's subjectivity rather than on unbiased observation and recording. "When the city of distorting mirrors revealed itself, through its districts and discriminations, I discovered more about London's past as a reworking of my own submerged history,"[14] admits Sinclair. Oscillating between documentary antiquarianism and psychology or psychoanalysis, psychogeography effectively combines historio-geographic scrutiny with psychological self-scrutiny, revelation of the city's unconsciousness together with that of the practitioner, phenomenalistic recording with aesthetic creation.

Ackroyd's Psychogeographic Antiquarianism

There are, among others, two major features of Ackroyd's conception of London and its representation in his writing that ally him with Sinclair: "an obsessive focus on the repressed history of the contemporary landscape, [...] a coherent project that is both gripping in and gripped by its fascination with particular territories, driven by its concern with the rival claims staked by those who would both make and tell the history of those territories," and the vision of the city as a "text that is endlessly recomposed,"[15] rewritten, inscribed on, and thus one over which an individual artist has only a limited, if any, control. Like Sinclair, Ackroyd is also convinced of the transhistorical power of *genius loci*, of the subterranean forces operating within certain places and areas in London due to which they have managed to retain their particular spirit and atmosphere across centuries till the present day – the old site of the Marshalsea Prison in Southwark, Lambeth and Limehouse, the most poverty-stricken parts of the East End, Nicolas Hawksmoor's churches, the British Museum and Clerkenwell. Also, like Sinclair, Ackroyd tries to demonstrate that the accumulation of human experience in these areas is reflected in the body of narratives which, creatively or not, record such experience. Therefore, he assumes that in and in between the individual layers of this palimpsestic city its essence might, if only partially, be revealed, mostly in textual form.

However, despite his concern for the obscure and occult and his insistence on the inherent interconnectedness between London and its inhabitants' collective as well as individual psyches, Ackroyd is by no

---

14   Iain Sinclair, *London: City of Disappearances*, 5.
15   Rod Mengham, "The Writing of Iain Sinclair," 56, 63.

means a prototypical representative of the contemporary psychogeographic tradition. Although he is, like many of his novels' protagonists, a keen London walker, his writing, including his non-fiction, lacks its overtly documentary form and narrative perspective, employing instead a combination of prophetic and visionary projections of a timeless and everlasting city in which certain recurrent events and mechanisms occur and operate in a space-time generated by cyclical and labyrinthine temporal patterns. Moreover, Ackroyd's and his characters' perambulations are not primarily politically subversive as he is chiefly interested in the intricate, subtle and often contradictory relationship between personal and official histories within the city as an aggregate of commonly shared experience. Therefore, regardless of Ackroyd's occasional tendency to espouse and promote certain unorthodox, irrational or even radical tendencies and phenomena, his concept of London is generally traditionalist: "Ackroyd's position is one of inherent conservatism in which all change is subsumed within this unending historical overview," and in his psychogeographic approach "political commitment is sacrificed to historical tradition."[16] His is a fundamentally idealistic vision of the city, one which is based on reconciliation rather than discord, integration rather than incongruity.

Paradoxically, although Ackroyd would definitely not label his writing as psychogeographic, "the publication of his mammoth *London: the Biography* in 2000 has been hailed as the moment when psychogeography entered the mainstream."[17] In its introduction Ackroyd invites his readers to accompany him on his roaming around London and across its history, yet he points out the ultimate inscrutability of the city, which inevitably renders the walker an inactive, astounded observer and receiver of countless stimuli who can only approach its immensity and obscurity through a series of epiphanies which may allow him or her, though mostly temporarily, to glance at the city in its complexity and diversity:

> The readers of this book must wander and wonder. They may become lost upon the way; they may experience moments of uncertainty, and on occasions strange fantasies or theories may bewilder them. On certain streets various eccentric or vulnerable people will pause beside them, pleading for attention. There will be anomalies and contradictions – London is so large and so wild that it contains no less than everything – just as there

16 Coverley, *Psychogeography*, 27.
17 Coverley, *Psychogeography*, 123–24.

will be irresolutions and ambiguities. But there will also be moments of revelation, when the city will be seen to harbour the secrets of the human world. Then it is wise to bow down before the immensity. (*LB*, 3)

Employing the methods of historiography, biography and topography, together with conjecture and poetic license, the book is a paean to a timeless London, an attempt at composing the city's many-sided yet ultimately fascinating literary image, a self-contained and self-sustained textual construct whose author's research and methods include the investigation of impacts of the urban milieu on its dwellers' mental processes.

Ackroyd's approach to London sees the aspects of its "unofficial" history as being as, or even more, important than "official" ones. Therefore, in accordance with contemporary narrative concern "with the abstract quality of provincial urban dynamics,"[18] *London: The Biography* always tries to discover and look into hidden, dubious, enigmatic or otherwise irrational forces, elements and mechanisms and, consequently, find their impact on the city's more apparent manifestations. As a result, certain discourses which are not grounded in rational reasoning become an inseparable part of his London's texture. By this focus on the dark sides of London, Ackroyd attempts to lay bare its latent, unconscious levels and processes, thus "developing a kind of gothic psychogeography that explores [...] the more extreme forms of behavioural response provoked by the city."[19] It is precisely the extremity of the obscure and the uncanny that he believes continually affects and underlines the city's orderly and mundane experience, a persuasion also to be found at the core of his London novels.

Having declared the composition of an exhaustive, continuous history of the city impossible, Ackroyd's concept of London is deliberately prone to fragmentation. The sequencing of historical events is reduced to a mere overall framework within which the book's inner structure can become loose, diversified, and sometimes even inconsistent, yet always interconnected through recurrent temporal patterns. Ackroyd calls this concept "chronological resonance" (EEL, 339), seeing this labyrinthine city as one in which the present always echoes and re-experiences the past, which shapes and prescribes not only the inhabitants' behaviour, but also their very character and identity. His method thus combines a psychogeographic approach with a kind of historico-mystical antiquar-

---

18   Philip Tew, *The Contemporary British Novel*, 89.
19   Coverley, *Psychogeography*, 124–25.

ianism whose "sense of endlessly recycled past negates any attempt by individuals to change the fundamental nature of their environment" as their "actions and beliefs [...] are seemingly of little or no consequence."[20] Ackroyd is concerned with the personality or character of the city, which involves and by far surpasses that of its dwellers:

> Thus, in his novels and biographies, Peter Ackroyd practices a 'phrenology' of London. He feels up the bumps of the city and so he defines its character and proclivities. To read Ackroyd is to become aware that while the physical and political structure of London may have mutated down the ages, as torrents of men and women coursed through its streets, yet their individuality is as nothing, set beside the city's own enduring personification.[21]

Though in both *London: The Biography* and his London novels Ackroyd elaborates on the idea of the city as a total sum of human experience and energy and focuses on an individual's perception of the urban milieu, it is London that remains his main hero because of its imprinting on its inhabitants' minds, its all-encompassing space-time continuum and all-pervading defining principle, which transcends and crucially determines the fates of all those ever involved with it. It is an infinite city which "goes beyond any boundary or convention" and "contains every wish or word ever spoken, every action or gesture ever made" (*LB*, 760). His psychogeographic antiquarianism consists in collecting a variety of texts and narratives, both official and private or popular, that he assumes have come into existence as a result of London's impact on its dwellers' mental processes, and exploring the related experience of those who have been, directly or not, affected by them. All these reflect its spirit, but in his novels Ackroyd is far from being a passive antiquarian or archivist as he, in order to compose a fictitious biographical history of his beloved city, always revels in exploiting the texts further by rewriting, recycling and juxtaposing them, drawing speculative connections between them, and also between them and their authors' and readers' individual as well as collective psyches.

---

20 Coverley, *Psychogeography*, 127.
21 Self, *Psychogeography*, 11.

Two Related Concepts

Interestingly, an approach to London truly related to Ackroyd's own can be found, not in the writings of the most acknowledged practitioners of psychogeography but in Michael Moorcock's *Mother London* (1988) and Penelope Lively's *City of the Mind* (1991). Moorcock's psychogeographic-antiquarian exploration of London, covering a timespan from the Blitz to the present, is articulated through the characters of Joseph Kiss and David Mummery whose physical and mental existence is inseparable from the city. Although Moorcock's novel follows the life stories of three main and several minor characters, London remains its crucial theme as well as its major protagonist, and as such it is even ascribed a parental dimension: "London is my mother, source of most of my ambivalences and most of my loyalties,"[22] claims the "urban anthropologist" (*ML*, 7) Mummery, suggesting that the city by far transcends the earthly reality of its inhabitants.

Both Kiss and Mummery are proud and obsessed London walkers who map the city through visiting its diverse commonplace topographical landmarks as well as sites of obscure happenings and eerie history. By doing so, they try to chronicle the city's development, spirit and nature through various forms of narratives which have, especially in the case of the one-time music hall performer Joseph Kiss, a notably theatrical character. As a result, *Mother London* presents a manifold and vivid image of the city which combines rational empiricism with imagination, facts with fiction, without privileging one over the other, and the fact that all the main protagonists are outpatients at a psychiatric hospital only adds to the novel's central conceit, that the distinctive character of the city calls for a revision of the conventional, supposedly clear-cut borderlines between opposites, such as truth-fabrication, reality-imagination, objectivity-subjectivity, or sanity-lunacy.

Moorcock's vision, like Ackroyd's, is of a sublime quality, emphasising the city's "exquisitely complex geometry, a geography passing beyond the natural to become metaphysical" (*ML*, 7). The two writers also espouse a very similar concept of time in and of the city in which the past, the present and the future are impossible to separate as each contains moments of the others, creating a perpetual continuum consisting of countless directions and passages, forming convoluted or even labyrinthine patterns, "like a faceted jewel with an infinity of planes and

---

22   Michael Moorcock, *Mother London*, 27. In all subsequent references to this novel the abbreviation *ML* is used in parentheses in the text.

layers impossible either to map or to contain" (*ML*, 486). The most apparent common feature of Ackroyd's and Moorcock's London is a belief in the intrinsic interconnectedness of the city and its inhabitants' psyches through the narratives it inspires them to create, be they diaries, myths, legends, tall tales, anecdotes or popular rhymes[23]. As they represent a crucial line of the city's continuity, they must be traced along old, forgotten, often obliterated routes and sites, which can only be disclosed by means of urban instinct, intuition and association. And so *Mother London* closes with a psychogeographic image, itself mythical and visionary, of the wanderer Nonny who chooses her paths "out of singular tensions, eccentric decisions, whimsical habit, so that she appears to move at random when actually she travels ancient and well-used arteries" (*ML*, 495), spreading her stories, old and recent, based on reality as well as fanciful, trading them for hospitality as she migrates from place to place. Through his antiquarian (re-)narrating of the city Moorcock contributes to and helps perpetuate this myth-making process, aware that "London endures" as long as "[h]er stories endure" (*ML*, 110–111).

Although Penelope Lively's fiction is rather noted for its middle-class, middle-aged heroines created "to frame her own survey of a fractured English society,"[24] *City of the Mind*, which thoroughly examines the various impacts of London on the mind of one of its sensitive walkers, shows a considerable affinity with Ackroyd's rendering of the interaction between the city and its inhabitants' psyches. Lively's London is based on a coexistence of various forms of time where the past, present and future perpetually collide and mingle. "For this is the city, in which everything is simultaneous. There is no yesterday, no tomorrow [...]. The city digests itself, and regurgitates. It melts away, and rears up once again more in another form."[25] It is a city which, despite all its decay and destructive forces, manages to rise again, partly intact, partly changed, yet always strong enough to preserve its vitality. This is an image similar to that which concludes Ackroyd's first novel, *The Great Fire of London*.

The concept of the simultaneous city is closely connected with its presence in each inhabitant's mind which "creates its own images, a bril-

---

23 Christoph Houswitschka in his article "This fabulous flotsam": Michael Moorcock's Urban Anthropology in "London under London," for instance, shows how various traumatic narratives of a number of the Blitz generation members shift the novel's emphasis "from the psychological condition of the individual that re-mythologises the prosaic geography as part of the generational collective" (64).

24 Dominic Head, *The Cambridge Introduction to Modern British Fiction, 1950–2000*, 79.

25 Penelope Lively, *City of the Mind*, 24. In all subsequent references to this novel the abbreviation *CM* is used in parentheses in the text.

liant mythic universe" (*CM*, 204). For Matthew Halland, an architect and the main protagonist, the city is a state of mind; being a Londoner is not only a matter of being physically present there but, above all, of letting the city enter and encapsulate one's mental world in order to prevent the reduction of one's existence to its physicality or instrumentality. Although its characters do not trespass on obscure, peripheral and off-limit territories, and their walks lack any political or subversive purpose, the motif of the vanishing city and its impacts on the protagonists' psyches make the novel a parallel to more distinctly psychogeographic narratives. Lively's London has a unique topography, which is not created merely by its actual landscape, but is determined also by its spiritual dimension – its *genius loci*, its atmosphere, its sense of its history and its invincible ability to survive. Similarly to Ackroyd's London, this city of the mind is a net of allusions to architecture, history, biology, multiethnicity and other historical, social, cultural and scientific phenomena, representing a guide to both intellectual and emotional selves, one of languages, narratives and practices which produce a great variety of discourses, and through which history asserts its undeniable voice to comment on the often senseless conquest of the present.

London of the Mind

In Ackroyd's London novels, the city "is posited as affecting not only the conscious development of its inhabitants, but also their unconscious gestures."[26] In his own antiquarian psychogeographical manner, Ackroyd thus shares the "belief that we must turn to the city in order to examine the distinctive conditions of contemporary life,"[27] which he demonstrates to the greatest extent on the large cast of characters in *The Great Fire of London*. The only "city" Little Arthur's mental disorder enables him to safely inhabit is his Fun City, a semi-virtual oasis of light and order over which, unlike the disorderly and insidious city outside, he can exercise sufficient control. For Audrey Skelton's fragile psyche the city becomes particularly hostile after she identifies herself as Little Dorrit and is dismissed from her job; she scarcely leaves her home at all, save for occasional night wanderings over the site of the old Marshalsea prison in order to discover who her newly emerging identity is, and the two occa-

---

26 Murray, *Recalling London: Literature and History in the work of Peter Ackroyd and Iain Sinclair*, 76.
27 Susan Brook, "Hedgemony? Suburban space in *The Buddha of Suburbia*," 209.

sions when she attempts to sabotage the film through which she believes "they" intend to take hold of the poor little girl's soul, the second of which results in her setting fire to the film's London sets. Symptomatically, she is assisted by those representing the underside of the city – the tramps who loiter around the area where the film sets are located. Audrey intuitively seeks help from these people, whose fates and, consequently, relationships with the city are in a way similar to hers, for the tramps "had been neglected so universally and for so long that they no longer felt responsible for their actions" (*GFL*, 161). It is this feeling of being neglected and downtrodden by the outside world, of which the city becomes the most convenient and obvious materialisation, that unites the paranoid, baffled girl with the homeless men in their incendiary act. In effect, though for different reasons, they all believe that by burning down the sets "[t]hey would be doing London a favour" (*GFL*, 162): making it a better place for Audrey/Dorrit by destroying the unnamed, nefarious machinery, and providing rightful vengeance for the tramps by doing to the city what it has done to them.

Rowan Philips is lured to the city by its otherness, openness and diversity, qualities that are always rewarding and easily obtainable, which is reflected in his initial enthusiastic and would-be worldly-wise approach to searching for where the Marshalsea prison used to be. His pre-experienced London is thus an idealised, fantasy construct inevitably doomed to be challenged in direct confrontation with reality. Therefore, when he realises how superficial and spiritually unfulfilling his one-night sexual adventures are for him, he blames London rather than his foolishness and naivety, as if in other big cities the effects of anonymous sex are different: "In other cities the night is full of movement and possibility; in London, it is like a cloth placed over the cage of a bird. But Rowan was attempting to escape from himself, and darkness was an appropriate cover" (*GFL*, 73). In actuality, no city is big enough to allow Rowan to hide from himself, from his inability to admit and accept the true cause of his despair. He understands this when he falls for Tim, yet when the drunk and emotionally frustrated Tim eventually agrees to intimate contact with Rowan, the latter feels uneasy and abashed again, this time from the possibility of getting what he has long yearned for, fearing potential disappointment, and comparing Tim, ironically enough, to the city that has already disappointed his expectations: "Tim had been an emblem of what for Rowan had always been unattainable, romantic even; that vast chaotic urban life which had before existed for him only in books. Now, however, the unattainable was becoming all too attainable" (*GFL*, 130).

Due to his obstinate dwelling in a world of fantasies and his unwillingness to abandon it and face up to a sometimes bitter reality, Rowan fails to understand both the city and Tim, who inevitably becomes for him a detached, theoretical construct, too perfect in its abstract form to retain its quality when given some practical shape.

Letty Spender's states of mind are also closely linked to how she perceives the city, its life and its inhabitants. When she starts her affair with Andrew Christopher she suddenly feels free to do what she likes regardless of the consequences for other people's lives, and she identifies this careless and morally evasive freedom with the condition of the metropolis. "She would brave the city" (*GFL*, 65), she thinks when she finds it audacious to stroll around London on Andrew's arm while she is still officially living with her husband, suggesting that her private morality, no matter how hypocritical, is superior to what she assumes to be the norm in the city. It is only the disclosure of what Andrew is really like that opens her eyes and she is able to look at the city in a less prejudiced way during her, now more and more frequent, long walks through the streets. Letty realises that her view of the city has been rather simplistic, and that its true nature could possibly be known only through direct experience:

> Reflections such as these occurred fitfully to her as she walked through London at the beginning of spring. She found herself attracted to tall, dark streets where the new season had for some reason been refused entry. And yet the streets seemed to spawn life: she had never before realised quite how many people surrounded her in the course of her own daily activities. It was only when she, as it were, dropped out, and wandered without direction or purpose, that the fullness of the city presented itself to her. (*GFL*, 116)

Letty strives to glance at herself in this great psychic mirror, and she soon understands that this is impossible with the outwardly knowing but emotionally shallow and spiritually sterile Andrew. At this point, she seems to understand that the city's vigour and energy stem not from the glamorous, dehumanised pomposity and vanity of the milieu of the rich and powerful, but from its common streets and the millions of ordinary people who inhabit them.

Letty's city transforms into the sum of all its denizens, their fates and experience, famous and ordinary alike, as these people transmute in her imagination into all the individual, defining features of modern urban life in which "[s]he could have drowned" (*GFL*, 134–135). In this process of drowning she thus becomes part of the collective psyche of the city which, in effect, becomes a city of her mind, her mind's reflection and indicator. When she feels abandoned and betrayed by Andrew, her despair is suddenly detectable from all she observes around, which intensifies her suffering but, at the same time, offers her certain comfort: "Everyone around looked shabby and dirty – the whole city was undergoing some fundamental deterioration which marked its inhabitants like the evidence of some ugly disease. [...] any corroboration of her condition was better than none. She did not want to be alone" (*GFL*, 135). Paradoxically, her awareness that the city produces pain and distress not only in herself but in other people brings consolation to Letty, especially when she reaches a deadlock concerning the direction her personal life should take. Therefore, in Letty's case the city assumes an ambivalent role – it is both a call for help and a source of rescue, a symptom of a malady as well as a means of its curing.

Once again, the parallel with Dickens and his London in *Little Dorrit* suggests itself here, as the mood and atmosphere of some of the novel's city scenes reflect its author's state of mind. In the final days of 1885, Dickens worked on the depiction of the heroine's passage though the wastes of London. It had been a hard year for the writer, he had been slowly recovering from a bad cold and eye infection, while simultaneously moving between London and Paris, and so he felt tired, overworked, and depressed, associating his distress with the urban milieu. Under these circumstances, he became absorbed in the gloomy tones of his narrative and it soon grew beyond its intended scope, "bringing with it all of the weariness and sadness which Dickens now associated with the city. [...] Here we may see in part the origins of that image of imprisonment which critics have detected running through the novel" (*D*, 390). Such imagery resembles Rowan's and Letty's mental images of the city. It is notable that the text which serves Ackroyd as the thread sewing together the unfortunate fates of his London characters was in part written for autotherapeutic purposes, one in which the city becomes a self-reflective metaphor of not only its characters' but also its author's troubled psyche.

The character who has the most optimistic, almost cordial, attitude to the city is Spenser Spender. For him, London is an infinitely fascinating puzzle whose diverse mechanisms no one can ever fully know, but which is still worth exploring. He is very sensitive to those elements of the city which are somewhat mysterious, obscure or ambiguous, or which defy purely rational explication, such as, for instance, the pentagram formed by the imaginary line drawn between all of Nicholas Hawksmoor's churches. Spenser also believes that Charles Dickens was one of the few who were close to understanding the city and its inhabitants' ways and acts. As a film director, his ambition is to make a film about his beloved city which would authentically capture its spirit, and so he chooses to film Dickens's *Little Dorrit*, from which he would remove all the parts that take place outside London. Having conceived this plan, he imagines the particular London scenes and sequences, as a result of which he becomes so excited that he suddenly sees himself part of the great London tradition, which endows him with an invincible vigour and vitality:

> Spenser Spender was filled with a sensation of lightness, as though his own body were moving out, too, across the water, implicated in the lives of these human beings who trudged slowly through the dark. Each human figure seemed to emit its own brightness, so that the bridge itself resembled a line of energy, and one of irresistible momentum and sweetness. Spenser Spender was too elated to reflect then upon this experience; but he knew that it would remain with him, if he took care to nourish it. (*GFL*, 37)

Spenser becomes aware that belonging to this immense continuum of experience and energy is not only unavoidable but, above all, beneficial for all those who are able and willing to recognise their role, cultivate it, and appreciate its consequences. Although rather intuitive and sensual than rational, Spenser's realisation makes him the only person in the novel who can actually relish the city and whose personality is the least susceptible to the impacts of its negative manifestations.

Spenser thus wishes his film to be a homage and a paean to London, a celebration of its diversity, energy and lack of restraint, though the idyll is violated by the Film Finance Board's decision to substantially cut his funding. Like the other characters, he contemplates his unhappiness while walking aimlessly and half absent-mindedly around London. At the moment of crisis, Spenser proves to be a strong personality, especially thanks to his open-minded and unbiased attitude toward the city. He is aware it is his mind, not the milieu, that has been affected by the bad news: "The street seemed the same, the traffic crawled past in its usual manner, but Spenser's relationship to the world has been subtly altered" (*GFL*, 153). Rather than blaming the city for his misfortune, he seeks support and refuge in it. However, he knows that the city can only help those who "deserve" it, only those who are mentally and emotionally strong and balanced enough to stand on their own feet. The shattered Spenser finds such balance in his love for Letty, which he finally realises after she leaves him. No matter how complicated the mechanisms of city life are, Ackroyd suggests that in order to cope with them people can always rely on the most essential, and thus universal, human and humanistic values. Equipped with a confidence and assertiveness springing from his regained love, feeling that his despondency "was replaced by a settled conviction that his own fate was simply one of millions upon millions tumbling upon each other like a mountain of crystals" (*GFL*, 155), Spenser is ready to move freely in his London again and fully enjoy this freedom of mind and spirit.

Spenser comes to understand that it is pointless to fight or defy the city rather than comply with its demands – if the city devours the weak and the insecure but caters for and props up the balanced and the self-assured, all one must do is to avoid being in the first category, and Spenser is suddenly filled with the persuasion that he is one of those who are capable of benefiting from the city's bright sides: "He had walked for some miles, and when he looked back he saw the sky glowing with that orange which is the city's reflected light. It was like a furnace burning and turning, destroying everything it touched, but becoming also a source of energy and light" (*GFL*, 155–156). Indeed, Spenser draws much of his creative and working energy from the city, and it is the city that gives him the strength and optimism for his planning of the final grand, panoramic London scene of his film. Though reconciled with the fact that his original project has been doomed, he still, at least in his imagination, projects a vision "of London, crowded, packed with life, with the figures of Little Dorrit, Mr Dorrit and Little Mother the simpleton moving haphazardly through the crowd – but not lost within that crowd, rather sustained by its energy and momentum, feeling the impetus of a shared life" (*GFL*, 157). Despite all the odds of his life, Spenser tries to comprehend, embody and creatively capture the very spirit of the city. All the more surprising then is the tragic fate which Ackroyd prepares for his hero, symbolically ruining all his professional hopes and aspirations. The novel's Great Fire of London thus also assumes a symbolic meaning apart from that of mere physical catastrophe:

> It destroyed much that was false and ugly, and much that was splendid and beautiful. Some longed for it to burn everything, but for others a new and disquieting sense of impermanence entered their lives. Eventually, legends were to grow around it. It was popularly believed to have been a visitation, a prophecy of yet more terrible things to come. (*GFL*, 165)

It is as if there is no justice in the London of the novel: on the one hand, the unhappy yet likeable characters such as Tim and Rowan are left without prospects or consolation, Little Arthur opens the doors of the prison for the other inmates to flow into the streets but stays motionless inside himself, and the only person who has shown some understanding and appreciation for the city dies during a futile attempt at saving the scenery from the fire. On the other hand, the irrational, subversive and obscure forces triumph: the insane Audrey manages to sabotage the sinister "conspiracy" of the outside world, the homeless vagrants complete their vendetta upon the indifferent and uncaring city, and the prisoners enjoy, at least temporarily, the air of freedom. The role of the fire is ambiguous, like the nature of the city – it is destructive as well as cleansing, it brings about devastation as well as rebirth, evoking Ackroyd's favourite image of a phoenix-like city, "translating itself and rising as other from its ashes to produce itself anew."[28] Yet, above all, it is a warning about what can happen if the heterogeneous elements of the city are suppressed, ignored and neglected for too long.

A different concept of the city of the mind can be found in *The Casebook of Victor Frankenstein*. It may read as a parody or pastiche of Mary Shelley's *Frankenstein*, yet Ackroyd's rendering of the classic myth is far from being a merely modernised version of the original since it challenges Frankenstein's role within the narrative, and, in consequence, his status as a narrator and the very credibility of the story told. The novel represents yet another attempt to exploit the genre of urban Gothic novel since it offers an imaginative rendering of a Gothic myth that combines a highly subjective confession with historiographic and psychogeographic perspectives. There is one defining feature of the urban Gothic that the novel in particular exemplifies: the imminent interference of the city's past into its present. "For Gothic *of* a city rather than just in a city, the city needs a concentration of memories and historical associations."[29] The city can thus be taken as a determining constituent of a collective psyche which projects itself into each of its dweller's conscious or unconscious psychic processes. Witchard and Phillips identify this property of the city as crucial for urban Gothic fiction, noting that "[t]he ancient and the modern live in uncomfortable proximity in the imaginary of London. The past is celebrated but has increasingly become something that can disturb, disrupt and dominate the contemporary inhabitant even as social and cultural progress inexorably shifts towards the 'new' fabric of the city."[30] Similarly, the London of *The Casebook of Victor Frankenstein* is

---

28 Julian Wolfreys, *Writing London. Volume 2: materialisty, memory, spectrality*, 14.

29 Robert Mighall, "Gothic Cities," 57.

30 Anne Witchard and Lawrence Phillips, "Introduction," 3.

full of such "spectres" of the past, be they those of its renowned personages' accomplishments which contemporaries struggle to rival, or ill-fated areas of recurrent vicious crimes whose *genii locorum* still discourage law-abiding city dwellers from setting foot in them.

At the same time, Ackroyd undermines some of the characteristic principles of the Gothic, especially by his deliberate abandoning of its temporal vagueness by setting his novel in a specific period and by incorporating genuine historical personalities into the story. The characters of the Shelleys, Byron, Polidori, Godwin and others not only make the story more interesting to read but, above all, give the novel the new dynamic of an autonomous work of art rather than of a mere literary joke, one that makes use of pastiche, parody, intertextuality and metafiction in order to offer another attempt at casting light on the rise of the great Romantic myth. By doing this, Ackroyd carefully prepares the ground for the central metaphor of the narrative – London as a state of mind, an indicator of the unbalanced mental disposition of the novel's main protagonist – by exploring and mapping the territories of the city's underbelly, which are peopled by the impoverished, the diseased, criminals, outlaws and other dubious individuals inhabiting areas safely remote from the city's "official" public zones. So Frankenstein comes into contact with London political radicals when he attends a Popular Reform League meeting; Daniel Westbrook shows him round the most miserable and deprived districts of the city's underworld; he meets the resurrectionists, or Doomsday Men, grave robbers lacking all human dignity whose status as citizens is not even officially acknowledged; he experiences the restless London crowd and mob, first in the theatre and then, in its worst form, during the trial and execution of Westbrook. The novel abounds with fearful images of urban civilisation's collective neurosis, foreshadowing thus its main subject matter – Frankenstein's progressive mental deterioration, well-disguised by his cunningly misleading narration delivered from the perspective of bewildered Christian humanity. Moreover, he searches for a place for his secret laboratory in "the less respectable areas of the city" (*CVF*, 119) of Wapping and Rotherhithe, overcrowded and squalid at that time[31], eventually finding suitably desolate premises in Limehouse right by the Thames, not far from the site of the famous Ratcliffe Highway murders of 1811. For an Ackroyd reader familiar with the author's belief in the power of the *genius loci*, this is a telling indication that Frankenstein (sub)consciously plunges into the

---

31   Ian Cunningham, *A Reader's Guide to Writers' London*, 181.

very depths of the city's madness and fury, and is doomed to be engulfed by its homicidal lines of force.

The city as a metaphor for the main protagonist's sick mind occurs very early in the novel, after Frankenstein attends the "galvanising" lecture of Humphry Davy. Having left the lecture room, he, for the first time, feels burdened by another self, a shadow that follows him through the streets of London and he experiences a strong urge "to escape the confines of the city" (*CVF*, 31). However, the phantasm pursues him beyond the edge of the city where it even "saves" him from falling down when Frankenstein stumbles on a root. When Frankenstein eventually regains consciousness after a nervous breakdown, his personality is altered: "I experienced a curious sense of acceptance – not of relief or gratitude – when I had no notion of any burden being taken from me. I believed that I have been marked out in a way that I could not then comprehend" (*CVF*, 32). He is not only fully aware of his disorder but takes it as a sign of his exclusivity, seeing himself as a person chosen for some higher mission. When he turns back to London, its frightening image is gone, its noise reminding him of "a confused but not inharmonious muttering [...] an inchoate roar of vast life momentary stilled" (*CVF*, 33), and he walks back towards the city peacefully. That the "inchoate roar" of the city parallels his inchoate madness appears to be plain enough. Throughout the novel, the city is recurrently employed as a reflection of his states of mind: he appreciates the soothing "immensity of London coming to life" (*CVF*, 156) after he has learnt the terrifying intensity of the electric fluid; he experiences the redeeming solitude of night walks in the otherwise "teeming city" (*CVF*, 165) while carrying out his experiments; when he is returning from a journey to the country, he can smell London as if he could smell the monster (*CVF*, 200); he walks absent-mindedly through the city during his hallucinations; and in the end, he walks through the streets accompanied by his "creation," casting a shadow that is "bent forward, hastening onwards as if it had an existence of its own" (*CVF*, 383), showing that his acts are far beyond his conscious control. For the possessed Frankenstein, the cityscape and its spirit perfectly mirror his wounded psyche. Ackroyd's Gothic London is a display of the various irrational aspects of the city but, above all, a terrain of lunacy, a reflection of the main protagonist's deranged mind.

What makes Ackroyd's version of *Frankenstein* original, apart from the conceit of the protagonist's double personality, is the employment of the unreliable "mad monologist" narrator complemented by the lively explorations of London's lowlife and irrationalities, developing the image of the city as a reflection of Frankenstein's progressing insanity. The city can thus be read as a metaphor of the essential unknowability and inconceivability of the narrator's obscured mind as it is depicted as "ultimately unknowable, for it rewrites itself and erases itself even in those moments of apprehension when its identity seems understood finally. However, this does not prohibit either the novelist or the reader's desire to trace the unreadable, in the effort to make connections."[32] Ackroyd's city of fear is much more complex than those typical of traditional Gothic fiction: it is a playful combination of the factual and the fictitious, of scenes from everyday early nineteenth-century London life and the delirious visions of one of its unfortunate inhabitants. The fact that Ackroyd makes no distinction between these two narrative modes gives the story a special atmosphere and dynamism, but also makes readers easily forget the various hints scattered in the text and read the novel as an ordinary horror story until the final twist brings them back to the enticing yet disturbing intertextual and metafictional reality of the author's fictional world.

Lawrence Phillips notes that "within the modern tradition of representing London [...] there is a constant pull towards both the tropic (image, memory) and the discursive (narrative, history) in creative tension with the physical presence and lived experience of the city,"[33] a tendency clearly identifiable, with various modifications, in Ackroyd's London fiction. *Chatterton*, for instance, not only presents a mental reflection of its characters' attitude to or relationship with the urban milieu and topography, but also links it with another image of the city as a place of eccentricity and excess, peopled by a number of peculiar and obscure characters such as comic Dickensian antique shop owners, the Lenos (whose name may immediately remind readers of the famous Victorian music-hall comedian Dan Leno), or oddly-behaving regular public library visitors. Charles Wychwood and Harriet Scrope are both writers and eccentric personalities, so the city for them is to a large extent a product of their imaginations, or at least material their imaginations can tailor into a world of their own. Thus Charles keeps addressing almost everything he encounters, while Harriet seeks the calming effect of walking the streets, in the process talking to random passers-by in an extravagant Mockney (mock-Cockney) accent, but also renaming the streets metaphorically in order to reflect her perception of these places: "In the course of these long and erratic journeys she had renamed all the

32   Jeremy Gibson and Julian Wolfreys, *Peter Ackroyd: The Ludic and Labyrinthine Text*, 172.
33   Phillips, *London Narratives: Post-War Fiction and the City*, 6.

familiar streets around her, and now it was through The Valley of Bones, Tarts' Paradise and The Boulevard of Broken Dreams that she made her way" (*C*, 29). The city of their mind is thus a half-real and half-imagined place, a dreamland of its kind, a world that needs to be animated or otherwise transformed into a more appealing one resembling that of their literary works.

For the novel's Chatterton, on the other hand, London becomes a symbol of his career as a writer, a place of countless opportunities, a promised land of a bright future. Bored and annoyed with the provinciality of his native Bristol, all his thoughts and hopes are pinned on London, and when he finally gets there he is "lost in a Maze of Admiration long before [he is] ever lost in the Maze of the Streets" (*C*, 88). For the young aspiring poet, the bustling city represents all he could have ever hoped for – an exhilarating life, success, and social status, which is why he enjoys being a part of the city's very texture. Such a London, however, is not a real city, but an abstract, projected one, as the idealistic and inexperienced boy is not yet able to distinguish between the two substantially different experiences of seeing the city from above and the actual walking of its streets. As Michel de Certeau comments on the first, "the panorama-city is a 'theoretical' (that is, visual) simulacrum, in short a picture, whose condition of possibility is an oblivion and a misunderstanding of practices,"[34] it is a voyeuristic, totalising construct of the city as a homogeneous, lucid and therefore graspable and controllable entity, a text that can be easily read and comprehended.

> He opens the window wide, breathing in the air. He can hear the sound of the cattle bellowing in Smithfield, and already the carriages are hurrying down High Holborn, but these noises delight him. They accompany the rush of his own pride and ambition as he faces the summer day, and in a strong melodic voice he sings out across the rooftops the latest comic song from the Vauxhall Gardens. (*C*, 191)

On the other hand, the practice of walking the streets shows that all one gets down on the ground are heterogeneously inconsistent and fragmentary images which can never compose any coherent whole. This in effect transforms the complacent, detached voyeurs into vulnerable walkers "whose bodies follow the thicks and thins of an urban 'text'

---

34   Michel de Certeau, *The Practice of Everyday Life*, 93.

they write without being able to read it."[35] Chatterton is soon to understand this difference when he encounters the physical manifestation of the city's misery and indifference to the suffering of those affected by poverty and other unfortunate strokes of fate, and realises his previous self-delusion. "When I first came to London I thought I had entered a new age of miracles, but these stinking alleys and close packed tenements seem to breed monsters. Monsters of our own making..." (*C*, 211), he notes after visiting a poverty-stricken East End area and experiencing what brooding and ghastly shapes the city in reality can assume. The naïve young man, unpractised in living in a big city, only slowly learns to read the topography of the London streets and not confuse his idealising self-projections and wishful thinking for the harsh reality, yet he is unaware of the fatal consequences such an awakening might have for his fragile and vulnerable consciousness.

Ackroyd's Lonely Londoners

One of the distinctive features of Ackroyd's London is the number of lonely or isolated individuals who inhabit his city. These loners, both forced and willing, fictitious and real historical personages, strive, with varying success, to make their way in the immense, and therefore sometimes alienating and hostile, metropolis. Some of them are lonely because of their unprivileged status, social, economic or both, some because of their introverted or shy character, some because they espouse values and ideas different from or even opposing the majority society's conventions and expectations. There are also characters who end up isolated because they become somehow possessed, in the good and the bad sense of the word, with an idea, a vision, or with what they perceive as a personal quest. Naturally, what can be found at the core of most of these people's loneliness is a profound unhappiness resulting from their feelings of frustration, deprivation and incomprehension and an awareness or feeling of their personal failure. Inhabiting London and unable or unwilling to leave it, they often find themselves in a paradoxical situation: they identify the city as one of the crucial causes of their despair, yet they seek refuge and solace exactly in the milieu they have been at odds with, as if hoping or subconsciously feeling that being reconciled with the city could help them reassemble their broken identity and perhaps also

---

35 de Certeau, *The Practice of Everyday Life*, 93.

find their way to other people. The role of Ackroyd's London is therefore ambiguous or even contradictory, breeding misery in its less fortunate inhabitants' lives and, at the same time, serving as an ultimate agent of healing their wounded psyches.

The theme and motif of loneliness and isolation permeates all Ackroyd's London novels, for the first time, and probably most notably, forming the story's fundamental background in *The Great Fire of London*. There is no one central protagonist in the novel but a cast of miscellaneous characters whose fates become gradually interconnected through their involvement, direct or indirect, conscious or unintentional, voluntary or imposed, in Spenser Spender's project of making a film version of *Little Dorrit*. Enclosed in their lonely, separate lives they are only (semi-)accidentally and momentarily brought together as the story progresses as "they meet and part like travellers in Dickens's inspirational image."[36] Therefore, the common denominator of all these characters is their feeling of being left alone in a world which seems to offer very little consolation for those who prove incapable of coping with the demands of modern city life. As a result, as they wrestle with their anxieties and frustrations, they look for or devise various escapist strategies and protective mechanisms, such as searching for new sexual relationships, having recourse to spiritualism, abusing alcohol, and devoting themselves entirely to their work, to which they desperately stick and in which they find refuge from what appears to them as a dead-end life situation. The effect, however, is mostly minute and short-lived, if not downright counterproductive, and they eventually find themselves even more alienated from their immediate environment.

The most grotesque member of this cast is Arthur Feather, or Little Arthur as he is nicknamed due to his dwarfish stature, a Dickensian caricatural half-wit. As such he can be listed along with other of Ackroyd's related London eccentrics or otherwise dubious individuals, such as the Lenos, the affectionate homosexual Pat, and Harriet Scrope in *Chatterton*, the Uncle in *Dan Leno and the Limehouse Golem*, or Hamo Fulberd in *The Clerkenwell Tales*. Little Arthur suffers not only from social isolation resulting from his physical handicap, but also from a serious form of psychosis which does not manifest itself only thanks to the fact that he devotes his whole existence to his job as an operator of the "Fun City" amusement arcade. When the arcade is closed Arthur's despair knows no limits, his wounded psyche soon loses touch with reality and his mental

---

36 Barry Lewis, *My Words Echo Thus: Possessing the Past in Peter Ackroyd*, 20.

disorder comes to the surface and he kills a little girl from the neighbour-hood in what he believes to be an act of saving her innocence from the snares of the hateful outside world. Yet, not even prison confinement restores peace to Arthur's semi-insane mind as, when the film crew arrive there to shoot some scenes for Spender's film, he identifies in the actress playing Little Dorrit the same girl he tried to "save" earlier and decides to repeat the altruistic act, this time by short-circuiting the electricity system of the prison, by which he sets the other inmates free.

Audrey Skelton is a young woman very much discontented with her life: she feels bored and unfulfilled in her job as a telephone operator and so she spends much of her time daydreaming about being some other person, rich and famous, imagining in detail what such a life would be like, a desire no one else around her seems to understand. As an ex-traordinarily sensitive person, Audrey is prone to succumbing to alluring fantasies and other outcomes of her vivid imagination which allow her to free herself from the constraints of her troublesome, conscious existence. She often lapses "into a kind of trance," as if "possessed," and thus repre-sents a mystery even "to those who knew, and loved, her best" (*GFL*, 8). After she visits the site where the prison which features in Dickens's novel used to stand, she at first starts dreaming about living in the novel's story and later, when she attends a spiritualist séance, she comes to believe her-self to be some sort of reincarnation of Amy Dorrit, a medium through which the poor little girl attempts to pass on some secret. This, however, throws Audrey into an even greater isolation as she becomes paranoid, fearing that "the clever ones" from the outside world want "to get hold of the secret" (*GFL*, 113), which she therefore must protect.

Thanks to his carefree and optimistic nature, Tim Coleman, Audrey's boyfriend, feels no worries concerning his life, most important-ly because he has an adorable and loving girlfriend. All this, however, proves to be very fragile and collapses like a house of cards when Audrey becomes possessed with the spirit of Amy Dorrit and loses all interest in her previous life, her boyfriend included. Having been repeatedly rejected or ignored by Audrey, Tim finds distraction and solace in the company of Rowan Phillips, at first in the form of searching for the lost London of Dickens's novels and later in drinking, followed by tentative, non-coital homosexual practices. However, when Rowan discovers that for Tim he is a mere intimate surrogate for the lost Audrey he refuses to see him again, which throws Tim into a more intensified state of helpless-ness and confusion, in which he so much identifies himself as a victim of external circumstances that he even comes to sympathise with Audrey and her peculiar behaviour. Filled with "feelings of rejection and uncertainty" (*GFL*, 142), hurt by how unjustly the outside world has been treating him, Tim desperately looks for any kind of crutch that would help him through his sudden emotional and sexual frustration. Audrey and Tim thus represent two different kinds of lonely Londoners who, in effect, face a similar situation – they have lost their former self somewhere in the tides of the city life's currents and are unable to recover it by themselves.

Rowan Phillips is no more successful in coping with the pressures of the city than Tim and Audrey. Dissatisfied with the provincialism and academic sterility of life in Cambridge, he goes to London with the belief that it can provide him with what will fulfil him most – sexual freedom and limitless opportunities to find an accessible object for his erotic fantasies. This he disguises under the "official" reason for moving to the city in order to be "close to his 'material'" (*GFL*, 19), that is Charles Dickens, about whom he is supposed to write a critical study. However, his frenetic searching for a sexual partner brings him no satisfaction or joy and he eventually really does turn to his work on Dickens, both for his study and the script of Spender's film, so as to "rescue himself from the day" (*GFL*, 21), from a growing sense of the emptiness and futility of his own miserable existence. Moreover, his despair deepens when he becomes strongly attracted to Tim, who cannot and does not return his affection in the manner he would like him to do. The frustrated Rowan bitterly realises that neither his night expeditions to gay bars nor his scholarly research can help him escape from himself, from his unhappiness resulting from the fact that what he actually longs for is not one-night, anonymous sex, but to care for someone who loves him back, which only intensifies his feelings of loneliness and rejection.

At first sight, Spenser Spender seems to be a different case as he has a job he likes, a wife he loves, and, moreover, is offered the chance to fulfil his professional dream of making his beloved Dickens's novel, *Little Dorrit*, into an artistically valuable feature film. He thus engages himself fully in realising his vision of making a film that would capture the very spirit of Dickensian London. However, he gradually becomes so absorbed in this project that he even starts to disregard his own wife, Laetitia, or Letty, who at first tries in vain to bring Spenser back to reality, and then seeks what she has been denied at home – attentiveness, tenderness and respect – from the polished and elegant, yet ultimately pompous and egotistical, Andrew Christopher, with whom she eventually moves in after she leaves her seemingly unconcerned husband. Spenser's personal loss is accompanied, as is often the case, with professional ones: the Film Finance Board cuts the funding for his film and he is forced to reduce the script and drastically limit his creative aspirations. On top of this, the film crew go on strike for better working conditions after one of the technicians gets hurt by a fallen arc-light in a minor accident. There is a gleam of hope for him when Letty, after a failed suicide attempt, returns to him and the two realise how much they love and need each other, yet Ackroyd lets him die in a futile attempt to save the film's London sets from burning in a fire set by the psychically disordered Audrey and a group of homeless vagrants whom she persuades to be her accomplices in this act of mindless arson.

The basis of *The Lambs of London*'s story is formed by the gripping depiction of the three main protagonists' personalities – Charles Lamb, his sister Mary and William Ireland. Charles is a young man in his early twenties who nourishes the dream of becoming a professional writer and sends his essays, with varying degrees of success, to several periodicals. In the meantime, to support his family he works as a clerk for the British East India Company, which bores him, and he seeks distraction in drinking with his colleagues or just by himself. Doubtful about his writing talent and frustrated by a job that does not fulfil him, Charles gets frequently moody, sinking easily from enthusiasm to sulkiness. Being eleven years her brother's senior, Mary is already past her marrying age and so she lives with her parents, helping her mother run the household, an activity for which she never receives appreciation from the other family members. She finds rare moments of happiness in reading and in looking after her irresponsible brother. As a disregarded, introverted, insecure and solitary person she is mentally vulnerable and prone to set her heart on whoever seems to show some concern for her little world. William Ireland, a youth of seventeen, is the least decipherable of the three. Equipped with gentlemanly manners and, for his age, a remarkable gift for handling the language, he manages to disguise his true character under a polished surface of polite kindheartedness. Hoping in vain for his writing to be published and acknowledged, feeling he is wasting his potential as a bookseller, envious of the success of others, his confidence further bruised by the dismissal of his talent and aspirations by his father, an insensitive man and "an unrepentant bardolator,"[37] the pragmatically unscrupulous Ireland is ready in his desperate ambition to make use of the Lambs for his own purposes.

---

37   Lewis, *My Words Echo Thus: Possessing the Past in Peter Ackroyd*, 140.

The novel proves Ackroyd's gift for creating strong, exciting and enticingly believable stories and characters. The central motif associated with all the story's major protagonists and, at the same time, the crucial means through which their fates become intertwined, is that of loneliness and isolation within the bustling life of the populous metropolis and the resulting feeling of frustration and despair, hinting at "Ackroyd's identification of cities with labyrinths" which "reinforces the interaction of these few characters as in some way localized, or disconnected from the metropolis as a whole."[38] Due to her social status and position as an unmarried woman, Mary Lamb is doomed to conform to the role of the dutiful daughter who rarely goes out into the city unaccompanied and remains for most of her time closed in the household she is supposed to look after, in the uninspiring company of her scornful and narrow-minded mother and the elderly, uneducated maid. There she feels "buried alive" (*LL*, 10), detached from the literary world of spiritual and intellectual stimuli she so much longs to be a part of. "The city is a great jakes" (*LL*, 1), she notes sadly, referring to how the city, despite the immense opportunities it offers, thwarts all her hopes and aspirations. She thus only lives through her independent reading and studying, the effects of which she shares with her brother, whose frequent departures from the house provoke in her "the strangest mixture of anger and loneliness" (*LL*, 11).

Charles Lamb fails to notice or understand his sister's unhappiness as he is too preoccupied with his own worries and insecurities, namely those concerning his aspiration to become a respectable and successful writer. Doing a job he does not like, and striving hard to get his writing published by following editors' demands and composing essays on subjects that do not interest him in the least, his frustration deepens as he fears his literary talent is not exploited properly and he might never receive recognition from London's literary circles. In order to escape disappointing reality, he spends most evenings drinking with his colleagues or alone, coming home drunk and sinking into oblivion as soon as his sister puts him to bed. As a result, even the more fortunate of the two siblings in terms of life opportunities often finds himself alone with his troubles and anxieties about having "no vision to sweep him past all the difficulties and disappointments of the literary life" (*LL*, 127). No matter how outwardly happy and confident he appears, there are occasions for the inwardly insecure and self-doubting Charles "when it merely reinforce[s] his sense of failure" (*LL*, 28). Similarly, William Ireland is also a loner,

---

38 Lawrence Phillips, *London Narratives: Post-War Fiction and the City*, 19.

one whose personality and life bear similarities to the Lambs: in terms of his, age, ambition and social status he is very like Charles Lamb, but unlike the more conventional and patient Lamb Ireland is much more discontented with his lot and refuses to "accept his youth and anonymity as handicaps."[39] Moreover, with a sensitivity, politeness and refined manners uncommon for a person of his age and social background, he is, like Mary, an old-fashioned figure, as if born out of his time, largely misunderstood, underestimated or even ignored, both in his own family as well as by other literary aspirants; and, though much less successful than Charles because of the class prejudice of the literati, his chief ambition is to become an acknowledged author despite the adversities of fate. Like Mary, Ireland thus lives in a forced, turned voluntary, isolation, yet in his case spiritual and mental rather than physical and social, and, like Charles, he sees the opportunities London offers, yet, simultaneously, he is well aware that the city can easily dash all his hopes.

Charles Wychwood, the main protagonist in *Chatterton*, is one of Ackroyd's most distinctive and charming characters. Although he is also, in a sense, a loner, his loneliness is of a different kind than that of Rowan Phillips, Spenser Spender, the Lambs or William Ireland for three main reasons. First, he is not essentially unhappy, though many circumstances actually suggest that he could easily be so: as an unrecognised and unpublished poet, suffering from writer's block, he fails to support his family and becomes dependent on his wife's income. Yet, he is convinced of his own poetic talent and the quality of his poetry, which speaks for itself and therefore needs no intercession or supplication to find its readership, devoting himself entirely to being a good father to his perceptive and quick-witted son Edward. Second, his relationships with his family and friends are far from dysfunctional: his son adores him and enjoys all the "adventures" and language games his father comes up with; his wife Vivien loves him tenderly and even protects him from intrusions from the outside world which could potentially distract him from writing; and his best friend, Philip Slack, another solitary, working in a public library "frequented by people as desperately lonely and shy as himself,"[40] is amiable, loyal and helpful whenever Charles needs him. And third, he finds himself under no obtrusive external pressure or oppression, economic, social or familial, which would force him to do what he does not like or approve of, or prevent him from doing what he would like to. Therefore,

39 Doug Steward, *The Boy Who Would Be Shakespeare: A Tale of Forgery and Folly*, 53.
40 Onega, *Peter Ackroyd*, 36.

everything he does he does out of his free will, interest and enthusiasm, and it is rather his wife who finds herself under emotional pressure relating to how to keep on running the household without disturbing her husband's poetic genius with shallow, uninspiring material concerns.

Charles's child-like, carefree, absent-minded nature makes him somewhat lonely in the adult world where his spontaneous enthusiasm, naïve credulity, daydreaming and compulsive playfulness are seen as signs of, at best, a silly eccentricity. He inhabits a distinct universe of his own which he animates and variegates with the help of his imagination – by telling stories to Edward, or, when walking alone, by conversing with himself and addressing almost everything he sees, from dogs to buildings. Yet, at the same time, there is something very mature in his visionary imagination, in his belief in a higher artistic and human purpose, consisting in freedom, individuality, creativity and pursuing and defending one's truths. He finds such a purpose in writing a book about the true fate of Thomas Chatterton, which would once and for all cast light on the mystery of the young forger's death, as well as clarify and fully appreciate his crucial role in the development of English Romantic poetry, believing that he will "rewrite history" and speculating "over the publicity that will greet his discovery, and the subsequent interest in his own poetry, lifting him out of poverty and anonymity."[41] In this quest, however, he remains alone as his son is too young to understand it and Philip lacks his friend's zeal and determination, while the other adult characters either do not understand him at all or, like Harriet Scrope, plan to take advantage of his enterprise for their own ends.

Excited by the project, Charles sits down to compose the preface of his study, whose words come to him all of a sudden in an epiphanic, dream-like manner, seeing all at once "the entire pattern of Chatterton's life" (C, 127), but is interrupted by a telephone call after which he finds himself unable to resume his work, a scene as if derived from the legend of Coleridge's creation of *Kubla Khan*. At this point he sees a ghostly figure lying on the bed; a few days later he reads this preface to Vivien, Philip, Scrope and Flint in a restaurant symptomatically called the Kubla Khan. This is followed by an argument about the eternity and transience of literature during which Charles gives a passionate speech to the pragmatic and sceptical Flint declaring that imaginative vision is what really drives people to write. It is after this speech that Charles sees

---

41 Alex Murray, *Recalling London: Literature and History in the work of Peter Ackroyd and Iain Sinclair*, 29.

Chatterton's ghost again, just before he dies of a brain tumour. However, the exact cause of Charles's death, and also probably of his hallucinations, is much less important than the urgency of his message – it is the vision, the imaginative, alternative rendering of reality that constitutes the very essence of great art. Charles's loneliness is that of a visionary person endowed with exceptional imagination and foresight.

The two crucial loners in *Three Brothers* are Daniel and Sam. Both brothers are predestined to solitude by their character disposition. Due to his "natural propensity for study, and a love for reading" (*TB*, 9), Daniel soon becomes a stranger in the Hanway household, even more so when he, out of contempt for the shabbiness and commonness of the working-class council estate where he lives, develops the habit of walking as far as possible from the place where he feels he does not belong intellectually. Moreover, as a homosexual with a profound dislike for any team sport activities he does not fit much among his schoolmates, and so it is in Cambridge that he believes his new life begins. Yet a purely academic career does not satisfy him and it is only on returning to London that Daniel discovers his true self as he gets acquainted with the city's gay community, and also gets into its literary circles when he becomes a scathing reviewer and later a published scholarly author writing about the city. And so for him London turns into "an unfamiliar city, brighter and more colourful than the one he had known as a youth. It had become a place of promise as well as of pleasure" (*TB*, 122), yet this idealised, isolated view of the city is just a small segment of the whole, which he is only able to approach theoretically in his book. It is only when he fails as a literary commentator in a television show that he manages, though only temporarily, to establish a sensual, instinctive connection with the city in its social and temporal complexity, suddenly feeling that "the obduracy of London began to enter him" (*TB*, 237), and that he was "held up by the remains of an unimaginable past" (*TB*, 238). He eventually repudiates his roots by rejecting his lover Sparkler, the last remaining link between him and his low London origin, though much of his book is devoted to lower-class influences upon London writers. The underclass city literally traces him when he dies of a stroke at seeing the rejected Sparkler, naked and beating small drums, sitting on the lawn beneath the window of his Cambridge office, as if reminding him that the past cannot be escaped fully.

Sam is even more solitary as he lives in a private, dreamy world and prefers his own company. A natural psychogeographer without knowing it, he spends most of his time in aimless and inconsistent wanderings around Camden, examining minute details and objects "with wonder and concentration, absorbing them within his being, before discarding them" (*TB*, 42). While Harry and Daniel see life as a struggle, Sam does not see any need to live his life by delimiting himself against someone else and is therefore happy. He is the only of the brothers who likes walking not only around his home estate but also in unfamiliar parts of the city, both in daytime and at night, talking freely to vagrants and beggars, giving them all the money he receives from his mother. He also likes his job as Ruppta's rent collector as he enjoys communicating with the poverty-stricken tenants in Britannia Street. And so, when his employer is killed he has no reason to stay and, as a genuine wanderer, he sets out for the city:

> So in the waning light he went towards London Bridge. The street lamps shone on the crowd, casting long shadows across the brightly lit hoardings and shopfronts. It was a procession in torchlight, celebrating all the haste and fervour of London. He walked into the middle of the crowd, and slowly his anxieties began to subside. The touch of the stone beneath his feet, and the presence of the people, calmed him. He could feel the forgetfulness of the city rising within him. It was as if individual fear had no place in this concourse, where the great general drama of the human spirit was being displayed in the light of the street lamps. (*TB*, 242)

Although he is not successful professionally or academically like his brothers, and, paradoxically perhaps, he would not be able to describe himself as such, Sam most fittingly and forcefully personifies what Ackroyd identifies as the London spirit or genius. He enjoys the city in its full swing, with all its heterogeneity of sounds, images, movements and people. At the same time, it fills him with a vision which he pursues regardless of other people's disapproval, dismissal, mistrust or lack of understanding, yet never by antagonising or hurting them, unconsciously and intuitively understanding what it takes to become part of London's supratemporal continuum of human experience and imaginative creativity, and is thus the only one of the brothers allowed to survive by and in the city.

A complete list of Ackroyd's fictional or semi-fictional lonely Londoners, however, would be much longer. As an example, the most important in terms of their position within their novel's plot can be named: Nicholas Dyer and Nicholas Hawksmoor in *Hawksmoor*, the former an architect but also a merciless Satanist slaughterer, the latter the almost archetypal

lonely police detective, misunderstood and underrated by his colleagues
and superiors; Elizabeth Cree and George Gissing in *Dan Leno and the
Limehouse Golem*, the former a bullied and abused, solitary child turned
music-hall performer turned serial killer, the latter a struggling young
writer isolated in his attempts to launch his career and earn some money
to overcome the unpleasant consequences of his youthful indiscretions
and idealism; or Victor Frankenstein in *The Casebook of Victor Frankenstein*,
a self-deluded, failed visionary scientist unable to admit his inability to
surpass the limits of nature, as well as his progressing mental illness.
What connects all Ackroyd's loners is that their unhappiness, isolation
and disturbed states of mind are always directly, literally as well as metaphorically, connected with the city they inhabit.

Ackroyd's Walkers

Walking about the city may assume different forms: apart from the daily
walking which has the practical aim of reaching a specific destination,
there is another kind of walking, which may be called "mythological" or
"dreamy," one which liberates from this aim as it requires abandoning customary routes, stepping out of everyday time and experiencing the city in
a different rhythm. If practiced repeatedly, such walking can be, like the
repetition of certain processes in alchemy, a source of the walker's initiat-
ing transmutation through offering him or her symbols and signs of its
mythical geography[42]. The brief account of Chatterton's ramblings is only
one of many of Ackroyd's images of such compulsive and sensitive London walkers. In *The Lambs of London*, Charles Lamb is the most faithful
and perceptive observer of the city. Despite his insecurities, worries about
inadequacy and fears of professional failure, he manages to retain an optimistic and enthusiastic attitude to London, which he sees as both a place
of countless opportunities as well as an inexhaustible source of artistic
inspiration. "Ackroyd draws upon Lamb's essays, especially the miscellaneous pieces written in the persona of Elia, to round out the portrait
of this true Londoner."[43] Therefore, although often volatile and doubtful
about his writing, Charles is very firm in his views of the city, which he
especially enjoys during his voyeuristic *flâneries*, walking slowly, watching
carefully and with enthusiasm all the details of the diverse city life:

---

42 Daniela Hodrová, *Citlivé město (eseje z mytopoetiky)*, 179–180.
43 Lewis, *My Words Echo Thus*, 138.

He joined the throng of carriages and pedestrians, all moving eastward into the City. It was for him a motley parade, part funeral procession and part pantomime, evincing to him the fullness and variety of life in all its aspects [...] The sounds of footsteps on the cobbles mingled with the rumble of the carriage wheels and the echo of horse hooves to make what Charles considered to be a uniquely city sound. It was the music of movement itself. (*LL*, 27–28)

Charles's London is thus a distinctive crossbreed of a physical and mental space, a cheerful cityscape containing projections of all his hopes, dreams and aspirations. Moreover, such a milieu always offers a multisensual experience, from the heterogeneous spectacles of the crowded streets to the euphonic sounds echoing the momentum of the city in full swing.

The title of the novel invites two contrary interpretations: on the one hand, there are the timid and neurotic Mary, and William Ireland, a gifted yet neglected boy too eager to prove his worth, who become the true victims, or sacrificial lambs, of the city; Charles, on the other hand, despite, or maybe because of, his carelessness and levity, survives in the city and becomes the Lamb of London through his career as a popular writer. Although he loves the city enormously, he is simultaneously aware of its destructive potential:

He was part of the crowd. There were times when this brought him comfort, when he considered himself to be part of the texture of life. There were occasions when it merely reinforced his sense of failure. More often than not, however, it spurred his ambition. He envisaged the days when, from his comfortable library or writing-room, he would be able to hear the crowd passing by. (*LL*, 28)

Feeling himself part of the mass of the city's collective experience, his mind associating the city with the promises of a bright future, Charles never ceases to believe in its potential to endow its dwellers with the freedom necessary to achieve their most secret goals. More than anything else, for Charles the city represents life in all its miscellaneous forms and, consequently, a challenge to meet. He may be light-hearted and youthfully irresponsible, at times prone to brief gloomy periods of self-doubt, but he always seems to possess the optimistic spirit and vigour essential for grasping the opportunities London offers to those who are bold and ready enough to take advantage of them. "I am always lucky in the London streets, Mary. I lead a charmed life in the city" (*LL*, 47), he replies when his sister makes the grim point that he could consider himself fortunate when he was robbed on one of his nightly returns from the pub but left uninjured, as if suggesting that the city would always spare those who resonate with its spirit. Once again, Ackroyd's London becomes a metaphor and the cornerstone of one's ability to keep one's head up even when things do not look particularly auspicious, as it is the only successful strategy for meeting challenges and surviving in the rapidity of the modern urban world.

William Ireland is a much differently motivated stroller. Unlike Charles Lamb, who takes delight in the spectacles of bustling life and thus seeks the crowded parts of the central city in daytime, William sets out into the London streets with the sole purpose of being alone, having time to mediate on the technicalities of his forgeries and their presentation to the outside world, for which he needs to remain hidden and unrecognised in the anonymity of the urban maze. Therefore, most of his walks are directed off the peopled thoroughfares, into the side streets and poor areas whose inhabitants have no idea what the Shakespeare Papers are or who their discoverer is. Moreover, his solitary, ruminative ramblings often take place at night, the only time when he feels unthreatened by the unwanted attention of inquisitive and doubting intruders. William's attitude to the city is necessarily ambiguous: he needs it for his aims as only there he can gain recognition and perhaps even fame, yet it simultaneously denies him what he needs most for a successful and smooth completion of his plans – peace and quiet for work, and as such it can easily ruin his life. His dialogue with De Quincey reveals that he is very well aware of the fact that the city which has made him may easily break him as well (*LL*, 185).

For William, London is reduced to a few places he is familiar with, which he likes because he feels secure in them, such as his room, his father's bookshop, or the library, but he is in fact at odds with it as a whole. The city of his walks is a mental image, a detached fantasy rather than a real, physical space since he takes little notice of his surroundings, being enclosed deep in his thoughts and aspirations. Rather than an avid spectator of the countless urban dramas he is a director using the city as a stage for his carefully designed, private performances, an alternative and essentially unnatural reality which, therefore, proves hard to sustain as the city will resist a long-term imposition of such an illusion and unveil its true state of affairs. The protagonist's inability to come to terms with the particularities and regularities of city life, Ackroyd seems to suggest, brings about his inevitable downfall.

The two distinctive walkers of London's streets in *Hawksmoor*, Nicholas Dyer and Nicholas Hawksmoor, make an interesting dyad. Although much separates them, in terms of their personalities they have much in common as they are both rational thinkers who rely on reason and logic, but who also strongly believe in their intuition, or some kind of a sixth sense, and, as a result, they admit that the world is impossible to comprehend fully merely by rational cognitive processes. The list of their similarities would be long, including identical features in their appearance and behaviour as well as in their feelings, such as "they both feel a strong wish at certain point to dress and behave like tramps [...], and they are darkly aware that they are undergoing a process of self-fragmentation and alienation from society."[44] Both are therefore more sensitive to various irrational, or rationally inexplicable, manifestations around them, possessing the capacity to recognise the diverse impacts of the city on the human psyche. Moreover, for the sake of their jobs, they need to be particularly well-acquainted with London's topography, and these factors make them exceptionally alert observers of the city and its less obvious and covert mechanisms and phenomena.

Young Dyer spends much of his free time reading captivating stories, mostly about scholars dealing with magic or supernatural forces, such as Marlowe's *Doctor Faustus* or Greene's *Friar Bacon and Friar Bungay*, but he shows little enthusiasm for reading the texts presented to him at school. However, the curious boy loves to explore and experience the world around him, and so, whenever he can, he rambles the streets tirelessly, carefully taking note of every single detail, from people to buildings, his imagination picturing the city of the past as well as projecting that of the future. For him, London is like an immense textbook to be studied and inspired by, much more interesting and effective than a school education. Therefore he often plays truant in order to absorb and understand the city's spirit. However, as he grows up and changes from an eager learner and Sir Christopher Wren's gifted pupil, into a misanthropic, secret Satanist, his perception of the city develops into that of a devilish creation of chaos and confusion, "the Capitol of Darknesse," "the Dungeon of Man's Desires," "the smokey grove of Moloch" (*H*, 47–8). Dyer sees bloated, unrestrained and uncontrollable London as an incarnation of the devil, an aggregate of all thinkable forms of human incompetence, evil and misery, breeding only pain and despair. The city which so inspired the youthful Dyer, whose passion for its topography and the par-

---

44 Susana Onega, *Metafiction and myth in the novels of Peter Ackroyd*, 46.

ticular designs of its streets and alleys made him at first an enthusiastic student and later a respected architect, gradually transforms, like his mind, into a place of doom and insanity; instead of offering learning and other professional challenges it fills him with the blinding desire to complete his great, magic designs, which are to bring him salvation, no matter how many killings and other forms of suffering they will require.

A crucial role in Dyer's vision of the urban inferno is played by his deluded persuasion that he himself is excluded from this material being, rectifying but not participating in the vicious circle of evil. As a "chosen" one, he understands his life as a kind of otherworldly presence in the earthbound reality, a prophetic and messianic mission whose aim is to open other people's eyes by showing them and making them worship and serve the proper deity. Yet, when others, for whatever reasons, fail to awaken and look through the haze of their misconception and folly, he resolves to save himself through locating his churches as seven vertexes in a mystical, occult pattern, and burying human sacrifices in their foundations to please his Saviour. As the living prove deaf to his appeals and revelations he eventually turns to the dead, which can be seen in the different nature of his later walks:

> I walked to the Chandlery and then, to still my beating Mind, I entered into the Church-Yard beside the Abbey. I take Delight in stalking along by my self on that dumb silent Ground, for if it be true that Time is a Wound then it is one that the Dead may Heal. And when I rest my Head upon the Graves I hear them speaking each to each [...] I hear them whispering, the long dead, in Cripplegate, in Farringdon, in Cordwainers Street and in Crutched Fryars: they are pack'd close together like Stones in the Mortar, and I hear them speak of the City that holds them fast. And yet still I burn at Walter's recent Words as this Thought comes to me: why do the Living still haunt me when I am among the Dead? (*H*, 88–89)

The cityscape of his strolls reflects the state of his mind and vice versa. He no longer walks in the city centre, in the peopled streets and markets, preferring places of isolation and solitude, churches and graveyards, as only there does he finds souls who share with him his experience of the cursed city's oppressive might. It is also where he hopes he can reach communion with what he considers to be the true voice of London, and, in consequence, also the *vox mundi*, a supratemporal echo of the wisdom of the dead which the doubting and blasphemous words of the living only shout down and stifle. It is the world of the dead he roams, it is the world of the dead his disturbed psyche starts to resemble, and it is the world of the dead he pays homage to and wishes to cross over to by his every act.

The CID detective Nicholas Hawksmoor badly needs to find the prime suspect of the long-investigated serial killings, the mysterious vagrant nicknamed the Architect. Therefore, as Hawksmoor believes that every perpetrator eventually returns to the scene of his or her crime, the chief purpose of his pensive walks in the vicinities of Dyer's churches is to stay close to the areas where this slayer has committed his acts, and, assuming that he will recognise him when he sees him, to hope that he will encounter or spot him there. During one of these walks, although, or perhaps because, he has previously broken his glasses, he catches sight of a suspicious tall vagrant on the other side of the street, but when he pursues him the vagrant gets nervous and starts running away, soon vanishing from the detective's sight. All Hawksmoor finds eventually is a harmless group of other vagrants who, however, show no willingness to cooperate and so he at least wreaks his anger on them by forcing them to put out their fire. The city of his mind thus becomes like that of the homeless tramps, meths-drinkers and ragpickers – a dreary, inconsolable landscape of desolation and solitude, whose worries and pleasures do not reach beyond the present moment.

The desperate Hawksmoor carries on with his walks, at first in order to devise a strategy which would help him catch the Architect, and later to clear his mind of various foolish and semi-delirious thoughts and fantasies. Although his consciousness strives to figure out a new, yet untried, way of solving the case, his unconscious instincts are powerfully at work too and drive him relentlessly to what his rational self deems futile or foolish. Therefore, no matter how aimless and randomly directed these ramblings are, he always ends up in the same areas where he has already been tracing his suspect.

> He took long walks in the evening in order to avoid such thoughts, but he found that he was treading the same paths as before. There was a time, for example, when he walked into the park behind St George's-in-the-East and sat upon a bench closed to the abandoned museum – it had been upon this bench that he had spoken to the father of the murdered child [...] And as he stared at the trees beside the church he contemplated the calm of a life which itself resembled a park with no people in it – then he might sit and stare at these trees until he died. But his momentary serenity unnerved him, for it seemed to imply that his life was already over. (*H*, 198)

Hawksmoor is much too captivated by his pursuit and the topography of the terrain where it is being carried out and by the reminders of his professional and personal inadequacy and failure to find solace and composure in an escapist, pastoral image of a still city life of a foreseeable future. The transient and illusory tranquility of the park behind one of the crime scenes does not deceive the experienced detective with a sudden lucid perception of the city and the case, on the contrary, it only convinces him that he has got stuck in a blind alley where there is "in any case no future and no past, only the unspeakable misery of his own self" (*H*, 199). His restless mind is thus doomed to wander the urban wasteland until it reaches peace through a mysterious, transtemporal connection with the mind of the killer, "his black emanation,"[45] inside the non-existent church of Little St Hugh, in what may be interpreted as both a mystical act of "a transcendent communion across the centuries"[46] within London's collective experience, and as another hallucinatory stage of Hawksmoor's progressing insanity.

Elizabeth Cree and George Gissing are two relentless walkers in *Dan Leno and the Limehouse Golem*, yet the motivation for their journeys is far from getting to know the city's back streets or feeling their unique atmosphere and spirit. Although they are in many respects different personalities, what drives them into the streets is strikingly similar: the dismal and depressing situation in their destitute homes. Other common features of their walks, though also determined by different circumstances, are that they mostly take place in the evening or at night and that they, in an unforeseen manner, crucially affect the walkers' future fates. Elizabeth's at first directionless ramblings soon find a purpose in the form of the prospective fulfillment of her childhood wish to see a popular variety show, an act denied to her by her bigoted mother's persuasion that all places of entertainment are accursed, sinful abodes of the devil's making. Once she sets out for the nearest music hall, her mood is suddenly completely unlike that when she takes sewed sailing cloths to the docks or accompanies her mother to the local chapel – she is cheerful, fearless and resolute, despite the dangers the vast night city holds for a lonely young woman. When she eventually reaches the saloon of varieties, its bright and colourful façade makes such a contrast to the plain-looking and run-down vicinity that it excites her as if she had found a diamond in a pile of dirt. And so, fascinated and attracted by

---

45   Onega, *Peter Ackroyd*, 47.
46   Lewis, *My Words Echo Thus*, 44.

the saloon she roams the neighbouring streets and alleys, mustering the courage to enter it.

It is there that the area's topography gets reflected in Elizabeth's mind: the shabby back streets full of drunkards, pimps and prostitutes remind her of her hard and miserable existence, the old churchyard of her mother's semi-delirious, malevolent bigotry, and so the music hall naturally becomes a place of both ease and thrills, an oasis of hope for a better and happier life set free from the restraints of narrow-mindedness and poverty. Later on, however, when she has to end her career as a music-hall performer, the same topography transforms into a mental background as well as a physical terrain for the realisation of her vengeful homicidal schemes, through which her disturbed psyche seeks to vent her accumulated frustration, yet which can be also understood "as particularly violent traces of the city's disturbing identity."[47] Her transformation into the Limehouse Golem thus symbolises "the emanation of London's spiritual sickness."[48] These nocturnal walks are no longer the aimless, desperate acts of a runaway victim of hardships, but those of a focused, cold-blooded predator in search of a prey for her deranged fantasies.

The motif of the cityscape as a projection of a murderer's and a writer's mind is introduced in *Dan Leno and the Limehouse Golem* through De Quincey's famous essay "On Murder Considered as One of the Fine Arts," in which John Williams, the Ratcliffe Highway murderer, is presented as a particular amalgam of romantic hero, outcast and original artist of a sort, "an urban Wordsworth, a poet of sublime impulse who rearranges (one might say executes) the natural world in order to reflect his own preoccupations" (*DLLG*, 37), thus featuring as London's "avenging angel" (*DLLG*, 38). Such an image of London, Ackroyd suggests, is rooted in De Quincey's early experience with life in the city, when the area around Oxford Street became for him one of sorrow, poverty and loneliness, and his misery and frustration also stood behind his first purchase of laudanum. Therefore, this city of suffering and despair even in his later writing represented "the landscape of his imagination" (*DLLG*, 39), the city of his mind. De Quincey's "On Murder Considered as One of the Fine Arts" then becomes a brooding presence behind the novel's plot as it influences, inspires or captivates several of its key protagonists, namely George Gissing, John Cree, Elizabeth Cree and Karl Marx. Most of them are reading De Quincey and

47 Gibson and Wolfreys, *Peter Ackroyd: The Ludic and Labyrinthine Text*, 205.
48 Onega, *Peter Ackroyd*, 68.

other London texts, and produce or are dreaming of producing a text of their own, in the Reading Room of the British Museum, a site which Ackroyd considers the spiritual centre of London, where the interconnection between the actual city, its literary representation and the city of one's imagination and consciousness can most naturally materialise. And so "the murmuring of all the inhabitants of the Reading Room rose towards the vast dome and set up a whispering echo like that of the voices in the fog of London" (*DLLG*, 47), just as the read texts echo the interaction between their authors' creative process and the city's mental and physical topography.

The reason behind Gissing's night expeditions through London streets is even more peculiar than that of Elizabeth Cree as he is actually often looking for his own wife Nell, who has recently resumed drinking and prostitution, hoping in vain that he can persuade her of the benefits and joys of decent family life. The desperate young writer thus spends nights chasing Nell around various parts of the East End, visiting all the existing brothels in the vicinity of where she could possibly be practising her preferred profession. However, saving Nell from the snare of vice and himself from public shame is not the only purpose of his walks, nor even the principal one – his walks around Limehouse and its neighbouring areas serve him as research for his article about Charles Babbage and his Analytical Engine. As Gissing does not understand the mathematical principle and technical mechanisms of the ingenious computing machine, he believes that he could approach Babbage's mental processes by a thorough exploration of places he was fascinated with, for instance, the Limehouse church of St Anne's with the large white pyramid erected in its front grounds. Feeling "a shrinking uneasiness" (*DLLG*, 120) in the presence of the mysterious apparatus, Gissing insists on its connection with the spirit of the unfortunate area in which it was constructed. And so, in a truly psychogeographic manner, Gissing arrives at scrutinising the interference between his own wounded psyche and the topography of the place he so much associates with his misery and degradation rather than the mind behind the invention. His writing of an essay on the Analytical Engine thus becomes an autotherapeutic means of his coming to terms with his failures by putting at least a part of the blame on the city which allowed them to happen to him. "Gissing is thus used by Ackroyd as a medium for the city, for its traces and its textual reconfigurations."[49] Ironically, nothing of this seems to have been spotted by his renowned,

---

49   Gibson and Wolfreys, *Peter Ackroyd: The Ludic and Labyrinthine Text*, 208.

leftist admirer, Karl Marx, who reads his essay solely for the technical details, thinking of the Engine's potential use for the benefits of communist society.

Ackroyd's Gissing is a character who is exceptionally sensitive to the *genius loci* of London and its impact on its citizens' lives and psyches, and as such he develops a highly ambiguous attitude to the city, one perpetually alternating between fascination and delight on the one hand, and indignation and repulsion on the other. He experiences the first on his way to the Reading Room and it is the area around the British Museum, "the locus for so many ethereal words and thoughts,"[50] that he feels to be most himself and happy again, as

> ... he always considered this area of London to be his true home [...] only within this small neighbourhood did he feel entirely at ease. It was the spirit of the district itself which, he supposed, affected him so profoundly. Even the tradesmen he passed on his walk to the museum [...] seemed to share his sense of place and to accommodate themselves to it. He knew the porters and the cab men, the strolling musicians and the casual street-sellers, and he considered them as part of some distinctive human family to which he also belonged. (*DLLG*, 138)

His is therefore a most telling example in the novel of how the atmosphere and spiritual connotations of a particular locality may affect a person who comes to inhabit or even only repeatedly move around it. The intellectual and creative climate of the Reading Room, with its accumulated wisdom, knowledge and experience, Gissing believes, spreads far beyond the walls of the building, making more thoughtful and self-reflective individuals feel elated and optimistic about their future accomplishments in its vicinity. However, when he once decides to set off in another direction, eastward towards the Strand, and finds himself in an unfamiliar maze of streets around Clare Market, his former dejection from the dark sides of the city returns as he walks around streets full of rubbish and excrement, past a dimly lit rag shop with naked and half-starved little children sitting on its filthy mud floor, and a factory smelling unbearably of lead and acid, in which several lines of hard-working women sing in unison in the overpowering din and billowing smoke. It is while he is hastily leaving this hellish place that he comes to understand that London consists precisely of such contradictory, seemingly incon-

---

50 Lewis, *My Words Echo Thus*, 87.

gruent elements, whose incessant clashes and encounters constitute the very fabric of the material and mental cityscapes:

Suddenly, he is filled with the optimistic belief that the perpetual, infinite London can be discovered, both in himself and in other people (*DLLG*, 246). At this moment the young writer experiences some sort of urban epiphany, an Ackroydian Cockney visionary revelation about the eternal, mystical London which comprises, stores, and therefore also transcends, every moment and act lived within its limits. It is as if he could find peace within the teeming and at times intrusive city, when he understands and accepts his subordinate position within this mass of collective experience and wisdom. It also suggests that he can only approach the city meaningfully, and thus be reconciled with it and reach contentment, even on a personal level, when he sets his mind free of any illusions, self-projections and preconceptions and lets this universal city reflect itself in his mind, and, in consequence, lets the city and his mind become one. Only such a passive yet receptive state enables him to raise himself above the mundane, tedious worries and affairs of everyday life.

Ackroyd's London walkers move around a place and space which transcend the limits of their rational understanding, whose immense physical and spiritual power and energy captures, if not overwhelms, its inhabitants' minds and therefore irreversibly affects their mental states and processes. All their acts of psychosomatic consummation of the streets, be they psychogeographic ramblings, antiquarian explorations, topographic naming and mapping, autotherapeutic soothing saunters, liberating escapes from the restraints of prejudice and convention, attempts at reconstructing their identity through self-scrutiny and self-discovery, desperate struggles to fulfil their dreams and hopes, or the unfolding of a disturbed psyche, reveal the very ambiguous nature of this cityscape, oscillating between familiarity and unfamiliarity, comprehensibility and incomprehensibility, intimacy and estrangement, immediateness and alienation. "What Peter Ackroyd strives to make us familiar with is that London remains ineffable. It resists definition, by being nothing more than the voices, the texts, the traces of itself, endlessly reconfigured and performed, time and time again."[51] Yet no matter how infinite and ultimately unknowable such a city is, to resign from ever trying to approach it, and possibly partly make sense of it, Ackroyd seems to suggest, means to defy its nature and course. Towards the end of *London: The Biography* he notes that London is not merely a state of mind, this being only one

51 Gibson and Wolfreys, *Peter Ackroyd: The Ludic and Labyrinthine Text*, 210.

of its many roles and manifestations, as it contains "a world or worlds within itself" (*LB*, 750). However, as the numerous examples from his novels demonstrate, it does represent a crucial aspect as people have always been, and always will be, drawn by the city's endurance and perpetuity to identify themselves with its genius regardless of how hostile and destructive it can be.

Chapter 5
Theatrical London

Thus the city repeats its life, identical, shifting up and down on its empty hessboard. The inhabitants repeat the same scenes, with the actors changed; they repeat the same speeches with variously combined accents; they open alternate mouths in identical yawns. [...] Mercury, god of the fickle, to whom the city is sacred, worked this ambiguous miracle.

Italo Calvino, *Invisible Cities*

"Where pathos and pantomime meet"

In the period from 1576 to 1649, between the opening of the first public playhouse and the closing of the theatres by the Puritans at the end of the Civil War, London became a truly theatrical city due to the "sheer range of spectacles and experiences enacted in the English capital," which testified to "the existence of a theatrical culture of conscious dramatisation on all of the public stages."[1] Therefore, since late Elizabethan times, London has been a city of theatres and, indeed, many argue that it has been the "theatre capital of the world for five centuries."[2] Theatres, however, have not been merely a source of entertainment, cultural institutions with the capacity to "compensate for the upheavals of economic change, particularly when they appeal to ideals of timelessness and universality,"[3] they have also constituted a tough business that made a "massive contribution to London's economy,"[4] yet they have

---

1 David L. Smith, Richard Strier and David Bevington, *The Theatrical City: Culture, Theatre and Politics in London, 1576–1649*, 14–15.
2 Paul Ibell, *Theatreland: A Journey through the Heart of London's Theatre*, xiii.
3 Michael McKinnie, *City Stages: Theatre and Urban Space in a Global City*, 10.
4 Ibell, *Theatreland: A Journey through the Heart of London's Theatre*, xv.

also often served as a powerful means of political campaigning as well as a catalyst of social change, and thus "historically contributed to the civic as a social and urban ideal."[5] As such, London theatre has always had to cater carefully for the changing tastes and preferences of the city's audiences, "so diverse that it is impossible to consider a generic audience"[6] and for whom the stage became both a reflection of their lives and an escape from them. Under such circumstances, it is only natural that this reflection and influence has not been a unilateral process and that some of the striking dramatic manifestations and devices have been deeply imprinted into the very texture of the city's mechanisms and habitual practices. The London of theatres has gradually developed into an essentially theatrical city, one in which acting and spectacle are not only a form of distraction but also an intrinsic element, or even an underlying condition, of everyday life.

Ackroyd acknowledges that the "city of London is itself theatrical, a performative phenomenon more accurately described not as a place, but as that which takes place,"[7] and the city's noticeable theatricality was highlighted in the past by many prominent English literati, scholars and other public figures, such as Charles Dickens, William Wordsworth, Charles Lamb, Thomas Babington Macaulay, James Boswell, Henry Fielding, Tobias Smollett and Joseph Addison. For all of these, whether they are Londoners "by birth or adoption, the theatricality of London is its single most important characteristic" (*LB*, 142). The parallel between city life and the stage is drawn especially because life in the crowded and prevailingly anonymous city offers almost limitless opportunities for play acting, disguise, self-fashioning, and thus the assumption of diverse identities for diverse purposes. Numerous authors have "depicted the bustling city centres [...] as platforms or stages upon which individuals continuously practised being 'somebody'."[8] "The more civilised men become, the more they become actors. They want to put on a show, and fabricate an illusion of their own identities,"[9] observed Immanuel Kant, and nowhere else is this tendency more apparent than in big cities where "[d]eveloping this double consciousness is the primary step towards recognizing that daily life is largely constituted from the management of the fluctuating tensions and ambigui-

---

5   McKinnie, *City Stages: Theatre and Urban Space in a Global City*, 29.

6   Jim Davis and Victor Emeljanow, "Victorian and Edwardian audiences," 93.

7   Jeremy Gibson and Julian Wolfreys, *Peter Ackroyd: The Ludic and Labyrinthine Text*, 170.

8   Joanne Finkelstein, *The Art of Self-Invention: Image and Identity in Popular Visual Culture*, 129

9   Immanuel Kant, *Anthropology from a Pragmatic Point of View*, 14–15.

ties that combine and recombine the various elements in play-acting, deception and invention."[10]

This property allows for a disruption of and disrespect for conventional social boundaries and hierarchies, and imparts to the urban milieu an indisputable democratic character. These subversive, carnivalesque tendencies account "precisely for the combination of egalitarianism and theatricality that is so characteristic of London" (LB, 145). This is in part also due to the fact that for most of its history London, unlike other European capitals which were perceived as conscious symbols of national glory, "served as an expression of private values rather than of public exhortation,"[11] thus allowing more space for the dramatic enactment of one's identity. This ongoing play-acting is frequently accompanied by countless excesses in both content and manner – by "extravagance, and hyperbole, and variety, in every form" (A, 313). Such extremities lead to character stereotyping and a psychological flatness of the assumed roles, whose performances bear considerable features of caricature and melodrama, and inevitably breed various eccentric individuals who no longer seem able to distinguish between playing a part and being themselves. "That is why London has always been considered to be the home of stock theatrical characters" (LB, 142), Ackroyd notes, and, following the Dickensian tradition, he peoples his London novels with distinctive representatives of this kind.

The underlying nature of life in the big city bears striking resemblances to acting, staging and theatre-going as it consists of countless chance meetings and unexpected and often unwished-for situations, to which an individual must react swiftly yet adequately. Similarly to theatre actors, city dwellers are thus forced to be almost permanently alert: even though they have a given, rough 'script' in the form of the prescribed societal rules, norms and conventions of appropriate and polite behaviour, they cannot be prepared for all of the situations that may arise and must be always ready to improvise and extemporise. Moreover, all of this is happening against a background of socially-diverse crowds, which only makes such encounters more stressful since any diversion from the general norm might immediately attract the attention of numerous unwanted onlookers. As soon as the private encounter, through some eccentricity, acquires the character of a public performance and the previously unconcerned crowd turns into an (over-)excited mob, the streets assume an unmistakable spectacle-audience paradigm and transform into a vast urban playhouse, in which the roles of the actor and spectator are far from firmly given and keep interchanging unrestrainedly.

Seen from this perspective, life in the city becomes de-contextualised and has the character of a continuous flow of miscellaneous actions consisting of generally unrelated, yet intrinsically interconnected, scenes and performances. Urban theatricality is an ongoing process mirroring people's pleasures, desires and anxieties; it is recurrent and haphazard rather than causal and disciplined, heterogeneous rather than homogeneous, intuitive rather than rationally intentional, and as such it captures perfectly the very essence and condition of London and its true artistic representation, which Ackroyd identifies as "a particular London sensibility that derives its energy from variety, from spectacle, and from display [...], a sensibility in which pathos and comedy, high tragedy and low farce, are effortlessly combined" (LLCV, 345). He believes that London is even more theatrical than other metropolises, which derives from the fact that it has not been a well-planned and designed city but has grown out of the "imperatives of money and power. [...] It has had a sort of natural organic growth which has taken a thousand different forms."[12] It is a city full of paradoxes and peculiarities, which cause its dwellers' lives to be driven by undercurrents over which they can exercise very little control, and whose incongruent energies thus instigate the city's performativeness:

> London has always had the reputation of being a city of contrast, where pathos and pantomime meet. [...] It is a world of theatre. The grand theatre of the human spirit which London most readily represents, and there is scenic detail and movement and passion and the action of crowds. It is quite different from other cities.[13]

This theatre of the human spirit is never still but always in motion – volatile, accidental and transient – for "it accommodates arbitrariness, inscrutability and endless change" (A, 320). Taking part in it requires a specific capacity of imagination and, simultaneously, it produces a distinctly urban imagination of its own kind which, in Ackroyd's view, by extension helps constitute the English imagination itself.

The parallel between the capital city and the theatre thus stands at the origins of a certain creative sensibility which is grounded in the fusion

---

12   Daisy Banks, "Peter Ackroyd on London," an interview with Peter Ackroyd, *The Browser*.
13   Banks, "Peter Ackroyd on London."

of contraries and contradictions, a weld of sentimental melodrama and grand spectacle which "allows pathos and sublimity" (*A*, 321), petty trifles as well as impressive, memorable acts. It is therefore of little surprise that the dramatic and fictional representations of the above-mentioned aspects of London's theatricality show identical features and vagaries. City dwellers have always liked to see satirical or parodic images of themselves in farcical city comedies whose protagonists are narrowly defined by the pragmatically stereotypical roles the members of the audience, willingly, or out of necessity, have to assume in their everyday lives. Such depiction, Ackroyd notes, was based on "sentimental characterisation, rather than psychological complexity" for "there is no depth or cons istency to melodramatic portraiture, and realism necessarily is displaced by spectacle and energetic movement" (*A*, 313). As a result, the dividing line between the fictitious world of the stage and the real world of the spectators was made less clear-cut as they were built on the same principles of caricature, excess and paradox.

A similar tendency can be traced in fiction, especially since *The History of Tom Jones, a Foundling* (1749), in which Henry Fielding, originally a playwright, combines the principles of the comic or mock epic with those of drama. This becomes most notable in the episodes taking place in London, where events become even more strongly determined by the unpredictable whims of fate that cast its population of disparate and socially-diverse individuals into uncontrollable situations in which they can rely only on their resourcefulness, quick-wittedness and readiness to improvise. Other London novels, Ackroyd observes, strive to capture this theatrical nature of the city's life through their, in places, topsy-turvy narrative structure as they depict events whose randomness makes them unable to conform to any "observable plan or pattern. This mutability is mimicked by the novels themselves, which shift unexpectedly from allegory to history, from heroism and high sentiment to pantomime and melodrama" (*A*, 320). Many London narratives thus resort to strategies that best represent this character of the city, namely genre and discourse mixture and montage; they oscillate between such extreme perspectives as philosophical contemplation and burlesque, and even further disrupt their narrative structure by including other media reflecting the city's variability, such as rhymes and songs.

An understanding of the theatricality of London life is one of the key attributes of the works of those artists whom Ackroyd calls Cockney Visionaries, as they all "were entranced by the scenic and the spectacular, in a city that is continually filled with the energetic display of people and institutions" (LLCV, 346). Even though he acknowledges that a certain performative randomness and unpredictability are intrinsic properties of the city, he does not share the persuasion that London and its life are necessarily and absolutely accidental and ungraspable, as this would mean giving up on any literary representations of the city other than those shaped by chaos and structural confusion. Ackroyd's vision is primarily inspired by Charles Dickens, who believed that the "mystery of London lay in its interconnectedness" (*A*, 320). The London of Ackroyd's novels thus embraces its innate combination of contrasts and opposites, but also seeks to disclose some unifying aspects that help to explicate the inseparability of what appears to be ultimately incongruous, and by doing so cast some light on the often inscrutable mechanisms of the accumulation of Londoners' "suffered or shared experience" (*A*, 320). At the heart of these underlying forces are two contradictory yet mutually interconnected tendencies: a carnivalesque, subversive, pleasurable or even sybaritic and therefore liberating one, and a limiting, oppressive, restrictive, and therefore incarcerating one. "London is both theatre and prison" (*LB*, 447), Ackroyd remarks, following the metaphor Thomas More chose to represent the condition of the city (*A*, 311–312), and the incessant oscillation between these two images constitutes the essence of his fictional metropolis.

London as a Stage and the Stage as London in *Dan Leno and the Limehouse Golem*

Dan Leno and the Limehouse Golem is the novel in which the theme of London's theatricality and the metaphor of the city as theatre are most forcefully articulated as it examines "problems arising from the intersection of theatrical and urban space."[14] Not only is it set in a period when "theatregoers were particularly fond of spectacle,"[15] and which was the culmination of the "first era of mass theatregoing,"[16] but it also occupies the territory of London's East End, notable in the nineteenth century for the carnivalesque nature of the life in its shabby streets. Moreover, Victorian London was dominated by a persistent middle-class fear of the poor, and consequently "places of public amusement [...] did what they could

---

14 McKinnie, *City Stages*, 16.
15 Ibell, *Theatreland*, 21.
16 David Mayer, "Encountering melodrama," 146.

to keep the classes decently apart,"[17] which is why there were many public places of dramatic entertainment catering specifically for the tastes of
the working class. Among the most popular were the so-called "Penny
Gaffs," shop-front theatres "hosting up to six shows an evening" that
"typically consisted of a musical performance, lewd dancing and a 'vulgar' comic,"[18] and were located in the poor areas, charging only a penny
for admission. "The potentially politicised performance of the 'rabble-
ment' would later become central to many aspects of an imagined East
End culture, visibly manifesting itself, for example, in the music-hall
tradition."[19] The theatricality of the area stems from its awareness of its
social and material deprivation and is thus reactionary, if not revolutionary, in essence. Moreover, in the context of the Victorian era's Puritan
moral ethos, the subversive potential of theatrical performance rests in
the fact that it "was considered to endanger by its very nature the Victorian belief in a stable identity,"[20] as the multiplicity of roles and identities
performed and assumed by the actors pointed to a "fluidity of character
that decompose[d] the uniform integrity of the self."[21]

Several scenes of the book take place directly onstage, depicting various performances or their rehearsals, as its main protagonist becomes
a member of a successful late-Victorian music hall acting troupe led by
Dan Leno, who himself plays a crucial role in one of the plotlines. Connected with this are the miserable conditions in which Elizabeth Cree
grows up and which drive her to seek refuge in the illusory music-hall
world, and the deliberate and ostentatious theatricality of the murders
she commits, which resemble an act in a mock-Gothic drama inspired
by Thomas De Quincey's essay "On Murder Considered as One of the
Fine Arts." Therefore, the novel's urban "performance is, at least in part,
a response to the city's violent moments"[22] and social injustice. Two other
characters, one fictional and one real, John Cree and George Gissing,
visit the British Museum Reading Room in order to write a play (the
former), use theatricality as a narrative device in his novel (the latter),

---

17 Olsen, *The City as a Work of Art*, 207.

18 Richard Guard, *Lost London*, 138–139.

19 Paul Newland, *The Cultural Construction of London's East End: Urban Iconography, Modernity and the Spatialisation of Englishness*, 43.

20 Sidia Fiorato, "Theatrical Role-Playing, Crime and Punishment in Peter Ackroyd's *Dan Leno and the Limehouse Golem* (1994)," 67.

21 Nina Auerbach, *Private Theatricals: The Lives of the Victorians*, 4. Quoted in Sidia Fiorato, "The-atrical Role-Playing, Crime and Punishment in Peter Ackroyd's *Dan Leno and the Limehouse Golem* (1994)," 67.

22 Gibson and Wolfreys, *Peter Ackroyd: The Ludic and Labyrinthine Text*, 173.

or at least to muse on the correlation between a dramatic piece and their own life experience (both). Moreover, even some of the minor characters, like Karl Marx or Solomon Weil, have a passion for popular theatre, the latter even having "acquired a collection of sheet music from Endell Street which specialised in the newest songs from the halls" (*DLLG*, 65). The analogy between the city's life and the theatre is further reinforced by showing how the music hall performances reflect not only the happenings in the city, but also the current atmosphere, mood and temper of its streets.

The central type of playhouse in the novel is the music hall, a specifically Victorian, and mostly London, theatrical phenomenon that "came into existence as the queen was crowned, flowered with her reign, and entered the twentieth century ready to decline."[23] The music halls developed separately from the official stages especially throughout the first half of the period, and they gradually became the primary Victorian theatrical institution of professional entertainment, offering a unique blend of lower- and upper-class dramatic performances, the former by far prevailing over the latter. These ranged from the exhibition of freaks, strongmen, circus artistry, farcical clowning, cross-dressing, costumed impersonations, and comic singing and dancing to witty dialogues, monologues, sketches, gags, sentimental and melodramatic scenes, burlesques and operettas[24]. As a result, such venues attracted working and lower-middle-class people, "especially those under thirty-five with disposable income, and middle- and upper-class men who rejected or were evading dominant conventional morality, accompanied by prostitutes rather than women of their own class,"[25] though the greatest music-hall comic stars, such as Dan Leno, managed to draw entire middle-class families into the auditorium. Due to its composition, the music hall audience yearned for novelties and dramatised topicalities, they revelled in hoaxes, exuberant gaiety and excessive spectacle, and naturally valued all kinds of pleasures over the traditional Victorian artistic values of realism, moral involvement and rationally informed detachment. Because of its heterogeneity, energy and subversive potential, Ackroyd believes music-hall culture is crucial for understanding London's theatricality and creative sensibility as it produced "the true melodies of London" (LLCV, 345).

Although the actual theatrical production depicted in the novel is music hall comedy, farce and variety show, the destinies of its main

23 Jacky Bratton, "The music hall," 164.
24 Bratton, "The music hall," 165–70.
25 Bratton, "The music hall," 167.

protagonists bear visible traits of melodrama, a theatrical "response to a world where things are seen to go wrong, where ideas of secular and divine justice and recompense are not always met, where suffering is not always acknowledged, and where the explanations for wrongs, injustices, and suffering are not altogether understandable."[26] Featuring a cast of stock characters, taking place in a variety of diverse settings, domestic as well as exotic, revolving around themes such as love, murder and betrayal, relying on abrupt and unexpected twists of fate, abounding with pathos and strong sentimentality, melodrama appealed to the spectators' emotions rather than intellect, and the concluding triumph of good over evil provided an escapist illusion of order and justice in a world of pain, chaos and daily calamities, thus addressing mostly the pressures of the urban working-class milieu. In *Dan Leno and the Limehouse Golem* the lives of George Gissing, Elizabeth Cree and John Cree are determined precisely by such inexplicable calamities, sufferings and sudden twists of fate, yet they lack any ultimate consolation through a reconciliatory resolution of their misfortunes, leaving them helpless in "finding their way in a rapidly changing, increasingly urban world."[27]

George Gissing is one of the characters in the novel through whom the theme of the theatricality of city life is explored. From one point of view, he is similar to Elizabeth Cree as his private life bears some striking features to a melodramatic piece: a young, promising, but inexperienced gentleman becomes infatuated with a teenage prostitute, Nell Harrison, whom he, "in the best theatrical tradition" (*DLLG*, 111), decides to save from the snares of what he sees as the impacts of the social machine's injustice and indifference. Having derived his views of the world from reading novels by Dickens and Zola, he idealistically projects himself as a literary hero whose moral mission is to rescue the unfortunate outcast, whether she wants it or not. However, due to its schematisation and naivety, this mission is rather conceived in the tradition of "pathetic drama" (*DLLG*, 111). In effect, his undertaking loses its original ethical dimension and turns into an empty, hypocritical gesture of self-centredness as it is motivated by the need to fit an illusory image of himself rather than by a genuine humanistic concern for the fallen girl. Upon their arrival in London, he pays bitterly for his naivety and unwillingness to acknowledge that he and his delusions are the true causes of his misfortunes. It is as if in the metropolis his petty, private burlesque finds a proper stage

---

26 Mayer, "Encountering melodrama," 148.
27 Mayer, "Encountering melodrama," 148.

on which to grow into a proper melodrama: Nell shows little interest in being liberated from her previous life, on the contrary, she discovers what opportunities the London streets offer in that respect, and so her drinking tendencies only increase and she soon takes up prostitution once again. Consequently, Gissing's despair deepens, he spends hours chasing his wife around the East End streets, pubs and brothels, and eventually ends up in a prison cell suspected of the murder of one of his wife's new "fellow-sufferers."

Having found himself trapped in such dramatic circumstances, Gissing's traumatic life experiences get reflected in his writing. Despite congratulating himself on following in the footsteps of the great European realistic and naturalistic novelists, his fiction shows distinct marks of the sentimental theatrical tradition, such as verbosity, picturesqueness, and a tendency to romanticise the gloomier aspects of life: "Within the narrative of *Workers in the Dawn*, for example, he had bathed the city in an iridescent glow and turned its inhabitants into stage heroes or stage crowds on the model of the sensation plays in the penny gaffs" (*DLLG*, 137). It is of little surprise that the melodramatic nature of Gissing's life found its way into his first novel, based in part on his negative marital experience, yet the fact that he transforms the whole of his fictional London into a music hall stage points to a certain over-sensitive, histrionic predisposition in his personality rather than merely to an immediate mood or state of mind. This is further supported by the fact that "[h]e had even thought of writing a novel upon a music-hall theme, but realised just in time that the subject was too light and frivolous for a serious artist" (*DLLG*, 137), which is yet another evidence of the perpetual inner struggle between his realistic and rational side and its sentimental and idealistic counterpart. His liking for variety drama also brings him into the auditorium on the opening night of *The Crees of Misery Junction*, but Ackroyd ironically makes him muse on his essay in progress entitled "Real Drama and Real Life." Unable to suppress the melodramatic tendencies in his interpretation of the world, young Gissing's London as theatre becomes a stage on which he is doomed to perform in a pulp drama over which he has given up all control.

However, it is the character of Elizabeth Cree that connects all the theatrical aspects of the city in the novel since she assumes almost all the possible roles within this thematic framework – first she is a keen music hall attender, then herself a music hall performer, and eventually a playwright, director and stage manager. At the same time she is a brutal serial killer, a forger of her husband's supposed diary, and one of the story's narrators. The anxious and frustrated Elizabeth notices the essential ambivalence of the music hall, which appears to imitate the real urban world, yet presents it in a different, lighter and therefore more enticing, fashion. Despite its realistic background, it is an ultimate fantasy world in which the everyday and commonplace are intensified and exaggerated so that the resulting image surpasses the life experience of any of the members of the audience. When Elizabeth sees a familiar London street scene on the stage, she realises that through play-acting, colourful scenery, disguise, cross-dressing, nonsensical dialogues and singing and dancing even the most miserable city image or event can be promptly and easily turned into a spectacular and amusing show: "here was a picture of the Strand along which she had just walked – but how much more glorious and iridescent it now seemed, with its red and blue shop-fronts and their goods piled high. This was better than any memory. [...] there was no more pain now, and no more suffering [...] She was conscious only of the strange comedy with which Leno had assuaged the misery of her life" (*DLLG*, 19–20). It is no wonder that she is so strongly lured into this world, which offers her the chance to forget her unfortunate fate by allowing her to live the illusion of being someone else through a series of gags, sketches and stand-up comedy. Although Ackroyd eschews direct social critique he does envisage a "positive role for mass culture in enabling the oppressed to endure what, in his view, cannot be changed."[28]

Ackroyd has his main protagonist accepted into the music hall theatrical guild by none other than Dan Leno himself, the "music hall monopolylinguist,"[29] the most popular late- Victorian comedian and a famous follower of the London entertainment tradition established by Joseph Grimaldi. As with some other real historical personages featuring in his novels, Ackroyd changes some biographical data for the sake of his narrative. Two of these changes are especially important: he makes his Dan Leno ten years older, born in 1850 while in reality he was born in 1860, as he needs him to be already a teenager when Elizabeth first meets him in 1864, and a fully grown-up man when giving his testimony to the police investigators in 1880 (yet, for no apparent reason Ackroyd also has Grimaldi, who is only briefly mentioned in the text, be born in 1779 instead of 1778). The dates of Leno's first night performances are also moved back in time as most of them were not staged during the time of the novel's story: Elizabeth, for instance, gets a role in *Babes in*

---

28 Alan Robinson, *Narrating the Past: Historiography, Memory and the Contemporary Novel*, 158–59.
29 Susana Onega, *Peter Ackroyd*, 72.

the Wood, first performed in 1888, which is seven years after her supposed execution. The second alteration concerns one of Leno's many stage-names – "The Great Little Leno, the Quintessence of Cockney Comedians" – which in reality did not contain the word "Cockney" but "Irish," even though a great number of his impersonations, or "appearing in character,"[30] were peculiar Cockney characters of both genders. Ackroyd presents him as a distinctly Cockney artist, which he indeed was, and so gives him the appropriate label as a visionary London performer who, through his countless impersonations, "came to symbolize all the life and energy and variety of the city itself" (LLCV, 341). It is alongside this fictitious Dan Leno that Elizabeth becomes a music hall starlet, playing Little Victor's Daughter and later, due to her rather mannish stature and manner, The Older Brother, a role in which she eventually feels truly happy.

Elizabeth thus comes to dramatise, satirise and mock the very conditions from which she came, which she hates and which so deformed her psychological development – extreme poverty, deprivation and parental neglect. The quasi-real, illusory theatrical East End world allows her to displace its real model and imagine herself only "dancing upon the stage with the beautiful picture of London behind" (*DLLG*, 56). Her desire to be someone completely other than herself results in her dressing as The Older Brother and strolling through Whitechapel, Shadwell and Limehouse streets at night, enjoying this new, masculine, more secure identity, and entertaining herself by observing the city's filth and wretchedness:

> The females of the street would whistle to him but he passed them and, if the worst of them tried to touch him, he would grip their wrists with his big hands and thrust them away. He was not so rough with the game boys, because he knew that they lusted after him in a purer fashion: they were looking for their double, and who could reflect them better than the Older Brother? No one ever saw Lambeth Marsh Lizzie or Little Victor's Daughter – she had gone away, and I liked to think of her sleeping peacefully somewhere. (*DLLG*, 154)

For Elizabeth, the dilapidated night-time East End streets become an extension of the music hall stage, where she turns into a celebrity actress inhabiting a world detached from that of the prostitutes, vagrants, drunkards and gamblers. These typical denizens of the nocturnal city

---

30 Peter Bailey, *Popular Culture and Performance in the Victorian City*, 131.

transform in her mind into a mere audience she can easily forget about or only watch unconcernedly as they appear to have little relevance to, or impact on, her newly assumed self. In this case, the city as theatre proves rather harmless as it serves as an escapist, auto-therapeutic device for a person whose dignity and self-esteem have been fatally damaged by a dysfunctional social and familial background.

Unable to function as a mature individual in an intimate social relationship, Elizabeth enters her marriage as if she were assuming yet another role in the stage drama of her life, this time that of dutiful wife. However, unlike the hilarious music hall sketches, a performance like hers is doomed to utter failure because it concerns the mundane, everyday business of a respectable middle-class household, in which there is very little, if any, place for excess, overacting and ironic distance. The role is also very strictly prescribed, including the compulsory aspects of middle-class femininity, docility and meekness, which are exactly those qualities her mother used to demand from her and which, therefore, she has been trying to expunge from her life through her acting, and it obviously offers no opportunity for arbitrary gender identity switching, cross-dressing or nonsense-based improvising, the only devices that ever gave her a sense of liberty and independence. Moreover, married life involves emotional and physical intimacy, another aspect of life she detests as a result of her upbringing by her prejudiced mother. Elizabeth's husband, John Cree, soon notices that the principal cause of his unhappiness in the marriage is that his wife is trying to play a role she is not suited for, that on occasion she "became 'wifely' with a fierceness and determination that were almost professional" (*DLLG*, 227). Elizabeth underestimates the complexity of her new role, which requires both a public and performable, as well as a private and offstage side that is far less achievable through theatrical means. Hating the thought of her own failure, she strives to reach perfection in the former, more public side in which, however, she turns out to be helpless without the support of the latter. As a result, she finds herself trapped in an intimate chamber drama in which she lacks all the chief attributes of her successful role-playing, namely the artistic freedom derived from a fluidity of gender and personal identity, and the generous spaciousness of the city-stage.

Elizabeth's nostalgic longing for her old music-hall self and her urban-acting *locus operandi* stands at the core of her ominous nightly expeditions, through which she also settles accounts with her unpleasant past. Suffocated by the daily routines of her married life, she discovers what she believes to be artistic freedom and an opportunity for dramatic self-expression in her deliberately showy homicidal acts. She carefully studies maps of London in order to become streetwise in plotting what she calls "all [her] exits and entrances" (*DLLG*, 27). She also gets inspired by De Quincey's "On Murder Considered as One of the Fine Arts," in which the author ironically romanticises the 1811 Ratcliffe Highway serial killer, John Williams, as a solitary artist whose acts have a strong aesthetic dimension and "who used London as the 'studio' to display his works" (*DLLG*, 30). Elizabeth sees herself in a similar light, only the role of painter is replaced by those of director and actor as she "performs" the murders as if they were bombastic scenes from a heroic drama: she spills as much blood around as possible, pays attention to every single morbid detail, arranges the crime scene and the pose of the victim, and leaves misleading clues pointing to Jewish lore. Thanks to this, she manages to achieve her aim of attracting crowds of curious spectators, from police officers and newspaper journalists to ordinary Londoners, and the East End, once again, becomes her stage.

Even the otherwise incompetent Inspector Kildare takes notice of the apparent showiness of the murders and suggests that their perpetrator might be an "actor playing a part. [...] This murderer, this Limehouse Golem as they call him, seems to be acting as if he were in a blood tub off the Old Kent Road. Everything is very messy and very theatrical. It is a curious thing" (*DLLG*, 204–5). Inspector Kildare's observation is confirmed by the most qualified expert of all, Dan Leno, who agrees that hearing about the murders is "like being in some kind of penny gaff or theatre of variety" (*DLLG*, 205). However, unwilling to accept Leno's suggestion that the murderer could be a woman, Kildare's investigation fizzles out as all of his suspects turn out to have irrefutable alibis, and Elizabeth Cree is eventually tried and sentenced for a homicide she actually did not plan to commit originally and whose theatricality she was, on the contrary, trying to avoid – the killing of her husband.

One of the sacrifices Elizabeth has to make in playing the role of a middle-class wife is to leave her music hall career behind, a step she perceives as particularly frustrating as it means cutting herself off from everything enjoyable and comforting she has ever experienced. An opportunity to be a part of the real drama-making process again and even to see it from the other side comes when Elizabeth finishes writing her husband's play, a socially critical melodrama about the London poor entitled *Misery Junction*, and then decides to put it on stage herself. Disturbed by the odd and callous behaviour of his wife, John Cree had found himself struck by writer's block, unable to continue working on the play in which he invested much of his hope for fame and recognition. When Elizabeth announces to him the completion of his play he feels angry and betrayed because she has taken from him the last remaining chance for his life's fulfilment. Ignoring his protests, she makes plans for the play to be rehearsed and staged, yet in a manner more appropriate to her current social status: no longer a music hall performance, but a "different type of production altogether," approached "in the proper spirit" (*DLLG*, 239). However, despite having made it repeatedly clear to the acting ensemble that they are not participating in a variety show but in a serious, if not tragic, dramatic piece, the public rehearsal turns into a light comedy performance because the actors are unwilling to take her seriously, and because the Limehouse audience have no interest in the gravely moralistic play and virtually cheer the actors into turning it into its own parody.

It is this humiliating failure as a playwright and director that prompts Elizabeth to conceive the last act of her unfortunate marriage – getting rid of her annoying husband. She first arranges the scene so that the emotionally and sexually frustrated man seeks refuge in the arms of the housemaid, Aveline Mortimer, so she can make a highly dramatic extempore of the scandalous disclosure of their affair, evoking sufficient pathos by exclaiming lines from the tragic scenes she used to perform. Then, in a similarly theatrical manner, she accuses him of being the cause of Aveline's pregnancy, by which she gains dominance over him and the desired mastery of the household. Eventually, she poisons him as he begins to suspect her involvement in sinister and evil schemes. Although she is tried and sentenced for the murder of her husband, she gains solace even in the death cell from the striking similarity between her story and the popular music hall drama, *The London Phantom*, a fact she confides to the confused priest, Father Lane, who has come to hear her confession. She thus indirectly pleads guilty also to the Limehouse Golem murders, whose dramatic perfection and undetectability she is so proud of. Elizabeth's city as theatre is no longer a self-soothing game displacing the world that allegedly bred her wretchedness. In her diseased imagination, the streets have been transformed into a vast stage for her own Gothic revenge tragedy bloodbath, in which she deludedly sees herself as personifying the spirit of London whose mission is to right the city's injustice by exterminating all its symptoms.

No matter how infallible and far-sighted Elizabeth believes herself to be, she does not foresee in the least that her final entrance on the city stage is yet to come. Eventually, "her" *Misery Junction* finds its way onto a bill not so much due to its artistic quality, but because its background – the authoress being a recently executed murderer of her husband and a former music hall performer – has provided sufficient promotion of the piece to pack the playhouse with an eager audience. The performance is a grand spectacle from beginning to end, but is very dissimilar to how Elizabeth would have imagined it: new lines as well as topical references are added, the name of the main actress is changed to Elizabeth Cree, the plot is modified in order to correspond to the authoress's fate, and the play is renamed *The Crees of Misery Junction*. By blending low comic elements with serious and tender scenes, the play follows perfectly the established patterns of comedy, in which the Victorian audience saw no incongruity[31]. Elizabeth thus gets on her beloved London stage again in what is an ultimate fusion of reality and dramatic illusion, something she longed for her whole adult life, yet it happens only after her death and in a cheap farce parodying everything she used to admire about herself. However, there is one moment she would have particularly enjoyed – when the stage machinery simulating the gallows gets jammed and Aveline Mortimer, the cast member who most revels in mocking the character she personifies, is hanged right on the stage. It is as if some superior power of London as theatre interfered, meting out its cruel justice by insisting the staged city tale be as faithful to the real version as possible.

The story of *Dan Leno and the Limehouse Golem* circulates around the city's double condition – "of performance and textuality, transformation and interpretation,"[32] yet the performative aspect is far more significant than in other of Ackroyd's London novels as the urban and theatrical worlds in it perpetually intertwine and thus borrow and adopt principles and features from each other. Ackroyd's Londoners are well aware of the potential theatricality of the city's public life, and although some of them find it annoying and irritating, most of them appreciate and relish the independence and imaginativeness the spectacles of the streets allow them to enjoy. At the same time, these citizens are often ardent theatregoers and what they love to see on stage, though only in random glimpses or isolated scenes, are precisely those gags and sketches dramatising, satirising and parodying scenes from their everyday lives. As the most dramatic topical London affairs quickly find their way from newspaper reports onto the play-bills of the popular music halls, they fill their auditoriums with thousands of curious and sensation-seeking spectators. Those

31   Michael Booth, "Comedy and farce," 130.
32   Gibson and Wolfreys, *Peter Ackroyd*, 201.

actors, comedians and impersonators who are skilled enough to work ingeniously on the borderline between reality and illusion by making it, as needed, either imperceptible or distinct have thus an immense, and mostly wholesome, influence on the audience, who willingly surrender to the charm of their mesmerising persuasiveness.

It is Dan Leno who therefore saves the night and manages to restore the dichotomy of the stage as a separate realm from the reality of the auditorium. Thanks to his exceptional ability to keep cool and improvise in every conceivable situation, he swiftly adopts a new guise and performs a comic gag about the hanged woman being restored to life. As the formerly terror-stricken, now relieved audience streams out into the tumultuous London streets, the theatrical and the urban worlds intersect profoundly in physical and metaphorical terms:

> They left the theatre in Limehouse and went their separate ways, to Lambeth or to Brixton, to Bayswater or to Whitechapel, to Hoxton or to Clerkenwell, all of them returning to the uproar of the eternal city. And even as they travelled homeward, many of them remembered the wonderful moment when Dan Leno had risen from the trapdoor and appeared in front of them. 'Ladies and gentlemen,' he had announced in his best mammoth comique manner, 'here we are *again*!' (*DLLG*, 282, emphasis in original)

Both London and its theatrical nature can thus be taken as ongoing processes running concurrently, though necessarily interconnected thematically as well structurally. The eternal city thus functions as a self-reflexive *theatrum urbis*, offering up all of its defining features, especially its subversive and heterogeneous forces and the recurrent nature of its happenings. In his final exclamation Dan Leno expresses exactly this common attribute of the city and the theatre: endings take turn with beginnings so frequently and seamlessly that the sense of an ending has become virtually indeterminate. The comic urban theatrical tradition, embodied by Joseph Grimaldi, Dan Leno and Charlie Chaplin, reflects the continuous character of the city's life: "the chaotic phase comes to an end, order is restored and life in London can begin a new cycle, for the city that has bred the Golem is also the city that has bred the comedian/magus capable of absorbing it and expelling it in the cathartic ritual of drama."[33] And so, as Leno knows, amidst death and suffering there is always the hint of a promise of something new and perhaps better, which

---

33 Onega, *Peter Ackroyd*, 72.

the music hall illustrates more efficiently than anything else: the Golem is gone to where it sent its victims, Elizabeth Cree is executed, Aveline Mortimer is dead, but those who have survived must go on living – the show is over, long live the show! The city and its dramatic representations, once *again*, become one.

The Might and Glory of the City Celebrated – *The Clerkenwell Tales*

Another of Ackroyd's works in which London's theatricality is foregrounded is *The Clerkenwell Tales*. This novel playfully, yet resourcefully, elaborates on the strong organic connectedness between medieval urban life and its numerous spiritual and material dramatic manifestations, those "brief but vivid intimations of London life" (*LTM*, 25), both organised and staged as well as spontaneous and unprompted. This conception of theatricality correlates with Ackroyd's persuasion that a combination of mythology and "materialistic forces that have [...] structured London's geographical development since Saxon times"[34] lies at the core of the city's complex fabric. Although civic life in medieval London to a large extent revolved around various performances and spectacular events, it was a specific kind of theatricality, especially due to its integrative and communal character, but also due to its more or less manifest political dimension. "Civic London in the fourteenth century was no mere administrative and economic unit; it was theatrically oriented, valuing public and private civic display, apparently above all for its political uses although surely also for entertainment's sake."[35] This polarity between politically motivated theatricality in the form of secret plotting, deliberate manipulation of the public and intrigues of power, and seemingly apolitical dramatic performances during various feasts, festivals, fairs and pageantries, whose primary aim was to offer a diversion to all involved, yet which also reinforced a sense of local community and celebrated characteristic aspects of the citizens' ordinary life as well as the most significant events in the Christian calendar, composes the fundamental axis of the novel's multiple plots.

Medieval plays and other dramatic events were mostly intended for public display in city streets, churches, on special playing fields and in

---

34 Robinson, *Narrating the Past: Historiography, Memory and the Contemporary Novel*, 154.
35 Anne Lancashire, *London Civic Theatre: City Drama and Pageantry from Roman Times to 1558*, 65.

market-places. The fact that neither the venues nor the actors and spectators were standardised or professionalised caused the distinctly diverse and heterogeneous character of the drama of that time. This was further determined by the fact that most of these open-air performances were moveable, staged on special pageant wagons drawn by horses, which circulated around the city and stopped at selected sites where large audiences could potentially gather. The size of the wagon represented a substantial limitation of the acting space, meaning that much of the weight of the message relied on rhetorically structured dialogues and speeches; related to this was the narrative and interactive, rather than purely performative and monological, nature of the plays, often resulting in characters' running commentaries or direct audience address[36]. At the same time, the whole event had a noticeably processional quality as the audiences could easily follow the pageant wagon to its next station. This was accompanied with banners, pennants, music, singing and dancing, mostly relating to the procession. Therefore, sheer spectacle was the effect most desired, a "sense of marvel following upon marvel."[37] The whole procession thus became, if only for a brief moment, a self-contained community of its own kind.

Many kinds of theatrical actions took place in medieval London throughout the year, religiously connoted as well as secular, the latter category including mummings, the feast of Midsummer Watch and the Lord Mayor's Show. Mummings were organised by the city magistrates in order to celebrate and impress the monarch or a member of the royal family. As such they required elaborate costumes, music and choreography, the disguises of higher social ranks, such as esquires, knights, emperors, popes, cardinals and legates[38]. The mummers rode on horseback, taking the route of London's "principal pageant stations of coronation entries,"[39] providing thus both a street spectacle and a distraction for the royalty. The Midsummer Watch originated in part as an ordinary security measure, and in part as a military muster[40], but in the late fourteenth century it developed into a civic festival popular until the sixteenth century. It is especially the disappearance of this tradition that the historian and antiquarian of London, John Stow, nostalgically mourns in his famous

---

36 Meg Twycross, "The theatricality of medieval English plays," 42.
37 Twycross, "The theatricality of medieval English plays," 47.
38 Lancashire, *London Civic Theatre: City Drama and Pageantry from Roman Times to 1558*, 42.
39 Lawrence Manley, "Of Sites and Rites," 43.
40 Lancashire, *London Civic Theatre*, 50.

and monumental *A Survey of London* (1598)[41], which provides a detailed survey of all the city's streets and their characteristics and history[42]. Yet its decline was the result of increasing concern for public order and the Midsummer watches were gradually replaced by the more controlled Lord Mayor's Procession, held "on the occasion of his return from his oath-taking in Westminster."[43] It celebrated the city representatives and reminded them of their obligations to the poor, but it was not open to the public and offered only a pale substitute for the Midsummer Watch in terms of the degree of communal participation.

The most significant example of a late medieval religious theatrical festival in London was the Clerkenwell Plays. Performed on an annual or at least very regular basis, the action lasted for several days and the plays were thematically based on biblical subject matter. They were sometimes concurrent with another large religious dramatic spectacle, the feast of Corpus Christi cycle, which had been inaugurated as a thanksgiving for Christ's sacrifice and whose "observance rapidly became a highpoint in the religious year, being celebrated in early summer with a street procession of clergy and lay dignitaries behind the Communion Host."[44] All these religious feasts contained a significant secular element, especially due to their interactive and processional character, which allowed the lay and low-born spectators to take an active part in their proceedings. Some of the medieval mystery plays thus became predecessors of modern popular comedies as they employed the same "low" comic devices, such as excessive violence, directed mostly at infants or representatives of authority, mockery of women, contempt for foreigners, and excremental or sexual jokes (*A*, 280), which made their religious background only supportive if not entirely subsidiary.

Most of the above mentioned theatrical events can be considered as what Bakhtin famously terms carnivalesque popular-festive forms, possessing several of their constitutive features: there is a people's initiative in the celebration, which requires no official acknowledgement or patron-

---

41 At the same time, Stow criticises the public theatres which "distress [him] with their heteroglot character and variegated audience" (Smith, Strier and Bevington, *The Theatrical City: Culture, Theatre and Politics in London, 1576–1649*, 4).

42 Ackroyd admits that Stow's *A Survey of London* proved enormously helpful in his preparation and researching for *London: The Biography*, as it provides a picture of not only Elizabethan but also medieval London whose aspects were still apparent in his lifetime. He praises Stow because he "was able to see beneath the crevices and was able to judge and describe the underlying structures of the city (Banks, "Peter Ackroyd on London").

43 Ian Archer, "The Nostalgia of John Stow," 24.

44 William Tydeman, "An introduction to medieval English theatre," 20.

age; there is no place for respect, sobriety, piousness or externally maintained order, only for ongoing and spontaneous merriment, tomfoolery and grotesque images of the body; the crowd is internally arranged by the people, outside of and contrary to existing forms of coercive mechanisms; the feast is based on the suspension of all hierarchical differences, which is replaced by a jovial familiarity offering liberation from the seriousness of ordinary life; the mode of action and discourse is prevailingly that of insults and abuse, of a universal rather than personal nature and aimed at the higher level of power and authority which is to be challenged, ridiculed, dethroned and replaced. Through costume change and travesty the king becomes the clown while the clown becomes the king[45]. The carnival thus represents a silently authorised subversion of law and order, a remedial and redemptive opportunity for the lowly and powerless to release their negative energy and act out a breakdown of all traditional social norms and assumptions. However, this moment of disorder and liberty is only illusory and temporary and as such it "provides a release of class tension that allows the reinstatement and maintenance of the same social order."[46]

Ackroyd deliberately chooses Clerkenwell as the setting for the ingeniously enigmatic plot of the novel, not only for its intense theatrical activity, but also because he considers this part of London to have been known, from medieval times, for its multifariousness, being a visionary and spiritual place, a refuge for the outcast and the outlaw, a site of vigorous radicalism, and a locus of lunatics and eccentrics living as if outside the city's official time. The heterogeneous character of the area was further reinforced by the fact that numerous events that always attracted a large number of participants and audiences took place there, such as fairs, festivals and other forms of public entertainment. These in fact created a simulacrum of the London of that time as they imitated and parodied the routines and practices of the city's life, especially those with the potential to undermine its well-established law and order. Consequently, these events represented "a symbol of disorder and anarchy, threatening to overwhelm the values of a humanised and civilised London with all its vulgar paraphernalia of," in Alexander Pope's words, "shews, machines, and dramatical entertainments, formerly agreeable only to the taste of the Rabble" (*LB*, 140). This often low and bawdy spectacle of the fair dramatised "a permanent aspect of London life" (*LB*, 141), as it helped perpetuate the inhabitants' feeling of temporary liberation from the re-

---

45   Mikhail Bakhtin, *Rabelais and His World*, 196–257.

46   Maggie Ann Bowers, *Magic(al) Realism*, 129.

straints of their daily routines, offering a "perpetual consolation from the violence of material inequality,"[47] while, at the same time, affirming their sense of belonging to the city's tradition.

Theatricality of diverse kinds permeates the coarse texture of Ackroyd's medieval London in *The Clerkenwell Tales,* both metaphorically and literally. The metaphorical level revolves around the ultimate discrepancy between the official and unofficial spheres of the lives of the city's elite citizens. The former includes their public image, connected with and derived from their influential position within the city's hierarchy of authority and power, while the latter refers to their private acts, deliberately concealed from any public scrutiny as they often disregard and subvert the values and principles they espouse as officials or magistrates. These acts range from relatively innocent ones, such as visiting brothels and other dissolute places, to secret political and religious plotting whose aim is to discredit or dispose of those who occupy the highest ranks in the establishment's hierarchy, foremost of all the king. William Exmewe is the most striking example of such a two-faced character. As an irredeemable conspirator, he not only plots against the king but also against the very conspiracy he organises. He is a pragmatic loner for whom life is an ongoing risky, adrenaline game in which he can play on as many sides as possible. He realises the necessity of play-acting and the flexible assumption of different roles in different situations and contexts, taking London as a stage, a realm of deception, "no more than a veil, a pageant cloth, which must be torn asunder to see the face of Christ shining" (*CT*, 21). Exmewe is thus the director of an urban drama in which he plays the main role, using the less gifted and more diffident as pawns to be unscrupulously indoctrinated, manipulated and sacrificed for his own ends. After his treacherous practices have been found too extreme for those holding official power, his punishment is carried out in the form of a grand spectacle in order to mask the true scheming; while the crowds are watching the condemned walking "barefoot to Dover carrying the cross before him" (*CT*, 203) where he is to repent and pray for a boat to take him from England, the high officials on the scaffold have already secured for him immediate transport to France and a comfortable house arrest in a small castle near Avignon. As such a dull existence will be torturous for someone with Exmewe's character, he is at least given one more chance to perform his part and enjoy being in the limelight in front of an enthusiastic audience.

---

47   Alex Murray, *Recalling London: Literature and History in the work of Peter Ackroyd and Iain Sinclair,* 131.

Even more astute and sophisticated is the collaboration between the Bishop of London and Sister Clarice, the "mad" nun of Clerkenwell convent. Sister Clarice's acting skills prove to be far more effective and convincing than Exmewe's and she manages to create around herself an air of being endowed with prophesying, visionary powers. She starts disseminating seemingly mad, apocalyptic visions about London and the kingdom which scares her mother superior who locks her up within the walls of the convent to prevent her from perturbing the public. However, rumours concerning her exceptional ability have been spreading all over the city and people's increasing curiosity to hear her prophecies sets her free from the confinement of her cell, which is precisely what she needs in order to carry out her mission – to turn public opinion against Richard II. Her warning speeches in various parts of the city are successful in stirring up her large audience's fear of the future under the current king and making them more approving of the invasion by Henry Bolingbroke, and upon his arrival at Westminster the streets are in an uproar. It is only when Clarice is summoned, imprisoned and interrogated by the bishop that she turns out to be not only perfectly sane but also an associate and instrument of Dominus, a secret group of clerical conspirators cooperating with Exmewe with the sole aim of dethroning the king. With the aid of Clarice's ranting, rhetorical performances Dominus help to depose the hated king and also get rid of Exmewe, an ally who would be too dangerous once they lost a common aim. And so, while Richard II is despatched "to the Tower for his own 'safety' against the supposed wrath of the London populace" (*CT*, 162), and Exmewe is arrested and charged with treason, the bishop and the nun "were raising cups of wine and congratulating one another on a drama well staged" (*CT*, 163).

The affiliation ordinary Londoners have with the city's theatricality is completely different from that of its dignitaries; it is more physical, less subtle, and associated with officially authorised events that contain a strong element of spectacle. This is chiefly because their ability to affect the public state of affairs is negligible and their everyday duties are too consuming and exhausting to leave them with any desire to play-act in their extremely limited spare time. Yet, as in the case of their more noble-born fellow citizens, behind their need for drama lies another kind of paradoxical inconsistency. What they look for on these theatrical occasions is a confirmation and celebration of the stable, recurrent, commonplace processes and happenings, the natural cycles that re-connect urban life with its rural roots, yet they also seek diversion and escape from the demands and monotony of their ordinary existence. That is why they like markets, fairs and religious festivals where the source of pleasure stems from the combination of abundance of produce and products and moderate, controlled amusement, but why they also revel in unrestrained pastimes, the Bakhtinian popular festive-forms, which offer both passive entertainment and, more importantly, a boisterous subversion and disruption of routine and order, immune from prosecution, in which everybody is allowed to actively participate and temporarily assume whatever identity he or she desires. Ackroyd is well-aware that a "rich round of ceremonies and rituals regulated the medieval world,"[48] and his rendering of late fourteenth-century London includes several scenes depicting such set events, always emphasising their carnivalesque character and the consequent socially liberating effect they produce.

The novel's portrayal of an annual cycle of mystery plays in Clerkenwell during the week of Corpus Christi is an example of the first mentioned commoners' theatrical diversion. It is a feast that addresses all people regardless of their social status and so it naturally attracts those who are not traditionally welcome at more venerable religious ceremonies, yet it is organised by the city authorities and therefore closely controlled and inspected by officials, which in reality means it is held "under the guidance and supervision of the guild of parish clerks" (CT, 77). As a result, the Clerkenwell plays are composed of a specific mixture of the religious and the secular, the sacral and the mundane, reverence and ridicule, loftiness and indecency. The plays are based on biblical stories and are officially conceived as "mummings and interludes that celebrated the cycle of the city's year" (CT, 81), but they bear striking comic, or even farcical, features, mostly satirising universal human temperaments and vices or commenting on or alluding to popular topical issues, using wide linguistic and dramatic registers ranging from ostentatious verbosity and scenes abounding with pathos and dramatic vividness to obscenities, vulgar invective and lascivious gestures.

In "The Reeve's Tale," Ackroyd manages to authentically capture this peculiar atmosphere of the mysteries in which veneration and solemnity naturally give way to hilarity and derision. On a special platform the story of Noah's Ark is being presented, concretely a scene in which God, walking on stilts and wearing a gilded mask, is conversing with Japhet, who is riding a donkey. The stage dialogues are frequently interrupted by loud comments from the crowd as most of the spectators know the identity of the performers and these shouts thus mockingly refer to their civil

---

48   Lewis, *My Words Echo Thus: Possessing the Past in Peter Ackroyd*, 130.

professions, personal traits and acting skills rather than to the play's action. Moreover, as the younger actor is notorious for his impudence and quick wit, the audience impatiently awaits some unscripted verbal exchange or rude remark. Its wish is soon granted with a series of obscenities passing between the boy and his donkey, "culminating in a mock attempt by the boy to penetrate the beast's rear end" (*CT*, 80). As everybody knows the story well, comicality and topicality are the piece's crucial qualities – it is the manner in which it is presented, together with all the spontaneously improvised additional elements, spiced with malice and ribaldry, that determine the success and reception of the play, while the logic and plausibility necessary for sustaining dramatic illusion in the modern sense prove insignificant:

> In the same rhythmic chant, which seemed to the audience to come from some source beyond speech and song, God commanded Noah to build an ark and to shelter there two of every beast or bird upon the earth. The fact that the ark could already be seen upon the green was of no consequence; past, present and future were intermingled in the small area of Clerkenwell. The audience assembled knew precisely what would occur in front of them, but they were always surprised and entertained by it. (*CT*, 82)

Despite its hallmark of institutional authorisation, the festival is actually governed by an unwritten rule: the audience is presented with light, undemanding entertainment packaged as serious liturgical drama, yet though they know precisely what they can expect, they always look taken aback and amused. It is thus a theatrical process that requires active dramatic contributions from both sides involved.

The public urban theatrical tendency of programmed excess and eccentricity best finds its vent in the rituals of the carnivalesque masquerades. These represent, paradoxical though it sounds, an institutionalised form of spontaneously subversive, and excessively hilarious acts as well as a short-term reversal of traditional social standings. The spontaneity and freedom of expression are, however, strictly limited by the temporariness and territoriality of the feast, and are severely punished if the exuberance of the participants transgresses these limits. *The Clerkenwell Tales* portrays one such occasion, the pageant celebrating the feast of Midsummer's Eve, and demonstrates its ultimate theatricality: central to the celebration is a gaudily painted stage which is being carried around Clerkenwell and on which a satirical scene about King Richard II and Providence is performed. Behind the stage goes a horse-drawn pageant wagon containing a glittering and coloured model of the universe on which an astrological scene is depicted. This moveable drama is followed by a large procession of respectable Londoners in every imaginable noble disguise, depicting lay as well as clerical dignitaries, some of them wearing robes and costumes borrowed from the mysteries, suggesting that rather than comprising separate, unrelated units the city's theatrical events compose one cyclical continuum in which it is difficult, if not wholly impossible, to distinguish between the religious and the secular in terms of the performances' forms and purposes.

The feast thus seamlessly fuses two differently, if not even contradictorily, motivated and socially targeted theatrical events – a comic play satirising, among other authorities, the king and intended chiefly for a lower-class audience, and the mummings, supposedly meant to pay tribute to the said monarch and involving mostly higher-ranked participants. Satire and mockery thus go hand in hand with dignity and solemnity as the stage, the wagon and the disguised citizens on horseback move slowly around the city as one mass. Thomas Gunter, the physician, observes the picturesque procession in detail:

> Gunter grimaced at the guns upon the walls and bulwarks were 'shot for joy,' in the phrase of the mayor, while the merchants of the several crafts walked in procession past the Great Cross of Cheapside. [...] There followed behind them a group of citizens riding in disguise, as if for a mummery. Some were dressed as knights, in coats and gowns of red, with visors upon their faces, one was arrayed as the emperor and after him, at some distance, came one like the Italian pope accompanied by twenty-four cardinals. In the rear were seven others masked with black visors, unamiable, as if they were in service of some foreign prince; they were hissed by the crowd of spectators, who were eager to enter the spirit of the proceedings. (*CT*, 114)

All this is accompanied by a cacophony of shouting and trumpet playing, the lighting of bonfires, the playing of music and singing of minstrels, and watched by an excited mob which is an integral part of this grand spectacle where "the might and glory of the city were celebrated" (*CT*, 114). Yet, although the carnival is an opportunity for the common people to assume the identity of noblemen and dignitaries, its egalitarianism is not unconditional as not all free Londoners are allowed to participate equally – while only worthy Londoners can participate in the official parade, the poor men, known as "masterless men" (*CT*, 115), are given their own procession, separated from that of their more respectable fellow-citizens. Spontaneous, broadminded and free-spirited as they strive to appear, the novel shows that the medieval carnivalesque revelries are still marked by the imprint of social hierarchies and their conventions.

The daily intersection of official and public ceremonies and other spectacular rituals is shown in "The Man of Law's Tale": at Westminster, Martin, a young man of law, assists his master and teacher, the sergeant-at-law Miles Vavasour, in putting on his ceremonial coat and a special round cap signifying his rank, and then accompanies him from the robing chamber to the court in the Great Hall. "Such rituals enhanced the dignity of office, just as they add to the verisimilitude of Ackroyd's fiction."[49] Upon leaving Westminster Hall, as it is St Helen's feast day, Martin observes the procession held in the saint's honour. A scene on the pageant wagon depicts the discovery and unearthing of the Holy Cross and features a man disguised as St Helen who, "in a most unsaintly fashion" blows "kisses to those assembled along the path" (*CT*, 173). Eventually, even this supposedly peaceful religious feast gets disturbed by a riot as some of the spectators take advantage of being in the area where the municipal and religious authorities reside and, armed with swords and staffs, they demand the release of the nun of Clerkenwell from the bishop's dungeon, while two other men mount the wagon and drive it against the rioting crowd. Despite its officially proclaimed religious and political functions, the medieval city's theatricality is shown as inseparable from popular entertainment often on the verge of immediate commotion and disturbance.

Because of the enormous size of the gatherings of mostly mutually unfamiliar people, the large-scale consummation of alcohol, and the seeming absence of official surveillance, both the discussed forms of the city life's dramatic manifestations always teeter on the edge of uncontrolled violence and rioting. Bogo, the summoner, experiences this personally, even though, aware of his being highly unpopular among many Londoners for performing the duties of his job, he instinctively avoids crowds. In an unguarded moment he is dragged into an ominous *danse macabre* that grows into a fierce lynching during which he is beaten up, his clothes and shoes are singed with fire, and his earlobe is bitten off in imitation of a street fight: "He howled and the women, sensing his pain, yelled in triumph. It was the savage yell, hard, prolonged, exultant, which often sounded through London. It was the cry of the city itself" (*CT*, 120). This

---

49   Lewis, *My Words Echo Thus*, 131.

vengeful, ritual punishment inflicted on an innocent representative of the executive power becomes a symbolic act of defiance of and a settling of accounts with the power itself. As the executive body is too abstract and beyond their reach, the mob make do with anybody on hand who is at least loosely associated with the impacts they perceive as being unfair. The Lollards who are recognised by the spectators during the Clerkenwell mysteries are far less fortunate than the summoner. As generally hated public enemies, within a burst of brief but all the more merciless rage, they are either killed or fatally wounded on the spot. The onlooking reeve observes the split-second metamorphosis of the peaceful crowd into a mindless mob: "the crowd became one living creature with a single purpose. It hurled itself against the assailants of the mystery" (*CT*, 86). The pathos, hysteria, violence and ridicule on the stage have a strong tendency to find their mirror images in the minds and acts of the originally uninvolved spectators, thus making the distinction between the actors and the audience of the street drama indistinct, if not utterly irrelevant.

Ackroyd's treatment of the theme of the theatre and theatricality in *The Clerkenwell Tales* differs substantially from that in his novels set in a more recent past. He aptly demonstrates, through separate scenes rather than a coherent storyline, that medieval theatre was very unlike its modern counterpart. Although the novel loosely follows the scheme of Chaucer's *The Canterbury Tales* by employing the same cast of characters, it lacks, among other things, the unifying common narrative framework of its predecessor. Ackroyd's characters are, more or less directly and consciously, drawn into actions and events whose course and consequences they are often unable to foresee or even comprehend. Rather than being relaxed and carefree pilgrims they find themselves caught up in the turbulent – exciting for some, menacing for others, yet dangerous for all – spectacle and drama of London at that time, a turbulence that stems from the underlying double-sidedness of the existence of all its dwellers. On the one hand, there are intrinsic discrepancies between the public image and personal desires and aspirations of those in power, which result in a hypocritical, treacherous world of political intrigue, pretence and unscrupulously pragmatic behaviour lacking the essential elements of humanity. On the other hand, the commoners' need for theatrical entertainment which can plausibly reflect their life, re-affirm its order and emphasise its stable institutional, social and religious framework, contrasts with their need for temporary escape in the form of spontaneous and boisterous, carnivalesque festivity. It is precisely this dramatic tension between the conflicting realms of the homogeneous, official and prescribed and the heterogeneous, private, and subversive that makes Ackroyd's fragmentary image of late fourteenth-century London in *The Clerkenwell Tales* so vivid and convincing, despite the novel's episodic structure.

The Horrific, the Spectacular and the Sublime

For Ackroyd, districts like Clerkenwell best embody the inseparable connection, conceived through London's fundamental theatricality, between joy and spectacular diversion on the one hand and violence and criminality on the other. One example can be found in the various kinds of violent rioting, which have been a "London tradition [...] since the early Middle Ages" and which "happen so frequently that they are almost part of London's texture."[50] The city thus becomes "a stage upon which were presented spectacles for the delight and terror of the urban audience" (*LB*, 275), through the unrefined mimesis of the most familiar aspects of their own lives, including felonious ones. Such an idea of the *urbs criminis theatrum* is explored in *Hawksmoor* when Nicholas Dyer is musing on how one of his churches stands right in the centre of a poverty-stricken area around the Ratcliffe Highway:

> ... this good and savoury Parish is the home of Hectors, Trapanners, Biters who all go under the general appelation of Rooks. Here are all the Jilts, Cracks, Prostitutes, Night-walkers, Whores, Linnen-lifters, who are like so many Jakes, Privies, Houses of Offices, Ordures, Excrements, Easments and piles of Sir-reverence [...] There are other such wretched Objects about these ruined Lanes, all of them lamentable Instances of Vengeance. And it is not strange (as some think) how they will haunt the same Districts and will not leave off their Crimes until they are apprehended, for these Streets are their Theatre. Theft, Whoredom and Homicide peep out of the very Windows of their Souls; Lying, Perjury, Fraud, Impudence and Misery are stamped upon their very Countenances as now they walk within the Shaddowe of my Church. (*H*, 94)

Dyer's view of the impoverished and crude life in the East End streets is derived from a series of loosely related scenes and performances whose common background is destitution, deprivation, anger, a sense of in-

---

50 Andy McSmith, "Rioting has been a London tradition for centuries," an interview with Peter Ackroyd. *The Independent*, 22 August 2011.

justice, and a resulting tendency towards the abuse of alcohol, violent behaviour and criminality. For the cynical and merciless architect these manifestations of London low life are merely an obtrusive spectacle he is forced to watch in the background of his lofty creation. Hypocritically and self-deludedly, he excludes himself from this spectacle, while, in reality, his acts of human sacrifice for the successful construction of his churches are nothing more than yet another part of the violent urban drama he appears to despise so ostentatiously.

Most of Ackroyd's other London novels also touch upon the theme and motif of the city's theatrical nature, though not in such a complex and thorough manner as *Dan Leno and the Limehouse Golem* and *The Clerkenwell Tales*. Theatre and dramatic performance also feature in *The Lambs of London*. Charles Lamb, known for his positive attitude to drama, was among the critics who valued theatre for its "capacity to unite people, humanize them, reconcile their conflicting interests and give them something to talk about."[51] In the novel, he and his friends and colleagues establish an amateur acting group and, for the sake of irony, they decide to rehearse the scenes featuring the Athenian mechanicals from *A Midsummer Night's Dream*. They also invite Mary Lamb to co-direct the rehearsals as Charles hopes it might make her forget William Ireland and, consequently, her alarming state of mind would be improved. However, the actual effect is the very opposite: the devoted Mary is disappointed with the frivolity and flippancy of the young gentlemen, their carefree theatrical attempts seem to her too detached from the intricate impediments of the outside world, treating the stage and real life as two separate realms that do not overlap. Moreover, the unfortunate situation of the young lovers due to their parents' disapproval of their relationship in the mechanicals' play, *The Legend of Pyramus and Thisbe,* only reminds her of her clandestine meetings with Ireland, their "covert outdoor assignations"[52] disapproved of by their parents, and only intensifies her desire to spend her time with the serious and ruminative young gentleman. The rehearsals are eventually cancelled because of Mary's mental breakdown, but Charles persuades some of his friends to resume them when she has been found insane and is confined to a lunatic asylum after she kills her mother as he, once again, hopes the social activity will serve a therapeutic purpose and help her to recover from her deepening apathy and rediscover her lost interest in focused intellectual and artistic enterprise.

---

51 William Hazlitt quoted in Jim Davis, "Spectatorship," 59.
52 Barry Lewis, *My Words Echo Thus*, 141.

A shortened version of the play is briefly rehearsed and performed in front of Mary and some other inmates. Yet, once again, the final effect is far from beneficial for her as she suddenly gets extremely disturbed by Oberon's speech about the lovers being ever true in loving each other, probably moved by a memory of her relationship with Ireland, and she dies. It is as if her heart, for so long used to a life of quiet seclusion, could not bear the powerful theatrical emotivity and pathos of the scene which so strongly reminded her of her own destiny.

The character through which the theatrical theme is elaborated on most is William Ireland. He is a keen, though less ardent than his father, admirer of William Shakespeare's dramatic works, and he also manages to imitate the Bard's language and style so well in his forged play, *Vortigen,* that many of his prominent contemporaries, including several scholars, publishers and literati, are firmly convinced of its authenticity. Despite the fact that the hungering of London's literary circles for new discoveries of Shakespeare's lost works and other memorabilia and collectibles represented a substantial part in the manuscript's reception, for a boy of seventeen and of very limited schooling it was more than a remarkable achievement, all the more so because the contemporary audience preferred new comedies to tragedies and several ambitious playwrights, including Tobias Smollett and Samuel Johnson, "[f]ound their tragedies rejected by managers, or witnessed the often ignominious failure of their play on stage."[53] Moreover, the widespread belief that *Vortigen* was an early tragedy by the greatest English playwright even prompted Richard Brinsley Sheridan to put it on the bill of his Drury Lane theatre, though only one performance was eventually staged.

In the chapters depicting the rehearsing and performing of the play, Ackroyd demonstrates how significant a role the theatre played in shaping public opinion in the city as well as its overall social, intellectual and cultural climate. The scenes taking place at Drury Lane, especially the actual production of *Vortigen*, abound with period details which "enhance the credibility of the setting," and "[w]e can almost hear the mechanical moon as it is winched into place by ropes and pulleys and see the helmeted, breastplated, and kilted figure of Charles Kemble as he waits in the wings to perform as the ancient British king."[54] Although the production is originally meant to be a serious one, due to various circumstances, namely the growing speculation concerning the play's genuineness and

53   Susan Staves, "Tragedy," 88.
54   Lewis, *My Words Echo Thus,* 138.

the main actor, Charles Kemble's[55], disrespect for what he considers to be an artless fake, it turns into a comic performance and the celebration of the newly discovered literary treasure soon becomes a music-hall style parody deliberately accentuating its imperfections. All this happens to the young forger's horror and shock, but to the delight of the derisive crowd of spectators. "We survived sir. We hit choppy waters, and we were holed beneath the deck, but we sailed on guns blazing! God bless the London stage!" (*LL*, 178), remarks the malicious but experienced Kemble to the desolate Ireland after the performance is over, suggesting that in the theatrical world the text of a play means very little if it is not successfully presented to the audience and confronted with their multifarious, and often contradictory, tastes and expectations. In the cheers and boos of the audience Ackroyd identifies the very materialisation of the city's spirit and sensibility. He thus shows affinity with, among others, Charles Lamb, a keen stroller of the London streets, who in his essay "The Londoner" (1802) declares that a "mob of happy faces crowding up at the pit-door of Drury Lane theatre [...] gives [him] ten thousand sincerer pleasures that [he] could ever receive from all the flocks of silly sheep that ever whitened the plains of Arcadia or Epsom Downs."[56]

The disappointment for William Ireland is all the more bitter when his love for acting and theatre-going is taken into account. Although he and Mary share many traits and interests, they differ in their attitude to the theatre. For Mary, watching a play is a pleasant pastime but it is no more than a source of entertainment as she finds it lacks the solemnity of reading and discussing classical literature and philosophy, and too light-hearted to offer an appropriate alleviation of the hardships of her everyday life. William, on the other hand, is fascinated by the possibilities of the theatrical world, especially that of creating the illusion of an alternative, more enjoyable reality. Lacking Mary's education and opportunities of social status, his reading consists entirely of works cherished by his father, which means those of Shakespeare. While Mary's resort to literature is a means of forgetting her troublesome duties as a conscientious daughter and sister, William's literary efforts are motivated almost solely by the desire to prove his worth and abilities to his dismissive father. Therefore, literature for him by no means represents a leisurely escape from reality; on the contrary, his writing is part of his struggle

---

55 This is in fact one of Ackroyd's many deviations from historical records as the main part of *Vortigen* was played by John Philip Kemble, while Charles Kemble, his younger brother, took the role of the king's son.

56 Charles Lamb quoted in Lewis, *My Words Echo Thus*, 139.

with the source of his frustrations and anxieties, one which makes him even more strenuous and tenacious rather than relaxed or fulfilled. What fills him with pleasure and contentment, however, are all the imaginable forms of theatricality, both on stage and in life.

Unlike that of the sincere and truthful Mary, William's life is one of continuous play-acting and deceiving, and the whole of the Shakespeare Papers case easily bears comparison with a well-plotted urban drama of intrigue: the timing of the findings, their increasing historical and literary value, the invention of a mysterious benefactor, the leaving of deliberately misleading clues, the manipulation of credulous literary enthusiasts, and the bringing of a forged play to the most prestigious stage in London. Although William claims that he does not care about publicity, he does revel in the various roles and identities he assumes within his astute performances, such as those of duly appreciated son to his proud father, a respected essayist, and an aspiring scholarly lecturer. It is therefore understandable that he, as an amateur actor and director more or less out of necessity, looks up to the professionals who are allowed to inhabit the alluring world of institutionalised illusion and deception. When he goes to Drury Lane to see a popular musical drama, he becomes absorbed by a different state of mind, feeling "himself to be dissolved in the haze of light and sound that hung over the auditorium [...] For William this was more beautiful – more intense, more brightly coloured – than the material world itself" (*LL*, 160). As he watches Kemble and his fellow actors with fascination, admiring the ease and facility with which they become someone other than themselves, he realises that he is witnessing a materialisation of his innermost dream, which gives him the hope that he too could attain his wished-for self. "This was the meaning of the theatre, as William now understood it. It allowed the spectators to rise out of their own selves in an act of communion" (*LL*, 161). For him the theatre is more than an escapist spectacle, for its meaning and effect transcend the simple actors-audience axis by adding the dimension of a collective identity and sense of belonging, which most city people lack in the experience of their everyday lives.

The Casebook of Victor Frankenstein captures the unique atmosphere of early nineteenth-century public theatre performance. Due to the increasingly accelerating democratising tendencies after the Restoration, at the turn of the eighteenth and nineteenth centuries English theatres resumed the Elizabethan tradition, both in terms of their size and the composition of the audience: by the 1790s big theatres like Drury Lane or Covent Garden Theatre could accommodate more than 3,000 spectators, and the separated realms of the pit, the boxes and the galleries contained audiences comprising a wide cross-section of society from all around London, from aristocratic patrons, including royal family members, to servants, footmen and sailors. The theatre was thus the largest secular indoor space where people of different social standing could meet, and the fact that the auditorium was fully lit throughout the performance, together with the peculiar theatrical tastes and sensibility of the time, considerably shaped the audience's responses. Although these spectators were very attentive, examples of rowdiness were not exceptional as they often used their liberty to express dissent, or even riot, when they were displeased with the performance[57]. Social rank, and its possibility of freedom of expression, thus was a determining element in the experience of the public theatre, which resulted in this milieu's peculiarly ambivalent climate of democratic egalitarianism and snobbish contempt, as the behaviour of the low-class members of the audience was simultaneously an "offence to their superiors" as well as a "source of pride in an English social system that did not countenance treating servants like 'slaves'."[58]

Although historically the story of *The Casebook of Victor Frankenstein* takes place only a few years after that of *The Lambs of London* ends, the novel explores the motif of the London mob, the ultimate spectatorial body of urban dramas, in a similar way as in the *The Clerkenwell Tales,* set more than four hundred years earlier. The first theatrical scene of the novel depicts the production of a Romantic melodrama, a dramatic genre which dominated the stage in that period and which was especially a domain of the lower classes since centrally important for this genre was the "beauty of humble virtue, the hegemonic interpellation of the poor as honest, [...] especially as the theatres responded to rising social consciousness."[59] Its Gothic variant grew in popularity in the early nineteenth century, following the great success of M. G. Lewis's *The Castle Spectre* (1797) and Gilbert de Pixérécourt's *A Tale of Mystery* (1802), staged at Drury Lane and Covent Garden respectively[60]. The young, inexperienced and timid Swiss student Victor Frankenstein is taken by his rebellious and worldly-wise friend, Percy Bysshe Shelley, to see a popular Gothic melodrama, *Melmoth the Wanderer*, at Drury Lane, where he is for the first time exposed to the frightening character of the monolithic, tumultuous crowd. "Despite the laughter, and the general mood of ani-

57 Davis, "Spectatorship," 57–59.
58 Kristina Strub, "The making of an English audience: the case of the footmen's gallery," 133.
59 Jacky Bratton, "The music hall," 119.
60 Bratton, "The music hall," 120–121.

mation, it resembled some restless creature in search of prey. Could many lives make up one life?" (*CVF*, 43), he wonders, aware of the sinister potential of the assembly's transformation, within a moment, from a set of individuals into a mindless mass of furious might, triggered by a single hysteria-evoking impulse. At this point he does not know that his worst experience of the crowd is yet to come, specifically during the trial of Daniel Westbrook and his subsequent execution. As Westbrook is poor and radical in thought, the spectators are not interested in a lengthy, though fair, process but are anxious for a swift condemnation of the accused to the most severe punishment available. The whole event is thus conceived as a dramatic music-hall performance rather than legal proceedings, in which, unfortunately for the tried person, the roles and parts are carefully laid out beforehand.

Accordingly, the courtroom and the composition of the audience correspond to the nature of such a show: Frankenstein observes that the room looks more like "a cardboard puppet theatre than a place of justice" (*CVF*, 43), and the audience is "made up of shopmen and apprentices, of vagrant boys and ballad singers, of anyone who had no other pastime or occupation that afternoon [...] all of them causing an incessant bustle and noise. It was very like watching the activity of a London street" (*CVF*, 44). The bloodthirsty rabble's calls for a morbid spectacle are eventually satisfied by Westbrook's public execution at Newgate Prison. This is where the crowd definitely changes into a grotesque mob, roaring, howling, dancing and guffawing frenetically in the face of death, shouting exclamations of abuse, ridicule and obscenity, and baying for the immediate punishment of the condemned man. Speechless with terror and disgust, Frankenstein muses on the inconceivably inhumane cruelty and viciousness of these supposedly human shapes:

> The English mob, screeching and laughing and yelling, is a thing of horror in what we deign to call the civilised world. The open space in front of the prison was taken up by men and women who had all the appearance of thieves and prostitutes, as well as other rogues and ruffians of every description. Their smell was insupportable. They whistled and imitated Mr Punch; they drank from bottles, and fought among themselves. Some of them urinated freely against the walls of the prison itself calling out, according to the London tradition, "In pain!" (*CVF*, 221)

These scenes of horror and dissolution make Frankenstein doubt that people were ever created in God's image, coming to the conclusion that "[t]he human form is not divine" (*CVF*, 222). The mob's idea of the city's theatricality was always that of the proverbial bread and circuses, craving only the spectacular show itself, ignoring the humane and ethical side of the matter, and London, as Ackroyd demonstrates, was no exception to this rule across the centuries.

Like *Dan Leno and the Limehouse Golem*, the novel also explores the close and interconnected relationship between London and its theatrical world, and the theatre is presented as a miniature version of the city, a microcosm controlled by the same mechanisms as the streets. "Everything begins and ends in Drury Lane" (*CVF*, 42), explains Shelley to the astounded Frankenstein upon their arrival at the theatre, pointing to the fact that the city's life is not only portrayed on the stage but also reflected in the auditorium: the bustling atmosphere is reminiscent of a market, fair, or anti-government demonstration with its noise, commotion and ribaldry, omnipresent disorder and tension, and a diverse audience ranging from noblemen and dignitaries to political radicals. This is, at least in part, an example of Ackroyd using artistic licence as in reality the literati like Lamb, Shelly and Byron "all disliked the contemporary theatre's emphasis on visual spectacle and music as opposed to words and hoped for a theatre in which the poet's words were primary."[61] Frankenstein is also impressed by the forceful dramatic effect of the performance, which is created more by external factors, such as the colourful scenery, rich costumes and convincing impersonations, than by the plot – it is the acting and the spectacle that create an image and illusion "more real than reality itself" (*CVF*, 45), making Shelley call it "the true thing" and "the full sublime" (*CVF*, 46). It is the inherent duality of a concurrent mimicking of and escape from reality that stands behind the mesmerising attractiveness of the stage. London theatres and music halls, however, do not dramatise only universal human and urban traits and vices, they also promptly react to topical issues, preferably scandalous and sensational ones adapted from newspaper reports which involve some notorious personages. And so the cynical Shelley enjoys watching "himself" in the Alhambra Theatre in an awkwardly rendered melodramatic piece entitled *The Atheist's Curse,* depicting the recent events that led to his girlfriend's murder.

Similarly to Ackroyd's other London novels, *The Casebook of Victor Frankenstein* presents the city, in somewhat loosely connected dramatic scenes, as a continuous spectacle of the streets, an incessant manifestation of its positive as well as negative energies. It is the excitingly per-

---

61 Susan Staves, "Tragedy," 100–101.

formative character of these daily encounters and happenings, in which one can become simultaneously a spectator as well as an actor, that was addressed in the celebratory words of Charles Lamb and Charles Dickens, who described the city as "a pantomime and masquerade," the "magic lantern" (*LB*, 142) that compelled them to walk the streets and filled their imagination with their everyday dramas, while James Boswell "was entranced by London precisely because it allowed him to assume a number of disguises and thus escape from his own identity" (*LB*, 145). Frankenstein soon realises that the spectacle of the streets follows his every step, but his attitude to it changes along with the transformation of his psyche. At first he is fascinated by its dynamism, diversity and extremeness, yet in the end it annoys him as obtrusive, vulgar and dreadful, as for instance the riotous events during the Covent Garden Sweep Fair:

> ... I saw a gaggle of climbing boys at the other end of the Piazza. They were a queer sight. Their clothes were in rags, so sooty and black that they betrayed their profession at once: they might just have been dragged out of a chimney, except that they were trailing white ribbons, tied to their arms and legs. As I walked closer to them, I could see patches of gold and silver foil plastered to their dirty clothes and faces; it was altogether a most forlorn spectacle. Then to the sound of drums, the boys began to march. They waved their climbing tools, their rods and brushes, in the air above their heads; they sang some frightful song, full of oaths and execrations, at which the spectators laughed. (*CVF*, 388–89)

As theatricality is an inherent component of the texture of city life, one's attitude to it unfolds according to one's open-mindedness and responsiveness to the city. Therefore, the more one needs to keep something secret and hidden from public view, the less comfortable and more vulnerable one feels when exposed to the permanent scrutiny and watchfulness of one's fellow citizens. Naturally, the last thing that Frankenstein needs for his dubious experiments and homicidal acts is a crowd of curious spectators. From the psychological perspective, though, it is as if the rational and pragmatic scientist from the early pages of the novel was captivated by the city's irrational and carnivalesque displays because watching these Dionysian pleasures suitably complemented and contrasted with his personality, while the manic, semi-lunatic wretch who sinks deeper and deeper into irrationality detests and fears them as they resemble too strongly scenes from his hallucinatory fantasies.

The Great Fire of London elaborates on the theme from the perspective of Charles Dickens's formative influence on contemporary London narratives, Ackroyd's included. Dickens was not only a keen theatregoer, he even had his own amateur company with which, for instance, he acted in Jonson's *Every Man in His Humour* in 1845[62]. What Ackroyd shares with Dickens, among other things, is a belief in the essentially theatrical nature of London, that "[s]pectacle and melodrama are intrinsic aspects of the London vision and thus, by extension, of the English imagination itself" (*A*, 320). Dickens believed London "filled his imagination with the glimpse of strange dramas and sudden spectacles" (*LB*, 112), providing him with an invaluable source of literary inspiration. Ackroyd's novel demonstrates much of this influence as it is full of "most vivid echoes of Dickens's original text,"[63] *Little Dorrit*, such as having the same settings, names derived from wordplay with those of the original characters, and similarly composed scenes. Moreover, this conception of urban theatricality reinforces another characteristic feature of the city's public life – egalitarianism: the city as an anonymous stage helps to remove some of the social differences between individuals as it allows them to escape from their identities and, at least for a short while, to present themselves as the persons they wish to be. The novel's very plotline reflects this aspect of London, which even makes Gibson and Wolfreys claim that in the novel "we find not a real world but one composed of mannerisms, performances" trying "to show a city full of interlocking coincidences leading inexorably to tragedy,"[64] as it is constructed as a series of scenes, short performative spectacles with often very ambiguous relevance to one another, and introduces a cast of characters insecure about their own identities, such as Rowan, Audrey and Letty, who try to find or recover their lost or wounded selves through assuming alternative roles in the city life.

Spenser Spender at first tries to do without these little dramatic scenes from Dickens's novel in his film since he considers them too pathetic and sentimental, but he soon realises how mistaken he has been: "It turned out that the melodramatic elements had been essential to the story of *Little Dorrit*, and Spenser had decided to make a cinematic virtue out of necessity by emphasising the theatrical, almost caricatured, elements in the plot" (*GFL*, 105–106). He understands that it is the theatricality of the city that would lend his film both the right atmosphere and an air

---

62 Jim de Young and John Miller, *London Theatre Walks*, 159.

63 Lewis, *My Words Echo Thus*, 19.

64 Gibson and Wolfreys, *Peter Ackroyd*, 84.

of authenticity. This is the reason why he also plans the last scene to be a complex, "final panoramic vision" (*LB*, 157) of a London pulsing with life, conceived as a series of rather juxtaposed, separate images or little performances which would dramatise and vivify the city's energy and diversity. Yet, simultaneously, there are the outcast characters, mostly reincarnations of Dickens's protagonists, such as Audrey, Little Arthur and Pally, who naturally lack Spenser's artistic detachment as they find themselves too mired in the city's misery, and who are alarmed at what they consider to be a mendacious interpretation of and, as such, an un-acceptable appropriation of the novel. Therefore, they eventually "be-come convinced that they must put an end to the filming of *Little Dorrit* because the film is hopelessly 'misreading' the real spirit of London."[65] Ackroyd's irony is that while Spenser's film remains unfinished because the director dies and the final scene is never filmed, the novel does have a panoramic finale, though of a different kind and design, yet not lacking in theatricality. The great fire becomes a focus around which several little scenes are staged: the tramps cheer and drink a toast to their act of rebel-lion; in her trance, Audrey at first gapes at the fire and then starts run-ning around, laughing insanely; Spenser throws himself into the flames in a vain attempt to save some of the film sets, watched by the motionless Rowan who is too afraid for his life to help him; and Rowan, annoyed at being stared at by Audrey and moved by his conscience, turns tail to the fire site. It is a drama in which madness, rage and impulsiveness prevail, as if suddenly everything breaks free from any kind of rational control, a scene whose sole director is the city itself.

London in *Chatterton* is also a city of theatrical eccentricity and ex-cess, peopled by a number of peculiar and obscure characters, such as comic antique shop owners, the Lenos (whose name may immediately remind the reader of Dan Leno), or oddly behaving public library visi-tors. Ackroyd even maintains that in this novel he was more interested in creating plot and characters while the city remained a subdued subject[66]. Harriet Scrope, the malicious elderly novelist, with her "striking inborn capacity of the London 'monopolylinguist' to assume different roles and voices and to mimic other characters" resembles a "Dickensian-cum-music-hall character," a particular "cross-breed of Dan Leno's 'Mother Goose' and Punch's Judy."[67] Symptomatically, she plagiarises *Stage Fire*, the second book by a forgotten Victorian novelist, Harrison Bentley, in

---

65 Onega, *Peter Ackroyd*, 29.
66 Peter Ackroyd quoted in Gibson and Wolfreys, *Peter Ackroyd*, 249.
67 Onega, *Peter Ackroyd*, 35.

order to overcome her writer's block. Bentley's book deals with an actor possessed by the spirits of his great predecessors and models, David Garrick and Edmund Kean, and she adopts the plot synopsis, merely changing the profession of the hero from actor to writer. Lewis notes that this novel also mimics certain aspects of *The Great Fire of London*, namely the "possession by a spirit, the reference to a fire, and the emphasis on theatricality."[68] This emphasis winds like a thread through Ackroyd's London novels and makes most of his protagonists attracted, fascinated, or even possessed by various forms of urban theatricality, performativity and the possibilities of play acting.

In terms of the city's spectacular potential, Ackroyd identifies with Virginia Woolf's belief that the "delightful thing about London was that it was always giving one something new to look at, something fresh to talk about. One only had to keep one's eyes open."[69] In *Chatterton*, a related attitude to the city's theatrical character is personified by George Meredith. An avid observer of life in all its variety, Meredith sees the city as an incessant, infinitely diverse and mutable *theatrum mundi* which never ceases to amaze and puzzle him. Insecure about the value of his poetry, a feeling caused by his gloomy discussion with Wallis on the impossibility of achieving originality in art and its transience, even the city-as-stage of fashionable Oxford Street offers him only a spectacle of a low sort:

> In the gathering darkness the faces of those he passed seemed more vivid, and in all their clothes and their movements they seemed to be showing him their histories, beseeching him to understand them. The city had become one vast theatre – not the theatre of his imagination, either, but that of Astley's or the Hippodrome, tawdry, garish, stifling, real. (*C*, 135)

Although Meredith resolutely refuses any responsibility for what kind of theatre he sees around him, his current mood and state of mind are, in fact, the true directors of this performance. It is for this reason that when in doubt about his potential to create what he considers to be serious art, the passers-by in Oxford Street remind him of ridiculous and pathetic characters from a popular music-hall performance. When a few moments later he is amused by the screaming of two small boys playing in the street, he suddenly feels more vigorous and finds himself

---

68   Lewis, *My Words Echo Thus*, 49.
69   Virginia Woolf, *The London Scene*, 82.

walking towards his house "with lighter tread" (*C*, 135). No matter what is actually happening in such theatre, its interpretation and meaning always originate in the eyes and minds of its audience. The theatre of the streets is ultimately the theatre of their dwellers' imaginations, in which they, mostly simultaneously, assume the roles of actors, directors and spectators. Whoever is watching is also being watched, whoever is interpreting or directing is also being interpreted or directed. Murray argues that for Ackroyd "history is constituted through its representation, whereby language becomes reality, and any attempt to posit an empirical historical reality is decisively rejected in favour of competing language games,"[70] yet these games, as can be concluded from this chapter, are not of a purely linguistic or discursive nature, but also display a substantial performative and theatrical dimension, both in terms of the characters' acts and the rendering of historical reality.

---

70   Murray, *Recalling London: Literature and History in the work of Peter Ackroyd and Iain Sinclair*, 36.

Chapter 6
Literary London

... the city must never be confused with the words that describe it. And yet between the one and the other there is a connection.

Italo Calvino, *Invisible Cities*

Ackroyd's London – uncanny, felonious, psychogeographic, antiquarian and theatrical – is essentially a literary city. It exists and is simultaneously reborn again and again through, within and between the countless texts which have been (and will be) written in it and about it. These texts do not merely document the city, they compose one of the levels of its multiple meanings by (re)presenting, rewriting, fictionalising, mythologising and parodying its various tendencies, manifestations and happenings, while alluding to other, somehow related, narratives, as well as self-reflectively commenting on themselves and the process of their creation. Such a city is itself a vast text, and a highly variable one as it is permanently in motion, in the process of (re)creation, without a beginning or end, reminiscent of Borges' infinite book, Leibniz's monad or Calvino's invisible city as it not only contains all texts about itself, but also reflects all other city-texts[1]. Ackroyd avidly stores up, juxtaposes, interconnects and also deliberately adapts and confuses all the possible London texts and narratives in order to disclose or extrapolate an at least partly credible and always vivid image of his beloved metropolis.

Believing that "[i]ntertextuality is not inimical to writing but an inextricable part of it,"[2] his fiction is consciously referential to other related textual production. His approach to rendering the past thus permanently balances between imaginary stories and reality or, more precisely, between fiction and historical facts, since his understanding of history is

---

1   Daniela Hodrová, *Citlivé město*, 18–21.
2   Brian Finney, "Peter Ackroyd, Postmodernist Play and Chatterton."

that it is an immense intertextual web and as such it can be traced and partly restored through its miscellaneous written records. As Bradbury puts it, "Ackroyd is a playful user of fiction, well aware of the contemporary devices in the postmodern novelist's repertory: pastiche, parody, punning, intertextuality."[3] Moreover, Ackroyd is consistent in his treatment of the literary city as in terms of method there are no substantial differences between his fiction and non-fiction works. In *London: The Biography* his narrative strategy is similar to that of his novels, only the imaginary, fictitious elements have been replaced by a great number of various quotations from and references to authentic texts and other materials – chronicles, historical records, descriptions of paintings, engravings and photographs, and the writings about the city by more, and less, famous writers and scholars. The author thus manages to combine his readable, light style with a scholarly approach supported by extensive reading and research.

In his London novels, however, literary and non-literary texts, real as well as fictitious, play other and more crucial roles than that of providing authentic pieces of historical evidence. They inspire and affect present-day events, as in *The Great Fire of London*, *Chatterton* and *The House of Doctor Dee*; they trigger some, usually vicious and ominous, action in the past, as in *Dan Leno and the Limehouse Golem* and *The Lambs of London*, or provide material for rewriting, as in *The Clerkenwell Tales* and *The Casebook of Victor Frankenstein*. Yet in all these cases they serve as constituting elements of an imaginative rendering and reenactment of the city's past and its relationship with the present. In *London: The Biography*, for example, Ackroyd picks a text connected with the city's condition and/or produced by a person inhabiting its territory in the past, and situates it into a context which, though it features real characters and events, is largely made-up. While in the non-fiction the speculative and hypothetical are reduced to occasional casual suggestions and supplementary commentaries, in the novels they assume greater significance as they form the backbone of the plotlines. As a result, various texts are shown to instigate or influence actions with which they have never previously been associated. Since each novel depicts only a fraction of the city's immense (inter)textual body and explores only a selection of the potential connections, but also since the texts used in them, as well as their authors, reflect at least some of the city's determining aspects, this London corresponds with the image of the city discussed in the preceding chapters.

---

3   Malcolm Bradbury, *The Modern British Novel*, 436.

This literary London is constructed through several dominant textual and discursive tendencies, related and thus mutually interconnected: it is intertextual, palimpsestical, metafictional and apocryphal, and all these qualities evince strong elements of pastiche. The first two need not be introduced any further as the city's intertextuality was discussed fully in the previous chapters, and its palimpsestic nature was illustrated on the process of rewriting crimes in chapter three and will be further elaborated upon later in this one. Ackroyd acknowledges that the act of writing and reading entails being thrown into a network of textual relations and thus forced to move between and make sense of a number of other texts, as a result of which each seemingly independent text "becomes the intertext."[4] Unlike an autonomous, delimited and coherent text, an intertext is defined precisely by attributes that exceed these qualities. An intertext is far from autonomous as it operates through references to countless other texts and therefore it is inherently unrestricted and has a "twofold coherence: an *intra*textual one which guarantees the immanent integrity of the text, and an *inter*textual one which creates structural relations between itself and other texts."[5] These attributes are at the core of the ambiguous nature of intertextuality and account for both its richness and its problematic character. On the one hand, it can produce multiple new meanings, relations and interpretations which cannot be generated within the confines of a single text, on the other hand, it may be prone to self-dissolution in its perpetual referencing of other texts and, in extreme cases, may lose its identity and disintegrate "into numerous text particles which only bear an extrinsic reference."[6] Ackroyd's novels make use of the fact that intertextuality defies the readers' desire for order, control, singularity and stability of meaning, making them aware "that all texts are potentially plural, reversible, open to the reader's own presuppositions, lacking in clear and defined boundaries, and always involved in the expression or repression of the dialogic 'voices' which exist within society."[7]

As was demonstrated in the preceding chapters, in terms of employment of intertextuality, Ackroyd's London novels may be loosely subdivided into two groups: those in which one text is central as it crucially and ultimately determines both plot and structure, and those which feature a network of more texts, none of them paramount, whose significance to the novel's meaning rests in their relationships and interconnectedness.

---

4   Graham Allen, *Intertextuality*, 1.

5   Heinrich F. Plett, "Intertextualities," 5.

6   Plett, "Intertextualities," 6.

7   Allen, *Intertextuality*, 209.

The first group includes *The Great Fire of London*, where Dickens's *Little Dorrit*, directly or not, affects the lives of all the novel's main protagonists and their attitudes to the city, and also *The Clerkenwell Tales* and *The Casebook of Victor Frankenstein,* which use the basic narrative framework and some characters from the original classics, Chaucer's *The Canterbury Tales* and Shelley's *Frankenstein*, but rewrite them as two distinct versions of the urban Gothic psychothriller. The rest fall into the second group, the one exception being *Dan Leno and the Limehouse Golem* which, as probably the most intertextually complex of his London novels, combines both the approaches. De Quincey's "On Murder Considered as One of the Fine Arts" represents a determining constituent of its plot as a text that influences most of the action, but it also stands at the centre of the novel's intertextual network of texts, real as well as fictitious, whose creation it inspired.

The process of writing as a theme or motif appears in most of Ackroyd's London novels, most explicitly in *Chatterton*, but metafiction as a specific constituent of the city's texture is also explored in *The Great Fire of London*, *Dan Leno and the Limehouse Golem*, *The House of Doctor Dee*, *The Lambs of London* and *The Casebook of Victor Frankenstein*. A narrative strategy related to metafiction is pastiche, both linguistic and textual, and this serves as one of Ackroyd's methods of imparting an air of authenticity and plausibility to his narratives. The most telling linguistic example is *The Last Testament of Oscar Wilde*, conceived as a pastiche of the eponymous writer's diary, but it can also be found in the Elizabethan, early eighteenth-century, Dickensian and music-hall English of John Dee, Nicholas Dyer, Audrey Skelton and Harriet Scrope respectively. Textual pastiche is even more frequent: the pastiche of the Victorian novel in *The Great Fire of London*, the medieval collection of tales in *The Clerkenwell Tales*, the urban Gothic thriller in *The Casebook of Victor Frankenstein*, the diaries in *Hawksmoor* and *Dan Leno and the Limehouse Golem*, or the interrogation and trial transcripts in the last mentioned to name the most prominent examples. Ackroyd's employment of pastiche often borders on parody, such as in the narratives of detection in *Hawksmoor*, *Chatterton* and *Dan Leno and the Limehouse Golem*, or the use of the minor eccentric Dickensian characters of Little Arthur, the Lenos and Mr. Joynson in *The Great Fire of London* and *Chatterton*. Moreover, as Amjad, Ilkhani and Aryan suggest, *Chatterton* can be read as a parody of the process of historiographic research in general, but also of autobiography and biography as its specific subdivisions[8].

---

8   Fazel Asadi Amjad, Sarah Catherine Ilkhani and Arya Aryan, "The Problematisation of the Representation of Reality in Peter Ackroyd's *Chatterton* in the Light of Postmodern Theories," 121–122.

The purpose of Ackroyd's pastiche is, however, more complex than merely to enrich and enliven the story – while it may increase the impression of the narrative's authenticity it also introduces the themes of originality, genuineness, plagiarism and counterfeit that permeate all his novels. They are most thoroughly exploited in *Chatterton* and *The Lambs of London*, whose plot revolves around various forms of forgeries, but also resonate loudly in *The House of Doctor Dee*, where, with a great deal of self-irony, Ackroyd toys with the various effects of the anxiety of influence: the author's fear of a lack of originality and subsequent stealing from someone else's plot is first expressed by an unnamed early twentieth-century writer in his diary, and echoed in the final chapter by Ackroyd's authorial voice casting doubt on the originality and authenticity of the creation of his semi-fictional character through his metacommentary:

> ... I do not understand how much of this history is known, and how much is my own invention. And what is the past, after all? Is it that which is created in the formal act of writing, or does it have some substantial reality? Am I discovering it, or inventing it? Or could it be that I am discovering it within myself, so that it bears both the authenticity of surviving evidence and the immediacy of present intuition? *The House of Doctor Dee* itself leads me to that conclusion: no doubt you expected it to be written by the author whose name appears on the cover and the title-page, but in fact many of the words and phrases are taken from John Dee himself. If they are not his words, they belong to his contemporaries. Just as he took a number of mechanical parts and out of them constructed a beetle that could fly, so I have taken a number of obscure texts and have fashioned a novel from their rearrangement. But is Doctor Dee no more than a projection of my own attitudes and obsessions, or is he an historical figure whom I have tried genuinely to recreate? (*HDD*, 275)

Ackroyd contests and destabilises the supposedly clear-cut borderline between the original and the imitation or borrowing and inverts the conventional hierarchy privileging the former over the latter as, following Barthes, he considers the meaning of a text comes into being through its interaction with already existing ones, all texts thus being "rearrangements of other texts" rather than "inventions of unique writers of genius."[9] He also uses the theme of originality as a significant point of departure in his exploration of another problematic binary opposition,

---

9   Finney, "Peter Ackroyd, Postmodernist Play and *Chatterton*."

that of history and fiction, revising both their intricate relationship as well as the question of their primacy. Therefore, just as fiction may sometimes precede and determine history, he demonstrates that imitation and fakery may prove more interesting and valuable than the original.

This, perhaps provocative, belief allows Ackroyd to introduce the device of an apocryphal text, that is a text of doubtful authenticity, a sham or counterfeit. Many of his novels feature a text that is unoriginal, inauthentic, yet which is shown in some respect to be more meaningful than those whose originality and authenticity are far less dubious. According to Jean-Pierre Audigier, this insistence on the meaningful relevance of apocrypha may be considered to be one of the better responses to the dilemma of all discourses: rather systematic apocrypha than pseudo-History, rather the true false than the false true[10]. The truthfulness of these texts, Ackroyd suggests, rests in their creators' motivation being far more ambitious and daring than that of a mediocre epigone – what may at first appear as mere imitation is in reality fuelled by the aspiration to become part of the timeless, imaginative creative process. Thomas Chatterton's poems inspired and perhaps helped instigate the English Romantic movement, and William-Henry Ireland's Shakespeare papers further immortalised the Bard and reinforced national pride in possessing such a unique cultural heritage. However, Ackroyd's use of apocrypha also complies with its two other meanings: the first is that of "not belonging to canonical literature," hence his emphasis on unofficial texts and discourses, both written and performed, which are for various reasons ignored, dismissed or denounced by the established political and cultural circles, such as murder accounts, occult writings, visionary prophecies and music hall sketches. The second is derived from the Greek *apocryphal*, meaning "hidden away, secret." Although Ackroyd's apocryphal texts do contain a meaning that proves crucial for understanding his novels, it is far from transparent and incessantly escapes pinning down. As Audigier notes, the meaning does not appear otherwise than hidden in the secret "architexture," literally encrypted, and thus they call for a new, apocryphal reading[11], one which would be conscious of the need for a careful and patient dismantling and disentangling of the architextural, encrypting construction of the texts in order to activate their revelatory potential, as in the case of Detective Hawksmoor's scrutiny of Dyer's secret diary.

---

10 Jean-Pierre Audigier, "L'apocryfe selon Ackroyd," 146.
11 Audigier, "L'apocryfe selon Ackroyd," 150.

Ackroyd's two London novels in which the tendencies discussed above are most thoroughly employed and contemplated are *Chatterton* and *The Lambs of London*. In the former, metafiction, intertextuality, apocryphal texts and the theme of counterfeiting and plagiarism help problematise the representation of past reality both in literary historiography and historical fiction, demonstrating that historical representation "requires creation and interpretation" and as such cannot be "an objective recounting as historiography and literary realism credit."[12] The latter uses the same means in order to reenact two past events by establishing and working out an undocumented connection between them. However, in both cases the novels deal with, and at the same time are examples of, texts which represent, re-present and render the city in which they come into being, thus contributing to its essentially palimpsestical nature. And so, while the past can only be rewritten in an inaccurate, biased or distorted way and thus never brought back to life as it actually was, Ackroyd's infinite London perpetuates itself, among other ways, through its dwellers' imaginations, and so it can only benefit from all its textual representations, often the more creative the better.

The Necessity of Imitation –
the Counterfeiting and Metafictional London of *Chatterton*

Although *Chatterton* is Ackroyd's only London novel which does not feature a murder, or at least a mysterious death likely to have been caused by the hand of another person, there is an underlying aspect of the story which could be classified as criminal, as it revolves around one of the most famous cases of forgery in the history of English literature – Thomas Chatterton's creation of the pseudo-medieval *Rowley Poems*, soon followed by the young forger's untimely death. However, unlike in *The Lambs of London* which is all set in the past and where William-Henry Ireland's Shakespeare forgeries are thematically linked with Mary Lamb's matricide and thus constitute the decisive component of the plot, in *Chatterton,* the eponymous poet's acts serve as both a trigger and a unifying element of the novel's multiple plotlines, which take place in several different, yet shown as parallelly interconnected, time periods. The novel thus exemplifies what Nick Bentley denotes as a "concentra-

---

12   Amjad, Ilkhani, Aryan, "The Problematisation of the Representation of Reality in Peter Ackroyd's *Chatterton* in the Light of Postmodern Theories," 123.

tion on alternative, marginalized and often competing perspectives on official histories,"[13] which, combined with Ackroyd's rather "disrespectful" treatment of real historical personages often results in what Richard Bradford terms an "iconoclastic brand of historical fiction."[14] Moreover, the themes of forgery, plagiarism, imitation and copying permeate the novel and this allows the author to add another much more crucial dimension to the story, a philosophical and metafictional one concerning issues such as the very possibility of authenticity and originality of artistic creation, the often indistinct borderline between inspiration and imitation, and, consequently, the moral and ethical limits of exploiting other people's work for one's own purposes.

The second common denominator of all of the novel's plotlines is the capital city, the only place where such fates could unfold: in 1770 Thomas Chatterton goes to London in the hope of gaining recognition as a poet and writer; about thirty years later Samuel Joynson forges Chatterton's manuscripts and his son paints a mock-portrait of the middle-aged Chatterton in order to prove that the poet had faked his own death and by doing so trick a rival bookseller; in 1856 George Meredith poses for his friend Henry Wallis who is to paint his famous *Death of Chatterton* and who later has an affair with Meredith's wife; and, more than a century later, Charles Wychwood accidentally gets hold of the faked portrait in an obscure London antique shop, which stirs his curiosity regarding the identity of the portrayed person and as a result causes a series of actions that bring together people whose interests in Chatterton, if any, are differently motivated and not always sincere. This London is primarily a literary city, a milieu fundamentally intertwined with writing: Chatterton attempts to make his name in literary circles by writing poems and satires; Meredith muses on the nature of literature and writing while sitting for Wallis; Charles Wychwood is an unpublished poet who still believes in his talent and the power of the imagination; his friend Philip Slack works as a librarian but nurses an ambition to write a novel; Andrew Flint, the schoolmate of Charles and Philip, is a best-selling author of popular novels who is about to write a biography of George Meredith; and the elderly, mean and spiteful novelist Harriet Scrope unsuccessfully tries to compose her memoirs and hires Charles as her "interpreter." In *Chatterton*, literary London with all its ambitions, rivalry, intrigues and other deceitful practices thus comes fully to life from three different temporal perspectives.

---

13   Nick Bentley, *British Fiction of the 1990s*, 12.
14   Richard Bradford, *The Novel Now*, 83.

It is not only the motifs of fraud, intertextual playfulness and London as a setting and theme that connect *Chatterton* with Ackroyd's other fictions, but also the theme of forgery. It is explored through the character of the gifted yet underestimated and misunderstood youthful forger and the speculative reworking of his fate, the use of multiple parallel plots, mixing real historical personages and events with fictitious ones and the main protagonist being a somewhat eccentric loner obsessed with, if not possessed by, a famous writer. However, what differentiates *Chatterton* is its strong metafictional focus – more than in any of his other novels Ackroyd here reflects on the nature of writing, its motivation, purpose, and goal, as well as its limitations. Rather than as an alternative rendering of the past, Ackroyd makes use of his literary and counterfeiting London as a backdrop for an in-depth exploration of the ethical concerns each creative process necessarily entails.

Forgery and plagiarism are the cornerstones of Ackroyd's London in *Chatterton*, as each of the novel's main protagonists are directly or indirectly associated with some act of imitation, borrowing, or even the outright stealing of someone else's creative work. The principal protagonist in the novel is Thomas Chatterton, the notorious teenage forger of late-medieval English poetry supposedly written by the fabricated Thomas Rowley, a fifteenth-century monk endowed with extraordinary poetic genius. Unlike his treatment of William-Henry Ireland, Ackroyd does not change any of the basic historical facts concerning Chatterton's family background, life and work, but toys with the most mysterious aspect of the young poet's story – his death by arsenic poisoning at the age of only seventeen, around which he builds three speculative theories. The first is that when Chatterton sees that the true origin of his poems might soon be exposed and that he will be seen as a forger and imposter, forever despised and condemned, he decides to save his literary career. With the help of Samuel Joynson, a Bristol bookseller and friend, he fakes his own death, after which he continues imitating poetry, but this time in the guise of his contemporaries, both living or recently deceased. This theory suggests that the authorship of certain works by poets such as Charles Churchill, Mark Akenside, Thomas Gray, Oliver Goldsmith, William Cowper, George Crabbe or even William Blake are thus to be attributed to Chatterton, as a result of which "our whole understanding of eighteenth century poetry will have to be revised" (*C*, 127). For the sake of this argument, Ackroyd concocts a study by an imaginary American professor, Homer Brillo, in which the scholar elaborates on the assumption that Chatterton had a decisive influence on the English Romantic poets, most notably on Blake's poetic vision. The second theory indicates that Chatterton actually dies in 1770 but has a serious dispute with Joynson before his death, accusing the bookseller of abusing him and his poetry. When the letters containing these accusations are published by a rival bookseller, Joynson, who up to that point has been making profits selling Chatterton's poetry, needs to blacken the forger's name, so he fakes the manuscripts in which Chatterton admits to having forged his own death, by which he deprives him of the aureole of a tragically lost marvellous prodigy. In order to support this, and partly as a hoax, Joynson's son then paints a mock-portrait of the poet in his early fifties.

The third theory speculates on the very circumstances of the forger's death: rather than a desperate suicidal act of a broken and disappointed man, it is presented as an unfortunate accident. "No one can touch me now [...] there will come a time when I will astonish the world" (*C*, 207, 216) claims Ackroyd's confident and optimistic Chatterton just before, having drunk too much brandy, he overdoses on arsenic in an attempt to cure himself of the venereal disease he has recently caught from his landlady. This theory, unlike the first two completely fabricated ones, is at least partly based on historical evidence. Chatterton really was confident and optimistic concerning his chances as a published writer, and Mrs Ballance, the cousin with whom he lodged for about two months after his arrival in the city, even described him as "proud as Lucifer."[15] This was true, however, only at the beginning of his London stay, as in his last few weeks, hungry and shabby, he was rather desperate and languishing. Similarly, it is probable that he was suffering from some venereal disease (due to his worsening financial situation he later moved to "29 Brooke Street in Holborn, then a neighbourhood of dubious character, the haunt of prostitutes and pickpockets"[16]), the cure of which must have been enormously unpleasant and painful, but there is no evidence that he caught it from his landlady, Mrs Angel, or that he killed himself accidentally while attempting to alleviate his suffering with arsenic.

Two other real historical personages, although their personalities and relationship are substantially fictionalised for the sake of the narrative, feature in another parallel plotline which takes place more than eighty years later – the poet and novelist George Meredith and the painter Henry Wallis. The Pre-Raphaelite painter is working on his mas-

---

15 Linda Kelly, *The Marvellous Boy: The Life and Myth of Thomas Chatterton*, 32.
16 Kelly, *The Marvellous Boy: The Life and Myth of Thomas Chatterton*, 34.

terpiece, *The Death of Chatterton*, which depicts the corpse of the eponymous forger, described by another famous representative of the English Pre-Raphaelite Movement, Dante Gabriel Rossetti, as "'the day spring' of English Romantic poetry,"[17] in the posture he was found in the morning after his death, and, as he needs a live model, he asks Meredith to pose for him. While impersonating the dead poet Meredith experiences the strangeness of pretending to be someone else, to become a forgery himself, which prompts him to muse thoughtfully on the ambiguous relationship between realism and imitation, authenticity and copying, inspiration and stealing, immortalisation and the loss of one's self in the process. Ironically, he is unable to recognise that his own marriage is based on pretence and emotional fakery and only too late does he understand how self-absorbed and dismissive to his wife he has been. By his pastiche-imitation of the conventions and voices of the Victorians, Ackroyd is faking a "contemporary authenticity, even while calling into question the notion of authorial authority and authenticity."[18]

In the contemporarily set plotline, the theme of plagiarism is most forcefully explored through the character of Harriet Scrope, a successful elderly novelist. The beginning of her career back in the 1950s hides a dark secret. As the achievement of an excellent and meticulous stylist, Scrope's first novel was appreciated only by narrow academic and critical circles but never gained any popularity with the reading public. The novel took her a long time to write and its content had very little to interest any mind other than her own. Aware that the time for highly subjective experimental fiction was long over, she understood that she needed a strong story which, however, she found herself incapable of conceiving. Desperate because her writing was at a deadlock and stressed by the expectations of critics and friends, it occurred to her to borrow a plot from some other source. She found this source in three books by a forgotten late nineteenth-century novelist, Harrison Bentley, another of Ackroyd's made-up "real" personae, whom she happened to come across in a second-hand bookshop and whose plots she used in her three novels "as a plain, admittedly inferior, vessel for her own style" (*C*, 102). She changed details such as names, jobs, social environment and relationship patterns, leaving only the basic plotlines which she "wrapped up" in her stylistically precise narratives. These three novels became a stepping stone for her subsequent career, as they removed her writer's block

17   Kelly, *The Marvellous Boy*, 116.
18   Alan Robinson, *Narrating the Past: Historiography, Memory and the Contemporary Novel*, 50.

and helped her to create her own stories. "The experience of employing a plot, even though it was the invention of some other writer, had liberated her imagination; and, from that time forward, all her novels were her own work" (*C*, 103). Her plagiarism could easily be taken as the unfortunate yet tolerable, if not forgivable, act of a young, fledgling writer, if it were not for the facts that not only had her conscience not troubled her at all since her plagiarism, but she is ready to do something similar if given a chance, such as stealing the Chatterton papers from Charles. The selfish, arrogant and disdainful Scrope worries only about her good name and reputation, and opportunistically makes use of other people as instruments for achieving her own goals. This makes her different and also ethically more contentious than the novel's other imitators and forgers.

An interconnected story is that of the famous and recently deceased painter Joseph Seymour and his last assistant, Stewart Merk. Seymour's paintings have long sold well and their price has even risen since his death, with his late works being especially appreciated and in demand. What nobody knows is that in his old age Seymour suffered from arthritis in his hands and therefore all his late-period pictures were painted by Merk, who had learnt to imitate his master's style and technique. The commercially most profitable paintings are those produced by an unknown imitator which should therefore be virtually worthless. When Sadlier, an experienced Seymour dealer, discovers that they are fakes, Merk, to Sadlier's surprise, reveals his role in the affair. Yet, for the sake of business they abandon all moral scruples and eventually agree to keep the truth a secret as Sadlier has fifteen more late-period "Seymour" paintings in stock which he has been waiting to sell when the painter's death would drive up the prices. Moreover, Harriet Scrope is a great admirer of Seymour's late-period work and is planning to purchase one soon in order to add style to her flat. And so, ironically enough, the pretentious plagiarist and copyist will own and boast of a forged artifact.

In the felonious, fraudulent, or at least morally dubious London in *Chatterton* the theme of plagiarism and forgery is primarily intertwined with that of writing. However, the metafictional aspect of the novel does not focus on specific writers and their works, like for instance the Lambs in *The Lambs of London* or George Gissing in *Dan Leno and the Limehouse Golem*, but rather generally revolves around the question of the originative and ethical limits of creative writing. Ackroyd himself tends to profess the medieval and Renaissance idea of originality and imitation which believed the "task of literature was to celebrate or to readjust the works of the past,"[19] and so the novel challenges the modern idea of originality and authenticity, according to which many great poets and writers of the past, including Shakespeare, might be seen as plagiarists and imitators. Moreover, he holds the position that there actually is not any substantial distinction between mimesis and invention[20]. "The truest Plagiarism is the truest Poetry" (C, 87), exclaims the novel's Chatterton, and, no matter how exaggerated this statement seems, Ackroyd is far from dismissing it as completely illusory when he lets Charles declare, in his enthusiasm, that Chatterton "was the greatest poet in history" (C, 94). *Chatterton* thus can be taken as a contribution to the ongoing discussion concerning the question of narrative authority, problematising the notion of the author as the source of originality and meaning, provoked some twenty years prior to the novel's publication especially by Roland Barthes's influential essay "The Death of the Author" (1967). Barthes notoriously argues that poetics should consist of suppressing the author as a source of originality and theological meaning and substituting him/her with language which acts and performs instead. He sees the text as a "space of many dimensions, in which are wedded and contested various kinds of writing, no one of which is original: the text is a tissue of citations, resulting from the thousand sources of culture." Each writer can therefore only imitate, copy and compile from already existing texts, "combine the different kinds of writing, to oppose some by others so as never to sustain himself by just one of them."[21] Despite Ackroyd's widely known dismissive attitude to postmodern theories and theorising, *Chatterton*, to a considerable extent, does read as a fictional rendering of Barthes's key ideas.

Several characters in the novel muse on the impossibility of ever coming up with something original in literature: "I never know what is mine any more" (C, 134), sighs Meredith when Wallis suggests that he should appropriate the effect of light by putting it into a poem; later on, Meredith stresses the dominant role of language in the writing process, expressing the persuasion that language alone rather than the author or outside reality shapes the text: "There is nothing more real

---

19 Anke Schütze, "I think after More I will do Turner and then I will probably do Shakespeare," an Interview with Peter Ackroyd.

20 "On the whole they tend to become the same thing. You can't have invention in vacuum; it always has to spring from, or in large part depend upon, the way other people use the language. So invention is a form of mimesis. On the other hand, the idea of transcribing or copying the external world in itself is a form of invention" (Patrick McGrath, "Peter Ackroyd: Interview").

21 Roland Barthes, "The Death of the Author," 313–316.

than words. They are reality. It is just as everything I do becomes an experiment – I really don't understand why and, please God, I never shall – and until it is completed I never know whether it will be worth a farthing" (*C*, 157), he says, admitting to being subject to language rather than authoritatively mastering it as a tool for expressing his ideas, and, in consequence, lacking narrative control over what he writes. "[N] ovelists don't work in a vacuum. We use many stories. But it's not where they come from, it's what we do with them" (*C*, 104), argues Harriet Scrope self-apologetically to Charles who, without intending to soothe her, sincerely assures her that naturally "everyone copies" (*C*, 106). The theme is, however, most articulately voiced by Philip Slack. When he discovers that Scrope borrowed her plots from an earlier novelist he is surprised but does not condemn or criticise her, rather seeing the world of literature as an immense intertextual web of texts and stories whose permutations and combinations generate new ones: "Philip believed that there were only a limited number of plots in the world (reality was finite, after all) and no doubt it was inevitable that they would be reproduced in a variety of contexts" (*C*, 70). This view was also affected by his own experience with writing a novel, a project he soon abandoned because he could see in his style too much influence of those writers and works he admired. As a result, his novel gave the impression of being a "patchwork of other voices and other styles" (*C*, 70) in which he did not recognise himself.

Philip thus represents Ackroyd's views, though intuitively and unconsciously rather than eruditely, when he opts to indulge in pastiche, parody, imitation and genre and discourse mixture, as these are strategies Ackroyd himself also employs in his fiction[22]. Brian Finney points out how Ackroyd plagiarises, both flagrantly and more subtly, his own books, namely *The Last Testament of Oscar Wilde* and *The Great Fire of London*, in the titles and stories of Harrison Bentley's novels, *The Last Testament* and *Stage Fire*[23]. He even confesses to enjoying conscious undeclared borrowing from all kinds of other texts[24]. To write inevitably means to cross the threshold into a world of words and voices, to enter a magnetic

---

22 On a dialogue from *Milton in America* which paraphrases or echoes similar conversations in *English Music* and *Chatterton, Jeremy* Gibson and Julian Wolfreys show how Ackroyd deliberately plagiarises himself "in games of 'postmodern' self-reflection" (*Peter Ackroyd: The Ludic and Labyrinthine Text*, 158–159).

23 Finney, "Peter Ackroyd, Postmodernist Play and Chatterton."

24 "I enjoy stealing things if I can. [...] A line from a film, for example, a sentence from television. [...] I'm rather like a collector of other people's trifles, other people's bits and pieces" (McGrath, "Peter Ackroyd: Interview").

field whose lines of force are other texts and stories. Therefore, it is absolutely legitimate, if not unavoidable, to borrow and imitate as long as this borrowing and imitation are not aims in themselves, but mere devices through which the author discovers his or her own voice. In the case of *Chatterton* this is self-referential since metafiction "can never be totally autonomous,"[25] as it always relates to the past and the outside reality, both textual and extratextual. The novel presents an ingenious defence of this process: "The poet does not merely recreate or describe the world. He actually creates it" (*C*, 157), notes Meredith, proving the point that in his forged poems Chatterton invented a whole historical period and its poetics and, in effect, influenced and significantly shaped the Romantic poetic sensibility; by loosely using Bentley's plots in her early novels Scrope established herself as a recognised writer; through retelling Charles's theory and investigation from his perspective, Philip had the hope that he might eventually be able to find his own voice and style as a novelist; and, last but not least, through the story of Thomas Chatterton, Ackroyd conceives a novel whose multiple levels of meaning by far transcend the limits of the traditional historical narrative.

The novel's London is a vast and dense intertextual and palimpsestical network[26], "the textual universe extending out in an infinite mass of associations that lie beyond any form of comprehension,"[27] a world of texts and stories and their ongoing interactions in which the works of the past crucially influence and affect authors of the present, regardless of their will, awareness or acknowledgement. Obviously this is a concept that makes the issue of originality and authenticity even more problematic, as, in accordance with Barthes's claim, it presents each new work as at least partly shaped by what has been written already. "Think of them all around us, watching us, Blake, Shelley, Coleridge [...] And Meredith. All of them influencing us" (*C*, 77), notes Charles Wychwood to Flint when he is trying to demonstrate how the said poets were themselves influenced by Chatterton, suggesting that such influence is unavoidable. Charles is the most outspoken proponent of this view, since he sees it not only as inevitable, but also as natural and even beneficial for the creative process. At the same time, he is aware that it can be seen as frustrating and intimidating by many aspiring

25 Patricia Waugh, *Metafiction: The Theory and Practice of Self-Conscious Fiction*, 100.

26 Barry Lewis, for instance, shows the novel's numerous quotations from and references to different works of T. S. Eliot (*My Words Echo Thus: Possessing the Past in Peter Ackroyd*, 46–50).

27 Alex Murray, *Recalling London: Literature and History in the works of Peter Ackroyd and Iain Sinclair*, 7.

writers, showing, for instance, his familiarity with Harold Bloom's theory. "It's called the anxiety of influence" (C, 100), he explains to Harriet Scrope when she contemplates how writers keep borrowing from other writers, though in her case she is not motivated by an interest in the general mechanisms of artistic creation, but by the need to seek justification for her own borrowings.

Through the use of the supra-sensual, *Chatterton* dramatises this invisible yet all-encompassing intertextual world of shadows and voices. First of all, there is the ghost-figure of Thomas Chatterton with whom several of the novel's protagonists come into contact: it saves young Meredith, desperate because his wife has recently left him, from suicide by poisoning by "standing over him and forbidding him to drink" (C, 70); Wallis is certain that his painting will be a triumph as he feels it has "been infused with the soul of Chatterton – a soul not trapped but joyful at its commemoration" (C, 170); it twice appears to Harriet Scrope, as if it were trying to warn her against stealing the findings of Charles's investigation from Vivien and Philip; and, most importantly, it twice reveals itself to Charles during his attempt to solve the mystery of the portrait. Such a world is also a supra-temporal one in which the past, the present and the future coexist and intermingle to such a degree that they are no longer distinguishable. Charles's soul leaves this world in order to join those of Chatterton and Meredith in the intertextual one; Chatterton lives on through his masterful forgeries and mysterious death, inspiring new people to study his life and write his biographies, yet each such biography seems to describe a "quite different poet" (C, 127), as they simultaneously always reflect the personalities of their authors; and Wallis's painting immortalises not only its author, the portrayed person and the model, but all those whose lives were somehow affected by it, including Charles, whom his son Edward still sees in the painting, thanks to which he believes that his father "would never wholly die" (C, 230). It is a psycho-physical world in which not time but visions, ideas, beliefs and dreams are the true measuring criteria of value and durability.

The London of *Chatterton* possesses all the typical features of Ackroyd's (semi-)fictitious construction of the urban world: it features real historical as well as made-up characters and events. The main protagonists, Thomas Chatterton and Charles Wychwood, are loners, both by choice and circumstance, enclosed in themselves not only due to their eccentricity, but mainly because they are endowed with the capacity and determination to pursue their vision even against the tide of the conventions and expectations of their surroundings. There is a crucial narrative constituent of a mystery, which includes elements bordering on the irrational – the mystical, occult and supernatural. The plot revolves around a crime, or at least a morally dubious act, which, however, is a mere pretext for the exploration of "more serious" themes such as the principles and ethical limits of artistic creation. Metafiction and intertextuality are at the heart of the city's texture – the themes of writing and the relationship between the city and its texts substantially determine the novel's plot and character construction. In terms of temporality it defies traditional chronology; the parallel plots as well as the different time periods become intertwined, affecting one another on both physical and mental levels, and certain patterns of events, acts and ideas cyclically recur across the centuries. As a result, the city assumes several different roles, from that of physical setting, *locus delicti*, and literary milieu to that of the reflection of its various protagonists' minds, their hopes, worries, despair and self-projections.

Although the role of the city within the narrative framework of *Chatterton* is indeed essential, it is different from that which it plays in *Hawksmoor* and *The House of Doctor Dee*, Ackroyd's two other London novels which have parallel yet historically different plotlines. In these two novels, London at first seemingly serves as a setting or platform for committing murders and carrying out occult practices respectively, but eventually it turns out that the city is in fact their main protagonist and they end with passages, openly celebratory in *The House of Doctor Dee*, in which the story smoothly transmutes into an affirmation of the city's indestructible spirit and eternity. *Chatterton*, on the other hand, elaborates on what the ending of *The House of Doctor Dee* only mentions: the power and timelessness of the imagination. "Reality is the invention of unimaginative people" (*C*, 39), Harriet Scrope remarks, and, accordingly, every page of the novel demonstrates Ackroyd's conviction that in the realm of artistic creation, imagination has a higher value than anything else, and a belief in an imaginative vision takes precedence over the moral and conventional norms of the outside world.

> [Charles's] belief had been the important thing. So the papers were imitations and the painting a forgery – yet the feelings they evoked in Charles, and now in Vivien, were still more important than any reality. 'You know,' [Philip] said softly, 'they don't have to be forgotten. We can keep the belief alive.' He looked at Vivien, and smiled. 'The important thing is what Charles imagined, and we can keep hold of that. That isn't an illusion. The imagination never dies'. (*C*, 231–232)

Acts of imitation, forgery or plagiarism are legitimate and justifiable as long as their purpose is not only to imitate and plagiarise, but to become a means of achieving something that by far transcends these acts. The traditional humanist idea of original creative genius is thus rejected "in favor of the medieval (or Blakean, Borgesian, and also 'modernist', in Ackroyd's terminology) notion of shared subjectivity/authorship."[28] Chatterton's forgeries allowed the young man to discover the poet in himself, but also helped to launch the Romantic espousal of medievalism and possibly even to shape its poetics, as "[t]o Wordsworth, Coleridge, Shelley and above all Keats [...], Chatterton was a source of inspiration not only as a symbol but as a poet"[29]; Scrope's plagiarism set her imagination free and she found her own style in her best, mature later works; and the fake Chatterton manuscripts and painting helped Charles make sense of his life which, in consequence, could help Philip fulfil his ambition of writing a novel. Rather than being a key character, this novel's London is thus an inexhaustible power field of creative energy which incessantly generates new imaginative and prophetic visions. *Chatterton* is a distinctive and original contemplation on the very nature and ethics of art, which is ironically and symptomatically based on a pastiche of other texts, stories and voices, a fact that more than effectively proves its author's point.

When William Met Mary: London as a Palimpsest in *The Lambs of London*

Ackroyd deliberately focuses on those aspects and phenomena which have proved most fruitful in inspiring people to write, even though they are not usually made part of the city's "official" history, and he shows how they are narrativised again and again, by different people, with different aims, for different purposes and from different perspectives. They are thus incessantly rewritten, new versions being inscribed onto older ones, transforming themselves into an ongoing process of forming a network of mutually overlapping texts, a palimpsest. Ackroyd acknowledges the metaphor of the city as an historical palimpsest of texts, one laid upon another, whose perpetual interactions constitute the very dynamism of London's literary history. "The city's topography is a palimpsest

---

28 Onega, *Metafiction and myth in the novels of Peter Ackroyd*, 185–186.
29 Kelly, *The Marvellous Boy*, xvii.

within which all the most magnificent or monstrous cities of the world can be discerned. It has been the home of both angels and devils striving for mastery. It has been the seat of miracles, and the harbour of savage paganism. Who can fathom the depths of London?" (*LB*, 753–754). In a manner close to New Historicism he then attempts to reveal as many of these layers as possible, to explore how they relate one to another and to their contemporaneous socio-historical reality, and consequently, perhaps, to discover something that they do not seem to convey in themselves, sharing the view that "[s]ocial actions are themselves always embedded in systems of public signification, always grasped, even by their makers, in acts of interpretation, while the words that constitute the works of literature [...] are by their very nature the manifest assurance of a similar embeddedness."[30]

However, Ackroyd goes even further and in his novels offers his own contributions to this process by rewriting the city's history through his alternative versions of selected past events, his "could-have-been" stories that, based on a combination of the factual and the fictitious, always balance on the narrow border between historiography and playful speculation.

> Ackroyd plays constantly: within a given text, across his own texts, and between the texts which his name signs and those to which he alludes, from which he cites or otherwise borrows, often wittily, with knowing gestures of pastiche and parody, as much from a sense of fun or jest as out of a sense of respect and inheritance. He plays quite seriously between the conventional constraints of the novel and biography, so as to interanimate and contaminate the genres respectively.[31]

Having been peopled with both fictional and real-life personalities, and having their plots revolve around real as well as fictional historical events, his novels contain a world where the boundaries between fact and fiction get blurred for the sake of the stories' attractiveness, although such "fabulation or Gothic repetition, [...] uncanny historical echoes or rhymes of earlier events, and apparent transhistorical identities of characters separated by centuries, destabilise historical reality."[32] Moreover, what has been said about the characters and events also applies to the texts, which often play a crucial role within the novels' plots. Most of these are authentic but some are made up for the purposes of

30   Stephen Greenblatt, *Renaissance Self-Fashioning: From More to Shakespeare*, 5.

31   Gibson and Wolfreys, *Peter Ackroyd: The Ludic and Labyrinthine Text*, 9.

32   Alan Robinson, *Narrating the Past: Historiography, Memory and the Contemporary Novel*, 31.

the narrative. Most of Ackroyd's London novels thus follow, by slightly different and less scholarly means, the pattern suggested in his biography of London – they re-enact the city's past through a palimpsestic layering of texts, discourses and narratives concerning selected events or personalities. *The Lambs of London* represents probably the most illustrative example of this approach and process.

Although the Lambs' story is intriguing enough as such, Ackroyd rewrites and reworks it by adding to it an imaginative "what if" dimension. His central aim in the novel is to offer an alternative version of how Mary Lamb killed her mother, to rewrite existing accounts from a fresh, though largely speculative and fabricated, perspective. For this purpose he adds a criminal dimension to his story: Charles Lamb gets robbed on his way home from a pub, two respectable clerics sexually abuse a Negro crossing-sweeper boy, and, most importantly, William Ireland forges Shakespeare's works and Mary Lamb kills her mother. The novel also includes newspaper reports of recently committed crimes in London, one of which, the murder of an elderly laundress whose killer has not yet been caught, Charles reads aloud to his sister, jokingly informing her that "[c]ities are places of death" and that he "read recently that the first cities were built upon graveyards" (*LL*, 193), unable to realise how disturbing such teasing might be for her oversensitive and unstable psyche. Around the tense and brittle situation in the Lambs' household, Ackroyd constructs a London as a web of miscellaneous crime narratives, and thus evokes an omnipresent atmosphere of physical, social and emotional suffocation with violence and murder in the wind, a sinister urban milieu in which "Mrs. Lamb becomes a sacrificial victim to the innate violence of the city."[33] By connecting the two famous offences, Mary Lamb's matricide, the true circumstances of which are still rather shrouded in mystery, and William Ireland's relatively well-recorded literary forgery, which substantially differ in their nature as well as in their social and legal consequences and implications, Ackroyd composes another layer of the palimpsest composed of the numerous attempts to provide more or less plausible and historically accurate narrative accounts of the crimes.

In conceiving his story, Ackroyd draws on the fact that very little is known about the true circumstances surrounding Mary Lamb's murder of her mother, as all the people involved "consciously kept private any information they had regarding Mary's actions and state of mental health," and that "[e]ven the public record lacks a clear indication of the steps

---

33 Lewis, *My Words Echo Thus*, 139.

taken to extricate Mary Lamb from any painful legal consequences."[34]
The absence of any reliable evidence concerning what precisely preceded
the fatal afternoon of 22 September, 1796 thus leaves room for various
speculations built around a few firm facts which, however, cannot fully
explain what prompted the otherwise mild and docile daughter to commit her violent act. On the other hand, more is known about the events
that followed the trial: the matricide was deemed a manifestation of the
perpetrator's lunacy and she was not confined to a prison or a mental
hospital. Her brother was designated her guardian and she lived under
his gentle care and supervision "as freely and productively as a woman
of her time and temperament could expect – maybe even more so."[35]
Mary shared not only her brother's home, but also his friends and literary career, and with his love and help created a happy and productive
life for herself, outliving him by more than twelve years and dying at the
venerable age of eighty-two, despite the recurrent periods of deep de-
pression which immobilised her for several months of nearly every year.
Though practically self-educated, as she received only a basic education
and her parents probably intended her for a life of service, along with
her brother she presided over an informal but influential literary circle
which included such prominent writers and intellectuals as Coleridge,
Wordsworth, Hazlitt and Godwin[36].

Their father died in 1799, which was something of a relief for Charles,
not only because John Lamb had been mentally incapacitated since suffering a serious stroke around 1792, but mainly because Mary could
then move in with her brother, which arrangement gradually developed
a taste for bachelorhood[37], until his death in 1834. Yet, even these events,
though they are only briefly mentioned in the form of a post-script in
the last chapter, are twisted by Ackroyd. In his version John Lamb dies
only "a few months after his wife's murder" (*LL*, 210), and, more importantly, Ackroyd lets his Mary Lamb die as early as in 1804, being thus
outlived by her brother. He remains faithful to only two historical facts:
that the two siblings collaborated on *Tales from Shakespeare* and that they
are buried in the same churchyard. However, the book was in reality
completed in 1807, thus three years after the death of Mary in the novel,
and the grave is not at St Andrew's, Holborn as the novel claims, but in
All Saints' Churchyard, Edmonton, which only proves how "consistent"

---

34 Susan Tyler Hitchcock, *Mad Mary Lamb: Lunacy and Murder in Literary London*, 18.
35 Hitchcock, *Mad Mary Lamb: Lunacy and Murder in Literary London*, 19.
36 Kathy Watson, *The Devil Kissed Her: The Story of Mary Lamb*, 3–4.
37 Hitchcock, *Mad Mary Lamb*, 94.

Ackroyd is in his toying with the past. Moreover, in Ackroyd's version the doctor is called Philip Girtin and he recommends institutionalising Mary in Hoxton House, "London's largest and longest-established private madhouse," while in reality the doctor's name was David Pitcarin and he advised Charles to place his sister in Fisher House, "a modestly priced, smaller private madhouse in Islington."[38] Ackroyd also makes Thomas De Quincey the person with whom Charles Lamb shares his feelings concerning the murder and its impact on his and his sister's psyches. It is true that Lamb and De Quincey knew each other very well, but his real "literary" confidant was his life-long friend Samuel Taylor Coleridge, who is never mentioned in the novel.

Ackroyd's fictional rendering of Mary Lamb's murder of her mother is based on a peculiar mixture of facts, speculations, conceits and imaginative constructs, whose blend is far more motivated by the desire to make the story interesting and readable than to follow historical records. Making De Quincey a few years older and Ireland a few years younger are therefore not the author's only historical or factual inaccuracies, and having his Mary stab her mother with a roasting fork rather than with a kitchen knife is another minor change. Ackroyd also changes the address of the house where the Lambs lived at the time of the murder, from Little Queen Street to Laystall Street, and he even omits from his account of the events one member of the household, Sarah Lamb, John Lamb's elder sister, who was also present in the house when the murder was committed. Concerning other aspects of the Lamb family background, *The Lambs of London* offers a combination of the factual and fictitious, which pragmatically selects only those facts that support and "legitimise" its author's reconstruction of what led to the crime. Therefore, it is interesting to compare Ackroyd's version with studies which use the available contemporaneous records and evidence to try to cast some light on this murder mystery.

The character of her act suggests that Mary Lamb suffered from some psychological dysfunction[39], most probably from manic-depression, or bipolar disorder. Yet her case was not all that rare, and many of her creative contemporaries, such as Goldsmith, Coleridge, Wollstonecraft, Blake and the Shelleys, are suspected of having suffered from a related mental dis-

---

38 Hitchcock, *Mad Mary Lamb*, 52, 53.
39 Interestingly, at the time of the murder there was an intense fascination in England with the topic of insanity and the nation's relationship to it because King George III suffered from alarming fits of insanity from 1788, and the head of state's mental condition became a subject of public discussion (Watson, *The Devil Kissed Her*, 63).

order[40]. Nevertheless, no matter how peculiar and eccentric most of these personages were, none of them ever overstepped the limits of socially, not to say legally, acceptable behaviour so greatly. The crucial question of what it was that provoked such an uncontrollable and fierce rage in the otherwise timid and forgiving young woman thus arises, whether it was merely her genetic predisposition towards mental instability, or whether some external factors contributed to her temporary, yet fatal, loss of control.

Unmarried and childless at the age of nearly thirty-two, Mary Lamb was condemned to a life of solitude and sacrifice, exposed to patronising compassion bordering on social scorn and confined to the household to look after her elders and serve the men around her. A significant change in the relatively prosperous, though still serving-class, life of the family came when John Lamb's employer and the family's generous benefactor, Samuel Salt, died in 1792. The family's income dropped significantly and they lost their home and had to move to a place more suited to their new economic reality. The situation was too devastating for John Lamb and he suffered a serious stroke at this time, lost his job and, due to his worsening mental and physical condition, demanded almost permanent care and supervision. During the same period of time, Elizabeth Lamb began to experience arthritic pains that eventually affected her whole body and she found it difficult even to stand and walk. The eldest household member, Aunt Sarah, ironically required the least care, yet she was an ill-tempered woman who had a very problematic relationship with her brother's wife, and the household suffered from various manifestations of the two sisters-in-law's intolerance of each other[41].

In the years preceding the murder, Mary Lamb's personal life was therefore far from enviable as she remained the only adult capable of running the household as her mother was basically paralysed and bedridden. In the tense atmosphere of the small flat Mary did almost all the chores, looked after her father during the day and after her mother, with whom she had even begun to share a bed, during the night, for which she received very little but ingratitude. She had to listen to and reconcile the wrangling of her mother and her dotty aunt, and, in the little leisure time she had, instead of her beloved reading, she did needlework in order to augment the family income. Late in 1795, Charles suffered a mental breakdown and spent six weeks as a patient in Hoxton House, London's best-known private asylum. The cause of this episode is unknown,

---

40   Hitchcock, *Mad Mary Lamb*, 277–78.
41   Hitchcock, *Mad Mary Lamb*, 25–26.

but owing to his problems with drinking it may have been triggered by his excessive indulgence in alcohol. Her older brother, John, lived elsewhere but early in the summer of 1796 he had an accident and hurt his leg so severely that he moved back in with his family for a while, adding thus one more soul for Mary to care for. Moreover, only a few days before the murder the family hired a nine-year-old apprentice who was supposed to help Mary with the chores and duties but who, due to her age and being unfamiliar with the new environment, may have quickly turned into a burden for Mary, and the girl in fact unintentionally initiated a series of causes and effects that led to the matricide[42]. Considering all her responsibilities and the difficult family situation, it is obvious that Mary must have been exposed to psychic pressure so intense and stressful that it could easily have struck down a person with a lesser genetic predisposition to mental instability than hers.

In Ackroyd's version the situation in the Lamb family differs in many respects: the father does suffer from some mental illness (the cause of which, however, remains a mystery) and rapidly progressing senility, talks nonsense and needs to be looked after permanently, Charles feels like a lonely outsider and has problems with alcohol, frequently coming home drunk late at night, and the mother never seems to understand her daughter or appreciate what she does, but the rest of the story is altered substantially. The family by no means leans entirely on Mary as her mother is physically perfectly capable and runs the household authoritatively while tending to her husband "with her powerful right arm" (*LL*, 3), the apprentice girl is removed from the murder scene, the wrangling aunt is replaced by a docile and kindhearted elderly spinster who is too frail to perform all the chores and Mary has to take on only "the most onerous duties" (*LL*, 6). Mary does not have to look after her mother day and night, she sleeps alone in her own bedroom, she can leave the house almost as she pleases, and she does not take up her needle to earn money when her parents have gone to bed but spends most of her free time reading Charles's books. Moreover, there is no reference to Charles's mental breakdown or any other similar problem (nor is the stammer that troubled him his whole life mentioned)[43], on the contrary, it is he who worries

---

42 Hitchcock, *Mad Mary Lamb*, 26–28. For a more detailed account of what immediately preceded the matricidal act, including the role the nine-year-old apprentice played in the course of events, see pp. 28–29.

43 Hitchcock discusses the social and personal consequences of Charles Lamb's stammer, which he eventually learnt to use to his advantage, and other minor physical defects such as a short stature and an uneven gait, mostly results of his childhood case of smallpox, on pp. 81–82.

about his sister's sudden changes of mood, her fits of hysteria alternating with periods of absent-mindedness, and her tendency to harm herself with a kitchen knife.

However, the most significant of these changes or speculations is acquainting William Ireland with Charles and Mary Lamb, a narrative act for which there is no basis in the historical records. William and Mary are drawn to each other thanks to several similar traits in their personalities and life situations: both are intelligent, thoughtful and sensitive people with a thirst for knowledge and learning, yet they both are, for different reasons, self-effacing loners overlooked and underestimated by those around them. As a result, they both dream of setting themselves free from what they perceive as an oppressive life of stereotypical convention, prejudice and hypocrisy. Ackroyd makes the insecure, yet ambitious and rather self-conscious, Ireland a close friend of Mary's, one who invites her to be his confidant and with whom he shares the secret of his new "findings." The credulous Mary soon experiences an extraordinary liking for this uncommonly contemplative young gentleman and defends him against all accusations that he has been far from honest with her and the literary world. She refuses to listen to her brother, who gradually develops a suspicion concerning the young man's trustworthiness, agreeing with De Quincey that "Ireland forges his feelings as he forges words" (*LL*, 183), and warns her that Ireland's motives might not be always sincere and honest. When she eventually discovers the true origin of the manuscripts it severely unsettles her fragile mental condition. Ackroyd's version suggests that Ireland could have been the deciding factor that caused the distress which preceded the murder and thus possibly played a crucial role in it. His Mary develops a close relationship with Ireland, one that borders on affection, and therefore takes his confession of forgery as an ultimate betrayal of their mutual trust, understanding and what she takes as an almost secret bond of spirit and soul. As a result, she suffers a mental breakdown after which she is "filled with an overpowering sense of his absence" (*LL*, 204), but still she feels an elated cheerfulness because of her sudden breaking free from all the responsibilities and conventions of her miserable existence, "discharged from life [...] after valiant service" (*LL*, 204), and only a few hours later she commits the murder. Ackroyd thus adds to the amalgam of personal and societal reasons for the matricide – Mary's anger towards and frustration with her mother, her overwhelming family duties, her repressed feelings and desires, namely being deprived of the classical education enjoyed by her brothers, and a genetic tendency towards mental instability – another significant component that actually triggers the family tragedy.

In the acknowledgement placed before the story, Ackroyd claims that he "changed the life of the Lamb family for the sake of the larger narrative," yet he does not say anything about his treatment of the Ireland family, whose fate he twists in a similar manner. Again, the basic factual framework of the events is retained: William-Henry Ireland[44], a young, much overlooked and underestimated boy, desperately longs to win the love and respect of his intransigent father, Samuel Ireland, a pretentious and ambitious writer, antiquarian, and passionate admirer of William Shakespeare who lusts after the great author's memorabilia. And so William forges several documents associated with or supposedly written by the Bard, such as a signed deed, a love letter, poems and an entirely new play, *Vortigen*, which was even staged by Sheridan at Drury Lane. Although the play is in places a clumsy pastiche of characters and scenes from Shakespeare's other plays, the teenage forger wrote his first drama almost as quickly and fluently as his model, and without a draft, in only six weeks[45]. As in the case of Mary and Charles Lamb, this story is simultaneously tragic and amusing, and is also partly unbelievable from the modern perspective as well as shrouded in mystery; unbelievable with regard to the enormous success of the forgeries, mysterious in terms of the forger's origin. Although the forged documents were rather amateurish as they were produced within a short period of several months by a teenager of limited education, poor mastery of his mother tongue (for instance, Ireland initially spelled by ear and never punctuated[46]), and only very superficial knowledge of English literature and history, and who in his own father's eyes was nothing more than a half-educated simpleton who lacked his father's intellect and sophistication[47], many literati, scholars and men of letters of the time, including Samuel Parr, Joseph Warton, R. B. Sheridan, Edmund Burke and James Boswell, believed that the "Shakespeare Papers" were authentic. The explanation could be that these people simply wanted the papers to be genuine.

The second half of the eighteenth century witnessed an increasing interest in Elizabethan and medieval literature, most notably in Shake-

---

44 In *The Lambs of London*, Ackroyd does not use the forger's middle name "Henry" although both the boy and his family commonly used it. The boy had been named "Henry" in honour of the Tory politician and writer Henry St John Bolingbroke, while his first name had probably been chosen as a homage to Shakespeare (Patricia Pierce, *The Great Shakespeare Fraud*, 21).

45 Doug Stewart, *The Boy Who Would Be Shakespeare: A Tale of Forgery and Folly*, 91.

46 Pierce, *The Great Shakespeare Fraud*, 232.

47 Stewart, *The Boy Who Would Be Shakespeare*, 65.

speare's life and work. As almost nothing written in his hand had ever been found many people believed that some more documents or even works of the Bard could still be discovered. The cult of Shakespeare, or "Bardolatry" as it was termed, was thus well established, although the level of Shakespearian scholarship was not; textual study was in its infancy and palaeography almost unknown – there was more enthusiasm and fascination than expertise, most experts being self-taught and self-appointed[48]. The rapidly expanding British Empire started to take pride in its cultural history and cherish its greatest literary genius as the trend towards Romanticism strengthened. The art of forgery in fact fully developed in the eighteenth century and was associated with the relatively new phenomena of professional authorship and a growing commercial publishing market. However, the "most significant connection is to be found between forgery and the burgeoning movement known as 'romanticism'" as "[t]he forged document and the 'romantic' personality are manifestations of the same change in taste" (A, 421). Therefore, it was also the time of famous and successful forgeries, especially James Macpherson's Ossian poems in the early 1760s and Thomas Chatterton's *Rowley Poems* a few years later. The story of Chatterton stirred William-Henry's imagination, particularly the striking similarities between the two boys' ages and backgrounds. He considereded Chatterton "an unrecognised genius much like himself,"[49] yet he did not choose to forge some "lost," obscure ancient poems by unknown authors but those by the most worshipped literary figure, an immensely daring act for an aspiring young writer.

On the personal level, there was uncertainty surrounding William-Henry's parentage, as he could not be sure whether either of the two adults who had brought him up, Samuel Ireland and his partner, Mrs. Freeman, were his biological parents, and although he repeatedly asked his father he never received any definite answer concerning his true origin[50]. Mrs. Freeman's maternal feelings were well concealed; she was a disagreeable, at times malicious woman whom Samuel Ireland treated as if she were a domestic servant and never married[51]. All this can also

---

48 Pierce, *The Great Shakespeare Fraud*, 3–4.

49 Pierce, *The Great Shakespeare Fraud*, 15, 33. For his whole life, and even more after the exposure of his forgeries, William-Henry Ireland continued to admire Chatterton, he devoted to him a book of poems entitled *Neglected Genius*, and he kept emphasising the close association between "the Rowleian Chatterton and the Shakespearean Ireland" (Kelly, *The Marvellous Boy*, 78–79).

50 Pierce, *The Great Shakespeare Fraud*, 19–20.

51 He never married her, in part because she had been the mistress of John Montagu, the notorious eighteenth-century English Casanova, Lord Sandwich, though her fortune (probably

explain Samuel's lack of warmth and interest in his son, which troubled William-Henry deeply and provoked in him an almost obsessive desire to please his father and gain his attention and recognition. Yet, no matter how successful his forgeries were, he never managed to achieve his main goal: the opportunist and foolishly obstinate Samuel Ireland grew interested not in his son, but in his own fame and profit, repeatedly ignored William-Henry's pleas not to exhibit and later publish the documents, and even after William-Henry's confession refused to believe, until the end of his life four years later, that the "precious" papers were produced by his dull-looking, incompetent, childlike son.

In *The Lambs of London*, Ackroyd makes use of the fact that the two crimes took place at more or less the same time, and that their main protagonists suffered from deprivations and frustrations resulting from an analogous social and personal situation. Also, the personality and character of his Samuel Ireland and the nature of the relationship between the father and the son more or less correspond with reality. However, as with the Lambs, the alterations he makes for the sake of his story fundamentally distort the available historical records. First, there are the household members: instead of the educated and well-read Mrs. Freeman, herself an aspiring writer who could potentially be William-Henry's real mother, Ackroyd's Samuel Ireland lives with the narrow-minded Rosa Ponting, whom he even secretly marries after the death of his first wife, who was William's true mother; Ackroyd also never mentions William's two older sisters. His William works as an assistant in his father's shop, while in reality he apprenticed as a law conveyancer. This William feels nothing when visiting Shakespeare's birthplace in Stratford, while the real one "became ecstatic with the sensation of being immersed in air the Bard breathed, the ground he had walked upon" and later admitted that the visit "greatly conducted to the subsequent production of the papers."[52] Ackroyd also changes the gender of the mysterious "source" of the papers, from a Mr H., for whom William-Henry, as a law clerk, as he claimed to his father, supposedly saved a considerable sum of money[53], to an unnamed widow.

His treatment of the role of real historical personages in the case is also eclectically inaccurate: while some are retained, like Dr. Samuel Parr, who strongly believed in the papers' authenticity, R. B. Sheridan,

---

received in compensation from the lord) was likely a reason why Samuel settled with her (Stewart, *The Boy Who Would Be Shakespeare*, 12–14).

52 Pierce, *The Great Shakespeare Fraud*, 36, 41.

53 Stewart, *The Boy Who Would Be Shakespeare*, 85.

who staged *Vortigen* even though he considered it an immature work by the young Shakespeare, or John Philip Kemble, the famous actor and manager "perhaps best known as the man who consolidated the managerships of Drury Lane and Covent Garden in the early 1800s,"[54] whose deliberately unprofessional acting heavily undermined the performance[55] though he normally "took tragedy immensely seriously,"[56] some are left out, such as James Boswell, Dr. Joseph Warton or George Steevens (though there is a Mr Stevens on the committee of inquiry), and some are changed. The most significant of these changes relates to the character of Edmond Malone, the most prominent Shakespearean scholar of that time, who in the novel thoroughly examines the papers and pronounces them to be genuine. In reality, Malone had serious doubts concerning the papers' authenticity from the very beginning (he had also been one of the first to attack Chatterton's poems thirty years earlier)[57]. He was a true professional who relied on precise and careful reading and research, but his wish to see the papers in private was repeatedly turned down by Samuel Ireland who had no desire to subject the documents to such an in-depth scrutiny, and so Malone had to wait until Samuel Ireland's *Miscellaneous Papers and Legal Instruments under the Hand and Seal of William Shakespeare* was published on 24 December, 1795, and on 10 January he sat down to write his response. He originally intended it to be a short pamphlet, but, as he assembled more and more pieces of evidence, the work grew into a 424-page book which methodically dismissed each of the forgeries. Malone's book was published on 31 March, 1796, only two days before *Vortigen* was to be staged, but 500 copies were sold during this short period and it negatively affected the performance[58], certainly much more than the "Rank Forgery" handbill distributed in front of the theatre in Ackroyd's version.

The list of differences could continue – for instance, William-Henry did not confess to his father, whose reaction he feared, but to his sisters and Mrs. Freeman, he did not set the house on fire while burning the papers but secretly moved out and for some time the family had no idea

54 Jim De Young and John Miller, *London Theatre Walks*, 208.

55 Kemble intended to put on the first performance of *Vortigen* on April Fools' Day, but the first night was eventually moved to 2 April.

56 Peter Thomson, "Acting and actors from Garrick to Kean," 12.

57 To his growing fury, Edmond Malone twice attempted unsuccessfully to have some of the papers removed temporarily from their public display in Norfolk Street in order to scrutinise them at home and with his friends. For a more detailed description of Malone's examination and disproval of the Shakespeare Papers see Pierce's *The Great Shakespeare Fraud*, pp.151–166.

58 Pierce, *The Great Shakespeare Fraud*, 160–64.

where he was, and he soon married a girl none of his friends and family had known existed[59], an event Ackroyd logically omits completely. Although William-Henry did set up a circulating library, it was not in Kennington but near Kensington Gardens, and he could hardly send out *Tales from Shakespeare* to his borrowers (*LL*, 216) as when the book was published he was no longer operating the library. Most importantly, in order to combine Mary Lamb's and William Ireland's stories, Ackroyd has to change the chronology of events, as in reality the murder took place on 22 September, but William-Henry had already confessed in May and married on 4 June. Moreover, he left London in late July, first for Wales and then he roamed around the country and was not back in the city until the end of October. At the time of the murder he was in Bristol, visiting the birthplace of Thomas Chatterton[60].

The intriguing stories of Mary Lamb and William-Henry Ireland have more in common than may seem at first sight: the protagonists are ignored and underestimated, they suffer from loneliness, frustration and despair resulting from a lack of parental love and respect as well as from the burden of conventions and expectations, their intellectual and literary aspirations are doomed to remain unfulfilled due to their social status, and so their subsequent crimes, which put them on the front pages of newspapers and at the centre of many public debates, in a way freed them from most of the restraints of their former existence. There is yet another aspect that connects the two affairs – they could have only happened in the capital city, not only because of its anonymity, but mainly because London is the economic, cultural and intellectual centre of the country, which crucially determines the values and moral attitudes of its inhabitants. Nowhere else could Mary have got away so easily with her matricide, lived peacefully in her brother's house, and even become a respectable literary personality and author of popular children's books; nowhere else could William-Henry have got away with the tale about his mysterious benefactor; and nowhere else would his forgeries have caused such a commotion far beyond literary and scholarly circles. The two stories aptly demonstrate how the city can easily make and destroy a person, how generous it can be in offering opportunities, but also how unpredictable and merciless when judging those who trespass its laws: paradoxically, even though William-Henry's offence was much less serious than Mary's, it was deemed so "unforgivable" that it ultimately spoiled

---

59   Pierce, *The Great Shakespeare Fraud*, 177–85.
60   Pierce, *The Great Shakespeare Fraud*, 186–94.

his chances as an actor, playwright and writer in London, forced him to leave England for France, and, despite his authorship of more than sixty books, prevented him from ever gaining any substantial recognition.

The Lambs of London exemplifies Ackroyd's conviction that biographies and fictions should not be understood as separate activities[61], and thus offers another contribution to the discussion over the possibility of imaginative or alternative literary history. Although the Lambs were very likely to have known about Ireland's forgeries from the daily press, the three young people most probably never met in person. By combining their fates Ackroyd fabricates a new, "what-if" dimension to the exciting literary and intellectual milieu of late eighteenth and early nineteenth-century London, and, by rewriting their life-stories, he simultaneously contributes a palimpsestic rewriting of the city and its biography. The fact that the past will never be known completely since it contains too many mysteries and gaps caused by the absence of reliable evidence serves as a double-edged sword: it tempts writers and scholars to come up with speculative versions which might, on the one hand, further obscure the original events and, in effect, impede their subsequent disclosure, but which, on the other hand, have the potential to draw more attention to these less well-known events and circumstances. And once questions are posed, answers are demanded as, for instance, a strictly "psychiatric diagnosis does not entirely satisfy our fascination with Mary Lamb."[62] *The Lambs of London* does not help literary scholars overcome the lack of clarity concerning Mary Lamb's mental disposition or William-Henry Ireland's parentage, but it undoubtedly brings the two unfortunate people's lives to the forefront of many readers' interest and thus, though only through the means of fictitious narrative, saves the first from forever being mentioned only in the footnotes of her brother's biographies, and the latter from forever staying in Chatterton's shadow. If Mary Lamb and William-Henry Ireland were guilty of their crimes, so is Ackroyd – those of "fakery, pastiche, and plagiarism,"[63] of blurring the novel and biography, of eclectic disrespect for recorded history, but, most of all, of making the literary texture of the city even more colourful and exciting.

---

61 Murray, *Recalling London*, 85.
62 Hitchcock, *Mad Mary Lamb*, 279.
63 Lewis, *My Words Echo Thus*, 141.

Towards Autobiographic Self-referencing: Literary London in *Three Brothers*

A different tendency in Ackroyd's treatment of London as a literary city – autobiographic self-referencing – can be found in *Three Brothers*. Like his other London novels, it presents the city as one which has provided a limitless source of inspiration for narratives. On an amateur and a sub-literary level, the novel presents the city's potential to incessantly generate material for storytelling through Sparkler and Harry, through whom the novel asserts its antiquarian dimension most forcefully. As his nickname indicates, the former keeps sparkling with stories and gossip about the various activities and members of the London underworld, jokingly suggesting that Daniel writes them down under the title "The Sparkler Papers" (*TB*, 83)[64]. "There is nothing about London I don't know. I'm on first-name terms with the sparrows and very chummy with the pigeons" (*TB*, 152–53), says the watchful and meddlesome petty thief to Daniel, pointing to the double function of his ability: his half true and half made up stories may show him in a better light while, simultaneously, entertain the listener, and thus perhaps contribute to the popular urban imagination and myth-making, but, much more importantly, they are only a by-product of his general survival strategy in the unscrupulous and callous criminal world – to have information someone else may need. Harry's transforming of the city's happenings into narratives, though differently motivated, is in fact similar in principle as his job is to report crimes and collect rumours about celebrities and politicians, at first for a local Camden journal and later for a more ambitious London newspaper. Being dismissive of literature, his reports have no other purpose than to increase sales by being amusing and sensational.

The truly literary aspect of the city is represented by Daniel, Ackroyd's parodic self-projection, who after completing his doctorate in English literature at Cambridge becomes not only a junior fellow and supervisor at his college, but also a reviewer for literary journals and supplements and a television commentator. Using his own experience as a book reviewer and broadcaster, Ackroyd satirically portrays the often pretentious, hypocritical and volatile milieu of London literary circles, especially the pomposity, rivalry and insidiousness of those who dominate them. Daniel's interest in the London literary tradition is instigated when he is asked, as an expert on English literature and Londoner

---

64 Which can be an anecdotal allusion to *The Plato Papers*.

born and raised, to write a book entitled "The Writers of London." In spite of his initial doubts concerning the academic profundity of such an enterprise, he gradually becomes fascinated by the theme. Unlike in Ackroyd's other novels, the literary London of *Three Brothers* is not very intertextual, palimpsestic or apocryphal[65], but rather self-reflectively metafictional, as it does not revolve around authors and/or their texts, but around a literary project and scholarly research strikingly similar to its author's own.

While carrying out his research, Daniel realises that a crucial component of the city's literary genius is to be found outside the domain of the official culture, in the experience and imagination of those on the margins of society, or in popular cultural forms. And so, even though in reality he is not concerned in the city's low-class idiosyncrasies in the least, in his research he concentrates on the novelists who in their works explored the nineteenth century Limehouse opium dens, and on London popular culture, such as penny dreadfuls and music halls, whose performers he calls "the real heroes of London," and whose songs he considers "[f]ar better than the poetry of the period" (*TB*, 184). Moreover, he becomes aware of the significance of the atavistic power concentrated in certain areas that causes similar events to take place there and similarly minded people to settle in them.

> One of the themes of Daniel's book concerned the patterns of association that linked the people of the city; he had found in the work of the novelists a preoccupation with the image of London as a web so taut and tightly drawn that the slightest movement of any part sent reverberations through the whole. A chance encounter might lead to terrible consequences, and a misheard word bring unintended good fortune. An impromptu answer to a sudden question might cause death. (*TB*, 185)

All these features echo loudly in Ackroyd's concept of London – the patterns of resonance and continuity, mythical time, the power of the *genii locorum*, the Cockney Visionaries, the music hall tradition invigorating the popular imagination and producing outstanding monopolylinguists, the city's spiritual radicalism and occultism – as if Daniel were his younger, less experienced alter ego. Only very slowly does Daniel come to understand that the city is a densely knit network, an immensely

---

65   Unless its title is counted as an implicit reference to Anton Chekhov's *Three Sisters*, with which, however, the novel does not bear any conspicuous affinity, perhaps save for the characters' longing to escape their unsatisfying life.

convoluted and heterogeneous system of relationships, influences, associations, energies and forces. This mechanism combines and reconciles opposites and contradictions, which cannot be separated from each other without losing their true meaning, and whose ongoing encountering generates the most unexpected coincidences. However, before he can grasp the city in its complexity, he becomes prey to one of its snares: his panic-stricken reaction to Sparkler's sudden declaration of love in effect brings about his untimely decease. And so, the novel in fact does contain a metafictional as well as intertextual element as it comments on a London writers' tendency which it later employs itself, and the expression "the great general drama of the human spirit" (*TB*, 242) by which Sam identifies what dominates the London streets around him at the end of the novel comes directly from Ackroyd's lecture "London Luminaries and Cockney Visionaries."

Although *Three Brothers* contains the defining attributes of Ackroyd's fictional London, such as lonely characters roaming its streets in order to either enjoy or cope with their solitude, a focus on the city's undersides including crime and criminals, various uncanny and irrational manifestations, a reflection of the urban experience in the protagonists' minds, an urge to transform this experience into stories and narratives, the city life's inherent theatricality, and London's distinctly literary nature, it bears a particularly strong affinity with his first novel, *The Great Fire of London*. They both take place entirely in the present time, or not so distant past, and do not have any features of a historical narrative. They present a cast of miscellaneous characters, many of them peculiar or eccentric, whose fates are brought together and interconnected through a central motif and a series of often improbable coincidences. This breaks the novel into several parallel plotlines conceived through often separate, more or less related, scenes in which these characters encounter one another, a narrative strategy also employed in *Chatterton* and *The Clerkenwell Tales*. Moreover, they both have unhappy endings in the form of the tragic death of one or more of the main protagonists who, in some way, become victims of their misconception or misapprehension of the city, while, at the same time, its heterogeneous and ungovernable forces, personified by Little Arthur, Sparkler and the vagrants, prevail and persist. Yet, in this respect, *Three Brothers* offers a more hopeful resolution as Sam, the brother most in accord and compliant with the city's nature, lives on to perpetuate his vision.

However, the most striking resemblance rests in the stories' autobiographic element which, with the exception of the self-ironic authorial voice in the final chapter of *The House of Doctor Dee*, does not appear in any of Ackroyd's other London novels. Central to this resemblance is the character of a gay literary scholar associated with Cambridge University whose interest is identical with its creator's. Rowan Phillips, an aspiring novelist and Cambridge-based scholar focusing on Dickens in *The Great Fire of London* "may be described as a parodic version of Peter Ackroyd."[66] However, he differs from his author in several respects: not only is he not a Londoner or even British, but Canadian, and his coming to London to be closer to the place where the subject of his academic research lived and wrote is merely a pretext for his true motivation – to enjoy the sexual freedom of London's gay community under the veil of the anonymity of a big city. Moreover, he is always at odds with the city life, he does not like its bustle and pace, his love life is a frustrating failure, as a result of which he not only feels lonely and alienated there, he also cannot fully understand Dickens's imagination no matter how much he studies his life and writing.

Daniel Hanway, on the other hand, resembles Ackroyd much more as he is a Londoner who graduated from Cambridge with excellent degrees, who works as a literary reviewer, critic and commentator, and who comes to be interested in writers who wrote in and about London. He is thus a differently parodic image of his creator, who puts in Daniel's mouth statements and phrases which seem to come directly from his own non-fiction texts about London, especially those about the city's undersides, about the music hall and its performers and songs, about the power of the *genius loci*, and the supratemporal "patterns of inheritance" (LLCV, 343). The most distinctly (self-)ironic feature about Daniel is his inability to transform his theoretical propositions and findings into practice and transfer them from his book to his own life, for which he is granted the most severe destiny by Ackroyd. While in Ackroyd's other London novels the literary aspect is built around the texts of writers such as Dickens, Chatterton, Gissing, De Quincey and Mary Shelley, in *Three Brothers* it centres around its author's own scholarly and literary production. Although the novel is gripping and fits perfectly into the body of his London novels, it does not offer much that is new and original and, in terms of the conception of its chronotope, is rather a reprise of the fictional London created by Ackroyd more than thirty years earlier. Perhaps symbolically, by replacing his beloved Dickens with himself, Ackroyd in a way intimates his own affiliation with what he identifies as the

---

66   Onega, *Peter Ackroyd*, 28.

city's Cockney visionary tradition. Nevertheless, with all due respect for Ackroyd's achievements and the legitimacy of such a claim, the absence of other than a self-referencing literary framework or a historical dimension means that *Three Brothers* lacks a great deal of the vividness and imaginative playfulness of its predecessors.

Conclusion:
Longing and Belonging

In Euxodia, which spreads both upward and down, with winding alleys,
steps, dead ends, hovels, a carpet is preserved in which you can observe
the city's true form. [...] All of Euxodia's confusion [...] is evident in the
incomplete perspective you grasp; but the carpet proves that there is
a point from which the city shows its true proportions, the geometrical
scheme implicit in its every, tiniest detail.

Italo Calvino, *Invisible Cities*

The London of Peter Ackroyd's novels is a highly idiosyncratic construct which reflects and derives from its author's ideas about the actual
city's character as well as his concept of the English literary sensibility
in general. First of all, it is a fundamentally heterogeneous city of enormous diversity and richness of human experience, moods and emotion,
of actions and events, and also of the tools through which these are (re)
presented and reenacted – styles, forms, languages and other means of
expression. This heterogeneity mostly originates outside the sites and
domains of the established or mainstream cultural production and social
norms and conventions, particularly in occult beliefs and practices, subversive acts and plotting of radical individuals or groups, criminal and
fraudulent activities of various kinds, dubious scientific experiments,
and the popular dramatic forms of ritual and entertainment whose permanent encounters with and contesting of the officially approved and
prescribed forms instigate the city's vitalising energy for dynamic change
and spiritual renewal. In order to render such diversity Ackroyd employs
a variety of stylistic and linguistic devices, such as the mixing up of genres, the alternation of narrative perspectives and the use of parody and
pastiche of styles, narrative forms and discourses. This London also does
not revolve along a chronological time axis as its development is domi-

nated by supratemporal and/or co-temporal paradigms of powers, tendencies and phenomena which float free and (re)emerge haphazardly across historical periods, and which are to be found actively operating underneath our present day consciousness and sensibility.

Due to the intrinsic interconnectedness of its material and immaterial sides, this London represents a distinctive space-time model, a particular chronotope whose spatial and temporal properties incessantly interact with each other and substantially affect the novels' plots as well as their characters' fates. However, there are two main reasons why Ackroyd's fictional urban realm exceeds the limits of the Bakhtinian chronotope: the first is his notion of time as non-directional, labyrinthine and non-sequential, in which different time layers can coexist, overlap or intertwine, most apparently in *Hawksmoor*, *Chatterton* and *The House of Doctor Dee*, as a result of which time gets divorced, at least temporarily, from space and the story's meaning shifts to a transcendental, perpetual plain where no physical laws apply; the second is the fact that as well as being a setting his London also assumes a meta-chronotopic role as a character, or even as an all-controlling principle, which, in terms of narrative significance, tends to predominate and overshadow the human characters and their acts, as can be seen especially in *The Great Fire of London*, *Hawksmoor*, *The House of Doctor Dee* and *Dan Leno and the Limehouse Golem*. Ackroyd's London chronotope is also internally diverse as it involves, and is crucially co-determined by, a set of minor heterotopic chronotopes of different types, both walled, enclosed and outdoor, counter-sites in and outside time which, thanks to their capacity for embracing contradictory and opposing qualities, are capable of reflecting other places, in and through which all the discussed principal attributes of the city – the uncanny, felonious, psychogeographic, theatrical and literary – most perceptibly manifest and perpetuate themselves. The most potent of these in Ackroyd's novels are Doctor Dee's house, the medieval Clerkenwell Green, the Reading Room of the British Museum, sites of confinement and the nineteenth-century music halls.

As a whole, that is including its human inhabitants, this chronotopic London constitutes a social space, or rather meta-space, which bears all the defining characteristics of Soja's Thirdspace (and Lefebvre's lived space). Most of all, it is a realm of extraordinary simultaneities which unites and appropriates opposites and contradictions, the real, the material, and the physical with the imagined, the metaphorical, and the spiritual, without privileging any by placing them into the established value hierarchies, or by marginalising any by banishing them to its periphery. This allows such a meta-space to display both familiarity and otherness, and by doing so to open up within itself numerous spaces of resistance, counter-power and liberation, where the dominant and the hegemonic are contested and undermined. In Ackroyd's novels such "counterspaces" of personal rather than ideological or overtly political radical struggle can be found almost everywhere, though they differ, deliberately or not, in terms of their public visibility. In several cases they coincide with the heterotopic chronotopes, for instance the Reading Room of the British Museum, the prisons, the medieval venues of popular folk theatrical performances, the music halls and theatres, but a majority of the others also evince at least some features of a heterotopia: the churches as sites of subversive criminal acts – personal, as in *Hawksmoor*, and political, as in *The Clerkenwell Tales*; the various secluded, concealed places, the sanctuaries of intellectual, spiritual or political radicalism, such as Dyer's, Chatterton's, Weil's and Ireland's study rooms, Dee's and Frankenstein's laboratories, Sister Clarice's convent cell, or the undercroft where the clandestine group known as Dominus meet to plan their conspiratorial activities. There are also mental spaces which are not tied to any specific physical locality but are carried from one place to another in the minds of their "possessors," such as Spender's project of immortalising Dickens's London in a film, Wychwood's idea of genuine poetry, Ireland's ambition of becoming a source of pride for his father and Sam Hanway's imaginary convent. Moreover, all Ackroyd's protagonists who manage to persist or even be happy in this London approach it in the same way that Soja characterises as the attitude of typical inhabitants of Thirdspace: rather than trying to unravel and understand its operating mechanisms and actively transform it, they try to appropriate the city by reading its symbolic communication, describing it, and finding and accepting their position and role in it. However, as the cases of Spender, Hawksmoor, Wychwood, Chatterton, the Lambs or Gissing illustrate, they are rarely granted, and if so then often only briefly, moments of earthly, mundane happiness, for the true reward lies elsewhere – in becoming part of the city's creative and visionary tradition.

It is impossible to approach Ackroyd's fictional London separately from his understanding of the English creative sensibility (and, in consequence, that of London), literary in particular, as both these conceptions are defined by the same principles and therefore are of the same nature and fabric. Ackroyd does not call for fundamentally radical revisions, he does not propose a wholly alternative canon or history, but he problematises conventional views of English creativity and of London's historical development by presenting them to be somewhat incomplete, and therefore at times simplifying and misleading, because they have deliberately overlooked and dismissed certain substantial factors and influences. The premise of his conviction is that both are composed of phenomena and tendencies that have been habitually and one-sidedly seen as opposite, contradictory, and as such incompatible and mutually exclusive: the rational and the irrational, the material and the immaterial, the tangible and the intangible, the manifest and the undercurrent, the orderly and the disorderly, the orthodox and the oppositional. While the first in these binary oppositions have become the cornerstone of the line of argument of the majority of historical and critical studies, the second have been considered as either insubstantial, marginal to the point of non-existence, or deleterious. The main reason for this, Ackroyd claims, is that they are subversive, and as such hard to grasp, control or categorise, due to which they prove useless or even counterproductive as a systematic means for any power-motivated purposes. However, without them the concept of any historical continuation turns out to be illusory, artificial and sterile. What Ackroyd does is, strictly speaking, very simple: he reveals, exposes and foregrounds these heterogeneous and dissident aspects, lets them interact with one another as well as with those which are generally approved, and tries to discover, or uncover, the yet unseen or almost inconceivable connections, continuities and consequences, and explore their corrective impact on the official versions.

This on no account means that Ackroyd would invert or disprove history at any cost or on principle: in English literary history he acknowledges canonical writers and texts, in the history of London he does not question factual accounts of events and developments, but he tries to see them in a new light, from different perspectives and in varying contexts by putting the long-ignored factors into play and demonstrating that they have influenced all the constitutional tendencies within these intrinsically interconnected traditions. He argues that the potential of the city and its creative sensibility rests in absorbing and adopting this heterogeneity and diversity, not in avoiding it and banishing it from view, and so the city's greatest visionaries and most extraordinary and enduring properties are such especially because they have successfully incorporated and reconciled all the so-called binary polarities and transformed them into concurrently directed evolutionary and creative agents operating in concord rather than in opposition. The essence of Ackroyd's method is therefore not merely deconstructive but productive and reconstructive, as his primary aim is to arrive at a definition and delineation of the tradition of the English (mostly yet not exclusively literary) imagination and, along with this, of the history and character of the capital, unburdened with bias, prejudice, political, ideological or religious motivation, and the implications of the power struggles of domination and submission.

In the fictional world of Ackroyd's London novels all these seemingly incongruous elements not only coexist but also collaborate, producing a diverse yet complementary image of a city, which he says for him is simultaneously "a horror and a beauty."[1] This London embraces and fuses enterprises and phenomena such as science and philosophy with occult teachings and practices, high-brow cultural production with popular entertainment forms, products of original genius with forgeries and plagiarisms, Protestant ethics with Catholic and pagan ones, the desire for a rational, orderly society with the urge for bodily excess and violence, and is depicted as being constituted by their interaction. By this he takes part in what Linda Hutcheon identifies as a productive dialogue between the modernist and postmodernist paradigms[2]. Although he does not acknowledge the legitimacy of the latter, his fiction is in accord with its postulates that "allow space for difference and particularity, for plurality and heterogeneity, [...] that investigate the production of meaning and 'truth' and question an unthinkable acceptance of historical, social, political and ethnic assumptions."[3] His dismissive attitude is rather a matter of perspective than content since he espouses these tendencies, but sees them as historically much older and merely falsely attributed to, or appropriated by, what denotes itself a postmodernist literary theory, as only a part of a "definite native London art [...] and a definite native London sensibility which goes back for many hundreds of years."[4]

Ackroyd's London, present and past, is firmly embedded in historical tradition, yet in one which is not based on sequential temporality and "logical" causality of events, but rather on unceasing, often invisible and rationally intangible lines of continuity that have affected the face of the city for ages, which helps elucidate even that which may appear either inexplicable or newly emerged, but it can do so only in its completeness and wholeness. He sees historical events, including very recent ones, as

1   Peter Watts, "Peter Ackroyd: interview." *Time Out*, 18 September 2008.

2   Gunilla Florby, Postscript: "So what about Postmodernism? Frederick Jameson vs Linda Hutcheon," 248.

3   Florby, Postscript: "So what about Postmodernism? Frederick Jameson vs Linda Hutcheon," 249.

4   Anke Schütze, "I think after More I will do Turner and then I will probably do Shakespeare," an Interview with Peter Ackroyd.

mere surface effects of these undercurrents, "all the more powerful for being undetected,"[5] as merely different manifestations of certain invariable forces, while London remains "always the same. It hasn't changed its essential nature for many centuries and it probably never will."[6] He therefore shows this tradition to be deeper, more complete, assorted and inspiring by clearing away the silt of hypocrisy, convention and disdain, thus laying bare and celebrating agents that have been operating unobserved within it, and demonstrating that some "(post)modern" phenomena are in fact not new as they have existed for long, only in slightly modified forms depending on the periods in which they occurred. Ackroyd believes that history is driven by "longing and belonging," that is by the need to be part of something that transcends one's physical existence, "the atavistic desire to find deep sources of identity."[7] His fictional London offers his novels' protagonists an opportunity to satisfy such needs, yet on condition that they are perceptive and sensitive enough to recognise and embrace its patterns of permanence and perpetuation, and to identify with and internalise the continuation they perpetuate.

Ackroyd's concept of the "mystical city universal" is thus in essence conservative and traditionalist. Despite his focus on its unorthodox and subterranean features Ackroyd's approach, unlike Sinclair's psychogeography, does not search for another, alternative London but for the "genuine" London in all its complexity, just as he does not search for another literary tradition but for the genuine, complex English sensibility. His celebration of the majestic and infinite metropolis is closely linked with establishing and defending the notion of Englishness, the English sensibility or genius as he prefers to call it. In his London novels the dominant tone is that of respect and admiration that at times inevitably borders on pathos and reverence, which may easily provoke critical voices pointing to its excessive sentimentality and lapses into artificial schematisation[8]. However, before he adopts such a stance he subjects London and its history to thorough revision and reassessment, which, necessarily, requires a certain redefinition of the city's character, and of Englishness in general as the former cannot be separated from the latter.

---

5   Peter Ackroyd, "My epic search for our turbulent roots." *The Telegraph*, 25 August 2011.

6   Daisy Banks, "Peter Ackroyd on London," an interview, *The Browser* (2013).

7   Ackroyd, "My epic search for our turbulent roots."

8   Ladislav Nagy, for instance, suggests that too strong an insistence on the ungraspable and paranormal might lure one into resigning from critical thinking, and that for Ackroyd one of the most dynamic European capitals thus serves for a pathetic defence of "true" Englishness (*Londýn stejný a jiný*, 27–28).

Ackroyd's call for such a redefinition stems from a different motivation than that of his contemporaries who deal with this theme, such as Julian Barnes, Kazuo Ishiguro, Salman Rushdie and Zadie Smith, but the result is to some extent similar: he sees them as convoluted, multilayered, even in a way hybridised, through their capacity to accommodate heterogeneity and diversity which comprise noticeability and familiarity as well as a wide range of otherness, both subliminal and consciously repressed.

The London of Ackroyd's novels is a yet more imaginative extension of how he describes the city in his non-fiction works, brought to life through his "incisive style and mordant wit,"[9] by which he manages to poeticise its more seamy and obscure manifestations as well as defamiliarise the mundane ones. Although some may view this world as idealistic and implausible, or object to its author's tendencies to pathos and a conservative insistence on the extensiveness of the domestic tradition, or claim that it reduces the protagonists' identities and diminishes the relevance of their acts[10], it is an integral and autonomous world which possesses what Milan Kundera identifies as the defining attributes of the novel – the spirit of complexity and the spirit of continuity, which distinguish it from the all-pervading hyper-reality of simplifications and stereotypes generated by the modern media[11]. Though based on the real city, Ackroyd's London is an imagined space which "seized upon by the imagination cannot remain indifferent space subject to the measures and estimates of the surveyor," a space conceived and lived in "with all the partiality of the imagination."[12] As such, it is one that is naturally susceptible to criticism, as well as one that appeals to many as "it concentrates being within limits that protect."[13] This intricate yet enclosed and self-contained fictional universe offers various pleasures but only for those readers who come to accept the ruling tenets of its imaginary security.

In all his novels London features as an all-affecting entity, and in some of them also as the main character, its role transcending and surpassing those of individuals, yet this does not mean that it is merely a spatial and temporal construct lacking a social dimension. This London is inseparable from the people who inhabit it, though they are often portrayed, in accordance with what Ackroyd identifies as properties of London writing, through hyperbole, caricature and dynamic action, and

---

9   Thomas Wright, "Introduction," xviii.

10   Nagy, *Londýn stejný a jiný*, 27.

11   Milan Kundera, *The Art of the Novel*, 18.

12   Gaston Bachelard, *The Poetics of Space*, xxxvi.

13   Bachelard, *The Poetics of Space*, xxxvi.

he sees the city's physical and human sides as being like communicating vessels: the former crucially influences the latter but, at the same time, cannot function without it as the city's transtemporal continuum is propelled and sustained primarily by its dwellers' creativity. His (hi)stories, based on a "what-if" conception as well as those set in the present, explore the dynamisms within such a system, that is, the various effects of the interaction between the city and its people under different, more or less imaginary and fanciful, circumstances and contexts. The question of whether London has ever really been such is thus irrelevant since novels, as Kundera claims, do not examine reality but rather existence as a realm of human possibilities, and so the main task of the novelist is to "draw up *the map of existence* by discovering this or that human possibility."[14] As in Italo Calvino's *Invisible Cities*, the actual sites of meaning and creative energy in Ackroyd's London novels can be found in the realm "[b]etween the perceived disorder of the world and the rationalizing structures attempting to map and order it," in the "*outopic*,"[15] displaced gap or interval between them within which the crucial disorderly and indomitable energies and tensions that shape this existence operate. In this sense, he is a distinct and particular London cartographer whose narratives represent a picturesque set of maps of possible human existence within, through and because of the disparate city.

Peter Ackroyd's idea of the task of literature is plain yet much easier to state than to achieve: "to entertain," while also conceiving an imaginary realm that would interest people and "make them see the world slightly differently."[16] This book has tried to demonstrate that his London novels meet all these criteria by picturing a fictional universe that is amusing and enticing precisely because it is simultaneously familiar and unknown, secure and perilous, predictable and volatile, contemporary and foregone. It is a complex, thirdspatial and heterotopic chronotope which stages actions and events that appear uncontrollable, mysterious, fragmentary and chaotic, yet which are shown as natural, or even possible to anticipate, as they are generated and conducted by recurrent perpetual patterns of forces running, undetected by the naked eye, beneath the surface of Londoners' everyday reality. Through this strategy Ackroyd manages not only to explore the less known or more obscure aspects of London's history, but also to lay bare what he sees as its true

---

14 Kundera, *The Art of the Novel*, 43, emphasis in original.
15 Kim Roberts, "Bridge, Mirror, Labyrinth: Shaping the Intervals of Calvino's *Invisible Cities*," 142.
16 Schütze, "I think after More I will do Turner and then I will probably do Shakespeare."

tradition in its wholeness, and create a city which casts light on the very nature of time and on how the present is always soaked with and submerged in the past. He is well aware that London as a theme and object of interest is too immense and multi-faceted to ever be fully captured within the confines of textual representation, no matter how voluminous and varied, which is why he stresses the importance of "the vision behind it."[17] His novels by no means attempt to provide an all-encompassing or panoramic image of London, but they do present a visionary city which is also a city of vision, an original and distinctive one, though Ackroyd would certainly argue that this vision has fuelled the city's imagination, latently perhaps, since time immemorial.

---

17   Five Minutes With: Peter Ackroyd, interviewed by Matthew Stadlen, BBC News website, 10 November 2013.

Summary

Peter Ackroyd is one of the foremost contemporary British "London writers". He focuses on the capital, its history, development and identity, both in his fiction and non-fiction. The London of his novels is thus a highly idiosyncratic construct which reflects and derives from its author's ideas about the actual city's nature as well as his concept of the English literary sensibility in general as he outlines them in his lectures and historical and literary studies. It is an exceptionally heterogeneous city of enormous diversity and richness of human experience, moods and emotion, of actions and events, and also of the tools through which these are (re)presented and reenacted. According to Ackroyd, this heterogeneity mostly originates outside the sites and domains of the established or mainstream cultural production and social norms and conventions, particularly in occult practices, subversive acts and the plotting of radical individuals or groups, criminal and fraudulent activities of various kinds, dubious scientific experiments, and the popular dramatic forms of ritual and entertainment whose permanent encounters with and contesting of the officially approved and prescribed forms instigate the city's vitalising energy for dynamic change and spiritual renewal. This book presents the world of Ackroyd's London novels as a distinct chronotope determined by specific spatial and temporal properties and their mutual interconnectedness. Although such a concept of urban space in its essence defies categorisation, the book is thematically organised around six defining aspects of the city as Ackroyd identifies them: the relationship between its past and present, its uncanny manifestations, its felonious tendencies, its inhabitants' psychogeographic and antiquarian strategies, its theatricality, and its inherently literary character.

Bibliography

Ackroyd, Peter. *The Great Fire of London*. London: Penguin Books, 1988.

Ackroyd, Peter. *Hawksmoor*. London: Penguin Books, 1993.

Ackroyd, Peter. *Chatterton*, New York: Grove Press, 1987.

Ackroyd, Peter. *Dickens*. London: Vintage, 2002.

Ackroyd, Peter. *Dan Leno and the Limehouse Golem*. London: Vintage, 1994.

Ackroyd, Peter. *The House of Doctor Dee*. London: Penguin Books, 1994.

Ackroyd, Peter. *The Life of Thomas More*. New York: Anchor, 1999.

Ackroyd, Peter. *Blake*. London: Vintage, 1999.

Ackroyd, Peter. *The Plato Papers*. London: Vintage, 2000.

Ackroyd, Peter. "The Englishness of English Literature." In *Peter Ackroyd: The Collection (Journalism, Reviews, Essays, Short Stories, Lectures)*. Edited by Thomas Wright. London: Vintage, 2002 (328–340).

Ackroyd, Peter. "The Future of English Prisons." In *Peter Ackroyd: The Collection (Journalism, Reviews, Essays, Short Stories, Lectures)*. Edited by Thomas Wright. London: Vintage, 2002 (74–78).

Ackroyd, Peter. "London Luminaries and Cockney Visionaries." In *Peter Ackroyd: The Collection (Journalism, Reviews, Essays, Short Stories, Lectures)*. Edited by Thomas Wright. London: Vintage, 2002 (341–351).

Ackroyd, Peter. "William Blake, A Spiritual Radical." In *Peter Ackroyd: The Collection (Journalism, Reviews, Essays, Short Stories, Lectures)*. Edited by Thomas Wright. London: Vintage, 2002 (352–364).

Ackroyd, Peter. "All the Time in the World." In *Peter Ackroyd: The Collection (Journalism, Reviews, Essays, Short Stories, Lectures)*. Edited by Thomas Wright. London: Vintage, 2002 (365–371).

Ackroyd, Peter. "A Manifesto for London." In *Peter Ackroyd: The Collection (Journalism, Reviews, Essays, Short Stories, Lectures)*. Edited by Thomas Wright. London: Vintage, 2002 (386–387).

Ackroyd, Peter. *London: The Biography*, New York: Anchor, 2003.

Ackroyd, Peter. *The Clerkenwell Tales*. Chatham: Quality Paperbacks Direct, 2003.

Ackroyd, Peter. *The Lambs of London*. London: Vintage, 2005.

Ackroyd, Peter. *Albion: The Origins of the English Imagination*, London: Vintage, 2004.

Ackroyd, Peter. *Newton*, London: Chatto & Windus, 2006.

Ackroyd, Peter. *Thames: Sacred River*. London: Vintage, 2008.

Ackroyd, Peter. *The Casebook of Victor Frankenstein*, 2008, London: Vintage, 2009.

Ackroyd, Peter. "My epic search for our turbulent roots." *The Telegraph*, 25 August 2011. http://www.telegraph.co.uk/culture/books/bookreviews/8722559/Peter-Ackroyd-on-History-My-epic-search-for-our-turbulent-roots.html (accessed September 2014).

Ackroyd, Peter. *London Under*. London: Vintage, 2012.

Ackroyd, Peter. *Three Brothers*, London: Chatto & Windus, 2013.

Alexander, Marguerite. *Flights from Realism: Themes and Strategies in Postmodernist British and American Fiction*. London: Edward Arnold, 1990.

Allen, Graham. *Intertextuality*. London: Routledge, 2010.

Amjad, Fazel Asadi, Ilkhani, Sarah Catherine and Arya Aryan. "The Problematisation of the Representation of Reality in Peter Ackroyd's *Chatterton* in the Light of Postmodern Theories." *International Journal of Humanities and Social Sciences*, Vol. 1, No. 10, 2011 (117–126).

Appadurai, Arjun. *Modernity at Large: Cultural Dimensions of Globalization*. Minneapolis: Minnesota University Press, 2005.

Archer, Ian. "The Nostalgia of John Stow." In *The Theatrical City: Culture, Theatre and Politics in London, 1576–1649*. Edited by David L. Smith, Richard Strier and David Bevington. Cambridge: Cambridge University Press, 1995 (17–34).

Atkins, Mark and Iain Sinclair. *Liquid City*. London: Reaktion Books, 1999.

Audiger, Jean-Pierre. "L'apocryfe selon Ackroyd." In *Historicité & Métafiction dans le roman contemporain des iles britaniques*. Edited by Max Duperray. Aix-en-Provence: Publications de l'Université de Provence, 1994 (139–150).

Auerbach, Nina. *Private Theatricals: The Lives of the Victorians*. Harvard: Harvard University Press, 1990.

Bachelard, Gaston. *The Poetics of Space*. (Trans. Maria Jolas). Boston: Beacon Press, 1994.

Bailey, Peter. *Popular Culture and Performance in the Victorian City*. Cambridge: Cambridge University Press, 1998.

Bakhtin, Mikhail. *The Dialogic Imagination*. (Trans. Caryl Emerson and Michael Holquist). Austin: University of Texas Press, 1981.

Bakhtin, Mikhail. *Rabelais and His World*. (Trans. Hélène Iswolsky). Bloomington: Indiana University Press, 1984.

Ball, John Clement. *Imagining London: Postcolonial Fiction and the Transnational Metropolis*. Toronto: University of Toronto Press, 2004.

Barnes, Julian. *A History of the World in 10 1/2 Chapters*. London: Picador, 2005.

Barthes, Roland. "The Death of the Author." In *Modern Criticism and Theory: A Reader* (Third Edition). Edited by David Lodge and Nigel Woods. Harlow: Pearson Education Ltd., 2008 (313–316).

Bentley, Nick. *British Fiction of the 1990s*. London: Routledge, 2005.

Beran, Zdeněk. "'Allied to the Bottom of the River': Stratification of the Urban Space in Charles Dickens's *Our Mutual Friend*." *Litteraria Pragensia*, Vol. 20, No. 40, 2010 (25–37).

Bergson, Henri. *An Introduction to Metaphysics*. (Trans. T. E. Hulme). Indianopolis and Cambridge: Hackett Publishing Company, 1999.

Blake, William. *Selected Poetry*. Oxford: Oxford University Press, 1994.

Bloom, Harold. "Cities of the Mind." In *Bloom's Literary Places: London*. Edited by Donna Dailey and John Tomedi. Philadelphia: Chelsea House Publishers, 2005 (vii–xi).

Booth, Michael R. "Comedy and farce." In *The Cambridge Companion to Victorian and Edwardian Theatre*. Edited by Kerry Powell. Cambridge: Cambridge University Press, 2004 (164–182).

Botting, Fred. "Aftergothic: Consumption, Machines, and Black Holes." In *The Cambridge Companion to Gothic Fiction*. Edited by Jerrold Hogle. Cambridge: Cambridge University Press, 2002, (277–300).

Bowers, Maggie Ann. *Magic(al) Realism*. London: Routledge, 2004.

Bradbury, Malcolm. *The Modern British Novel*. London: Penguin Books, 1994.

Bradbury, Malcolm. *The Atlas of Literature*. London: De Agostini Editions Griffin House, 1996.

Bradford, Richard. *The Novel Now*. Oxford: Blackwell Publishing, 2007.

Bratton, Jacky. "The music hall." In *The Cambridge Companion to Victorian and Edwardian Theatre*. Edited by Kerry Powell. Cambridge: Cambridge University Press, 2004 (93–108).

Bratton, Jacky. "Romantic melodrama." In *The Cambridge Companion to British Theatre, 1730–1830*. Edited by Jane Moody and Daniel O'Quinn. Cambridge: Cambridge University Press, (115–27).

Brook, Susan. "Hedgemony? Suburban space in *The Buddha of Suburbia*." In *British Fiction of the 1990s*. Edited by Nick Bentley. London: Routledge, 2005 (209–225).

Byatt, A. S. *On Histories and Stories: Selected Essays*. London: Chatto & Windus, 2000.

Calvino, Italo. *Invisible Cities*. (Trans. by William Weaver). London: Vintage, 1997.

Certeau, Michel de. *The Practice of Everyday Life*. (Trans. Steven Rendall). Berkeley and Los Angeles: University of California Press, 1988.

Certeau, Michel de. *The Writing of History*. (Trans. Tom Conley). New York: Columbia University Press, 1992.

Chalupský, Petr and Anna Grmelová. "Introduction: Urban Spaces in Literature." *Litteraria Pragensia*, Vol. 20, No. 40, 2010 (1–7).

Chapman, Siobhan and Christopher Routledge. "The Pragmatics of Detection: Paul Auster's City of Glass." *Language and Literature*, Vol. 8, No. 3, 1999, (241–253).

Charnick, David. "Peter Ackroyd: *The Plato Papers*." *Londonfictions* online, 2010. http://www.londonfictions.com/peter-ackroyd-the-plato-papers.html (accessed August 2014).

Charnick, David. "Peter Ackroyd's Imaginary Projections: A Context for the Creature of *The Casebook of Victor Frankenstein*." *Modern Language Review*, Vol. 108, Part 1. London: Modern Humanities Research Association, 2013 (52–67).

Charnick, David. "Out of time: Peter Ackroyd's perpetual London." Conference paper given at *"Ages of London" – Representations of London in Literature: An Interdisciplinary Conference* organised by The Literary London Society and The Institute of English Studies, University of London, 23–25 July, 2014.

Colombino, Laura. *Spatial Politics in Contemporary London Literature: Writing Architecture and the Body*. London, New York: Routledge, 2013.

Coverley, Merlin. *London Writing*. Harpenden: Pocket Essentials, 2005.

Coverley, Merlin. *Psychogeography*. Harpenden: Pocket Essentials, 2006.

Coverley, Merlin. *Occult London*. Harpenden: Pocket Essentials, 2008.

Cowley, Robert. "Introduction." In *What if?* Edited by Robert Cowley. London: Pan, 2001, (xi–xiv).

Cunningham, Ian. *A Reader's Guide to Writers' London*. London: Prion Books, 2001.

Dailey, Donna and John Tomedi. *Bloom's Literary Places: London*. Philadelphia: Chelsea House Publishers, 2005.

Davies, Charles Maurice. *Mystic London: or, Phases of Occult Life in the Metropolis*. London: Forgotten Books, 2012.

Davis, Jim and Victor Emeljanow. "Victorian and Edwardian audiences." In *The Cambridge Companion to Victorian and Edwardian Theatre*. Edited by Kerry Powell. Cambridge: Cambridge University Press, 2004 (93–108).

Davis, Jim. "Spectatorship." In *The Cambridge Companion to British Theatre, 1730–1830*. Edited by Jane Moody and Daniel O'Quinn. Cambridge: Cambridge University Press, 2007 (57–69).

Debord, Guy. "Introduction to a Critique of Urban Geography." In *Situationist International Anthology*. Edited by Ken Knabb. Berkeley CA: Bureau of Public Secrets, 1981 (8–11).

De Young, Jim and John Miller. *London Theatre Walks*. New York: Applause Theatre & Cinema Books, 2003.

Donald, James. *Imagining the Modern City*. Minneapolis: University of Minnesota Press, 1999.

Eagleton, Terry. *The English Novel*. Oxford: Blackwell Publishing, 2005.

Eliot, T. S. *The Complete Poems and Plays*. London: Faber and Faber, 2004.

English, J. F. (ed.). *A Concise Companion to Contemporary British Fiction*. Oxford: Blackwell Publishing, 2006.

Ferguson, Niall. "Introduction." In *Virtual History*. Edited by Niall Ferguson. New York: Basic Books, 1999, (1–91).

Fiorato, Sidia. "Theatrical Role-Playing, Crime and Punishment in Peter Ackroyd's *Dan Leno and the Limehouse Golem* (1994)." *Pólemos: Journal of Law, Literature and Culture*. Vol. 6, No. 1. De Gruyter Online, 2012 (65–81).

Finkelstein, Joanne. *The Art of Self-Invention: Image and Identity in Popular Visual Culture*. London: I. B. Tauris & Co Ltd, 2007.

Finney, Brian. "Peter Ackroyd, Postmodernist Play and Chatterton." *Twentieth Century Literature*, Vol. 38, No. 2, 1992, (240–261). http://www.csulb .edu/~bhfinney/ackroyd.html (accessed May 2014).

Florby, Gunilla. "Postscript: So what about Postmodernism? Frederick Jameson vs Linda Hutcheon." In *Rethinking Modernism*. Edited by Marianne Thormählen. Basingstoke: Palgrave Macmillan, 2003 (239–251).

Foucault, Michel. *Discipline and Punish*. (Trans. Alan Sheridan). Harmondsworth: Penguin Books, 1979.

Foucault, Michel. *Power/Knowledge*. (Trans. Colin Gordon, Leo Marshall, John Mepham and Kate Soper). New York: Pantheon, 1981.

Foucault, Michel. "Of Other Spaces." (Trans. Jay Miskowiec). *Diacritics*, Vol. 16, 1986 (22–27).

Gibson, Jeremy and Julian Wolfreys. *Peter Ackroyd: The Ludic and Labyrinthine Text*. London: Macmillan Press Ltd., 2000.

Glinert, Ed. *East End Chronicles*. London: Penguin Books, 2005.

Greenblatt, Stephen. *Renaissance Self-Fashioning: From More to Shakespeare*. Chicago: The University of Chicago Press, 1980.

Gregoriou, Christiana. *Deviance in Contemporary Crime Fiction*. London: Palgrave Macmillan, 2007.

Groot, Jerome de. *The Historical Novel*. London: Routledge, 2010.

Guard, Richard. *Lost London*. London: Michael O'Mara Books Limited, 2012.

Hardy, Stephen. *Relations of Place: Aspects of Late 20th Century Fiction and Theory*. Brno: Masarykova univerzita, 2008.

Hart, Vaughan. *Nicholas Hawksmoor: Rebuilding Ancient Wonders*. New Haven and London: Yale University Press, 2007.

Hayes, M. Hunter. *Understanding Will Self*. Columbia: University of South Carolina Press, 2007.

Hazlitt, William. "Our National Theatres." In *William Hazlitt: Selected Writings*. Edited by Jon Cook. Oxford: Oxford University Press, 1991 (155–156).

Head, Dominic. *The Cambridge Introduction to Modern British Fiction, 1950–2000*. Cambridge: Cambridge University Press, 2002.

Hitchcock, Susan Tyler. *Mad Mary Lamb: Lunacy and Murder in Literary London*. London: W. W. Norton & Company, 2005.

Hodrová, Daniela. *Citlivé město (eseje z mytopoetiky)*. Prague: Akropolis, 2006.

Horsley, Lee. *Twentieth Century Crime Fiction*. Oxford: Oxford University Press, 2005.

hooks, bell. *Yearning*. Boston: South End Press, 1990.

Houswitschka, Christoph. "'This fabulous flotsam': Michael Moorcock's Urban Anthropology in 'London under London.'" Prague Journal of English Studies, Vol. 4, No. 1, 2015 (61–75). Hutcheon, Linda. *A Poetics of Postmodernism*, London: Routledge, 1992.

Ibell, Paul. *Theatreland: A journey through the heart of London's theatre*. London: Continuum, 2009.

Jeffries, Stuart. Interview with Iain Sinclair. *The Guardian*, 24 April, 2004.

Jenkins, Keith. *Re-thinking History*, London: Routledge, 1991.

Kalaga, Wojciech and Jacek Mydla. (eds.). *Mapping Literary Spaces: Memory, Place, Locality*. Katowice: Wydawnictwo Uniwersytetu Śląskiego, 2009.

Kant, Immanuel. *Anthropology from a Pragmatic Point of View*. (Trans. Mary J. Gregor). The Hague: Martinus Nijhoff, 1974.

Keen, Suzanne. "The Historical Turn in British Fiction." In *Contemporary British Fiction*. Edited by James F. English. Oxford: Blackwell Publishing, 2006 (167–187).

Kelly, Linda. *The Marvellous Boy: The Life and Myth of Thomas Chatterton*. London: Faber and Faber, 2008.

Kundera, Milan. *The Art of the Novel*. (Trans. Linda Asher). London: Faber and Faber, 1986.

Lachman, Gary (ed.). *The Dedalus Book of the Occult: A Dark Muse*. Cambridge: Dedalus, 2003.

Lamb, Charles. "The Londoner." *Quotidiana*. Edited by Patrick Madlen. http://essays.quotidiana.org/lamb/londoner (accessed May 2014).

Lancashire, Anne. *London Civic Theatre: City Drama and Pageantry from Roman Times to 1558*. Cambridge: Cambridge University Press, 2002.

Lefebvre, Henri. *The Production of Space*. (Trans. Donald Nicholson-Smith). Oxford: Blackwell Publishers, 1991.

Lewis, Barry. *My Words Echo Thus: Possessing the Past in Peter Ackroyd*. Columbia: University of South Carolina Press, 2007.

Lively, Penelope. *City of the Mind*. London: Penguin Books, 1992.

Lowenthal, David. *The Past is a Foreign Country*. Cambridge: Cambridge University Press, 1985.

Lowenthal, David. *The Heritage Crusade*. Cambridge: Cambridge University Press, 1998.

Lutwack, Leonard. *The Role of Place in Literature*. Syracuse: Syracuse University Press, 1984.

Malmgren, Carl Darryl. *Fictional Space in the Modernist and Postmodernist American Novel*. London and Toronto: Associated University Presses, 1985.

Manley, Lawrence. "Of Sites and Rites." In *The Theatrical City: Culture, Theatre and Politics in London, 1576–1649*. Edited by David L. Smith, Richard Strier and David Bevington. Cambridge: Cambridge University Press, 1995 (35–54).

Mayer, David. "Encountering melodrama." In *The Cambridge Companion to Victorian and Edwardian Theatre*. Edited by Kerry Powell. Cambridge: Cambridge University Press, 2004 (145–164).

McKinnie, Michael. *City Stages: Theatre and Urban Space in a Global City*. Toronto: University of Toronto Press, 2007.

Mengham, Rod (ed.). *An Introduction to Contemporary Fiction*. Cambridge: Polity Press, 1999.

Mengham, Rod. "The Writing of Iain Sinclair." In *Contemporary British Fiction*. Edited by Richard J. Lane, Rod Mengham and Philip Tew. Cambridge: Polity Press, 2003 (56–67).

Mighall, Robert. "Gothic Cities." In *The Routledge Companion to Gothic*. Edited by Catherine Spooner and Emma McEvoy. London: Routledge, 2007 (54–62).

Moorcock, Michael. *Mother London*. London: Pocket Books, 2004.

Munslow, Alun. *Deconstructing History*. London: Routledge, 2006.

Munslow, Alun. *The Future of History*. London: Palgrave Macmillan, 2010.

Murray, Alex. *Recalling London: Literature and History in the work of Peter Ackroyd and Iain Sinclair*. London: Continuum, 2007.

Nagy, Ladislav. *Londýn stejný a jiný*. Prgue: Arbor vitae, 2004.

Newland, Paul. *The Cultural Construction of London's East End: Urban Iconography, Modernity and the Spatialisation of Englishness*. Amsterdam: Rodopi, 2008.

Olsen, Donald J. *The City as a Work of Art: London, Paris, Vinna*. New Haven and London: Yale University Press, 1986.

Onega, Susana. *Peter Ackroyd*, Plymouth: Northcote House, 1998.

Onega, Susana. *Metafiction and myth in the novels of Peter Ackroyd*. Columbia, SC: Camden House, 1999.

Palmer, Jerry. *Thrillers. Genesis and Structure of a Popular Genre*, London: Edward Arnold Publisher, 1978.

Phillips, Lawrence. "Introduction." In *The Swarming Streets: The Twentieth-Century Literary Representations of London*. Edited by Lawrence Philips. Amsterdam-New York: Rodopi, 2004 (1–6).

Phillips, Lawrence. *London Narratives: Post-War Fiction and the City*. London: Continuum, 2011.

Pierce, Patricia. *The Great Shakespeare Fraud*. Gloucestershire: Sutton Publishing, 2004.

Plett, Heinrich F. "Intertextualities." In *Intertextuality*. Edited by Heinrich F. Plett. Berlin: Walter de Gruyter, 1991 (3–29).

Porter, Dennis. *The Pursuit of Crime: Art and Ideology in Detective Fiction*. New Haven: Yale University Press, 1981.

Priestman, Martin. "P. D. James and the Distinguished Thing." In *On Modern British Fiction*. Edited by Zachary Leader. Oxford: Oxford University Press, 2002 (234–257).

Punter, David and Glennis Byron. *The Gothic*. Oxford: Blackwell, 2004.

Roberts, Kim. "Bridge, Mirror, Labyrinth: Shaping the Intervals of Calvino's *Invisible Cities*." In *Frameworks, Artworks, Place: The Space of Perception in the Modern World*. Edited by Tim Mehigan. Amsterdam-New York: Rodopi, 2008 (137–158).

Robinson, Alan. *Narrating the Past: Historiography, Memory and the Contemporary Novel*. London: Palgrave Macmillan, 2011.

Sağlam, Berkem Gürenci. *"The Mystical City Universal": Representations of London in Peter Ackroyd's Fiction*. Lewiston: Edwin Mellen Press, 2011.

Self, Will. *Psychogeography*. London: Bloomsbury Publishing, 2007.

Sinclair, Iain. *Lights Out for the Territory*. London: Penguin Books, 2003.

Sinclair Iain (ed.). *London: City of Disappearances*. London: Penguin Books, 2007.

Sinclair, Iain. *Lud Heat: a book of the dead hamlets*. Cheltenham: Skylight Press, 2012.

Smith, Andrew. *Gothic Literature*. Edinburgh: Edinburgh University Press, 2007.

Smith, David L., Strier, Richard and David Bevington. (eds.). *The Theatrical City: Culture, Theatre and Politics in London, 1576–1649*. Cambridge: Cambridge University Press, 1995.

Smethurst, Paul. *The Postmodern Chronotype: Reading Space and Time in Contemporary Fiction*. Amsterdam: Rodopi, 2000.

Soja, Edward W. *Thirdspace: Journeys to Los Angeles and Other Real-and-Imagined Places*. Oxford: Blackwell Publisher, 1996.

Stanford, Michael. *An Introduction to the Philosophy of History*. Oxford: Blackwell Publishers, 1998.

Staves, Susan. "Tragedy." In *The Cambridge Companion to British Theatre, 1730–1830*. Edited by Jane Moody and Daniel O'Quinn. Cambridge: Cambridge University Press, 2007 (87–102).

Stewart, Doug. *The Boy Who Would Be Shakespeare: A Tale of Forgery and Folly*. Cambridge (US): Da Capo Press, 2010.

Strachan, Francoise (ed.). *The Aquarian Guide Occult, Mystical, Religious, Magical London and Around*. London: The Aquarian Press, 1970.

Straub, Kristina. "The making of an English audience: the case of the footmen's gallery." In *The Cambridge Companion to British Theatre, 1730–1830*. Edited by Jane Moody and Daniel O'Quinn. Cambridge: Cambridge University Press, 2007 (131–143).

Swales, Martin. "Introduction." In *The Art of Detective Fiction*. Edited by Warren Cherniak, Martin Wales and Robert Vilain. New York: Saint Martin's Press Inc, 2000 (xi–xv).

Taube, Aleksejs. "London's East End in Peter Ackroyd's *Dan Leno and the Limehouse Golem*." Edited by Lieven AmEEL, Jason Finch and Markku Salmela. Basingstoke: Palgrave Macmillan, 2015 (93–110).

Tew, Philip. *The Contemporary British Novel*. London: Continuum, 2004.

Thomson, Peter. "Acting and actors from Garrick to Kean." In *The Cambridge Companion to British Theatre, 1730–1830*. Edited by Jane Moody and Daniel O'Quinn. Cambridge: Cambridge University Press, 2007 (3–19).

Twycross, Meg. "The theatricality of medieval English plays." In *The Cambridge Companion to Medieval English Theatre*. Edited by Richard Beadle. Cambridge: Cambridge University Press, 1994 (37–84).

Tydeman, William. "An introduction to medieval English theatre." In *The Cambridge Companion to Medieval English Theatre*. Edited by Richard Beadle. Cambridge: Cambridge University Press, 1994 (1–36).

Vernyik, Zénó. *Cities of Saviors: The Representation of Urban Space in E. E. Cumming's Complete Poems, 1904–1962 and Peter Ackroyd's Hawksmoor*. Szeged: Americana eBooks, 2015.

Versluis, Arthur. *Restoring Paradise: Western Esotericism, Literature, Art, and Consciousness*. Albany: State University of New York Press, 2004.

Watson, Kathy. *The Devil Kissed Her: The Story of Mary Lamb*. London: Bloomsbury Publishing, 2004.

Warner, Marina. *Managing Monsters: Six myths of our time*. London: Vintage, 1994.

Warner, Marina. *Phantasmagoria: Spirit Visions, Metaphors and Media into the Twenty-first Century*. Oxford: Oxford University Press, 2006.

Waugh, Patricia. *Metafiction: The Theory and Practice of Self-Conscious Fiction*. London: Routledge, 1986.

Weiss, Rudolf. "'Hell is a city much like London': Postmodern Urban Gothic in Charles Higson's *Getting Rid of Mister Kitchen*." *Litteraria Pragensia*, Vol. 20, No. 40, 2010 (54–69).

White, Edmund. *The Flâneur: A Stroll through the Paradoxes of Paris*. London: Bloomsbury Publishing, 2001.

White, Hayden. *Tropics of Discourse: Essays in Cultural Criticism*. Baltimore: Johns Hopkins University Press, 1978.

White, Jerry. *London in the Twentieth Century: A City and Its People*. London: Vintage Books, 2008.

Winks, Robin W. (ed.). *Detective Fiction, A Collection of Critical Essays*. New Jersey: Prentice Hall, 1980.

Witchard, Anne and Phillips, Lawrence. "Introduction." In *London Gothic: Place, Space and the Gothic Imagination*. Edited by Lawrence Phillips and Anne Witchard. London: Continuum, 2010 (1–8).

Wolfreys, Julian. *Writing London. Volume 2: materiality, memory, spectrality*. Basingstoke: Palgrave Macmillan, 2004.

Woolf, Virginia. *The London Scene*, London: Snowbooks Ltd., 1975.

Woolley, Benjamin. *The Queen's Conjuror: The Life and Magic of Dr Dee*. London: Flamingo, 2002.

Wright, Thomas (ed.). *Peter Ackroyd: The Collection (Journalism, Reviews, Essays, Short Stories, Lectures)*. London: Vintage, 2002.

Interviews with and articles about Peter Ackroyd

Banks, Daisy. "Peter Ackroyd on London," an interview. *The Browser* (2013). http://fivebooks.com/interviews/peter-ackroyd-on-london (accessed February 2014).

Ferguson, Euan. "I just want to tell a story," an interview with Peter Ackroyd. *The Observer*, 25 August 2011. http://www.theguardian.com/books/2011/aug/25/peter-ackroyd-interview-foundation-england (accessed August 2014).

Hattenstone, Simon. "Tales of the city," an interview with Peter Ackroyd. *The Guardian*, 11 August 2003. http://www.theguardian.com/education/2003/aug/11/highereducation.fiction.

Lacey, Hester, "The Inventory: Peter Ackroyd," an interview with Peter Ackroyd. *The Financial Times Magazine*, 28 September 2012. http://www.ft.com/intl/cms/s/2/05ab3878-b623-11e1-a14a-00144feabdc0.html#axzz3EnEOKrXA (accessed September 2014).

Mann, Emily, "Tales of the city." *The Guardian*, 15 September 2007. http://www.theguardian.com/books/2007/sep/15/biography.fiction (accessed August 2014).

McGrath, Patrick. "Peter Ackroyd: Interview." *BOMB Magazine*, Vol. 26, Winter 1989. http://bombmagazine.org/article/1168/peter-ackroyd (accessed September 2014).

McSmith, Andy, "Rioting has been a London tradition for centuries," an interview

with Peter Ackroyd. *The Independent*, 22 August 2011. http://www.independent
.co.uk/news/people/profiles/peter-ackroyd-rioting-has-been-a-london-tradi-
tion-for-centuries-2341673.html (accessed September 2014)

O'Mahony, John. "London calling." *The Guardian*, 3 July 2004. http://www.guardian
.co.uk/books/2004/jul/03/biography.fiction (accessed July 2014).

Preston, John. "My work matters more to me than love," an interview with
Peter Ackroyd. *The Telegraph*, 20 August 2006. http://www.telegraph.co.uk
/culture/3654738/My-work-matters-more-to-me-than-love.html (accessed September 2014)

Rosen, Jody. "Peter Ackroyd's London Calling." *The New York Times*, 12 September
2013. http://tmagazine.blogs.nytimes.com/2013/09/12/arts-and-letters-peter-ack-
royds-london-calling/?_php=true&_type=blogs&_r=0 (accessed January 2014).

Schütze, Anke. "I think after More I will do Turner and then I will probably
do Shakespeare." An Interview with Peter Ackroyd, 1995. http://webdoc.sub
.gwdg.de/edoc/ia/eese/articles/schuetze/8_95.html (accessed January 2014).

Vianu, Lidia. "The mind is the soul," an interview with Peter Ackroyd, 5 October
2001. http://lidiavianu.scriptmania.com/peter_ackroyd.htm (accessed January
2014).

Watts, Peter. "Peter Ackroyd: interview." *Time Out*, 18 September 2008. http:
//www.timeout.com/london/things-to-do/peter-ackroyd-interview (accessed
August 2014).

Wintle, Angela. "Petr Ackroyd: My family values." *The Guardian*, 29 November
2013. http://www.theguardian.com/lifeandstyle/2013/nov/29/peter-ackroyd-my
-family-values-writer_(accessed September 2014).

"Each book is a different reason to exist," Lidia Vianu's students' videoconference
interview with Peter Ackroyd, 9 May 2006. http://lidiavianu.scriptmania.com
/peter_ackroyd.htm (accessed September 2014).

"An interview with Peter Ackroyd." *Bold Type*, an online literary magazine, Vol. 2.8,
October–November 1998. https://www.randomhouse.com/boldtype/1098
/ackroyd/interview.html (accessed January 2014).

"Retire? Only if my arms are chopped off first," an interview with Peter Ackroyd.
The Independent, 12 July 2009. http://www.independent.co.uk/news/people/
profiles/peter-ackroyd-retire-only-if-my-arms-are-chopped-off-first-1742766.html
(accessed August 2014).

"Peter Ackroyd speaking at Royal Festival Hall," Part 1, 10 October 2011. http://
www.youtube.com/watch?v=DhSbFdQc34A (accessed January 2014).

"Five Minutes With: Peter Ackroyd, interviewed by Matthew Stadlen," BBC
News website, 10 November 2013. http://www.bbc.com/news/entertainment-
arts-17790481 (accessed January 2014).

Index